Dreamweaver 3 | H·O·T

lynda.com/books

By Lynda Weinman and Garo Green

Design: Ali Karp

Dreamweaver 3 | H·O·T Hands-On Training
By Lynda Weinman and Garo Green

lynda.com/books | Peachpit Press
1249 Eighth Street • Berkeley, CA • 94710
800.283.9444 • 510.524.2178 •
510.524.2221 (fax)
http://www.lynda.com/books
http://www.peachpit.com

lynda.com/books is published in
association with Peachpit Press
Peachpit Press is a division of
Addison Wesley Longman
Copyright ©2000 by lynda.com

ISBN 0-201-70276-2

0 9 8 7 6 5 4 3 2 1
Printed and bound in the
United States of America

H•O•T | Credits

Book Design: Ali Karp (alink@earthlink.net)

Peachpit Editor: Cary Norsworthy

Peachpit Production Coordinator: Amy Changar

lynda.com Editor: Joan Morley

lynda.com Production Coordinator: Sean Blumenthal

lynda.com Production Artist: Heidi Goodspeed

Cover Illustration: Bruce Heavin (bruce@stink.com)

Indexer: Steve Rath

H•O•T | Colophon

The preliminary art direction for *Dreamweaver 3 H•O•T* was sketched on paper. The layout was heavily influenced by online communication–merging a traditional book format with a modern Web aesthetic.

The text in *Dreamweaver 3 H•O•T* was set in Akzidenz Grotesk from Adobe and Triplex from Emigre. The cover illustration was painted in Adobe Photoshop 5.5 and Adobe Illustrator 8.0.

This book was created using QuarkXPress 4.1, Adobe Photoshop 5.5, Microsoft Office 98, and Dreamweaver 3 on a Macintosh G3, running MacOS 9. It was printed on 60lb. Arbor Smooth, at Edwards Brothers, Ann Arbor, Michigan.

Dreamweaver 3 H•O•T_____Table of Contents

Introduction_____x

About the Authors	xii
Our Team	xiii
Acknowledgements from Lynda	xiv
Acknowledgements from Garo	xv
How to Use This Book	xvi
HTML vs. HTM	xvii
Macintosh and Windows Interface Screen Captures	xvii
Mac and Windows System Differences	xvii
Making Exercise Files Editable on Windows Systems	xix
Making File Extensions Visible on Windows Systems	xxi
Creating New Documents	xxiv
Dreamweaver System Requirements	xxiv
What's on the CD-ROM	xxv

I. Background_____2

Roundtrip HTML	3
Do You Need to Learn HTML to Use Dreamweaver?	4
HMTL Resources	5
What Does HTML Do?	6
What Does HTML Look Like?	7
HTML Deconstructed	8
File-Naming Conventions	9
File Name Extensions	10
Extending Dreamweaver	11
What is DHTML?	12
What is XML?	13
What is JavaScript?	13

2. Interface _____ 14

A Tour of the Interface	15
The Objects Palette	16
Type of Objects	18
The Properties Inspector	20
The Launcher and Mini-Launcher	21
The Document Window	24
Preferences	25
External Editors	26
Preset Window Sizes	27
How to Define Browser of Your Choice	28
Shortcut Keys	29

3. Site Control _____ 30

What is a Root Folder?	31
Exercise 1_Defining a Site	33
Exercise 2_Relative and Absolute Links	36
Exercise 3_File and Folder Management	40
Exercise 4_Understanding the Path Structure	42
Exercise 5_Creating a Site Map	46
Exercise 6_Creating a Site from Nothing	48

4. Basics _____ 50

Exercise 1_Defining the Site	52
Exercise 2_Creating and Saving a Document	54
Exercise 3_Inserting Images	58
Exercise 4_Inserting Text	60
Exercise 5_Centering Images and Text	63
Exercise 6_Modifying Page Properties	64
Exercise 7_Creating Links with Images and Text	70
Exercise 8_Meta Tags	74
Exercise 9_Looking at the HTML	78

5. Linking _____ 80

Exercise 1_Linking with Point-to-File	81
Exercise 2_Browse for File and the Link History	85
Exercise 3_Linking to New Source Files	91
Exercise 4_Creating Email Links	96
Exercise 5_Named Anchors	101
Exercise 6_Image Maps	116

6. HTML _____ 120

Exercise 1_HTML Source Window	121
Exercise 2_Editing with the HTML Source Window	126
Exercise 3_External HTML Editors	129
Exercise 4_Quick Tag Editor	137
Exercise 5_Clean-up HTML	142
Exercise 6_Clean-up Word HTML	148

7. Typography _____ 152

A Word about FONT FACE	153
Exercise 1_Creating and Formatting HTML Text	155
Exercise 2_Font Lists	159
Exercise 3_Aligning Text	165
Exercise 4_Using the <PRE> Tag	168
Exercise 5_Ordered, Unordered, and Definition lists	174
Exercise 6_Color Schemes	176
Exercise 7_Formatting Text in Tables	178
Exercise 8_Repeat Last Action	180
Exercise 9_Character Entities	183
Exercise 10_Blockquotes and Non-Breaking Spaces	186

8. Layout _____ 190

Exercise 1_Applying a Tracing Image	192
Exercise 2_Tracing Images, Background Colors, and Images	199
Exercise 3_Converting Layers to Tables	207
Exercise 4_Converting Tables to Layers	211
Exercise 5_Using Margin Tags	216

9. Tables_____220

Exercise 1_Changing the Border of a Table   222
Exercise 2_Sorting the Table   226
Exercise 3_Changing the Color Scheme   228
Exercise 4_Creating and Modifying a Table   232
Exercise 5_Aligning Images and Text with Tables   237
Exercise 6_Percentage-Based Table Alignment   246
Exercise 7_Seamless Image Assembly   251
Exercise 8_Combining Pixels and Percentages   255
Exercise 9_Insert Tab-Delimited Data   258

10. Cascading Style Sheets_____262

Exercise 1_Redefining HTML Styles with Style Sheets 264
Exercise 2_Defining a Custom Class   271
Exercise 3_Using Selectors to Group Tags   275
Exercise 4_Affecting Links with Selectors   277
Exercise 5_Linking to a Style Sheet   281
Exercise 6_From CSS to HTML   286

11. Templates / Libraries_____288

Exercise 1_Templates in Action   290
Exercise 2_Creating a New Template   296
Exercise 3_Modifying a Template   303
Exercise 4_Library Items in Action   307
Exercise 5_Creating a Library Item   310
Exercise 6_Modifying a Library Item   312

12. Frames_____314

Frames: A Love-or-Hate Proposition   316
Exercise 1_Saving Your First Frameset   318
Exercise 2_Coloring Frames   325
Exercise 3_Links and Targets   328
Exercise 4_Adding a Background Image   334
Exercise 5_Seamless Background Across Two Frames   342
Exercise 6_Frames Object Palette   346

13. Rollovers _____ 352

Exercise 1_Creating a Simple Rollover   354

Exercise 2_Animated Rollovers   357

Exercise 3_Creating Pointer Rollovers   361

Exercise 4_Creating Multiple-Event Rollovers   368

Exercise 5_Inserting a Navigation Bar Rollover   374

Exercise 6_Inserting a Simple Rollover from Fireworks   385

14. Automation _____ 388

Exercise 1_Using the History Palette for Undo/Redo   389

Exercise 2_Copying and Pasting History   394

Exercise 3_Applying HTML Styles   398

Exercise 4_Creating Keyboard Shortcuts   406

15. Forms _____ 412

Form Objects   414

Exercise 1_Working with Form Objects   416

Exercise 2_Creating a Form   424

Exercise 3_Creating a Jump Menu   430

16. DHTML _____ 438

Exercise 1_Dragging Layers   440

Exercise 2_Using a Timeline for Animation   446

Exercise 3_Playing, Stopping, and Resetting the Timeline   452

17. Behaviors _____ 456

Exercise 1_Creating a Check Browser Behavior   458

Exercise 2_Creating a Set Text of Status Bar Behavior   467

Exercise 3_Creating a Set Text of Text Field Behavior   471

Exercise 4_Opening a New Browser Window   477

Exercise 5_Installing the Extension Manager   481

Exercise 6_Inserting ImageReady HTML   484

Exercise 7_Downloading from Macromedia Exchange   491

18. Commands _____ 500

Getting More Commands	501
Exercise 1_Color Schemes	504
Exercise 2_Create Web Photo Album Command	506
Exercise 3_Optimize Image in Fireworks Command	512
Exercise 4_Mailto Command, Using the History Palette	517

19. Plug-Ins _____ 522

Exercise 1_Linking to Sounds	524
Exercise 2_Embedding Sounds	528
Exercise 3_Inserting Flash Content	531
Exercise 4_Inserting Director (Shockwave) Content	533
Exercise 5_Inserting a QuickTime Movie	536

20. Getting it Online _____ 538

Free Web Hosting with GeoCities	539
Exercise 1_Setting Up with GeoCities	540
Exercise 2_Setting the FTP Preferences	544
Exercise 3_Putting Files to the Web Server	547
Exercise 4_File Synchronization	552

Troubleshooting FAQ (Appendix A)	558
Online Resources (Appendix B)	566
Technical Support (Appendix C)	570
Index	572

Introduction

A Note from Lynda	About the Authors	Our Team
Acknowledgements	How to Use this Book
HTML Versus HTM	Interface Screen Captures
System Differences	A Note to Windows Users
Making Exercise Files Editable on Windows Systems
Dreamweaver System Requirements	H·O·T CD-ROM Contents

H·O·T
_____
Dreamweaver 3

A Note From Lynda Weinman

In my opinion, most people buy computer books in order to learn, yet it is amazing how few of these books are actually written by teachers. My co-author, Garo Green, and I take pride in the fact that this book was written by experienced teachers who are familiar with training students in this subject matter. In this book, you will find carefully developed lessons and exercises to help you learn Dreamweaver 3 – one of the most well-respected HTML editors on the planet.

This book is targeted towards beginning to intermediate level Web developers who are looking for a great tool to speed up production, offer workflow flexibility, and create great code and results. The premise of the hands-on exercise approach is to get you up to speed quickly in Dreamweaver 3, while actively working through the book's lessons. It's one thing to read about a product, and an entirely other experience to try the product and get measurable results.

Many exercise-based books take a paint-by-numbers approach to teaching. While this approach works, it's often difficult to figure out how to apply those lessons to a real-world situation, or understand why or when you would use the technique again. What sets this book apart is that the lessons contain lots of background information and insights into each given subject, which are designed to help you understand the process as well as the exercise.

At times, pictures are worth a lot more than words. When necessary, we have also included short QuickTime movies to show any process that's difficult to explain with words. These files are located on the **H•O•T CD-ROM** inside a folder called **movies**. It's my style to approach teaching from many different angles since I know that some people are visual learners, others like to read, and still others like to get out there and try things. This book combines a lot of teaching approaches so you can learn Dreamweaver 3 as thoroughly as you want to.

This book didn't set out to cover every single aspect of Dreamweaver. The manual, and many other reference books are great for that! What we saw missing from the bookshelves was a process-oriented book that taught readers core principles, techniques, and tips in a hands-on training format.

We welcome your comments at dw3hot@lynda.com. Please visit our Web site as well, at http://www.lynda.com. The support URL for this book is http://www.lynda.com/books/dw3hot/.

It's Garo's and my hope that this book will raise your skills in Web design, HTML, JavaScript, and publishing. If it does, then we will have accomplished the job we set out to do!

-**Lynda Weinman**

Note | **About lynda.com/books and lynda.com**

lynda.com/books is dedicated to helping Web designers and developers understand tools and design principles. **lynda.com** offers hands-on workshops, training seminars, on-site training, training videos, training CDs, and "expert tips" for Web design and development. To learn more about our training programs, books, and products, be sure to give our site a visit at http://www.lynda.com.

About the Authors

Lynda Weinman

Lynda has been practicing computer design and animation since 1984, when she bought one of the first Macintosh computers. She worked as an animator and motion graphics director in the special effects industry for seven years before having a daughter in 1989. At that time, she was asked to teach her first workshop in multimedia animation, and eventually became a full-time faculty member at Art Center College of Design in Pasadena, California.

Lynda has been a beta tester for imaging and animation software packages since 1984, and has worked as a consultant for Adobe, Macromedia, and Microsoft. She has conducted workshops at Disney, Microsoft, Adobe, and Macromedia, and has been a highly sought-after keynote speaker, moderator and/or speaker at numerous design, broadcast design, animation, Web design, and computer graphics conferences.

Lynda is the co-founder of lynda.com, which specializes in Web design training via hands-on classes, seminars, training videos, books, Web tips, and CD-ROMs. Visit her site, http://www.lynda.com to learn more....

Garo Green

Garo Green is the Director of Training at lynda.com in Ojai, California. His responsibilities include course and curriculum development, faculty selection/training, as well as managing on-site training. Prior to joining lynda.com, Garo was a software instructor and Intranet developer for State Farm Insurance Company.

Garo has worked extensively in the development of custom curriculum and courseware for software training. He has over five years of teaching experience in both hardware and software applications. In addition, he has an extensive knowledge of HTML, computer graphics, and Web design. He is well versed in Dreamweaver, Fireworks, Flash, Freehand, Photoshop, GoLive, and ImageReady.

Garo is the co-author of the Dreamweaver 3 H•O•T book and Learning Dreamweaver 3 CD-ROM. He has also been a featured speaker at the Web99 and FlashForward2000 conferences.

In his spare time... (well, he doesn't have much of that anymore, but that's OK) he has found that his passion for teaching and sharing what he knows is very fulfilling. He does sneak away, several times a day, to the local coffeehouse for a double-latte with hazelnut. Of course this might explain why he talks so fast. ;-)

_____**Our Team**

Lynda and Garo take a break from their
busy schedules to smile at the camera.

The lynda.com training center offers classes
in Dreamweaver, Flash, Fireworks, Photoshop, ImageReady, GoLive, and Web design
principles. Visit www.lynda.com/classes for
more information.

A blurry Bruce and Lynda at their
training center via digital camera.

Lynda's daughter Jaimie
in a very serious mood
(as usual).

Lynda with book designer, Ali Karp
at their combination book signing
and photography exhibit.

_____Acknowledgements from Lynda

I could not have written this book without the help of several key people.
Special thanks to:

My **writing partner** on this project, **Garo Green**, who is not only someone I'm proud to call a dear friend, but who has an amazing gift for educating and sharing his vast knowledge with others.

My **book designer**, the always incredible **Ali Karp**, who not only laid out pages, but also beta tested, took a Dreamweaver workshop from us, and gave her usual 200% to this project. This is the 12th book that Ali and I have collaborated on in five years. Wow.

My **husband**, **Bruce Heavin**, who made the cover art, put up with the countless hours it took to complete this project, and was always there for moral support (and the ever-important foot massages!).

My **daughter**, **Jamie**, who provided ever-important cuddle time with her mom after a hard day's work on the book. Thanks for being so understanding and always sharing your sense of humor with me.

My **editor at Peachpit**, **Cary Norsworthy**, who contributed numerous great ideas, and whose opinion I always valued and appreciated. It's a rare treat to get to work with such a fine mind and kind soul. Thanks, Cary.

Our **developmental editor**, the brilliant **Lisa Brenneis**, who is not only smart, but has good taste in music and hometowns. She's da bomb.

Our **production artists, Heidi Goodspeed, Sean Blumenthal**, and **David Reeser**. Thanks for making the job of assembling all the images for this book more manageable for everyone. And I must also thank **Pamela Nye** and **Sean Dowey** for all the "photocopying," and "overnight shipping." It was a lot of work!

Our beloved **copy editor**, **Joan Morley**, who worked endless hours on this very complicated manuscript.

The **folks at Macromedia** who made this amazing HTML editor – especially the honorable **Kevin Lynch**, whose brilliance and vision is undisputed by all.

All of our fantastic **lynda.com staff**. You all make having a business much more fun than working out of my garage. ;-)

Acknowledgements from Garo

This book, and every other book you read, could not have been possible without a strong team of dedicated, enthusiastic, and talented individuals. I was fortunate enough to work with the best.

My deepest thanks and appreciation to:

My **co-author** and dear friend, **Lynda Weinman**. Thank you for putting me on your shoulders, so I could catch my dreams. Your friendship and support made writing this book a pleasure.

My **developmental editor** (and occasional therapist), **Lisa Brenneis**. If behind every great man there is a great woman, then behind every great author there is a great developmental editor. You always managed to make me smile and keep me inspired, even when the box of Cocoa Pebbles started talking to me. I hope we will be friends for a long time.

My **editor at Peachpit, Cary Norsworthy**, who could find a needle in a haystack any day! Your comments and suggestions were always great. Thank you so much for all of your hard work and extra effort on this book.

My **book designer, Ali Karp**, who would spend many sleepless nights laying out the pages, chapter after chapter. Thank you for making my words look so good. You friendship and support carried me through the good and hard times of writing this book.

My **editor, Joan Morley**. Boy, it's a good thing you were there to keep me from crossing my I's and dotting my T's. You did such a great job, even under the tightest deadlines.

My **beta testers, Dina Pielaet, Garrick Chow, Ellen Norgard, Cheri Hackett**, and **Kymberlee Weil**. I want to thank you guys for working so hard and quickly. Your valuable and humorous comments made it so much fun to write this book, even when it meant rewriting an entire exercise!

My **layout assistants, Heidi Goodspeed, Sean Blumenthal**, and **David Reeser** who helped make sure that all of my images were in order and looked good. I don't know how you guys did it, but thank you so much!

My **friends at Macromedia, Beth Davis, Eric Ott, Mike Sundymeyer**, and all of the Dreamweaver Engineers. Thanks for making such an amazing product! I have really enjoyed working with you guys.

The entire **lynda.com staff. Pamela Nye, Tony Winecoff, Heather Rowe**, and **Ramey McCullough**. You guys make coming to work each day fun; what more could a person ask for?

How To Use This Book

Please read this section—it contains important information that's going to help you as you use this book. The chart below outlines the information we cover:

Dreamweaver 3 H•O•T
Information in this Chapter:
The Formatting in This Book
HTML versus HTM
Macintosh and Windows Interface Screen Captures
Mac and Windows System Differences
• Choose versus Select
• Choose on MacOS 8 versus Open on MacOS 9
A Note to Windows Users
• Making Exercise Files Editable on Windows Systems
• Making File Extensions Visible on Windows Systems
• Creating New Documents
Dreamweaver System Requirements
H•O•T CD-ROM Contents

Note | The Formatting in This Book

This book has several components, including step-by-step exercises, commentary, notes, tips, warnings, and movies. Step-by-step exercises are numbered, and file names and command keys are bolded so they pop out more easily. You might notice that certain words are capitalized, such as Tables, Frames, Layers, etc. We chose to capitalize these terms to call more attention to them, and to mimic how the terms appear in Dreamweaver.

Captions and commentary are in italicized text: *This is a caption..* File names/folders, Command keys, and Menu commands are bolded: **images** folder, **Ctrl+Click**, and **File > Open…**. Code is in a monospace font: `<html></html>`. And URLs are in light serif font: http://www.lynda.com.

HTML Versus HTM

All of the HTML exercise files on the CD-ROM end with an .html extension. Windows users might be more used to naming files with an .htm extension. You can name your files either way, and a Web browser will be able to read them. The choice to name them with the four-letter extension represents a personal bias that we prefer. The shorter .htm suffix is a throwback to the old days of DOS when file names were limited to the eight-dot-three convention. That meant that file names could be no longer than eight characters, and had to end with a dot and a three-letter extension. Those days are history since the advent of Windows 95/98/2000, so we named all the files with the more accurate four-letter extension. It does, after all, stand for **H**yper**T**ext **M**arkup **L**anguage, not HyperText Markup! Now you know why we chose to name the files this way, but the bottom line of this explanation is that you can use either naming method and your HTML files will still work as long as they have been referenced this way in the links. We simply made a choice to use the four-letter extension because that's what we prefer to use.

Macintosh and Windows Interface Screen Captures

Most of the screen captures in the book were taken on a Macintosh. The only time Windows shots were taken was when the interface differed from the Macintosh. We made this decision because we do most of our design work and writing on a Macintosh. We also own and use a Windows system, so we noted important differences when they occurred, and took screen captures accordingly.

Mac and Windows System Differences

Macromedia has done a great job of ensuring that Dreamweaver looks and works the same between the Macintosh and Windows operating systems. However, there are still some differences that should be noted. If you are using this book with one of the Windows operating systems, please be sure to read the following section, titled *"A Note to Windows Users,"* carefully.

Warning | "Choose" for Mac and "Select" for Windows

Throughout this book, you will be instructed to click the **Choose** button. This is the correct way to do it on the Macintosh with OS 8.6. On the PC with Windows, you will instead see a **Select** button. The two buttons are interchangeable and do the same thing.

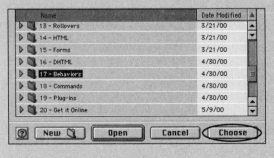 

Click **Choose** on a Macintosh.   Click **Select** on Windows.

Warning | "Choose" on Mac System 8 Replaced by "Open" on System 9

As we were writing this book, a new version of the Macintosh operating system, System 9, was released. Since some of you will be using System 8 and others 9, it is necessary to be aware of the following difference. When you **Browse for Files**, System 8 will display a **Choose** button, whereas System 9 will display an **Open** button. Both buttons perform the same function, even though they have different names.

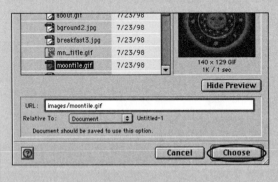 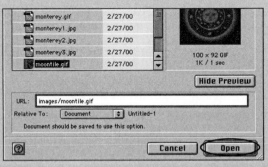

System 8 displays a **Choose** button.   System 9 displays an **Open** button.

A Note to Windows Users

This section contains essential information about making your exercise folders editable, making file extensions visible, and creating new Dreamweaver documents from the document window versus the Site window.

Making Exercise Files Editable on Windows Systems

By default, when you copy files from a CD-ROM to your Windows 95/98/2000 hard drive, they are set to read-only (write protected). This will cause a problem with the exercise files, because you will need to write over some of them. When you define a site (you will learn to do this in Chapter 3, *"Site Control"*), you will notice that the files have a small lock next to them which means the files have been set to read-only. To remove this setting and make them editable, follow the short procedure below:

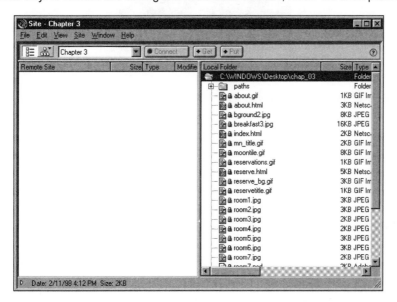

1. Define your site using the folder you copied from the **H•O•T CD-ROM**. When the Site window opens, you will see little locks next to all of the files.

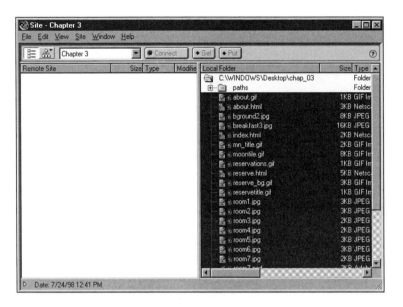

2. Ctrl+Click on each of the files that has a lock next to it.

3. Once you have all of the files selected, select **File > Turn Off Read Only**.

Making File Extensions Visible on Windows Systems

In this section, you'll see three different examples of how to turn on file extensions for Windows 95, Windows 98, and Windows 2000. By default, Windows 95/98/2000 users will not be able to see file extension names such as .gif, .jpg, or .html. Don't worry, you can change this setting!

Windows 95 Users:

1. Double-click on the **My Computer** icon on your desktop. **Note:** If you (or someone else) have changed the name, it will not say **My Computer**.

2. Select **View > Options**. This will open the **Options** dialog box.

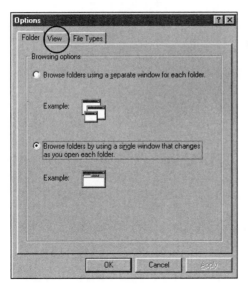 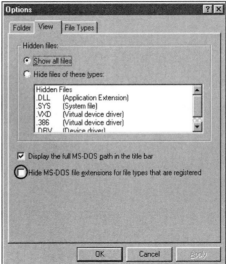

3. Click on the **View** tab at the top. This will open the **View** options screen so you can change the view settings of Windows 95.

4. Make sure there is no checkmark in the **Hide MS-DOS file extensions for file types that are registered** box. This will ensure that the file extensions are visible, which will help you better understand the exercises in this book!

Windows 98 Users:

1. Double-click on the **My Computer** icon on your desktop. **Note:** If you (or someone else) have changed the name, it will not say **My Computer**.

2. Select **View > Folder Options**. This will open the **Folder Options** dialog box.

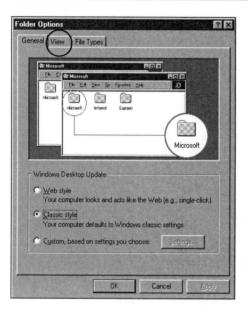 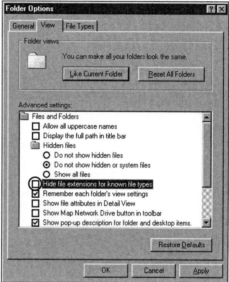

3. Click on the **View** tab at the top. This will open the **View** options screen so you can change the view settings of Windows 98.

4. Uncheck the **Hide File extensions for known file types** checkbox. This will make all of the file extensions visible.

Windows 2000 Users:

---

1. Double-click on the **My Computer** icon on your desktop. **Note:** If you (or someone else) have changed the name, it will not say **My Computer**.

---

2. Select **Tools > Folder Options**. This will open the **Folder Options** dialog box.

---

3. Click on the **View** tab at the top. This will open the **View** options screen so you can change the view settings of Windows 2000.

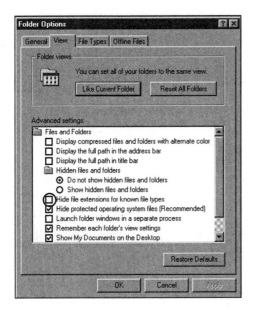

4. Make sure there is no checkmark next to the **Hide File extensions for known file types** option. This will make all of the file extensions visible.

Creating New Documents

Creating a new document in Dreamweaver can vary a little, depending on whether you are in the document window or the Site window.

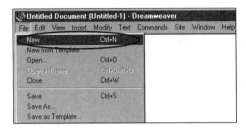

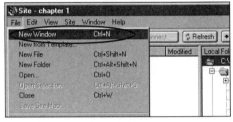

• To create a new document with the document window open, select **File > New** or press **Ctrl + N**.

• To create a new document that opens as a blank document window from the Site window, select **File > New Window**. If you were to select **File > New File**, the document would only appear in the Site window, and not as a new Untitled Document.

Dreamweaver System Requirements

This book requires that you use either a Macintosh operating system (Power Macintosh running System 8.1 or later) or Windows 95, Windows 98, or Windows NT 4.0. You also will need a color monitor capable of 800 x 600 resolution and a CD-ROM drive. We suggest that you have at least 64 MB of RAM in your system, because it's optimal if you can open Dreamweaver and a Web browser at the same time. More RAM than that is even better, especially on Macintosh computers, which do not dynamically allocate RAM like Windows. Here's a little chart that cites Macromedia's RAM requirements, along with our recommendations:

Dreamweaver RAM Requirements		
	Dreamweaver	**We Recommend**
Mac	32 MB	64 MB
Windows 95/98/NT	32 MB	64 MB

What's on the CD-ROM?

Exercise Files and the H•O•T CD-ROM

Your course files are located inside a folder called **exercise_files** on the **H•O•T CD-ROM**. These files are divided into chapter folders, and you will be instructed to copy the chapter folders to your hard drive during many of the exercises. Unfortunately, when files originate from a CD-ROM, the Windows operating system defaults to making them write-protected, meaning that you cannot alter them. You will need to alter them to follow the exercises, so please read the Note to Windows Users on pages xix and xx for instructions on how to convert them to read-and-write formatting.

Demo Files on the CD-ROM

In addition to the exercise files, the **H•O•T CD-ROM** also contains free 30-day trial versions of several software applications for Mac or Windows. All software is located inside the **software** folder on the **H•O•T CD-ROM**. We have included trial versions of:

- Macromedia Dreamweaver 3.0 + (3.01 Update)
- Macromedia Extension Manager
- Macromedia Fireworks 3.0
- Netscape Navigator 3.0 • Netscape Navigator 4.7
- Internet Explorer 3.0 • Internet Explorer 4.5 • Internet Explorer 5.0

We also have included several plug-ins on the **H•O•T CD-ROM**. If you don't have these plug-ins installed already, you should do that before working with any exercise in this book that calls for one of them. All of the plug-ins are located inside the **software** folder. We have included the following:

- Flash 4.0 plug-in
- Shockwave 8.0 plug-in
- QuickTime 4.1.2 plug-in

I.

Background

Roundtrip HTML	HTML
File Naming	Extending Dreamweaver
DHTML	XML	JavaScript

H•O•T

Hands-On-Training

We could start this book with lots of exercises, throwing you right into working with Dreamweaver without any preparation. But then you would be flying blind, without understanding basic Web-design fundamentals such as HTML, DHTML, XML, and JavaScript. Instead, we are starting you off with some definitions, concepts, and guidelines to help with your hands-on Dreamweaver training. Feel free to scan this chapter for information, in the event you already know some of what is here or want the instant gratification of getting started.

What Is Dreamweaver?

Dreamweaver is a WYSIWYG (**W**hat **Y**ou **S**ee **I**s **W**hat **Y**ou **G**et) HTML generator. This means if you change something on the screen inside Dreamweaver, it will show you the results instantly. In contrast, if you were to code the HTML by hand, you would have to look at the code inside a Web browser to see the results. The instant feedback of a live design environment such as Dreamweaver speeds up your workflow tremendously, because you can see whether you like the results while you are working.

Roundtrip HTML

Dreamweaver has gained a lot of great reviews and customer loyalty because of its invention of roundtrip HTML. Roundtrip HTML means you can alter the code that Dreamweaver automatically writes. Virtually all other WYSIWYG HTML editors today do not let you alter the code they produce. That's because they need to work with code that's written in a specific way, so they can offer all the WYSIWYG features. In other words, the code is self-serving to help the program, not to create the HTML.

Why is roundtrip HTML important? Because you can alter the code that Dreamweaver writes, and it will leave your changes alone, even if it doesn't understand them. This respect for your changes is key, because the program doesn't assume it knows what you want better than you do. Don't you wish all programs were so respectful?

Roundtrip HTML is especially important because HTML isn't yet a stable standard. If you have been watching the development of HTML, you might have noticed that it's changed a lot since it was first introduced in 1993. The inventors of the markup language didn't really expect that the Web would catch on as it has or that people would want to do full-scale multimedia with HTML.

To put it politely, HTML was extremely limited when it was first released. Browsers, such as Mosaic, Netscape Navigator, and Microsoft Internet Explorer, pushed the early boundaries of developing HTML without the consent of the Web's formal standards committee (the World Wide Web Consortium, or W3C). This meant that if you were using a WYSIWYG editor that didn't allow you to write your own code, you were prevented from trying some of the new markup that wasn't officially part of HTML. So many people who started with visual HTML editors, such as Adobe PageMill, Claris HomePage, NetObjects Fusion, and Microsoft Front-Page, couldn't always take advantage of the latest features that were supported by browsers.

It was like having a tool that handcuffed you in time to whatever was possible at the moment it was released. Roundtrip HTML, on the other hand, allows you to try things that aren't even invented yet. That's pretty cool.

Programmers have looked at HTML editors with dubious eyes because of the inflexibility of these tools and their inclusion of nonstandard HTML code. Dreamweaver is the first HTML editor to win the approval of programmers and designers alike. Programmers like the product because they are not tied to writing code in a rigid manner. Designers like Dreamweaver because it writes clean code without a lot of proprietary and self-serving tags, and it allows them to do a lot of great visual layout without understanding even a line of code. Hard to believe there could be a tool to please both of these divergent groups, but there is, and Dreamweaver is it.

Do You Need to Learn HTML to Use Dreamweaver?

For most people, HTML is quite intimidating at first glance — your first reaction may be to avoid it at all costs. In order to do design work in Photoshop, QuarkXPress, or PageMaker, it isn't necessary to look at raw PostScript code anymore. However, the early pioneers of desktop publishing had to know how to program in PostScript just to create a page layout! Because we are actually still in the infancy of the Web and HTML development, most early Web developers have been programmers, not artists, because it was necessary to write the raw code to create a Web page.

HTML has come a long way since its inception, and many of its features have become standardized while others have not. In the past, if you didn't know some HTML, you were at the mercy of a programmer who might have more control over your design than you liked. Today, with Dreamweaver, you can get by without understanding or writing a single line of code. Attractive though it might be, we recommend that you do understand HTML at its simplest, so you aren't afraid of it. No one likes to work in fear, and we find that most people who don't take the time to learn a little HTML are at a disadvantage in the workplace. When you don't understand HTML, it's sort of like having a secret that you hope no one will discover, or feeling like a fake and worrying that you will be found out. No one likes that feeling!

How do you learn HTML? The best way is to view the source code of pages that you like. Most of the HTML jocks we've met have taught themselves in this way. One of the best things about HTML is that "learn by doing" is possible. If you were to try to learn other computer languages this way, you most likely could not, because the code would be compiled and hidden from your view. In HTML, the code is visible to everyone and is parsed on-the-fly by the Web browser itself. To view the source code of a page, look under your browser's **Edit** menu and choose **View > Page Source** (Netscape) or **View > View Source** (Explorer). This will show you the raw HTML, and once you get comfortable with some of the tags, you will likely be able to deconstruct how these pages were made.

HTML Resources

There are many great resources, online and off, for learning HTML. Here are some online sites that are worth checking out.

NCSA: A Beginner's Guide to HTML Home Page
http://www.ncsa.uiuc.edu/General/Internet/WWW/HTMLPrimer.html

HTML: An Interactive Tutorial for Beginners
http://www.davesite.com/webstation/html/

The WDVL: HTML – The Hypertext Markup Language
http://www.stars.com/Tutorial/HTML/

Webmonkey: HTML Tutorial
http://www.hotwired.com/webmonkey/teachingtool/index.html

NCDesign: HTML Design Guide v4.0
http://www.ncdesign.org/html/

Index DOT HTML: The Advanced HTML Reference
http://home.webmonster.net/mirrors/bloo-html/

The HTML Writers Guild: A Resource List
http://www.hwg.org/resourceshtml/intros.html

What Does HTML Do?

HTML stands for HyperText Markup Language. It is a derivative of SGML (Standard Generalized Markup Language), an international standard for representing text in an electronic form that can be used for exchanging documents in an independent manner.

When Lynda first touched computers, (way) back in 1980, people had to use a form of markup in word processor documents. If you wanted something to have a bold face, for example, you had to tag it with the symbol <B> in order to create that formatting. You would never see the actual boldfaced text until the file was printed; back then, bold type could not even be displayed on the computer screen!

We've come a long way since then, and so has HTML. That's why programs such as Dreamweaver are starting to become viable alternatives to writing all the tags by hand. With maturity and established standards, HTML in its raw form will likely become as hidden away as the markup behind word processors is today.

At its heart, HTML allows for the markup of text and the inclusion of images, as well as the ability to link documents together. Hyperlinks, which are at the core of HTML's success, are what allow us to flip between pages in a site, or to view pages in outside sites. These hyperlinks are references that are contained within the markup. If the source of the link moves or the reference to the link is misspelled, it won't work. One of the great attributes of Dreamweaver is its site-management capabilities, which will help you manage your internal links so they are automatically updated if they change or are moved.

What Does HTML Look Like?

HTML uses a combination of tags, attributes, and values to generate its results. Here is a sample line of code that uses a tag, an attribute, and a value.

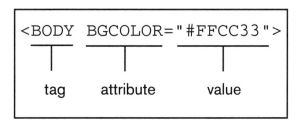

In this line of code, the tag is <BODY>, the attribute is BGCOLOR, and the value is FFCC33. When put together, this collection of items within the brackets < > is called an **element**.

Many tags require **opening** and **closing containers**, as marked here for the <BODY> elements.

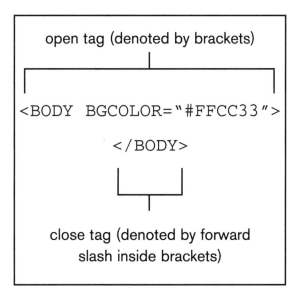

HTML Deconstructed

All HTML pages follow a basic structure. Each page must contain the HTML, HEAD, TITLE, and BODY tags. Whenever you open a new Untitled Document in Dreamweaver, this framework is already written. It is deconstructed for you below. Fortunately, you don't have to worry about getting this structure right. It is automatically built in to any page you create in Dreamweaver.

1. `<HTML>`
2. `<HEAD>`
3. `<TITLE>Untitled Document</TITLE>`
4. `<META HTTP-EQUIV="Content-Type" CONTENT="text/html; charset=iso-8859-1">`
5. `</HEAD>`
6. `<BODY BGCOLOR="#FFFFFF">`
7. `</BODY>`
8. `</HTML>`

1. Notice how the `<HTML>` tag is at the beginning of the document? It signifies that this is an HTML page. Without this tag, a browser cannot read the page. See line 8, the close `</HTML>` tag? This tag requires an open and a close tag. Both tags are required for most HTML tags, but not all.

2. The `<HEAD>` element of the document contains the HEAD information. In this case, the TITLE tag and the META tag are contained within the HEAD.

3. The `<TITLE>` is what appears at the top of the page inside a browser. If you leave the title **Untitled Document**, as in the example above, that is exactly what will appear! Dreamweaver has a setting for easily changing this title. We will get to this setting in Chapter 4, *"Basics."*

4. META tags are HEAD elements that record information about the current page, such as the character encoding, author, copyright, and keywords. Many properties can be set here, which you will learn about in Chapter 4, *"Basics."*

5. Here's the close tag for the HEAD element. Notice that the TITLE and META tags were nested within the HEAD tag.

6. The BODY tag is specifying that this page will be white, instead of the default gray. If you don't enter a BGCOLOR value here, the page will defer to browser defaults.

7. This is the close tag for BODY.

8. This is the close tag for HTML.

File-Naming Conventions

Working with HTML is much more restrictive than working with other types of computer media. The strictest part about HTML is its file-naming conventions.

Don't use spaces: It's best if you save your files using no spaces in between the file name elements. For example, the file name **about lynda.html** would be considered illegal because of the space between the words **about** and **lynda**. Instead, you would write this file name as **about_lynda.html** or **aboutlynda.html**.

Avoid capital letters: It is best to avoid capitalization in your file names. Although **AboutLynda.html** will work as a file name, anytime you link to the file you will have to remember the correct capitalization because many UNIX servers are case sensitive. It is far easier to simply use all lowercase letters.

Avoid illegal characters: The chart below contains a list of characters to avoid when naming files.

File-Naming Conventions	
Character	**Usage**
.(dot)	Periods are reserved for file name extensions or suffixes, for example .gif and .jpg.
"	Quotes are reserved for HTML to indicate the value of tags and attributes.
/ or \	Forward slashes (/) indicate that the files are nested in folders. If you include a forward slash in your file name, HTML may lose your references, thinking you are specifying a folder. A backslash (\) isn't allowed on MS-Windows servers.
:	Colons are used to separate certain script commands on Macs and Windows. Avoid them in your file names so as not to confuse a file name with a script command.
!	Exclamation marks are used in comment tags.

File Name Extensions

You may be curious about the many extensions used after the dot at the end of file names. Below is a chart which lists the meaning of some extensions you'll commonly run across.

File Name Extensions	
Extension	**Usage**
.html, .htm	These two extensions are commonly used to denote an HTML file. The three-letter extension works just as well as the four-letter version. Older DOS systems didn't allow for four-letter extensions, which is why you sometimes see .html abbreviated as .htm. Dreamweaver defaults to using .htm.
.gif	GIF images
.jpg	JPEG images
.swf	Flash files
.mov	QuickTime movie files
.avi	AVI movie files
.aif	AIFF sound files

Extending Dreamweaver

One of the neatest things about the Dreamweaver community is the way people share **Objects**, **Commands**, and **Behaviors**. These pre-built elements can be shared and distributed, much the way Photoshop Plug-Ins work. If you visit the Dreamweaver section of the Macromedia site, you'll find numerous listings for shared resources. Here are a few of our favorites.

Dreamweaver Depot

http://people.netscape.com/andreww/dreamweaver/
This is one of the largest repositories of Dreamweaver Objects, Commands, and Actions on the Internet. Many of them were developed by the site's owner, Andrew Woodbridge.

Dreamweaver Extensions Database

http://www.idest.com/cgi-bin/database.cgi
At this site, you are able to search an extensive database, which includes all of the Dreamweaver extensions.

Yaromat

http://www.yaromat.com/dw/index.htm
A personal home page that contains several very useful Dreamweaver extensions, including a great one for importing Fireworks-created rollovers.

Massimo's Corner of the Web

http://www.massimocorner.com
A great resource for Dreamweaver extensions, Objects, Commands, and Behaviors. It has an interesting DHTML interface, too!

What Is DHTML?

DHTML (**D**ynamic **HTML**) is a collection of different technologies. This can include any combination of HTML, JavaScript, CSS (**C**ascading **S**tyle **S**heets), and DOM (**D**ocument **O**bject **M**odel). The purpose of combining these technologies is to allow the authoring of more dynamic content than what basic HTML affords.

Some of the things possible with DHTML include animation, drag-and-drop, and complicated rollovers (buttons that change when a mouse moves over them). Dreamweaver uses DHTML to enable you to create pages with buttons that change in more than one place on the screen at the same time.

Just like HTML, if you program DHTML effects in Dreamweaver, most of the coding occurs behind the scenes. You don't have to see it unless you choose to.

There are, however, some serious cross-platform issues with DHTML, because it is supported quite differently by Netscape and Explorer (the two leading browsers). Fortunately, Dreamweaver lets you target specific browsers, as well as test the cross-browser compatibility of your DHTML effects.

DHTML Combinations

DHTML uses a combination of HTML, JavaScript, CSS, and DOM. Below is a chart with a short definition of each.

DHTML Terms	
Technology	**Explanation**
HTML	(**H**yper**T**ext **M**arkup **L**anguage) The default markup for basic Web pages and the root of DHTML
JavaScript	A scripting language that extends the capabilities of HTML
CSS	(**C**ascading **S**tyle **S**heets) A page-layout system supported by newer Web browsers, which allows for better control over the appearance and positioning of elements on a Web page
DOM	(**D**ocument **O**bject **M**odel) A hook to outside scripting protocols, such as ActiveX, or external Plug-Ins, such as Shockwave or Flash. It allows scripts and programs to address and update documents.

What Is XML?

XML stands for **Ex**tensible **M**arkup **L**anguage. The specifications for XML are still in development, but many people are looking to XML as a solution to improve interactivity between Web sites and databases. XML would make it possible, for example, to sort a list of names alphabetically online. It would also enable much more sophisticated searching of data, making it a boon to many Web-based forms and databases.

Dreamweaver supports templates, covered in Chapter 11, *"Templates/Library Items."* One of the advanced features of Dreamweaver 3 is the ability to import XML databases through a template. Because XML is so new, and the use of databases is outside the scope of this book, we don't include any XML exercises in any of the chapters. But you can investigate XML extensibility at the developer's area of the Dreamweaver site.

Macromedia Developer's Site

http://www.macromedia.com/support/dreamweaver/

World Wide Web Consortium

http://www.w3.org/xml/

What is JavaScript?

JavaScript was developed by Netscape in 1996 and has become almost as popular as HTML. It actually has nothing to do with the Java programming language, but Netscape licensed the name from Sun Microsystems in hopes of increasing acceptance of the new scripting protocol. We're not sure if it was the name that did the trick, but JavaScript has become almost as widely adopted as HTML itself! The most common uses of JavaScript allow for rollovers, resizing of browser windows, and checking for browser compatibility.

Most of the JavaScript routines are accessed by Dreamweaver's Behaviors palette, which you will learn about in Chapter 13, *"Rollovers,"* and Chapter 16, *"DHTML."* This is one area of Dreamweaver's product that must be previewed in a browser to be visible. This book covers many JavaScript techniques, including rollovers (Chapter 13, *"Rollovers"*), browser-sniffing (Chapter 10, *"Cascading Style Sheets"*), and launching external browser windows (Chapter 15, *"Forms"*).

You will not have to learn to write JavaScript by hand in order to use it within Dreamweaver. This is very fortunate for those of us who are not programmers, because JavaScript programming is more complicated than HTML.

2.

Interface

| Interface Tour | Objects Palette |
| Launcher and Mini-Launcher |
| Properties Inspector |
| Document Window | Preferences |

H•O•T

Hands-On-Training

We are both big fans of the Dreamweaver 3 interface. Other HTML editors that we've used require that you open a lot of windows and palettes in order to reach all of the features. Instead, Dreamweaver uses a few primary windows and palettes that change depending on the context of what you are doing. This saves screen real estate and makes learning the interface a lot easier than with other comparable programs. Although you might believe at this point that learning Dreamweaver represents a big learning curve, understanding the interface is probably one of the easier challenges ahead of you.

This chapter will take you through the basic concepts of the program's interface. In addition to a tour through the interface features, we've also shared how to set up our favorite Dreamweaver **Preferences** settings and configurations.

You might be antsy to start in on some of the step-by-step exercises contained in later chapters, but this chapter is needed first to establish how to use the interface.

A Tour of the Interface

The features that Dreamweaver 3 offers are very sophisticated, but its interface is actually quite simple. There are five main parts to this program, as illustrated below.

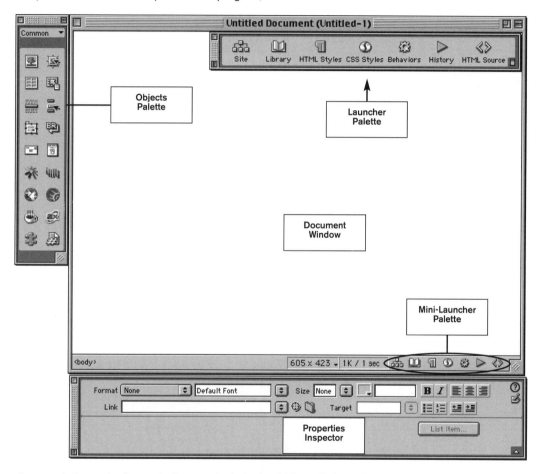

*As stated above, the five main features include the **Objects Palette**, **Properties Inspector**, **Launcher**, **Mini-Launcher**, and **Document Window**. Whenever you open Dreamweaver, it defaults to opening a new **Untitled Document**, as shown here.*

The Objects Palette

The Objects palette is used as a one-click stop for many operations. If you move your mouse over the Objects palette and pause for a moment, you will see what each one of the icons stands for. You may alter the appearance of this palette in your Dreamweaver Preferences, if you would like.

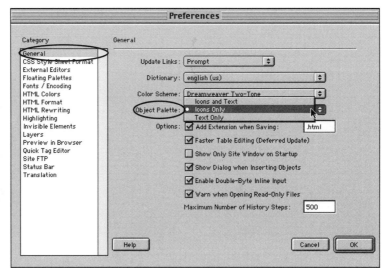

*The Objects palette shown above is in its default mode. To change the appearance of the Objects palette, select Edit > Preferences… > General > Object Palette. The Objects palette's setting can be changed to **Icons and Text**, **Icons Only**, or **Text Only**.*

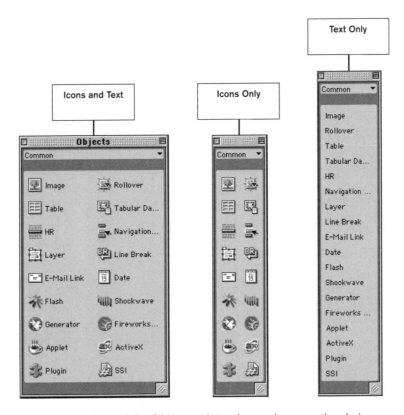

The three versions of the Objects palette shown above are the choices available in the Preferences. As you examine the Objects palette, you'll see that it allows you to access essential functions, such as inserting an image, a table, a horizontal rule, and so on. Note: These functions are called Objects in the Dreamweaver 3 Objects palette.

Many items that exist as objects are also found under the Insert menu in the top menu bar. The Objects palette provides a one-click alternative to using that menu bar. Some people are more comfortable clicking the icons, and others prefer the menu access. There is no right or wrong way to do this; it's just a matter of personal preference.

Important Note: Windows users – the underlined letters in the menu names and command names represent the **Alt+key** shortcuts you can use. For example, to insert an image, you can first hit **Alt+I** (for the **Insert** menu) and then press I again for the Image command. The I is underlined for both the menu and command. Sadly, Mac menus cannot be accessed using this method.

Types of Objects

Like many of the toolbars in Dreamweaver, the Objects palette is context sensitive. It defaults to showing what Dreamweaver calls the **Common** elements. You can change the Objects palette to show other categories of objects when you need them.

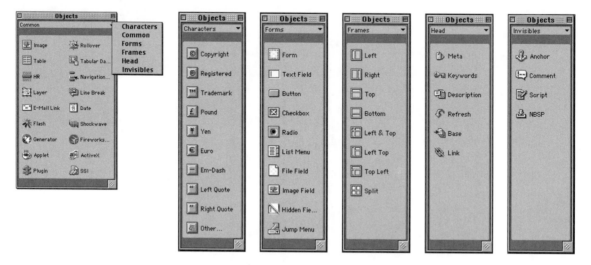

*When you hold your mouse down on the arrow at the top of the Objects palette, notice that it says Common. That tells you you're looking at the Common elements on this toolbar. To show the other types of objects, click and hold the mouse on the pop-up menu arrow. You'll see a list of the other palettes called **Characters**, **Forms**, **Frames**, **Head**, and **Invisibles**.*

Objects Palette Types	
Palette	**Description**
Characters	The **Characters** palette contains frequently used character entities, such as the ®, ©, and ™ symbols, so you no longer have to memorize tricky keyboard commands. This palette is a new feature in Dreamweaver 3.
Common	The **Common** palette contains the most frequently used objects in Dreamweaver, including **Images**, **Tables**, **Layers**, simple **Rollovers**, **Insert Fireworks HTML**, etc. You will use this palette a lot. This palette has been updated for Dreamweaver 3.
Forms	The **Forms** palette contains all of the objects essential for creating Forms for your Web page. These objects include text boxes, buttons, menus, etc. You'll learn about these items in Chapter 15, *"Forms."*
Frames	The **Frames** palette contains several preset framesets. With a click of the mouse, you can add any number of different framesets. This is a new feature in Dreamweaver 3.
Head	The **Head** palette contains objects that are inserted in the HEAD tag of your Web page. These elements, even though not visible on the page, can be an important part of your pages. These objects include META tags, such as **Keywords** and **Descriptions**. Many of these tags are used for search operations.
Invisibles	The **Invisibles** palette is probably used the least, but it's still important. Invisible objects include Named **Anchors**, **Server-Side Includes**, **Non-Breaking Spaces**, etc. You will get a chance to work with some of the invisible elements in exercises later in the book.

The Properties Inspector

Like the Objects palette, the Properties Inspector is context sensitive, meaning it constantly changes depending on what type of element is selected. The Properties Inspector controls many settings, including those for text, tables, alignment, and images. Because Dreamweaver defaults to opening a blank page with the text-insertion symbol blinking, the Properties Inspector defaults to displaying text properties, as shown below.

*The **Properties Inspector** changes depending on what is being edited on screen. Because these elements change depending on context, future chapters will cover the various properties on this bar in depth.*

Movie | **properties_inspector.mov**

To view a movie that demonstrates how to change the context of the Properties Inspector, check out **properties_inspector.mov** from the **movies** folder on the Dreamweaver 3 **H•O•T CD-ROM**.

The Launcher and Mini-Launcher

The Launcher allows you to access several aspects of Dreamweaver with a single click. It basically "launches" the **Site**, **Library**, **HTML Styles**, **CSS Styles**, **Behaviors**, **History**, and **HTML Source** areas of the interface. Go ahead and try clicking each of the buttons to see what they do. You can't hurt anything, we promise! Click the button again, and the feature will go away.

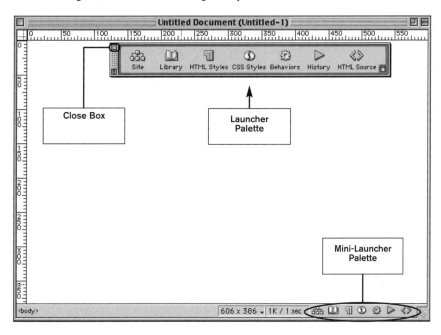

*The Mini-Launcher at the bottom of the screen works identically to its larger counterpart. Try clicking each of its buttons to see what we mean. If you can train yourself to understand what the icons on the Mini-Launcher represent, then you can close the larger Launcher (by clicking its close box) to make more room on your screen. You can open the larger Launcher at any time by selecting **Window >** **Launcher**.*

Launcher and Mini-Launcher Features

Site	Opens the **Site** palette, where you will control Dreamweaver's powerful site-management features. This window is covered in detail in Chapter 3, *"Site Control."*
Library	Opens the **Library** palette. You can create **Library Items** that are shared across your site and update them with ease. **Library Items** are helpful when you have elements of your site that are used on many pages, such as copyright notices or navigation bars. By converting these sorts of elements into Dreamweaver **Library Items**, you can make a single change, and it will ripple across every page in which the element is present. You will learn a lot more about this in Chapter 11, *"Templates/Library Items."*
HTML Styles	**HTML** Styles are a new feature in Dreamweaver 3. They are similar to **Cascading Style Sheets** (CSS) in function, except that they work on any browser.
CSS Styles	The **CSS Styles** button opens the **CSS Styles** palette. CSS is an advanced feature of Dreamweaver. This feature will be covered in Chapter 10, *"Cascading Style Sheets."*
Behaviors	Opens the **Behaviors** palette. This feature allows you to add JavaScript to your pages, even if you are not a programmer. Some of the **Behaviors** features will be covered a lot more in Chapter 17, *"Behaviors."*
History	Opens the **History** palette, which is used to orchestrate animation using Dynamic HTML. You will learn about this feature in Chapter 16, *"DHTML."*
HTML Source	Opens the **HTML Source** palette, where you can view the actual code generated by Dreamweaver 3. You can even watch the HTML code being generated as you create objects on your page! You will learn about this feature in Chapter 4, *"Basics."*

Launcher Shortcuts

All of the Launcher features are available as items under the **Window** menu. In addition, the following function-key shortcuts are available for both Mac and Windows users.

If you memorize the F-keys for the Launcher items, you'll probably never need the large Launcher palette again. For example, we use the Site and HTML palettes more often than the others, so we have memorized **F5** and **F10** as keyboard shortcuts. Below is a handy chart of the Launcher shortcuts.

Shortcuts	
Key	**Function**
F5	Site Files
F6	Library
F7	CSS Styles
F8	Behaviors
F9	History
F10	HTML Source

Warning | Redundancy in the Interface

Truth be told, there is some redundancy in the Dreamweaver 3 interface. For example, you can insert an image by clicking on the Objects palette or by choosing the Insert Image command from the Insert menu. You can often align objects using the Properties Inspector or using a command on a menu. Though it's convenient at times to have different options, it can be confusing to learn a program that has two or three ways to accomplish the same task. Throughout the book, we'll be citing our favorite ways to access features, but if you prefer an alternate method, don't let us stop you!

The Document Window

The **document** window is where all the action happens. This is where you assemble your page elements and design your pages. The document window is similar in appearance to the browser window when viewed from Netscape or Explorer. On both the Mac and Windows, Dreamweaver 3 will create a blank Untitled Document each time you open the application.

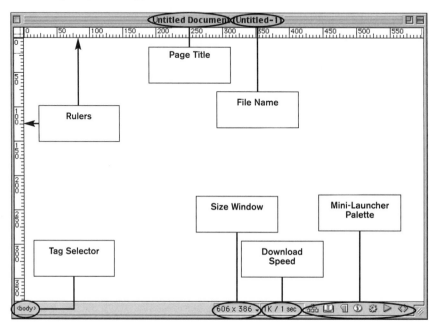

Document Window Features	
Feature	**Description**
Title Bar	Contains the name of your Web page (for instance, "My Web Page") and the file name of your document (for example, webpage.html).
Rulers	You can show or hide rulers by selecting **View > Rulers** and checking **Show** on or off.
Tag Selector	If you select visual elements on your screen, the Tag Selector highlights the corresponding HTML code. It's a fast and easy way to select different items on your page.
Window Size	This pop-up menu lets you resize your window to various preset or custom pixel dimensions.
Download Time	This gives you the approximate size (kilobytes) and download time for the current page.
Mini-Launcher	A small version of the **Launcher** toolbar, it gives you access to various key features within Dreamweaver.

Preferences

There are many different Preferences that you can change to make Dreamweaver 3 your very own custom HTML editor. These settings can be changed at any time in your workflow. To access the Preferences dialog box, select **Edit > Preferences…**. Under the **General** category are settings that determine the appearance and operation of Dreamweaver as a whole. For example, you might consider changing the Objects palette's appearance setting to **Icons and Text**, as described earlier in the chapter, until you become more familiar with the icons representing the various Dreamweaver objects. The next few pages will explore Preferences that may be set for external editors, preset window sizes, and browser choices.

External Editors

You can specify **External Editors** for HTML and image editing, if you want. This means that another HTML editor like BBEdit or HomeSite can be specified to edit the code Dreamweaver generates. This book does not cover the use of external HTML editors; they are mostly used by programmers who want to more tightly control the code that Dreamweaver automatically generates. Dreamweaver 3 ships with BBEdit (for Mac) and HomeSite (for Windows), so these will be preset as the default external HTML editors. In addition, you can specify external image editors. This means you can launch Fireworks or other image-editing applications from right inside Dreamweaver 3 by double-clicking an image file in the Site window or on the page.

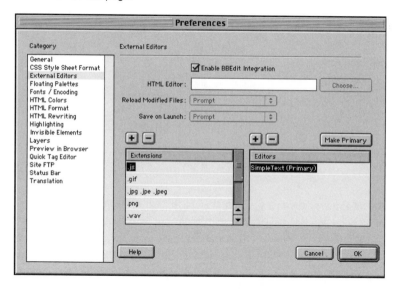

*You can specify an External Editor by choosing **Edit > Preferences...** and clicking the External Editors category. A separate editor can be specified for different types of files. For example, a .gif or .jpg file can be edited in Fireworks or Photoshop, while a .mov file could be opened in Adobe Premiere or Apple's Media Player.*

Preset Window Sizes

One of the pitfalls of Web design is that your page's look will change depending on the size of the monitor that displays it. Dreamweaver has a handy feature – the **Window Sizes** option – to help you design more accurately for a specific monitor size.

The Window Sizes menu offers a variety of preset sizes for the Document window. For example, if you want to design for a **640 x 480** pixel screen, you can select this setting, and Dreamweaver will automatically resize your window. This helps you visualize how your designs will look in browser windows of various sizes. You will learn how to restrict the size of the HTML window by using a Behavior in Chapter 17, *"Behaviors."*

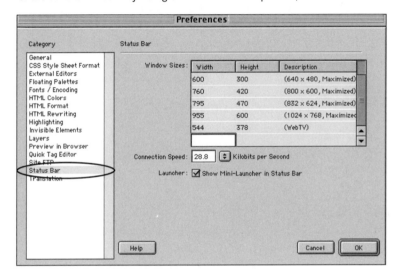

*You can set your own Window Sizes settings by choosing **Edit > Preferences...** and clicking the **Status Bar** category.*

*You can click the Window Sizes menu on the Status Bar to access the various default dimensions. If you choose **Edit Sizes...** you can add your own size presets.*

I. _____**How to Define Your Browser of Choice**

Netscape 4.7 was used in all the screen captures for this book, and has been provided for you on the **H•O•T CD-ROM**. You are welcome to use the browser of your choice for the exercises in this book. **Warning:** A few exercise steps will not work in earlier browser versions. To set up your browser Preference, follow the steps below:

1. Choose **Edit > Preferences...**.

2. Under **Category**, click on **Preview in Browser**.

3. Click the plus sign, minus sign, or **Edit...** to add, remove, or change a browser from the list of choices. **Note:** The Primary Browser defines which browser will launch using the **F12** shortcut key. The Secondary Browser defines which browser can be launched using **Cmd+F12** (Mac) or **Ctrl+F12** (Windows).

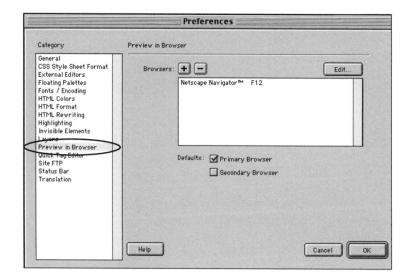

The Preview in Browser Preference sets the Primary Browser to open with the **F12** shortcut key.

Shortcut Keys

There are lots and lots of shortcut keys in Dreamweaver, and all of them are listed in your manual. Below is a chart that lists our favorite ones.

Shortcuts in Dreamweaver		
Command	**Mac**	**Window**
New Document	Cmd+N	Ctrl+Shift+N
Line Break	Shift+Enter	Shift+Enter
Page Properties	Cmd+J	Ctrl+J
Select a Word	Double-click	Double-click
Check Spelling	Shift+F7	Shift+F7
Find	Cmd+F	Ctrl+F
Convert Layers to Table	Cmd+Shift+F6	Ctrl+Shift+F6
Convert Tables to Layers	Cmd+F6	Ctrl+F6
Preview in Primary Browser	F12	F12
Preview in Secondary Browser	Cmd+F12	Ctrl+F12
Objects	Cmd+F2	Ctrl+F2
Properties	Cmd+F3	Ctrl+F3
Launcher	Shift+F4	Shift+F4
Library	F6	F6
CSS Styles	F7	F7
HTML Styles	Cmd+F7	Ctrl+F7
Behaviors	F8	F8
History	F9	F9
Timelines	Cmd+F9	Ctrl+F9
HTML Source	F10	F10
Layers	F11	F11
Frames	Cmd+F10	Ctrl+F10
Templates	Cmd+F11	Ctrl+F11

3.

Site Control

| Defining a Site | Relative and Absolute Links |
| Understanding Paths | Site Maps |

chap_3

Dreamweaver 3
H•O•T CD-ROM

Those of you who have already built Web pages will likely agree that file management is one of the greatest challenges of this medium. What is file management? The organization, folder structure, and naming conventions of all the pages and graphics in your Web site. Few other disciplines require the creation of so many documents at once, because Web pages are usually comprised of numerous text and image files.

To compound the difficulty of managing numerous files, most people build Web sites from their hard drive, and when they're finished they upload these files to a Web server so that the files can be viewed from the WWW. Let's say that you created a folder on your hard drive and called it **HTML** and created another folder called **graphics**. If you put your HTML and graphics files inside those two folders, you would have to replicate this exact folder hierarchy when you uploaded those files to your Web server, or your links to those files would break. In this chapter, you will learn how to avoid such misfortune, by building your Dreamweaver site-management skills.

What is a Root Folder?

Dreamweaver has a site-management scheme that requires that you keep all your files within one main **Root Folder**, so you can easily duplicate the folder hierarchy that's on your hard drive when you upload to a Web server. A Root Folder is no different than any other kind of folder on your hard drive, except that you have specified to Dreamweaver that this is where all HTML and media files for your site reside.

If you think of the Root Folder as the folder from which all other files stem, just like the roots of a tree, then you will understand its function. A Root Folder can contain many subfolders, but Dreamweaver cannot keep track of elements unless they are stored inside the Root Folder.

Taking the concept further, let's say that you decided midstream to change the folder hierarchy of your site by adding a folder or changing a folder name. If you were hand-coding the pages, it would be a hassle to make these changes. Dreamweaver makes this process painless, as long as you work within its site-management structure.

By the time you are through these exercises, you will have learned to define a site and a Root Folder, create a site map, and reorganize files and folders. Not bad for a day's work!

Warning | Site Management!

You might think that Site Management in Dreamweaver is a neat but optional feature, and that you would rather skip it now to return later when you're in the mood. Don't do it! Site Management is actually integral to Dreamweaver 3, and the program kicks up quite a fuss if you don't use it properly. This book will ask that you define a site with each new chapter, because if you have files outside your defined area, you will be constantly plagued by warnings. If you choose to ignore this, you will not be using Dreamweaver properly.

Note | Mac and Windows Differences

For the most part, Dreamweaver has the identical interface for both Mac and Windows platforms. The one case where this is untrue is with Site Management. For this reason, this chapter sometimes contains different directives for the Mac and the Windows user.

I. _____Defining a Site

This exercise will show you how to define sites in Dreamweaver. You will be working with a folder of HTML and image files from the **H•O•T CD-ROM** that you will transfer to your hard drive. Once you've finished this exercise, Dreamweaver's site-management feature will catalogue all the files inside this folder. This exercise teaches you how to define a site from an existing Web site. You would use this identical process if you wanted to use Dreamweaver on a site that you or someone else had created outside Dreamweaver. At the end of the chapter, you'll complete an exercise that will show you how to define a site from an empty folder, which will more likely simulate your approach when you are starting a new site from scratch.

1. Copy the contents of the **chap_03** folder to your hard drive. For clarity, it's best if you leave this folder named **chap_03**.

The folder contains images and HTML files that are requested throughout this chapter. You will be asked to add and change files, which requires that you have all of the files on your hard drive.

2. Open Dreamweaver and press **F5** to bring up the **Site** window. On the pop-up menu; select **Define Sites....** This will open the **Site Definition** window. **Note:** If you've worked in Dreamweaver before, and have already defined other sites, you will see the **Define Sites** dialog box. Click **New...** to define a new site.

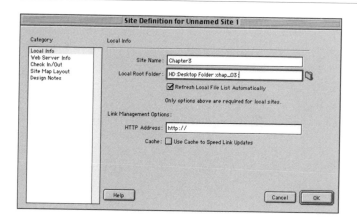

The Site Definition window.

3. Type **Chapter 3** for the **Site Name**.

This is an internal naming convention, so you can use any kind of name you want without worrying about spaces or capitalization. Think of it as your own pet name for your project, just like you give a folder or hard drive a custom name.

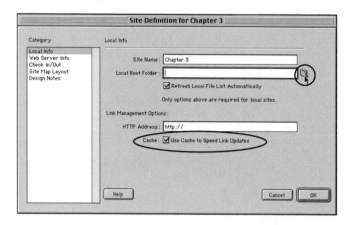

4. Click the small folder icon to the right of the **Local Root Folder** text box. Browse to the **chap_03** folder that you copied to your hard disk and click **Choose** (Mac) or **Open > Select** (Windows). Make sure to put a check in the **Use Cache to Speed Link Updates** checkbox. This will increase the speed with which Dreamweaver performs its link-management features.

5. Click **OK**.

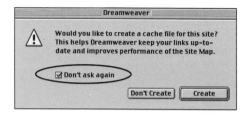

A message box will appear, indicating that the initial site cache needs to be created. You can choose to not have this message displayed in the future by clicking the checkbox (highly recommended!).

6. Click **Create**. After the site cache has been created, you will be brought back to the Define Sites dialog box.

7. Click **Done**.

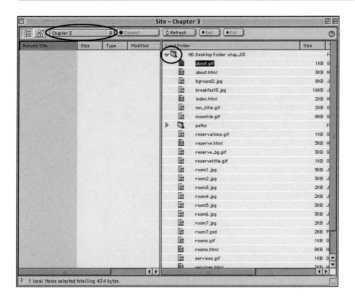

*The Site window is now defined as **Chapter 3**. The right side of the window displays the **Local Folder**. This is the folder on your hard disk that contains all of your HTML files and images. The list represents all the files on your hard drive within the **chap_03** folder. The left side of the window displays the **Remote Site** or the **Site Map** information. Nothing is displayed right now because you haven't gotten to that exercise yet. **Windows Users Note:** If you see locks next to the file names, refer to Chapter 1, "Introduction".*

Tip | Local Root Folder, Root Folder, Root

As you work through Dreamweaver, you will notice references to a Local Root Folder, a Root Folder, and Root. All these terms are interchangeable. Each refers to a folder on your hard drive that contains all of the HTML, images, etc. for your Web site. This can be any folder on your computer. It can be empty, or it can have an entirely completed Web site. We did not want this slight difference in terminology to cause any unnecessary confusion.

2. _____**Relative and Absolute Links**

This exercise will help you understand two different types of links – those that are **relative** and those that are **absolute**. Relative links reference files that are relative to your site. All the files that you see in the Local Folder of your Site window are internal files and can be referenced as relative links. If you want to link to an external file, such as someone else's site, you have to use an absolute link. If you don't understand the difference between these two types of links, read on.

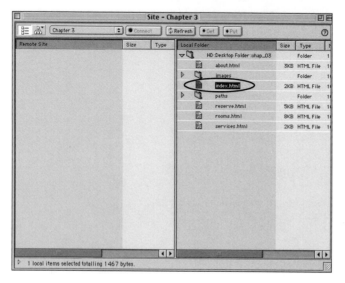

1. If your Site window isn't still open, press **F5**. Look on its right side to the Local Folder and double-click **index.html** to open it. Alternately, you could choose **File > Open** and browse to the **chap_ 03** folder to locate **index.html**.

We suggest that you train yourself to open HTML files from the Site window instead of your hard drive. If you do, it will ensure that you have defined a site and that Dreamweaver's site-management features are being enforced. Believe us, this will save you a lot of pain!

2. Click the "**about the inn**" (**about.gif**) image at the bottom of the screen to select it.

3. With the image selected, look at the Properties Inspector and notice that this image links to **about.html**. **Tip:** If your Properties Inspector is smaller than the one shown here, click the arrow at the bottom-right corner to expand it. The link **about.html** is a relative link. It does not have additional information in front of it, such as **http://www.moonsnestinn.com/about.html**. The file does not need that information because the file name is relative to other internal files in the site.

 Movie | **inspector_context.mov**

To view a movie that demonstrates how the Properties Inspector changes depending on context, check out **inspector_ context.mov** in the **movies** folder on the Dreamweaver 3 **H•O•T CD-ROM**.

4. Highlight the word "**ojai**" at the bottom of the document window. **Tip:** You can double-click the word to select it!

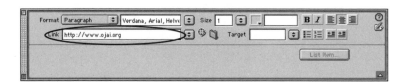

5. In the Properties Inspector, notice that this image links to **http://www.ojai.org**. This is an external link to another site on the Internet. This type of link is referred to as an absolute link. It needs the additional information to specify its location because it is not relative to any internal documents, and it exists on its own server, separate from the **moon's nest inn** site.

6. Close the file.

Note | Absolute and Relative URLs

The term URL stands for **U**niform **R**esource **L**ocator. In plain English, URLs are the addresses you use when you go to a Web site. Some are simple, such as http://www.lynda.com, while others are very complicated and hard to remember, such as http://www.lynda.com/dw3hot/lessons/chapterone. Regardless of whether a URL is short or long, there are two different types: absolute and relative.

An absolute URL looks like this:
http://www.lynda.com/index.html

An absolute URL is a complete URL that specifies the exact location of the object on the Web, including the protocol that's being used (in this case, http), the host name (in this case, www. lynda.com), and the exact path to that location (in this case, /index.html). Absolute URLs are always used when you want to link to a site outside your own.

You can use absolute URLs within your own site, but it's not necessary, and most Web publishers opt to use relative URLs instead. If you use relative URLs for internal documents, it's easier to move them if you change your domain name.

A sample relative URL looks like this:
index.html

If we were linking from pageone.html of our site to pagetwo.html of our site, we wouldn't need to insert the entire http://www.lynda.com part anymore. It's actually more flexible to move relative files around your site than to code them with external path names.

3. _____File and Folder Management

From within Dreamweaver's Site window, you can create new folders and files, as well as move them around. When you do this, you're actually adding folders and files to your hard drive, as this exercise will demonstrate. Accessing your hard drive from within Dreamweaver is essential to site-management practices because Dreamweaver can then keep track of where the files have been moved or added. This exercise will show you how to add folders and files to the Chapter 3 site.

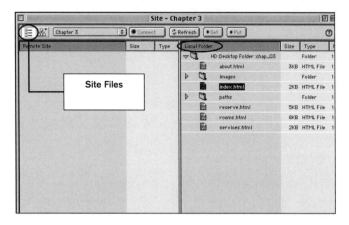

1. Make sure the Site window is open (**F5**) and click the **Site Files** button located in the upper-left corner.

2. Select the folder at the top of the Local Folder view.

3. Choose **Site > Site Files View > New Folder** (Mac) or **File > New Folder** (Windows). This will add a new folder to the Local Folder and your hard disk.

4. Type **html** for the folder name and press **Return** (Mac) or **Enter** (Windows).

5. Now you need to select the files to be moved into the folder you just created. Here, you'll learn how to select discontinuous files – files that are not adjacent to one another.

   •(Mac) Click **about.html**, then **Cmd+Click reserve.html**, **rooms.html**, and **services.html**. (Hold down the **Cmd** key as you click the last three file names).

   •(Windows) Click **about.html**, then **Ctrl+Click reserve.html**, **rooms.html**, and **services.html**. (Hold down the **Ctrl** key as you click the last three file names).

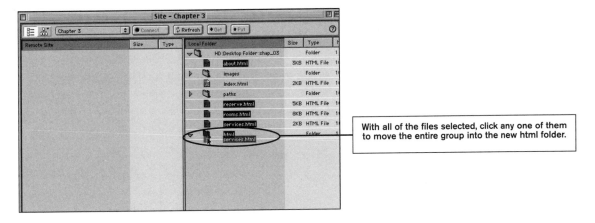

With all of the files selected, click any one of them to move the entire group into the new html folder.

6. Once you have all four files selected, drag them to the **html** folder that you just created. This will move all four files into this new location.

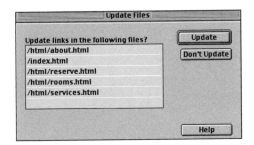

7. When you move files, Dreamweaver will prompt you to update their links. Click **Update**. Dreamweaver will list all the different files whose links were affected by the files you just moved. Once you click **Update**, these files will be rewritten automatically to reflect the change in file structure.

Warning | Use the Site Window!

If you want to add, modify, move, or delete files or folders in your Web site, do it inside Dreamweaver's Site window, as shown in Exercise 3. If you make these folder changes on your hard drive without opening Dreamweaver, you'll have to go in and repair the links manually by relinking each page. If you make your changes inside the Site window, then Dreamweaver will keep track of them and automatically update your pages.

Understanding the Path Structure

This next exercise builds on Dreamweaver's Site window features, and shows how path structures are altered if you move files around. A path structure is simply the path to different files in your site. Both relative and absolute URLs can be configured in a variety of different path structures. In this exercise, you will reference files in three distinct ways, each demonstrating the different type of path structures you might encounter.

In this first example, you will simply insert a file that is within the same folder.

1. Make sure the Site window is open (**F5**).

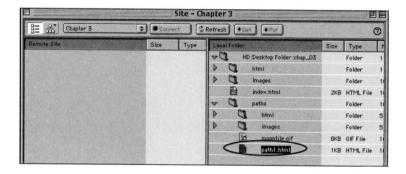

2. Under the Local Folder column, double-click the **paths** folder.

3 Open **path1.html**, by double-clicking it in the Site window.

4. Choose **Insert > Image**. Select **moontile.gif** and click **Open**.

5. Once you have inserted this image, look at the Properties Inspector. Notice that the **Src** is set to **moontile.gif**. As you become more experienced with building Web pages, you will begin to notice that a file name with no slash in front of it means that the file is in the same folder as the HTML that referenced it.

In this second example, you will insert an image that is inside another folder.

---

6. In the document window, delete the image that you just inserted by selecting it (clicking it once) and pressing the **Delete** key.

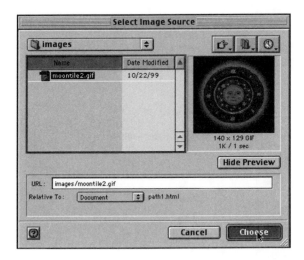

7. Choose **Insert > Image** and open the other **images** folder, the one nested inside the **paths** folder, to select **moontile2.gif**. Click **Choose**.

8. Once you have inserted this image, look at the Properties Inspector again. Notice that the **Src** is now set to **images/moontile2.gif**. The slash means that the file is nested inside another folder.

---

9. Select **File > Save** to save your changes. Close **path1.html**.

In this example, you will open an HTML document that is inside a folder and insert an image that is outside a folder.

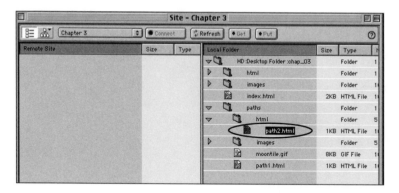

10. From the Site window (**F5**) open **path2.html** from the **html** folder nested within the **paths** folder.

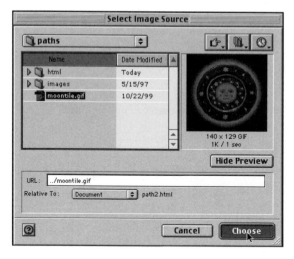

11. Choose **Insert > Image** and navigate outside the **html** folder, to find **moontile.gif**. Click **Choose**.

12. Once you have inserted this image, look at the **Properties Inspector** again. Notice that the **Src** is now set to **../moontile.gif**. The two dots before the slash indicate that the image was one folder up from the HTML document that referenced it.

13. Save and close the file.

Different Path Notations

When you reference files in HTML, it is necessary to specify exactly where the document is. Dreamweaver writes the HTML for you, and inserts different path structures depending on where the files are located. Below is a chart to reference how path structures are specified within HTML.

Path Notations in Dreamweaver	
Path Notation	**Description**
document.gif	No slash (/) or dots (..) indicates that the file is inside the same folder as the referring HTML file.
images/document.gif	The forward slash (/) indicates that the file is inside the images folder or the file is located one level down from the referring HTML file.
../images/document.gif	The two dots (..) indicate that the folder is one level up from the referring HTML file.

Creating a Site Map

The **Site Map** is a great way to examine the structure of your Web site. It allows you to see the different levels and what is contained within those levels. Many people use Site Maps to show their client how the site looks from a structural viewpoint. It's handy that Dreamweaver can easily create Site Maps, and even render them as PICT (Mac) or BMP (Windows) files. If you change the structure of the site, the Site Map will change as well. There is no right or wrong time to make a a Site Map, it is simply a convenience to have this feature available when you want one. This exercise will show you how to create and save a Site Map.

1. Press **F5** to open the Site window.

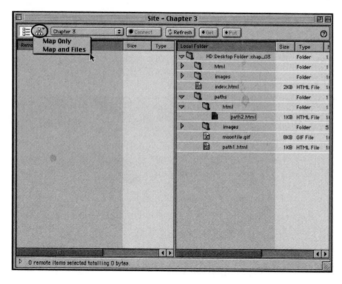

2. Click **Site Map** in the upper-left corner of the Site window. A pull-down menu lets you choose between two options, Map Only or Map and Files. Select **Map and Files**.

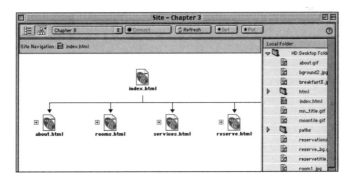

The Site Map view, set to Map and Files, will open in the left side of the window. The Site Map view is great if you want to see the overall structure of your Web site and how the different pages link to each other.

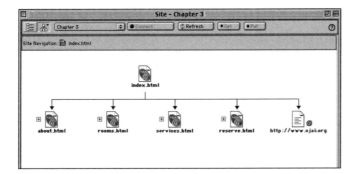

Here in the Map Only view, you can see the absolute and relative links displayed side by side. The absolute links are in blue and have a small globe to their right. The relative links have a small plus sign on their left.

3. Save this view as an image file.

　• (Mac) Select **Site > Site Map View > Save Site Map > Save Site Map as PICT....**

　• (Windows) Select **File > Save Site Map....** A **Save As** dialog box will appear so you can name the map.

4. Press **F5** to close the Site window.

6. _____Creating a Site from Nothing

So far, you've had a chance to work with Dreamweaver's site-management window by defining a site based on folders and files from the **H•O•T CD-ROM**. What about when you finish this book and go to create your own Web site? You might know how to define a Web site that already exists, but not know how to go about creating a site from scratch. We wouldn't want that to happen to you, so this next exercise will walk you through the steps of defining a site before you have any content to put in it.

1. Leave Dreamweaver open, but go to the desktop of your computer. Create a new empty folder on your desktop and name it **website**.

2. There are different directives for defining a site for Mac and Windows users.

• (Mac) Return to Dreamweaver and choose **Site > Define Sites...** from the top menu. In the **Define Sites** dialog box that will open up, click **New...**.

• (Windows) Press **F5** to open the Site window (if it isn't open). Choose **Site > Define Sites...** from the menu bar at the top of the Site window. Click New. **Note:** The Site menu item is not available from any other window except the Site window.

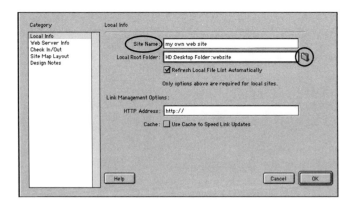

3. Fill in the **Site name** (we chose **my own web site**, but you may name it what you want). For the **Local Root Folder**, click the folder icon and navigate to the empty folder you created on your desktop called **website**. Click **Choose**, then **OK**.

4. If a dialog box pops up, indicating that the initial site cache needs to be created, check "**Don't ask again**", and click **Create**.

5. Click **Done**.

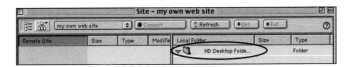

6. This is what your Site window will look like now that you have created a new site based on an empty folder. Notice there's nothing in the Site window. Dreamweaver is doing an accurate job of displaying the contents of an empty folder.

7. You can add files and folders directly from Dreamweaver! Make sure you highlight the Local Root Folder at the top of the Site window first, then:

- (Mac) Choose **Site > Site Files View > New File**. The file will appear inside the Site window as **untitled.htm**

- (Windows) Choose **File > New File**. The file will appear inside the Site window as **untitled.htm**

Note: You can name the file from the Site window, just as you can name an Untitled document on your hard drive. If you double-click the highlighted file, a blank Dreamweaver document will appear.

8. Leave Dreamweaver open. Look on the desktop of your computer and open the **website** folder. Lo and behold, there is an HTML document called **untitled.htm** in there! The same HTML file that appeared in the Site window is also on your hard drive.

9. Try moving some other files into this folder. When you return to Dreamweaver, these other files will appear in the Site window. The Site window is simply a mirror of what exists on your hard drive.

10. When you are finished, close all open files. It doesn't matter if you save your changes, you won't be using any of these files for the rest of the book.

In summary, Dreamweaver allows you to create files and folders directly from its Site window. Some Web designers create a lot of images first and throw them into a folder and define that as a site inside Dreamweaver. Others might start with an empty folder and build empty HTML files first, then create and add images later. There is no right or wrong way to start a Web site, but Dreamweaver is flexible enough to work from scratch with an empty folder or to create a site around existing files.

4.
Basics

File Name Versus Title Name	Significance of index.html
Inserting Images and Text	Page Properties
Links	META Tags	Looking at HTML

chap_4

Dreamweaver 3
H•O•T CD-ROM

If you're the impatient type (as we would frankly characterize ourselves), this is the chapter you've been waiting for. The following exercises are going to teach you how to create and save a page, insert and align images and text, link images and text, color text links, insert META information (such as Keywords and Descriptions for search engines), and view the HTML that Dreamweaver 3 created. Covering this much material may seem overwhelming, but if that seems like a lot to cover, it isn't. Dreamweaver makes most of these operations as simple as accessing a menu or property bar.

In the past the basics of creating a Web Page involved knowing HTML and making sure every letter of every tag was correct. While Dreamweaver shields you from writing HTML from scratch, it's generating complex code automatically in the background. This chapter will help clarify the relationship between the visual changes on your screen and the HTML code behind them.

Saving a document in Dreamweaver is similar to saving in any other program. However, it is always a good practice to save before you start inserting elements on a page. That's because Dreamweaver's site-management capabilities depend on the program's familiarity with the name and location of the page as you are building it.

Page Properties window:

- Title: Untitled Document
- Background Image: [ ] Choose...
- Background: [ ] #FFFFFF
- Text: [ ]   Visited Links: [ ]
- Links: [ ]   Active Links: [ ]
- Left Margin: [ ]   Margin Width: [ ]
- Top Margin: [ ]   Margin Height: [ ]
- Document Encoding: Western (Latin1)   Reload
- Tracing Image: [ ] Choose...
- Image ———————▽ 100%
  Transparent   Opaque
- Document Folder: HD:Desktop Folder:chap_04:
- Site Folder: HD:Desktop Folder:chap_04:

Buttons: OK, Apply, Cancel, Help

This chapter will introduce you to the **Page Properties** window of Dreamweaver, which is where the page title and all the colors for your text are set. The handy **Color Picker** palette allows you to set any color you want or choose a color from an image on your page. This function is great for flawlessly matching background colors to image colors.

By the time you are done with this chapter, your Dreamweaver feet will finally be wet, and you will be well on your way to a better understanding of the interface for creating pages and sites. The exercises here will be your foundation for building more complex pages in future chapters.

I. _____Defining the Site

With each new chapter, you will be copying exercises from the **H•O•T CD-ROM** files to a folder on your hard drive, and defining a new site based on the contents of the folder. This will familiarize you with setting up Dreamweaver's site-management features and help you troubleshoot problems that will develop if the site is not defined. Since each chapter of this book features different files, each chapter is considered a new site. Normally, if you were working on a single site, you would most likely define your site once. If you switched projects, however, you would need to define a new site. Dreamweaver allows you to manage multiple sites. This is helpful if you have multiple clients or projects for which you plan to use the program.

1. Copy the contents of the **chap_04** folder to your hard drive.

2. Make sure the Site window is open. If it's not, press **F5**.

3. Click the pop-up menu at the top of the Site window and select **Define Sites....**

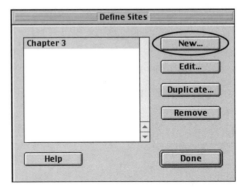

4. Click **New....**

5. In the Site window type **Chapter 4** for the **Site Name**.

6. Click the small folder and then select **chap_04** as the Local Root Folder.

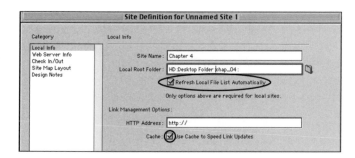

*The **Refresh Local File List Automatically** option is new to Dreamweaver 3. It is checked by default to automatically refresh the Site window when files are copied. To ensure that you see your changes as you make them, we suggest you leave this option checked.*

7. Make sure to check the **Use Cache to Speed Link Updates** checkbox. Click **OK**.

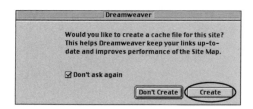

8. If the **Create Site Cache** dialog box opens, click **Create** and check **Don't ask again** so this dialog box doesn't appear repeatedly.

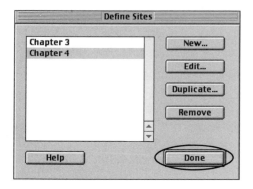

9. When the **Define Sites** dialog box opens, click **Done**. You will not need the Site window right now, so press **F5** to close it.

2. _____Creating and Saving a Document

This exercise will show you how to create and save a document in Dreamweaver. You will be naming this document **index.html**, which has special significance in HTML, and almost always means that it is the beginning page of a site. Additionally, you will learn to set the title of this document to **Moon's Nest Inn**.

1. A blank document should be visible; if not, select **File > New**.

2. Select **Modify > Page Properties....**

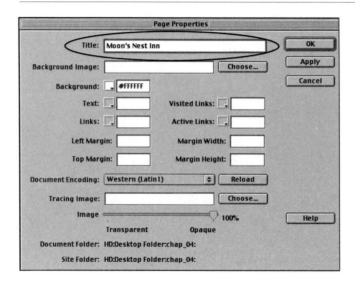

3. Type **Title: Moon's Nest Inn**. Leave the other options at their default values. Click **OK**.

You will be returned to the document window. The page is blank, but you're going to turn it into a cool and functional Web page in a jiffy.

Before you get started, it is very important that you save your file first. All of the site-management features introduced in the last chapter depend on Dreamweaver knowing the name of your file. With this ability, the program constantly notifies you if you are working on an unsaved document. Besides, no one wants to unexpectedly lose work, and this practice is good insurance against system crashes and/or a power outage.

4. Select **File > Save As…**. Name the file **index.html** and save it inside the **chap_04** folder on your hard disk. Leave this file open; you will be using it in the next exercise.

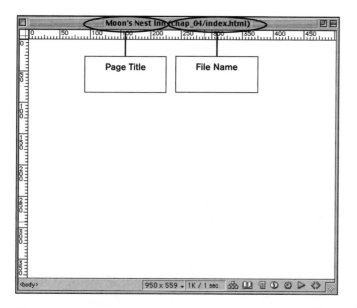

*There are two names in the title bar of your document window. The first is the title of the document (**Moon's Nest Inn**). The second name is the file name (**index.html**), which shows up to the right of the title. The title can be different from the file name, as in the example shown above.*

File Names Versus Titles

As you create Web pages with Dreamweaver, you will need to specify various names for your files, folders, sites, etc. This might not seem tricky at first glance, but there are actually two different names associated with HTML files – the file name and the title.

When you save a document, you will be assigning its file name. The file name must always end with the .htm or .html extension. There is another name associated with the document, too, and it is called the title. The file **index.html** here, for example, has the title of **Moon's Nest Inn**.

It's essential that you pay attention to spaces and capitalization in your file names. Page titles, however, are much more flexible and should be more descriptive than the file name. When the page is viewed from a Web browser, the title will be much more visible to your end user than your file name. Also, where end users bookmark this page, the title will appear in their bookmark list.

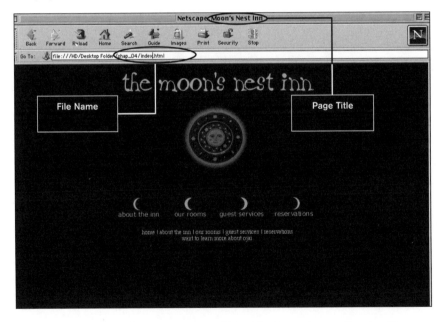

In the above example (which you will build in this chapter), note that the title appears in the browser's title bar, while the file name appears in the URL. The file name allows the page you create to appear to your end users. Titles are also important, because they determine the order in which your files are listed in search engines.

The Significance of index.html

You just created a document called **index.html**. What you may or may not appreciate is that this particular file name has special significance. Most Web servers recognize the **index.html** as the default home page. If you type the URL http://www.lynda.com, for example, what you will really see is http://www.lynda.com/index.html, even though you didn't type it that way. The Web server knows to open the **index.html** file automatically without requiring the full URL to be typed. Therefore, if you name the opening page of your Web site with the file name **index.html**, the Web server will know to automatically display this file first.

Taking this concept one step further, you can have an opening page to each section of your Web site, not just to your home page. This feature has definite advantages. Visitors to your site will no longer have to remember long URLs or type **index.html** time and again. Also, they won't find themselves looking at a generic index, like the example below.

This is why the file name **index.html** is so significant. It's also the reason most professional Web developers use it as the **Root File** name, although on some servers a different name is used, such as **default.html**. What you may not realize is that you are not limited to just one **index.html** on your site. You can have an **index.html** inside each folder that represents a category for your site, such as **Company**, **Services**, **Store**, and **Products**.

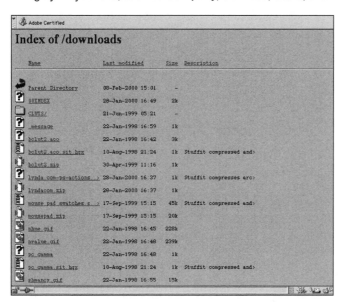

*If you do not have an **index.html**, browsers will display a general list of your files, such as the above example.*

3.————————————————Inserting Images

In this exercise, you will continue working with the **index.html** file and learn to insert images for your page's headline, logo, and navigation bar.

1. Click the **Insert Image** object in the Objects palette. **Note:** You may also choose **Insert > Image** from the menu bar, or use the shortcut key combination **Opt+Cmd+I** (Mac) or **Alt+Ctrl+I** (Windows).

---

2. Browse to **mn_title.gif** inside the **images** folder. Click **Choose**. If you are not familiar with the extension **.gif**, refer to Chapter 1, "*Background*."

---

3. In the document window, click off the image to deselect it, and press **Return** or **Enter** to create a paragraph break, causing a space to form between the headline graphic and the next image.

---

4. Click the **Insert Image** object in the Objects palette again. Browse to **moontile.gif** inside the **images** folder. Click **Choose**.

---

5. Click off the image to deselect it, and then press **Return** or **Enter** twice. This inserts two paragraph breaks into the formatting of the page.

---

6. Click the **Insert Image** object in the Objects palette, and browse to **about.gif** inside the **images** folder. Click **Choose**.

---

7. Click the **Insert Image** object, and browse to **rooms.gif** inside the **images** folder. Click **Choose**.

---

8. Click the **Insert Image** object, and browse to **services.gif** inside the **images** folder. Click **Choose**.

---

9. Click the **Insert Image** object, and browse to **reservations.gif** inside the **images** folder. Click **Choose**.

---

10. Save your file and leave it open for the next exercise.

This is what your page should look like at this point.

Inserting Text

Adding text to your Web page is simple in Dreamweaver. Just like your favorite word processor, you can simply start typing text on your page and the text will appear.

In this exercise, you will add some text at the bottom of your page as an alternative navigation system, which is useful to users who might have their images turned off in their browser settings or be browsing in a non-graphical browser (such as sight-impaired audiences).

1. Click to the right of the images you inserted in the last exercise and press **Return** to create a paragraph break. Type **home**, press the **Spacebar**, press **Shift+Backslash** to insert a small vertical line (|), or "pipe," and press the **Spacebar** again.

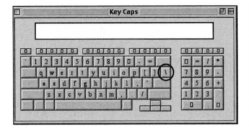
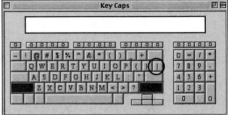

*Without the **Shift** key pressed.*   *With the **Shift** key pressed.*

*Note: The **Backslash** key is located in different spots on different keyboards.*

2. Type **about the inn**, press the **Spacebar**, press **Shift+Backslash** to insert a pipe, and press the **Spacebar** again.

3. Type **our rooms**, press the **Spacebar**, press **Shift+Backslash** to insert a pipe, and press the **Spacebar** again.

4. Type **guest services**, press the **Spacebar**, press **Shift+Backslash** to insert a pipe, and press the **Spacebar** again.

5. Type **reservations**.

6. Press **Shift+Return** to create a line break. This puts your type-insertion cursor on the next line without introducing a two-line paragraph return.

7. Type **want to learn more about ojai**?

8. Save your file.

home | about the inn | our rooms | guest services | reservations
want to learn more about ojai?

This is the result you should get at the end of typing in the items.

This is what your page should look like now.

Note | Paragraph Versus Line Breaks

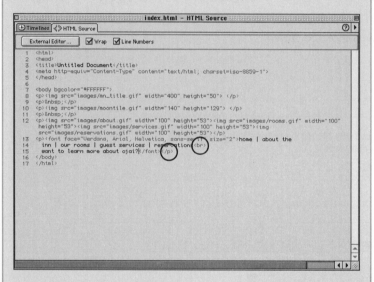

You may have noticed that each time you pressed the **Return** or **Enter** key, Dreamweaver skipped down the page two lines. Pressing the **Return** or **Enter** key inserts a single paragraph break. The HTML tag for a paragraph break is <P>. This is useful when you want to increase the space between different paragraphs. However, there will be times when you just want to go to one line directly below the one you are working on without introducing extra space. Pressing **Shift+Return** (or **Shift+Enter**) inserts a line break instead. The HTML tag for a line break is <BR>. Knowing the difference between a <P> and a <BR> will allow you to control the spacing between lines of text.

5. Centering Images and Text

Now that you have added the images and text to your page, it's time to learn how to center them. The next section shows you how to use centering procedures with text and images.

1. Select the "**moon's nest inn**" logo image from the previous exercise (**mn_title.gif**) at the top of the screen.

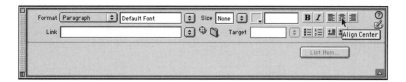

2. Click the **Align Center** button in the Properties Inspector. This will snap the "**moon's nest inn**" logo to the center of the screen.

3. Use your **Shift** key to multiple-select the images **moontile.gif** (the round image), **about.gif** "**about the inn**," rooms.gif "**our rooms**," **services.gif** "**guest services**," and **reservations.gif** "**reservations**." With the **Shift** key still depressed, select the text at the bottom of the screen.

4. Click the **Align Center** button in the Properties Inspector.

Your page should look like this at the end of the exercise.

5. Save the file and leave it open for the next exercise.

6. _____Modifying Page Properties

This exercise will walk you through changing the colors of your page, using the **Page Properties** window. The Page Properties feature controls many important attributes of your page, including the document title (which we looked at in Exercise 2), and the colors you set for your text and links.

1. Select **Modify > Page Properties...** or use the shortcut to access Page Properties, **Cmd+J** (Mac) or **Ctrl+J** (Windows).

2. Move this window to the side so you can see the Page Properties and your document at the same time.

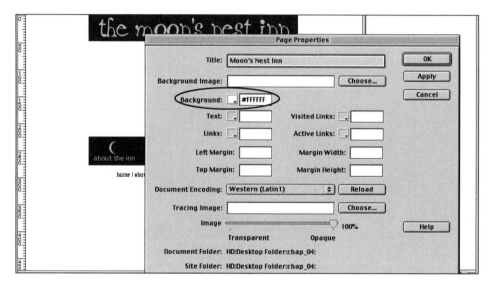

3. Click the small box to the right of the word **Background**. This will open the Dreamweaver Color palette shown on the next page.

Note | What is Browser-Safe Color?

Browser-safe colors are the 216 colors supported by browsers across platforms (Mac and Windows). If you use the browser-safe colors inside the Page Properties settings, you reduce the risk of having your colors shift when people view your Web pages.

The Dreamweaver Color Palette

All of the colors in the Color palette are browser-safe, and they're arranged in a manner that shows the darkest colors at the bottom and the lightest colors at the top. You can use the **Eye Dropper** to select from these colors. To understand each function of the Color palette buttons, see the chart below.

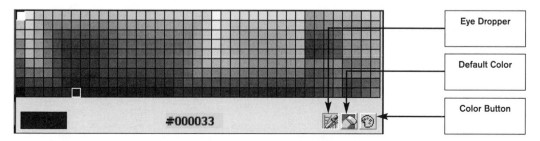

Color Palette Buttons	
Eye Dropper	The **Eye Dropper** allows you to select any color visible on your screen. When you click the **Eye Dropper** button, any color you eye-drop on snaps to the nearest Web-safe color. If you don't press this button, Dreamweaver will pick up the actual color, which may not be browser safe!
Default Color	The **Default Color** resets the color to its default value. You would use this if you picked a color and then changed your mind. Think of it as the equivalent of a **Cancel** button.
Color Button	The **Color** button launches the (Mac) **Apple System Color Picker** or the (Windows) **Color** dialog box. If you use the **Color** button, you will increase the odds of not picking a browser-safe color.

 Movie | **page_properties_eyedropper.mov**

To learn more about using the Eye Dropper to set a page's Background Color to match the edge of an image, check out **page_properties_eyedropper.mov** located in the **movies** folder on the Dreamweaver 3 **H•O•T CD-ROM**.

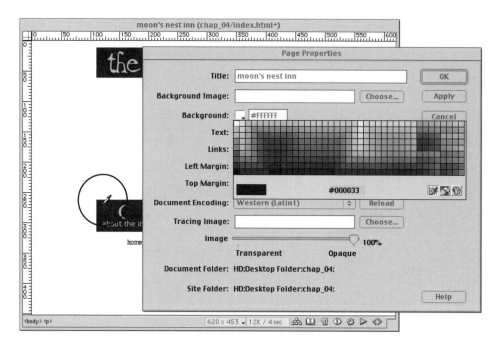

4. With your mouse depressed, move the Eye Dropper outside of the Page Properties window to release the mouse on the "**about the inn**" image. This will set the Background Color of your page to match the edge of this image. To instantly see the results, click **Apply**. Don't click **OK** yet, because there are still more colors to set in the upcoming steps.

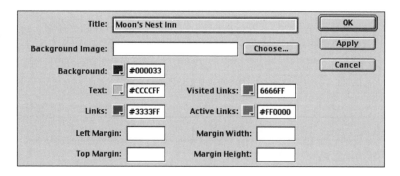

To set other colors, you can insert your own values.

5. Click inside the text box next to the **Text** option. Type #CCCCFF. You just colored all your text light blue in this document. Again, to preview, click **Apply**. The Apply button is actually accepting your changes, it is not merely a preview. Clicking it is the same as clicking **OK**, except that it does not close the window.

6. Type #3333FF for the **Links** option. All the text in this document that contains a link will be bright blue. Type #6666FF for the **Visited Links** option. After someone has visited a link it will turn blue, letting him or her know that that link has already been viewed.

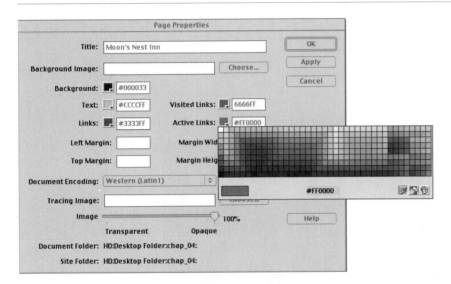

7. You could also choose a color by sight, instead of typing in a hexadecimal value. Click the box to the right of the words **Active Links** and the Color palette will open. Select a red color. This will set the active link color to red. The only time an Active Link color shows is when the mouse is depressed on the link.

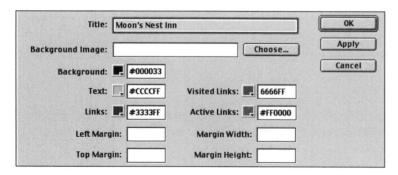

The Page Properties window should look something like this. **Note:** *You might have a different red for Active Links than shown here, since you selected this color by sight, not numeric value.*

8. Click **OK**.

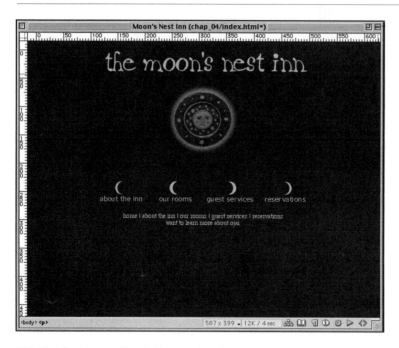

This is what the results of this exercise should look like.

9. Save the document and leave it open for the next exercise.

The Page Properties Window

The Page Properties window does more than just set the colors of the links and your document title. See the chart below for an explanation of all its features.

Page Properties	
Properties	**Description**
Title	The **Title** of your page is what will appear in the title bar of the Web browser and when your page is bookmarked. This name can contain as many characters as you want, including special characters, such as %(#*!.
Background Image	If you want a **Background Image** for your Web page, you would specify it here. A **Background Image** can be any GIF or JPEG file. If the image is smaller than the Web browser window, then it will repeat (tile).
Background	Sets the **Background** color. The values can be in hexadecimal format or by name, for example red, white, etc.
Text	Sets the default **Text** color. It can be overwritten for specific areas of text.
Links	Sets the color for **Links**. This option can be overwritten for specific links.
Visited Links	Sets the color for **Visited Links**. A **Visited Link** color specifies how the link will appear after a visitor has clicked it.
Active Links	Sets the color for **Active Links**. The **Active Link** color specifies how the link will appear while someone clicks it.
Document Encoding	Specifies the language for the characters and fonts used in the document.
Tracing Image	**Tracing Images** are used as guides to set up the layout of your page. They can be any GIF, JPEG, or PNG file. You will learn to work with **Tracing Images** in Chapter 8, *"Layout."*
Transparency	Sets the **Transparency** level of your **Tracing Image**.
Left Margin	Sets the **Left Margin** value. This attribute is only supported in Internet Explorer 4.0 or later. This option is new to Dreamweaver 3.
Top Margin	Sets the **Top Margin** value. This attribute is only supported in Internet Explorer 4.0 or later. This option is new to Dreamweaver 3.
Margin Width	Sets the **Margin Width** value. This attribute is only supported in Netscape Navigator 4.0 or later. This option is new to Dreamweaver 3.
Margin Height	Sets the **Margin Height** value. This attribute is only supported in Netscape Navigator 4.0 or later. This is yet another new option in Dreamweaver 3.

7._____**Creating Links with Images and Text**

The ability to link to pages and sites is what makes the Web dynamic. This chapter will show you how to set up links using Dreamweaver's Properties Inspector.

1. Select the **moontile.gif** image in the center of the screen.

2. Click the Browse for File icon, next to the **Link** option, in the Properties Inspector. **Note:** If your Properties Inspector window is smaller than what is shown here, click the arrow at the bottom right corner to expand it.

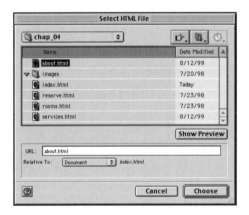

3. Browse to **about.html** and click **Choose**. Congratulations, you have just created your first relative image link. Why was it relative? It is relative simply because it linked to a document within this site, not to an external Web site.

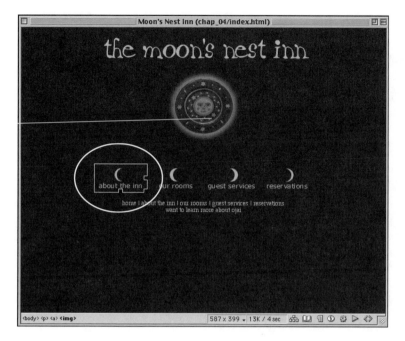

4. Highlight the **about.gif** ("**about the inn**") image at the bottom of the screen.

---

5. Click the small folder next to the Link option in the Properties Inspector.

---

6. Browse once again to **about.html**. Click **Choose**. Now **moontile.gif** and **about.gif** are linked to **about.html**.

---

7. Now repeat this process for the remaining navigation icons. Select the **rooms.gif** ("**our rooms**") image and link it to **rooms.html**. Click **Choose**. Select the **services.gif** ("**guest services**") image and link it to **services.html**. Click **Choose**. Select the **reservations.gif** ("**reservations**") image and link it to **reserve.html**. Click **Choose**.

*You have just successfully added links to all the images on this page! If you want to preview the links in a browser, press **F12** and click any of the images.*

Next, you will create some links using text. The process is almost identical, except you will be selecting text instead of images.

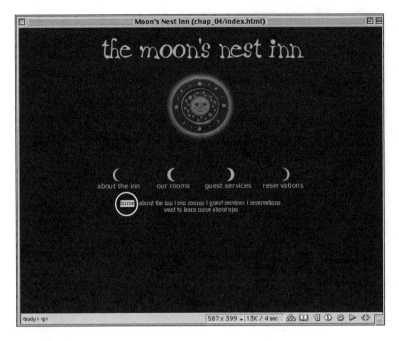

8. Highlight the word **"home"** at the bottom of the page.

9. Click the small folder next to the Link option in the Properties Inspector.

10. Browse to **index.html**. Click **Choose**.

11. Repeat this process for each word in the text navigation bar at the bottom of the screen. (You can select each word easily by double-clicking it). Once selected, link the **"about the inn"** text to **about.html**, the **"our rooms"** text to **rooms.html**, the **"guest services"** text to **services.html**, and the **"reservations"** text to **reserve.html**.

As you create the text links, you will notice the color of the text change. This happens because you set the Links color option in the Page Properties to blue, and Dreamweaver is previewing that setting for you.

12. Highlight the word "**ojai**" at the bottom of the page.

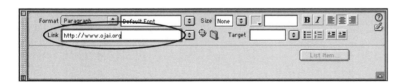

13. Type **http://www.ojai.org** into the Link option in the Properties Inspector. Congratulations, you just created your first absolute link. It's an absolute link because it begins with an **http** header and includes the full address.

14. Select **File > Save**. You don't want to lose any of your work!

15. If you want to preview all of your links, press **F12** to launch a browser and try them out. **Note:** Only the links you created on the **index.html** page will be working. You will learn some effective and fancy ways to work with linking in Chapter 5, "*Linking*."

8. _____META Tags

One of the big challenges (aside from building a Web site) is letting the search engines know that your site exists. There are two steps to getting your site listed: the first is to list it with all the various search engines out there, and the other is to insert META tags into your HTML so the search engines can find you on their own and correctly index your site. Many search engines send robots (also called spiders) out to search the Web for content. When you insert certain META tags into your document, you make it much easier for the search-engine robots to understand how to categorize your site. This exercise will show you how to enter META tags with specific attributes, so you can make your Web page more search-engine friendly.

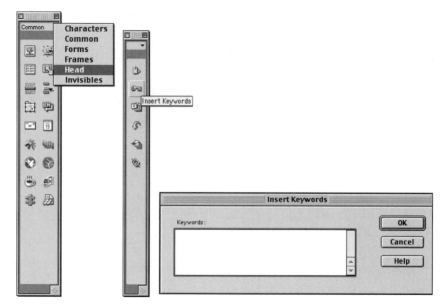

1. Click the arrow at the top of the Objects palette. This will reveal a small pop-up menu, which contains the following options: Characters, Common, Forms, Frames, Head, and Invisibles. Select the **Head** option. You are going to work with the **Head** option, because it contains the META elements.

---

2. Click the **Insert Keywords** object. A dialog box will be displayed for you to enter in the keywords for your page.

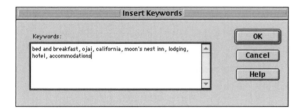

3. Type **bed and breakfast, ojai, california, moon's nest inn, lodging, hotel, accommodations**. Basically, you're listing words that someone might use in a search engine to bring up your site.

4. Click **OK**.

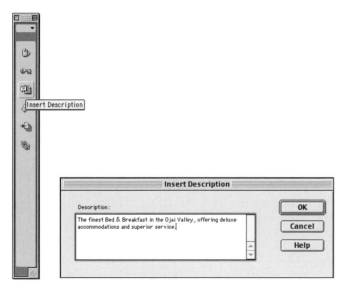

5. Click the **Insert Description** button. A dialog box will appear in which you can enter the description of your Web page.

6. Type **The finest Bed & Breakfast in the Ojai Valley, offering deluxe accommodations and superior service.**

7. Click **OK**.

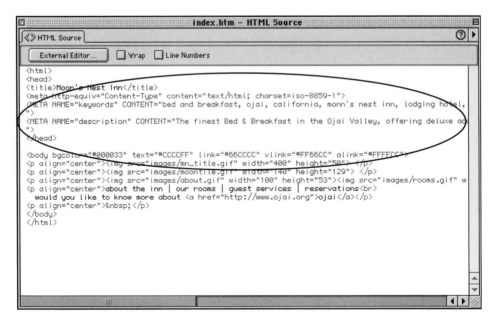

8. Press **F10** to view the HTML in this document. See the META information inside the HEAD tag? Visitors to your site won't be able to see the META tag information because it's only visible inside your HTML. It's a part of authoring the page that has nothing to do with appearance – and everything to do with helping the search engines find your site.

9. Save and leave this document open for the next exercise.

Warning | Keywords and Descriptions

Keywords are META tag values that specify certain words to help Internet search engines index your site. Many search engines limit the number of keywords you can use. Choose your words wisely and use no more than 10 to 15 keywords that best describe your site's contents.

Descriptions are META tag values that also help various search engines index your site. Some search engines will actually use in their directory the very descriptions you specify to describe your site. Again, some search engines limit the number of characters indexed, so keep it short and simple! If you would like more information about META tags, check out these URLs:

Web Developer — META Tag Resources
http://www.webdeveloper.com/html/html_metatag_res.html

META Builder 2
http://vancouver-webpages.com/META/mk-metas.html

9. _____Looking at the HTML

You briefly looked at raw HTML code in the last exercise. This exercise will help you understand the relationship between the images and text on your page, and the HTML code that Dreamweaver generated.

1. You can view the HTML generated in Dreamweaver by clicking the **HTML Source** button in the Launcher or by pressing **F10**, as you just did at the end of the last exercise.

*The HTML Source window is somewhat self-explanatory in Dreamweaver 3. However, there are a few options you should know about that definitely make it easier for you to view code. The **Wrap** checkbox causes the text to wrap to the next line based upon the size of the HTML Source window. This eliminates the need to scroll to the right to view all the code. The **Line Numbers** option displays a number next to each line of code. This is helpful when you are troubleshooting errors in specific lines of your code. These line numbers only appear in Dreamweaver, not in the final code*

2. Make sure there is a check in the Wrap checkbox, and place a check in the Line Numbers checkbox as well.

3. Press **F10** to close the window.

4. Select the **moontile.gif** image, in the middle of the page, by clicking it.

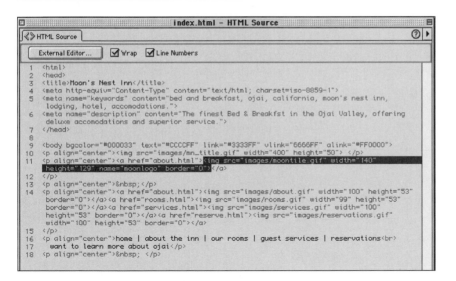

5. Press **F10** to return to the HTML Source window. Notice that the HTML code for the image is highlighted. This is very helpful when you want to look at specific HTML code in your page! You can actually teach yourself HTML by deconstructing your code in this way.

6. Close and save your changes. You won't be working with this file any longer.

5.
Linking

| Linking with Point to File |
| Browse for File and Link History |
| Linking to New Source Files | Email Links |
| Named Anchors | Image Maps |

chap_5

Dreamweaver 3
H•O•T CD-ROM

In Chapter 4, "*Basics*," you learned how to create links by clicking the **Browse for File** button and browsing to the **HTML** file on your hard drive. There are a few other ways to create links as well, and this chapter covers them.

For example, in this chapter you'll learn about **Point to File**, which allows you to point to a file inside your Site window and create the link based on your selection. This is helpful because it forces you to select files only within your Local Root Folder, which ensures better link integrity. In addition to creating links to HTML files, you can also use Point to File to select new image files and replace ones already on your page.

Another type of link is an email link. This special type of link launches your end-user's email program and automatically enters a recipient address. You will also learn how to use the **Link History** to quickly replicate links across your site, which can save you time and effort. Another new type of link you'll work with here is called **Named Anchors**, which work in conjunction with links to allow you to jump to different sections of one page. This can be very helpful when you have a large amount of text or information to navigate through. The final type of link that this chapter demonstrates how to make an image map. Image maps are useful when you want a single image to contain multiple links. If this all sounds abstract, dive into the chapter so you can get the hands-on experience that will make these new concepts understandable.

I. _____Linking with Point to File

The Point to File feature is an alternate way to create links on your Web pages. This feature forces you to select files that are within your Local Root Folder, which eliminates the unwanted possibility of linking to files that are outside the Root. Here's how it's done.

1. Copy **chap_05** to your hard drive. Define your site for Chapter 5 using the **chap_05** folder as the Local Root Folder. If you need a refresher on this process, visit Exercise 1 in Chapter 3, "*Site Control.*"

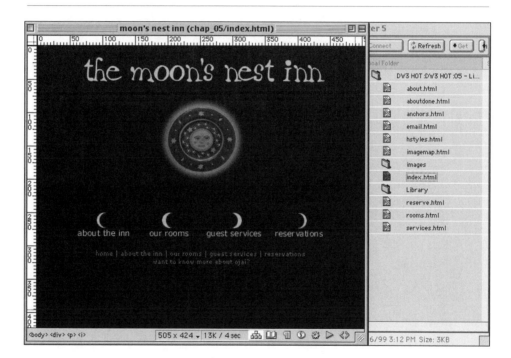

2. Open **index.html**. This file is complete except that it does not contain any links. You will create them using the Point to File feature.

3. The Site window does not have to be in the foreground, just open and visible in the background on your screen. Click **index.html** to make it active.

4. Click the **about.gif** image so that it is highlighted. Before you can create any link, you must first have the image or text selected.

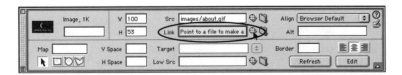

5. In the Properties Inspector, click and hold the Point to File icon next to the Link field. When you click and hold the mouse button down, the Link field will fill in with some text, telling you to point to a file to create a link.

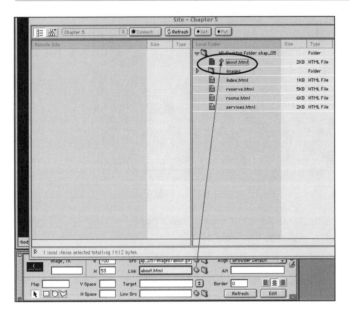

6. Click and drag your cursor over any part of the Site window. This will cause the Site window to come to the front on top of the document window. Move your mouse over **about.html**, so that it is highlighted, and release the mouse button. This will create a link to **about.html**.

7. The **Link** field will display the file you are linking to. This is a good place to look if you forget what file you linked to.

8. Click your document window to bring that forward.

9. Click the **rooms.gif** (**"our rooms"**) image so that it is highlighted.

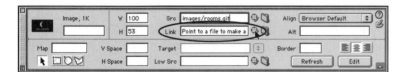

10. In the Properties Inspector, click and hold the Point to File icon again. When you click and hold the mouse button down, the **Link** field will fill in with some text.

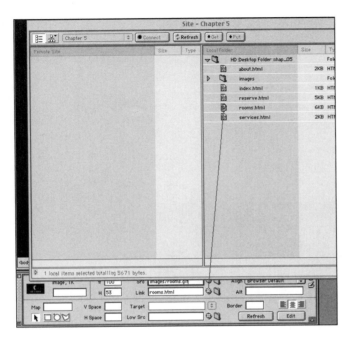

11. Click and drag your cursor over any part of the Site window. This will cause the Site window to come to the front, on top of the document window. Move your mouse over **rooms.html**, so that it is highlighted, and release the mouse button. This will create a link to **rooms.html**.

12. Using the Point to File feature, create a link for the **services.gif** ("**guest services**") image to **services.html** and a link for the **reserve.gif** ("**reservations**") image to **reserve.html**.

13. Press **F12** to preview the page in a browser. Click any of the images you linked to see if they work. When you are finished, return to Dreamweaver.

14. Choose **File > Save** to save the changes you've made, and leave it open for the next exercise.

2. _____Browse for File and the Link History

The Link History is one of those features that you probably are not aware of, but it can save you time and ensure that links are entered properly throughout your site. Unfortunately, the Link History will only remember links that you created using the Browse for File feature. It will not remember links that you created with the Point to File feature. If you want to enjoy the convenience of the Link History (and we know you will), you should create your links using the Browse for File feature.

This exercise will show you how to use the Link History to reproduce links throughout many pages in your site.

1. Make sure you have **index.html** open from the previous exercise.

2. Highlight the words "**about the inn**" at the bottom of the page. You are going to start with this text rather than "**home**" because you are already on the home page, so you don't need to create a link to that page.

3. In the Properties Inspector, click **Browse for File**.

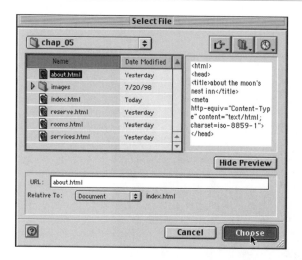

4. Browse to **about.html** and click **Choose**. This will create a link to that HTML file.

5. Highlight the words "**our rooms**" at the bottom of the page.

6. Click **Browse for File** again.

7. Browse to **rooms.html** and click **Choose**. This will create a link to that HTML file.

8. Using the Browse for File method, create a link for the words "**guest services**" to **services.html** and for "**reservations**" to **reserve.html**.

Now that you have created the links for your site, you are ready to begin using the Link History.

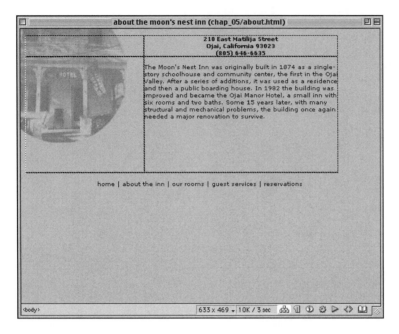

9. Open **about.html**. The text at the bottom of the page needs to be converted to links. You will use the Link History to do this very quickly.

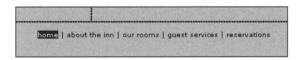

10. Highlight the word "**home**" at the bottom of the page. Because you didn't create a link for this on the **index.html** page, let's do that now so it will be in the Link History for later use.

11. In the Properties Inspector, use the Browse for File method to browse to **index.html**, inside the **chap_05** folder, and click **Choose** to create a link to **index.html**.

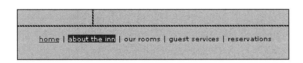

12. Highlight the words "**about the inn**."

*You have already created a link to this file on the **index.html** page, so it is recorded in the Link History.*

13. In the Properties Inspector, click the Link History pop-up menu and choose **about.html**. This will create a link to that HTML file. Notice that each link you created using the Browse for File method is listed in the Link History.

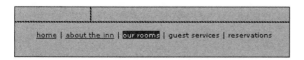

14. Highlight the words "**our rooms.**"

15. Click the **Link History** pop-up menu and choose **rooms.html**. This creates a link to that HTML file.

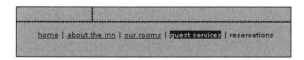

16. Highlight the words "**guest services.**"

17. Click the **Link History** pop-up menu and choose **services.html**. This will create a link to that HTML file.

18. Highlight the word "**reservations**."

19. Click the **Link History** pop-up menu and choose **reserve.html**. This will create a link to that **HTML** file.

*By now, you should be able to see how much time you can save by using the Link History. If you want more practice using the Link History, open **rooms.html**, **services.html**, and **reserve.html** and create links for the text at the bottom of each page. When you are finished with that, you will be a Link History expert ;-).*

20. Press **F12** to preview your page in a browser. Make sure you check the links you created at the bottom of each page.

21. Return to Dreamweaver and save and close the file.

You did all that work in just a few minutes and no typing, browsing, or pointing was needed. Sweet!

3. ————————————————— **Linking to New Source Files**

So far you have learned how to use the Point to File feature to create links on your pages. While this is the most common use of this feature, there are other ways to use it. You can use the Point to File feature to quickly replace images on your page. Because this feature ensures that you select only those files within your Local Root Folder, you will avoid missing files when you upload the files to a Web server. Please note that using Point to File is an alternate method to using the **Insert Image** object on the Objects palette, which you learned about in Chapter 4, "*Basics*." Sometimes there is more than one way to do the same thing in Dreamweaver. You'll find that you will develop your own preferences for which method to use as you gain experience in the program.

1. Open **newsource.html**. This HTML file contains a background, a table, and placeholders.

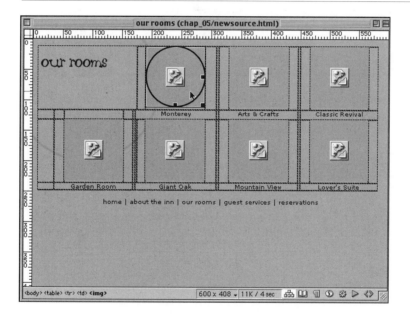

2. Click the **Placeholder** in the upper-left corner of the page to highlight it.

> ## Note | What Is a Placeholder?
>
> A Placeholder is an object that you add to your page to represent where final images will be inserted. You can resize the Placeholder so that it matches the dimensions of the image that will replace it. Placeholders are helpful in a workgroup where one person designs the page and another adds the content. Not everyone uses Placeholders. Some people like to add the images to their page as it is created. You can add a Placeholder by holding down the **Option** (Mac) or **Alt** (Windows) key while clicking the Insert Image object in the **Objects** palette. Then, you can resize the Placeholder by clicking it so that it is selected and then changing its height and width values in the Properties Inspector.

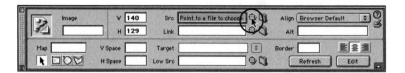

3. In the Properties Inspector, click the **Point to File** icon next to the **Src** option and drag it over the corner of the Site window. This causes Site window to come to the front of the document window.

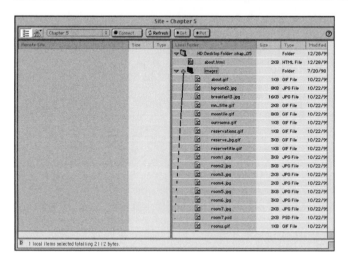

4. Hold the cursor over the **images** folder until it expands to reveal all the images inside.

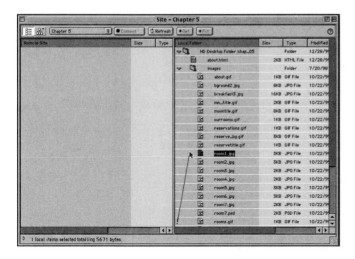

5. Move your cursor over the **room1.jpg** image and release the mouse button. This will select that image to replace the Placeholder currently on your page.

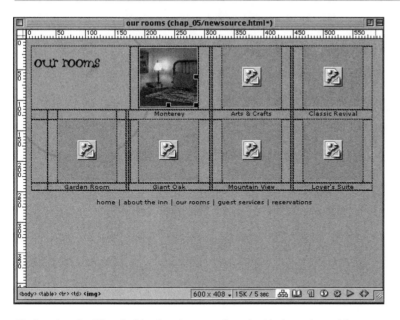

Notice that the Placeholder has been replaced with the selected image.

6. Click the Placeholder to the right of the image you just replaced to highlight it.

7. In the Properties Inspector, click the **Point to File** icon next to the **Src** option and drag it over the corner of the Site window, causing the Site window to come to the front of the document window.

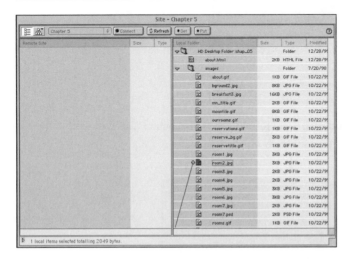

8. Move the cursor over **room2.jpg** and release the mouse button. This will replace the Placeholder with **room2.jpg** on your page. **Tip:** If you can't see **room2.jpg**, hold your cursor over the images folder until its contents are revealed.

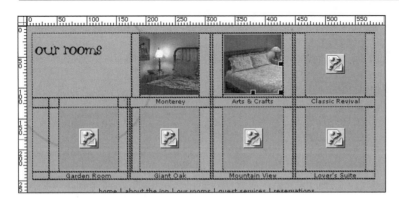

*Notice that the second Placeholder has now been replaced with the **room2.jpg** image.*

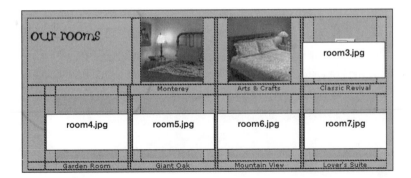

9. Replace the other five images on this page, using the Point to File feature (and the image above as a guideline). When you are finished, your page should look like the one below.

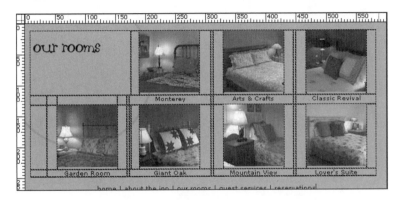

10. Choose **File > Save** to save your work. You can close this file, as you won't need it for any other exercises in this book.

4.————————————**Creating Email Links**

An **email** link will launch your end-user's email application and insert the recipient's address into the **To:** field. This is convenient and doesn't require the end user to remember complex and lengthy email addresses. This exercise will show you how to create an email link.

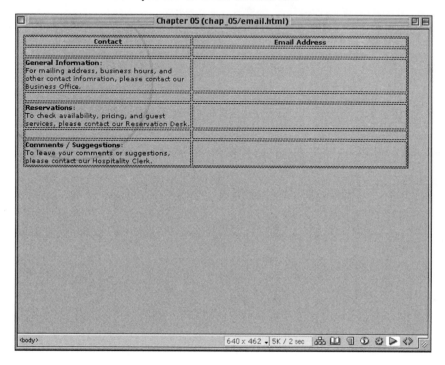

1. Open **email.html**. This file contains a table with some text and spaces for some email links. You will create those links in this exercise.

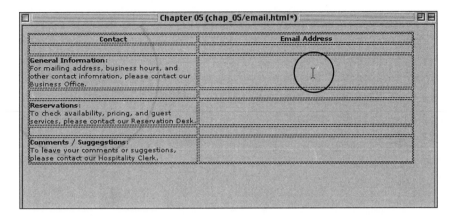

2. Click inside the cell to the right of the "**General Information**" column.

3. Click **Insert E-Mail Link** in the **Objects** palette. This will open the **Insert E-Mail Link** dialog box.

4. Enter **Text: General Information** and press **Tab**. Enter **E-Mail: information@moonsnestinn.com**. Click **OK**.

5. Click anywhere on the email link you just inserted on the page. In the Properties Inspector, notice that the **Link** field reads **mailto:information@moonsnestinn.com**. This is the correct format for creating email links.

> ## Note | Text versus Email
>
> The **Text** field determines what text will be displayed on the page, whereas the **EMail** field sets the actual email address for the recipient. Sometimes, you might want to put the email address in both fields, to allow someone to copy and paste the actual email link into another document or email application.

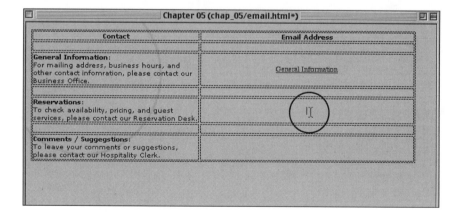

6. Click inside the cell to the right of the "**Reservations**" cell.

7. Click **Insert E-Mail Link** in the Objects palette.

8. Enter **Text: reservations@moonsnestinn.com** and press **Tab**. Enter **E-Mail: reservations@moonsnestinn.com**. Since Dreamweaver 3 will automatically insert any email address that you used previously, **information@moonsnestinn.com** will appear in the **E-Mail:** field. Click **OK**. This will insert an email link into the empty cell.

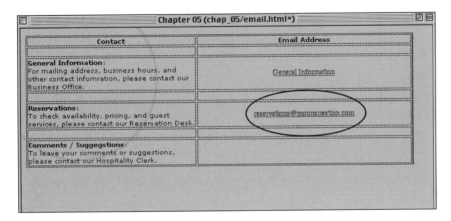

This will create an email link that displays the email address on the page.

9. An alternate way to create an email link is to avoid the **Insert E-Mail Link** object and do it manually. To do this, first click inside the cell to the right of the "**Comments / Suggestions**" cell.

10. Type **comments@moonsnestinn.com** inside the empty cell.

11. Click and drag over **comments@moonsnestinn.com** to highlight the text.

12. In the Properties Inspector, type **mailto:comments@moonsnestinn.com** in the Link field and press **Return/Enter**. This will create an email link from the selected text.

*You see, once again there are two ways to do the same operation. You learned how to create the email link using the **Insert E-Mail Link** object and how to manually insert an email link. Again, as your skills build in Dreamweaver, you will develop your own personal preferences for creating email links, just as you will develop your own preferences for assigning links.*

13. Press **F12** to preview this page in your default browser. You can click each of the email links to make sure they work.

14. When you are finished, return to Dreamweaver so you can save and close this file.

5. ——————————— Named Anchors

Named Anchors are a type of link. They are used infrequently, but when they're appropriate there's no other link quite like them. Named Anchors have two components – the **anchor** and the **link**. The time to use them is when you want to link to sections within a long page of content. Working together, they make it easy to jump to specific areas of your page. This exercise will show you how to set up anchors on your page.

1. Open **anchors.html**. This file has a table with some images that extend down the page.

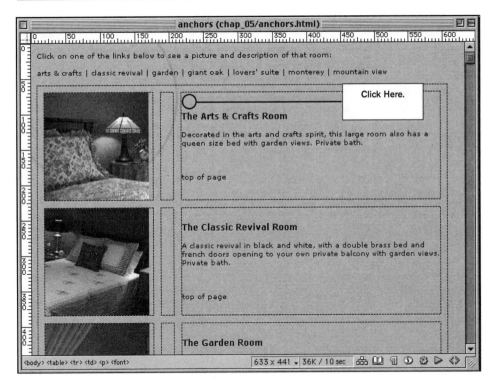

2. Click above the words "**The Arts & Crafts Room**." You will learn next how to insert a Named Anchor here, so users can easily jump to the photo and description of this room.

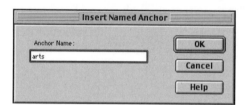

3. Choose **Insert > Named Anchor**. This will open the **Insert Named Anchor** dialog box. Type **arts** and then click **OK**.

 Movie | **anchor.mov**

To learn more about using Named Anchors, check out **anchor.mov** located in the **movies** folder on the Dreamweaver 3 **H•O•T CD-ROM**.

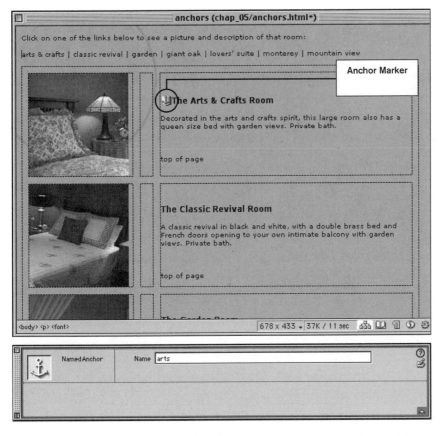

*Notice the small yellow Anchor Marker that appears on your page where you inserted the Named Anchor tag? If you ever want to change the name that you've set for your Named Anchor, click this **Anchor Marker** to access its name in the Properties Inspector in order to modify it.*

4. Click above the words "**The Classic Revival Room**." You will insert another Named Anchor here, so users can easily jump to the photo and description of this room.

---

5. Choose **Insert > Named Anchor**. This will open the **Insert Named Anchor** dialog box. Type **classic**, and then click **OK**.

---

6. Click above the words "**The Garden Room**." You will insert another Named Anchor here so users can easily jump to the photo and description of this room.

---

7. Choose **Insert > Named Anchor**. This will open the **Insert Named Anchor** dialog box. Type **garden** and then click **OK**.

---

8. Click above the words "**The Giant Oak Room**." You will insert another Named Anchor here, so users can easily jump to the photo and description of this room.

---

9. Choose **Insert > Named Anchor**. This will open the **Insert Named Anchor** dialog box. Type **giant** and then click **OK**.

---

10. Click above the words the "**The Lovers' Suite**." You will insert another Named Anchor here, so users can easily jump to the photo and description of this room.

---

11. Choose **Insert > Named Anchor**. This will open the **Insert Named Anchor** dialog box. Type **lovers** and then click **OK**. **Note:** Named Anchors cannot contain special characters like apostrophes.

---

12. Click above the words "**The Monterey Room**." You will insert another Named Anchor here, so users can easily jump to the photo and description of this room.

---

13. Choose **Insert > Named Anchor**. This will open the **Insert Named Anchor** dialog box. Type **monterey** and then click **OK**.

14. Click above the words "**The Mountain View Room**." You will insert another Named Anchor here, so users can easily jump to the photo and description of this room.

15. Choose **Insert > Named Anchor**. This will open the **Insert Named Anchor** dialog box. Type **mountain** and then click **OK**.

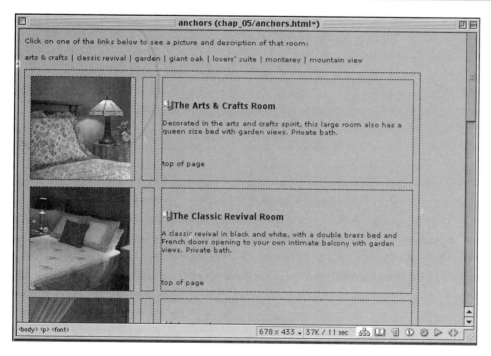

When you are finished, your page should look something like this. There should be a small Anchor Marker at the end of each room title.

16. Click and drag to highlight the words "**arts & crafts**" at the top of the page. Now that you have set up all of your Named Anchors, you need to create links to each of them.

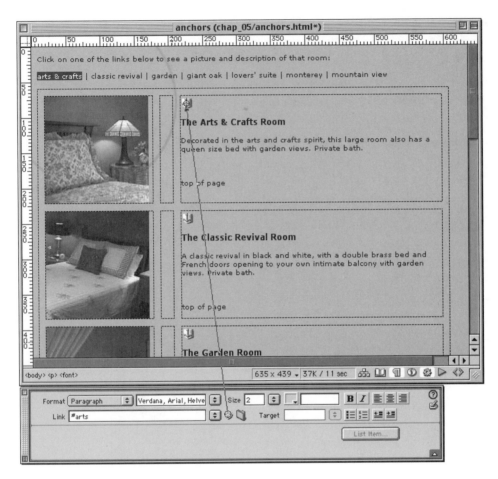

17. In the Properties Inspector, using the Point to File option, click and drag to the Anchor Marker above the text "**The Arts and Crafts Room**." Release the mouse button to create the link. **Note:** Links to anchor points always begin with a **#** sign.

18. Click and drag to highlight the words "**classic revival**" at the top of the page.

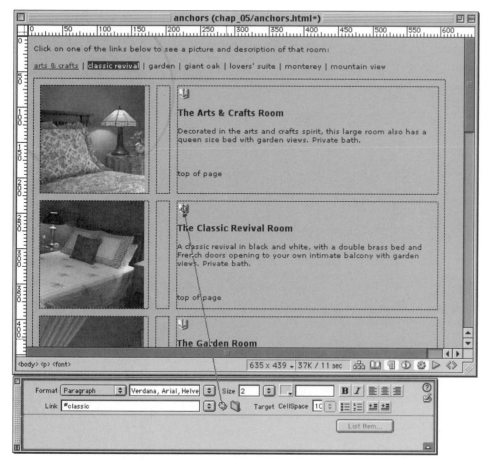

19. In the Properties Inspector, using the Point to File option, click and drag to the Anchor Marker above the text "**The Classic Revival Room**." Release the mouse button to create the link.

20. Click and drag to highlight the word "**garden**" at the top of the page.

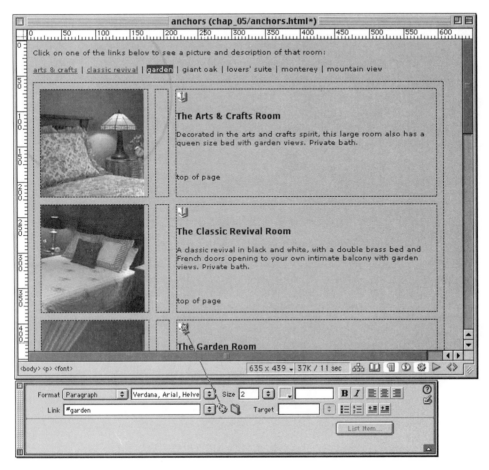

21. In the Properties Inspector, using the Point to File option, click and drag to the Anchor Marker above the text "**The Garden Room**." Release the mouse button to create the link.

22. Click and drag to highlight the words "**giant oak**" at the top of the page.

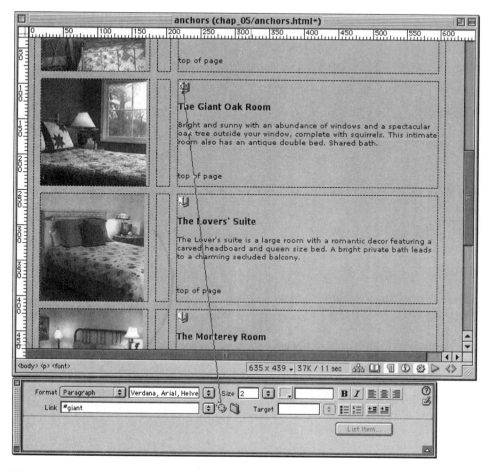

23. In the Properties Inspector, using the Point to File option, click and drag to the Anchor Marker above the text "**The Giant Oak Room**." Release the mouse button to create the link.

24. Click and drag to highlight the words "**lovers' suite**" at the top of the page.

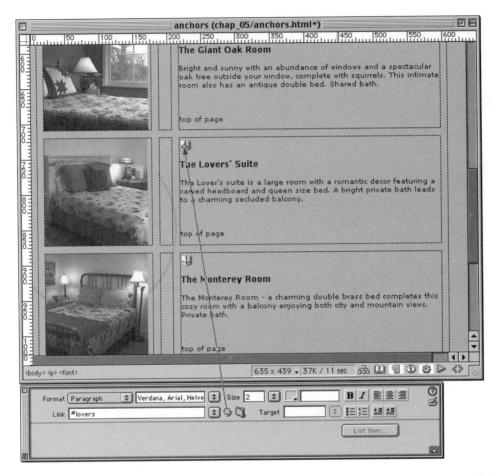

25. In the Properties Inspector, using the Point to File option, click and drag to the Anchor Marker above the text "**The Lovers' Suite**." Release the mouse button to crate the link.

26. Click and drag to highlight the words "**monterey**" at the top of the page.

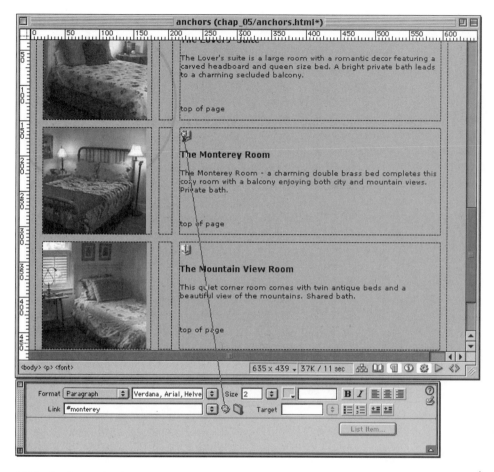

27. In the Properties Inspector, using the Point to File option, click and drag to the Anchor Marker above the text "**The Monterey Room.**" Release the mouse button to create the link.

---

28. Click and drag to highlight the words "**mountain view**" at the top of the page.

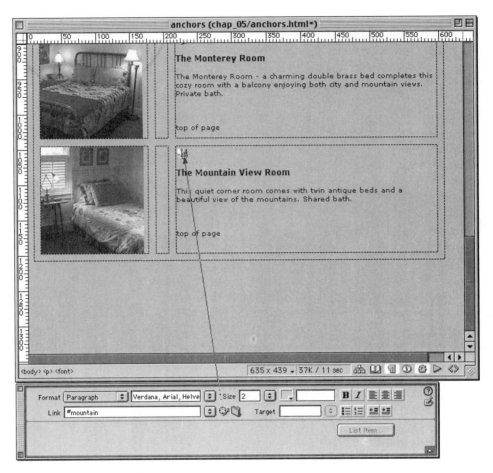

29. In the Properties Inspector, using the Point to File option, click and drag to the Anchor Marker above the text "**The Mountain View Room**." Release the mouse button to create the link.

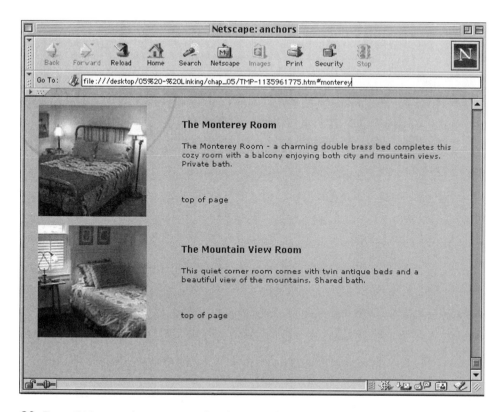

30. Press **F12** to preview your page in a browser. Click each of the links at the top to see how the Named Anchors work.

As you can see, this is a nice way to jump to different sections within a single page. Once you are at the bottom of the page, wouldn't it be nice if you had a link to a Named Anchor that would take you back to the top of the page? Well, you will create just that in the next few steps.

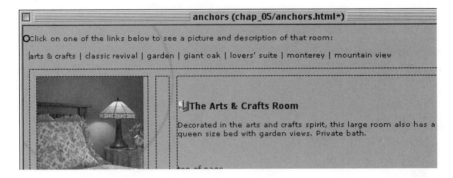

31. Return to Dreamweaver and click just to the left of the word "**Click**" at the top of the page.

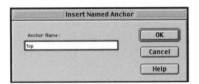

32. Choose **Insert > Named Anchor**. Type **top** for the name and click **OK**. This will insert an Anchor Marker at the top of your page.

33. Highlight the words "**top of page**" under the description of the "**The Arts & Crafts Room**."

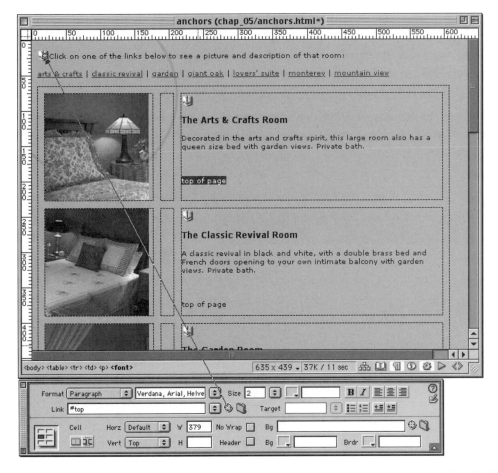

34. In the Properties Inspector, using the Point to File option, click and drag to the Anchor Marker next to the word "**Click.**" at the top of the page. Release the mouse button. This will create a link to the top Anchor Marker.

---

35. Repeat this process for each block of text that reads "**top of page.**" This will create a link to the top Anchor Marker, so users have a quick and easy way to get back to the top of your page.

---

36. Press **F12** to preview your page in a browser. Click the "**monterey**" link. This will take you to the bottom of the page. Next, click the "**top of page**" link. This will take you back up to the top. Pretty slick!

---

37. Return to Dreamweaver. Save and close all the work you've done in this file.

6._____Image Maps

An **image map** contains invisible coordinates that allow you to assign multiple links to a single image. With image maps, you can specify multiple regions of a single image and have each of those areas link to a different URL. This exercise will show you how to create an image map.

1. Open **imagemap.html**. This file contains a single image that will serve as a navigation bar for the site. In the following steps, you will create an image map so this single image can link to multiple pages.

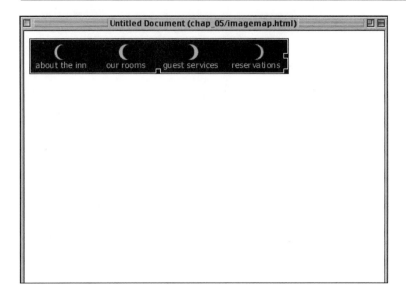

2. Click the image so that it is selected.

With an image selected, the Properties Inspector changes to reflect options for images, which include the image map settings.

3. In the **Map** field, enter **navbar**. By doing this, you are assigning a name to the image map, which is required and becomes even more important if you have multiple image maps on a single page.

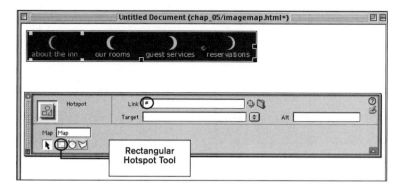

4. Click the **Rectangular Hotspot Tool**. Click and drag a rectangle around the words "**about the inn**" and the image of the crescent moon. By doing this, you are defining what area of the image you want to serve as a link. When you release the mouse, you will notice a light blue box around the image and the options in your Properties Inspector will have changed.

*Note: The # mark in the **Link:** field is used as a Placeholder for the real link. If you don't remove this or add your own link, the users will still see the link icon, the little hand, when they move their cursor over the image map.*

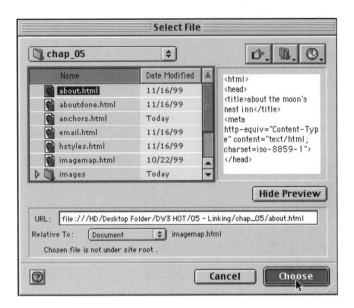

5. With the light blue rectangle selected, click **Browse for File** and browse to **about.html**. Click **Choose**. This will create a link for this specific area of the image map.

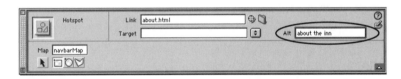

6. With that image map still selected, type "**about the inn**" in the **Alt** field in the Properties Inspector and press **Enter/Return**. In some browsers this will display a small help tag when the user hovers over the hot area of the image map. You don't have to put anything here if you don't want to.

Tip | Help Tags

Have you ever held your mouse over an image map only to discover that a little tag pops up with some text inside it? Well, that is no trick, it is simply the **ALT** attribute of the **HREF** tag being displayed. If you don't see this tag, either the **ALT** attribute wasn't used at all or you are using Navigator on a Macintosh, which doesn't display these cute little help tags. If you want to add an **ALT** tag to your image map, simply give each link a message inside the **ALT** field of the Properties Inspector, as shown in Step 6.

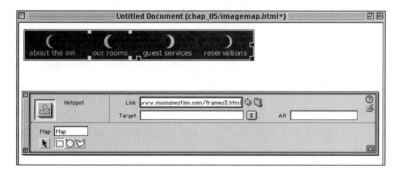

7. Click the **Rectangular Hotspot Tool** again. Click and drag a rectangle around the words "**our rooms**" and the image of the crescent moon.

8. In the **Properties Inspector Link** field, type **http://www.moonsnestinn.com/frames3.html**. This will create an external link in this part of the image map.

9. Press **F12** to preview the links in a browser. Like other links, they cannot be previewed from within Dreamweaver; they must be viewed through a browser.

10. When you are finished, return to Dreamweaver. Save and close this file.

In the real world, you would finish this by creating links to the other navigation options. However, since this is just an exercise, you can move on to the next chapter ;-).

6.

HTML

HTML Source Window	Editing with the HTML Source Window
External HTML Editors	Quick Tag Editor
Clean Up HTML	Clean Up Word HTML

chap_6

Dreamweaver 3
H•O•T CD-ROM

At our hands-on courses we are frequently asked if it's necessary to know HTML to be a successful Web designer. A few years ago, the answer was a resounding "yes," because Web pages were put together by writing HTML code. With the introduction of WYSIWYG HTML editors like Dreamweaver, Web developers are shielded from writing the HTML code and can create Web pages in a completely visual environment. The invention of the WYSIWYG editor brought Web page publishing within the reach of almost anyone. However, it's still our belief that a basic understanding of HTML is beneficial to anyone planning to work in this field professionally.

This chapter will show you how to interact with HTML in Dreamweaver. A lot of what is covered in this chapter will appeal to people who already know how to hand-code their pages, but don't be afraid to read on and dig into the exercises in this chapter, even if you are not familiar with HTML. The step-by-step tutorials will walk novices as well as experienced HTML coders through the process of editing HTML.

I. HTML Source Window

The **HTML Source** window in Dreamweaver allows you to access the HTML code generated for your page. The ability to quickly toggle between editing your code and then returning to the visual editing environment is really convenient. For those of you that are familiar with HTML code, you won't feel so far from home when using Dreamweaver. For those of you less familiar with HTML, you can watch Dreamweaver create the HTML code as you use the visual editing environment. Observing this process is actually a great way to teach yourself HTML.

This first exercise will expose you to the HTML Source window and show you how to edit your HTML code. Even if you don't know a whole lot about HTML, you should still work through this exercise. It's not that hard, and it will show you that learning HTML is truly within your reach.

1. Copy **chap_06** to your hard drive. Define your site for Chapter 6 using the **chap_06** folder as the Local Root Folder. If you need a refresher on this process, visit Chapter 3, *"Site Control."*

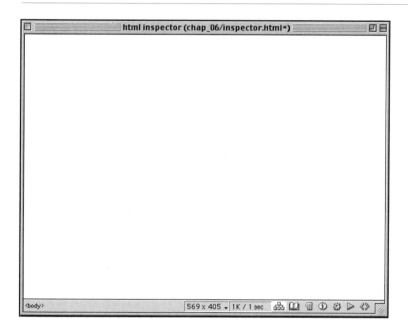

2. Open the **inspector.html** file located inside the **chap_06** folder. This is just a blank file that has been saved for you.

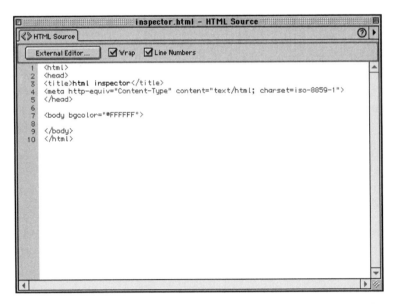

3. Select **Window > HTML Source** to access the HTML Source window. You could alternatively press **F10**, which is a valuable shortcut to memorize if you plan to look at the code of your document frequently. This window doesn't have much in it, but neither does your page yet!

4. To close the **HTML Source** window Press **F10**. This shortcut toggles the HTML Source window on or off.

Note | HTML Source Window Options

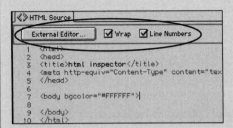

There are three options available in the HTML Source window: **External Editor...**, **Wrap**, and **Line Numbers**. The External Editor option will be discussed in the next section. The Wrap and Line Numbers are important to know about right away. Checking the **Wrap** option will force the HTML code lines to wrap to the size of the HTML Source window. This is very useful when you start working with large amounts of code. The **Line Numbers** option will place a number next to each line of code, along the left side of the HTML Source window. This is good when you need to refer to specific lines of code. The line numbers are only visible in the HTML Source window, and don't affect the integrity of the code at all.

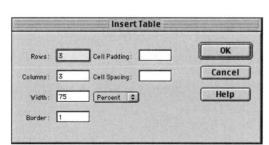

5. Click on the **Insert Table** in the Objects palette. When the **Insert Table** dialog box appears, make sure settings match the dialog box above and then click **OK**.

6. Press **F10** to re-open the HTML Source window. Check out all the code that was generated to create the Table. How would you like to type all that code? Your answer most likely is heck, no!

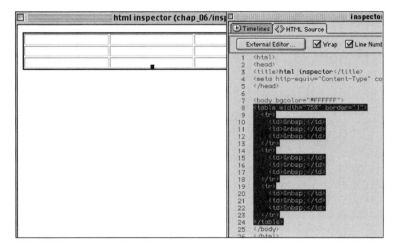

7. Move the **HTML Source** window over so that you can see it and the table on your page at the same time.

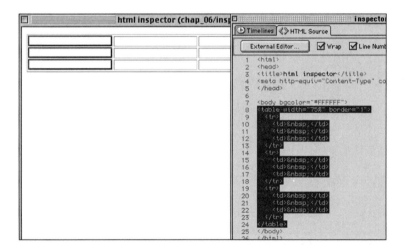

8. Click in the first cell and drag down. This will let you select all three rows in the table.

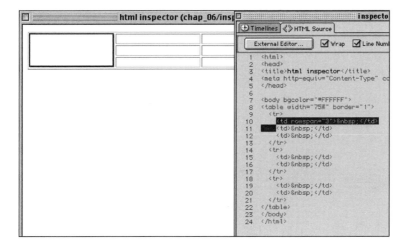

9. Select **Modify > Table > Merge Cells**. This will merge the cells you have selected.

Look at the HTML Source window. See how the HTML code is updated to reflect the changes you just made? This is a great way to learn HTML. You can literally watch the code being generated and modified as you add, modify, and remove content from your page. Go ahead and make some more changes to your page, but leave the HTML Source window open so you can watch all of the HTML being created. To think that people used to type all of this by hand! Phew, we are sure glad we don't have to do that anymore.

---

10. When you are finished, save your changes and leave the file open for the next exercise.

---

2. _____**Editing with the HTML Source Window**

Now that you have an idea of how the HTML Source window works, you will learn how to use it to modify your page. In fact, if you wanted to hand-code, you could create your entire page right within the HTML Source window.

In this exercise, you will use the HTML Source window to add content to your page and then make modifications to it. The purpose of this exercise is to make you more comfortable with the HTML Source window.

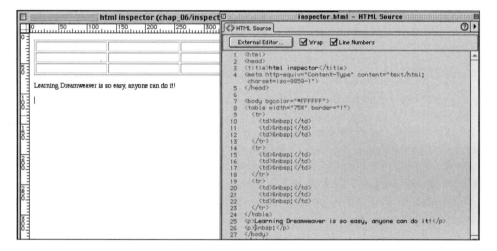

1. Click anywhere below the table and type **Learning Dreamweaver is so easy, anyone can do it!**. Look inside the HTML Source window and watch as your text is created. Press **Return** to add a paragraph break, when you are finished typing.

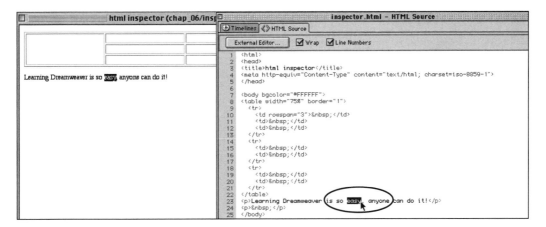

2. Inside the HTML Source window, click and drag to select the word "**easy**." Once you have it selected, type **simple**. When you are done typing, click anywhere in the document window to see the changes updated.

Tip | Updating with HTML Source Window

There are a few things to know about using the HTML Source window to make updates to your pages. When you initially open the HTML Source window, it will have a gray background. If you click anywhere inside the HTML Source window, it will turn the background white. This means that you can now make changes to the actual code. Anytime you make changes inside the HTML Source window, you will not see the changes until you click inside the document window. So, don't worry, if you don't see your changes as you make them in the HTML Source window, you will as soon as you return to the document window.

3. In the document window, click and drag to highlight the word "**simple**." With the word highlighted, use the Properties Inspector to make the word **bold**. Notice that the <b> tags were added around the word in the HTML Source window, which shows you the tag required to achieve bolding of text.

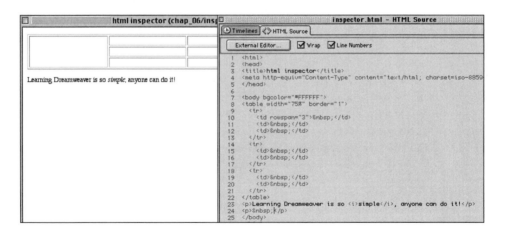

4. In the HTML Source window, change the <b> tags so they have an **i** in the middle instead of a **b**. The <i> tag will format the text so it's in *italics* instead of **bold**.

5. Click anywhere in your document window and your changes will be updated. You can begin to see how the document window and HTML Source window may be used in tandem to create and modify your documents.

6. When you are finished, save your changes and close this file.

3. _____External HTML Editors

While the HTML Source window gives you the ability to create and modify HTML code, it is not nearly as robust as other dedicated text-based HTML editors, such as BBEdit and Allaire HomeSite. These editors give you more control and options for generating and modifying code than Dreamweaver. In Dreamweaver, you can specify an external HTML editor that will open with the click of a button.

This exercise will show you how to set up an external HTML editor within Dreamweaver. You will also learn how to access this external editor inside Dreamweaver. Not everyone will need to set up an external HTML editor, but we wanted to make sure you know how, just in case.

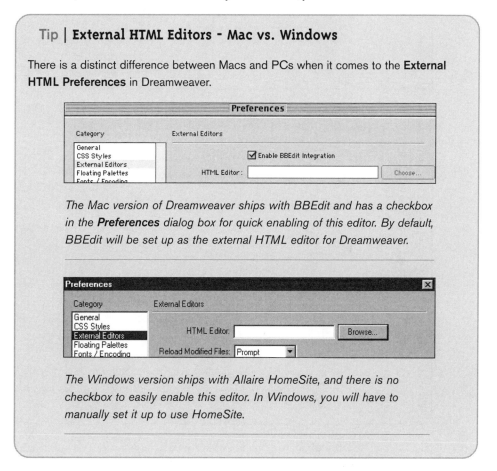

Tip | **External HTML Editors - Mac vs. Windows**

There is a distinct difference between Macs and PCs when it comes to the **External HTML Preferences** in Dreamweaver.

*The Mac version of Dreamweaver ships with BBEdit and has a checkbox in the **Preferences** dialog box for quick enabling of this editor. By default, BBEdit will be set up as the external HTML editor for Dreamweaver.*

The Windows version ships with Allaire HomeSite, and there is no checkbox to easily enable this editor. In Windows, you will have to manually set it up to use HomeSite.

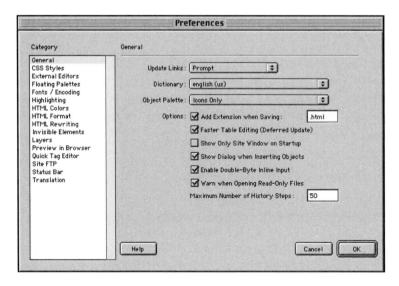

1. To access the **Preferences** dialog box, select **Edit > Preferences**. You could also press **Cmd+U** (Mac) or **Ctrl+U** (Windows).

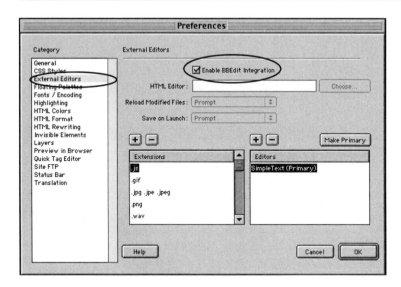

2. Click on the **External Editors** option under the **Category** option. This will cause the options for this category to appear. By default on the Mac, **Enable BBEdit Integration** will be checked.

3. Mac users should uncheck the **Enable BBEdit Integration** checkbox to disable this feature. This will allow you to browse to another application that you want to use as your external HTML editor.

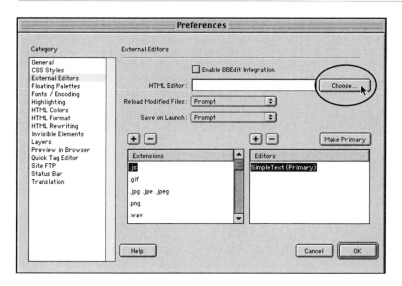

4. Click on the **Choose...** button (Mac) or the **Browse...** button (Windows). This will open a window that will allow you to browse to the application you want to use to edit your HTML code.

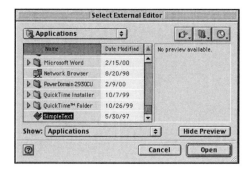 

5. On the Mac, browse to the **SimpleText** application and select that. On Windows, browse to the **NotePad** application and select that. When you are done, click **Open**. Click **OK** to close the **Preferences** dialog box. There, you have just specified a custom external HTML editor for Dreamweaver.

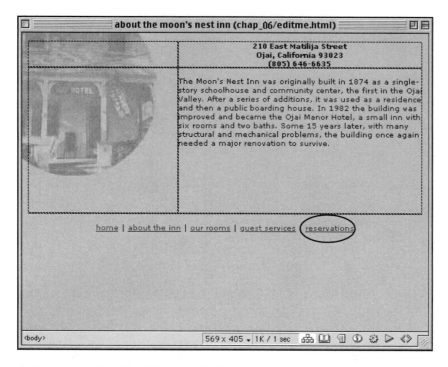

6. Open the **editme.html** file located inside the **chap_06** folder. You will work with this file using the external HTML editor you just specified.

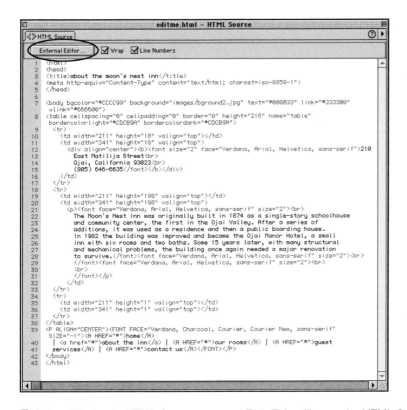

7. Select **Window > HTML Source** or press **F10**. This will open the HTML Source window, where you can view the code for this page.

```
                        editme.html
<html>
<head>
<title>about the moon's nest inn</title>
<meta http-equiv="Content-Type" content="text/html; charset=iso-8859-1">
</head>

<body bgcolor="#CCCC99" background="images/bground2.jpg" text="#000033" link="#333300"
vlink="#666600">
<table cellspacing="0" cellpadding="0" border="0" height="216" name="table"
bordercolorlight="#CDCB9A" bordercolordark="#CDCB9A">
  <tr>
    <td width="211" height="18" valign="top"></td>
    <td width="341" height="18" valign="top">
      <div align="center"><b><font size="2" face="Verdana, Arial, Helvetica, sans-serif">210
      East Matilija Street<br>
      Ojai, California 93023<br>
      (805) 646-6635</font></b></div>
    </td>
  </tr>
  <tr>
    <td width="211" height="198" valign="top"></td>
    <td width="341" height="198" valign="top">
      <p><font face="Verdana, Arial, Helvetica, sans-serif" size="2"><br>
      The Moon's Nest Inn was originally built in 1874 as a single-story schoolhouse
      and community center, the first in the Ojai Valley. After a series of
      additions, it was used as a residence and then a public boarding house.
      In 1982 the building was improved and became the Ojai Manor Hotel, a small
      inn with six rooms and two baths. Some 15 years later, with many structural
      and mechanical problems, the building once again needed a major renovation
      to survive.</font><font face="Verdana, Arial, Helvetica, sans-serif" size="2"><br>
      </font><font face="Verdana, Arial, Helvetica, sans-serif" size="2"><br>
      <br>
      </font></p>
    </td>
  </tr>
  <tr>
    <td width="211" height="1" valign="top"></td>
    <td width="341" height="1" valign="top"></td>
  </tr>
</table>
<P ALIGN="CENTER"><FONT FACE="Verdana, Charcoal, Courier, Courier New, sans-serif"
SIZE="-1"><A HREF="#">home</A>
 | <a href="#">about the inn</a> | <A HREF="#">our rooms</A> | <A HREF="#">guest
```

The document viewed in SimpleText on the Macintosh.

8. Click on the **External Editor...** button at the top of the window. This will automatically open the document in the external editor you specified. On the Mac, it should open in SimpleText, and in Windows, it should open in NotePad or WordPad.

```
</tr>
  <tr>
   <td width="211" height="1" valign="top"></td>
   <td width="341" height="1" valign="top"></td>
  </tr>
</table>
<P ALIGN="CENTER"><FONT FACE="Verdana, Charcoal, Courier, Courier New, sans-serif"
SIZE="-1"><A HREF="#">home</A>
 I <a href="#">about the inn</a> I <A HREF="#">our rooms</A> I <A HREF="#">guest
 services</A> I <A HREF="#">reservations</A></FONT></P>
</body>
</html>
```

9. Scroll to the bottom of the document until you see the word "**reservations**." Click and drag over the word "**reservations**" so that it is highlighted.

```
</tr>
  <tr>
   <td width="211" height="1" valign="top"></td>
   <td width="341" height="1" valign="top"></td>
  </tr>
</table>
<P ALIGN="CENTER"><FONT FACE="Verdana, Charcoal, Courier, Courier New, sans-serif"
SIZE="-1"><A HREF="#">home</A>
 I <a href="#">about the inn</a> I <A HREF="#">our rooms</A> I <A HREF="#">guest
 services</A> I <A HREF="#">contact us</A></FONT></P>
</body>
</html>
```

10. Type **contact us**. This will replace the word "**reservations**" with the words "**contact us**."

11. Close this file. When you are prompted to save your changes, click **Save**.

12. Return to Dreamweaver. You will be prompted immediately that the file you have opened has been modified outside of Dreamweaver. Click **Yes** to update the open file, so you can see the changes you made in the external editor.

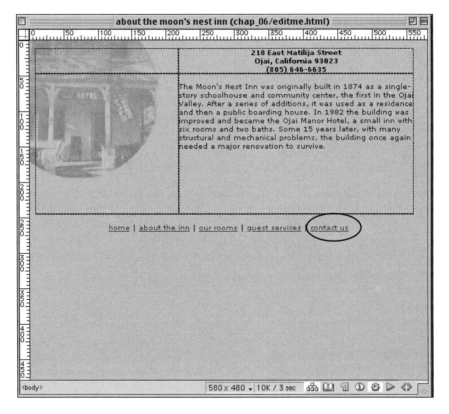

13. If the HTML Source window is open, close it by pressing **F10**. Notice that the link at the bottom of the page now says "**contact us**." You can start to see how easy it is to work with other applications and Dreamweaver. Close this file, since you won't need it any more.

4. _____Quick Tag Editor

Even if you are using a WYSIWYG HTML editor and like to code by hand, sometimes you still want quick access to the raw HTML code. The **Quick Tag Editor**, a new feature in Dreamweaver 3, gives you instant access to the HTML code on your page without forcing you to access the HTML Source window or an external HTML editor. This is great if you want to make a quick change to a tag or attribute. This exercise will show you how to use the Quick Tag Editor to make changes to a file.

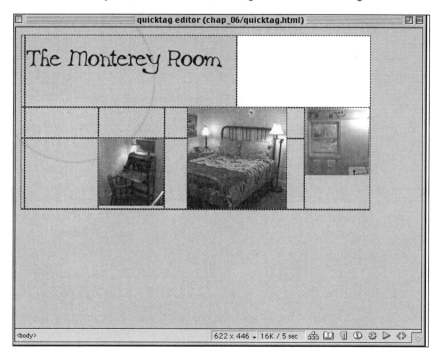

1. Open the **quicktag.html** file located inside the **chap_06** folder. This file needs a few changes. First, the large cell at the top has a white background and is not allowing the tan background to show through. Second, the image of the window is aligned to the top of the table cell and should be aligned to the bottom of the table cell. These problems can be easily fixed with the Quick Tag Editor.

2. Click inside the large white cell at the top of the table so your cursor is blinking inside the cell. Next, click on the **<td>** (**T**able **D**ata) tag in the **Tag Selector**, at the bottom of the document window. This will select the entire large white cell.

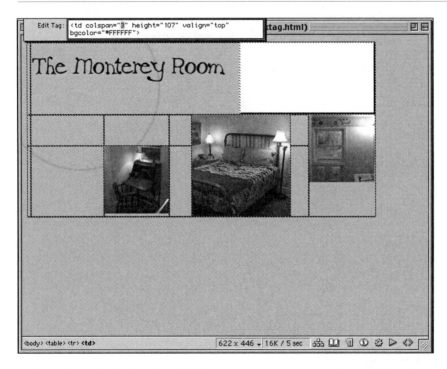

3. Press **Cmd+T** (Mac) or **Ctrl+T** (Windows) to access the **Quick Tag Editor**. (You could alternatively choose **Modify > Quick Tag Editor**.) The Quick Tag Editor will appear at the top of the document window. It currently displays the active attribute settings for the selected <td> tag. Notice that the bgcolor attribute is set to #FFFFFF, which is the hexadecimal value for white.

> ### Note | What are HTML Attributes?
>
> HTML consists of a series of HTML tags. These tags define how your page is formatted in a browser. Attributes attach to these HTML tags to further define the appearance of your page. For example, <TABLE> is a standard HTML tag. The <TABLE> tag has several different attributes that can be used to further define its appearance, such as width, height, bgcolor, etc.
>
> For some great references on HTML and their associated tags, make sure you check out the following links:
>
> http://www.w3.org/MarkUp/
> http://www.htmlhelp.com/

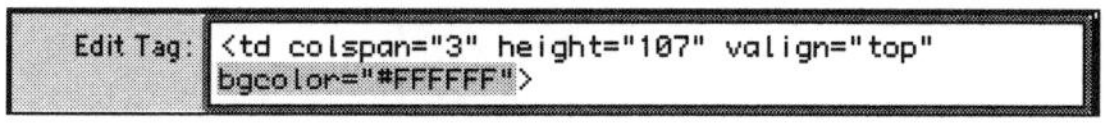

```
Edit Tag:  <td colspan="3" height="107" valign="top"
           bgcolor="#FFFFFF">
```

Select the tag exactly as shown here.

---

4. Click and drag inside the **Quick Tag Editor** to select the **bgcolor** attribute. Press the **Delete** key to remove this attribute. Press **Return** or **Enter** to accept the changes you made. With the bgcolor attribute removed, the tan background is allowed to show through the table cell.

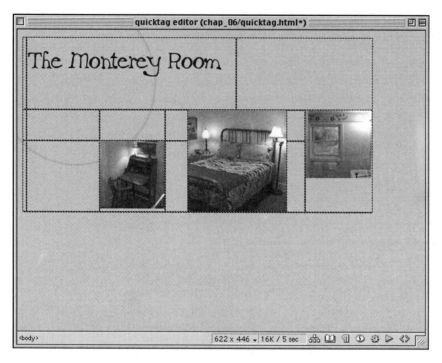

This is what your page should look like with the bgcolor *attribute removed.*

5. Click on the window image (on the right), which is currently aligned to the **top**. With the image selected, click on the **<td>** tag in the **Tag Selector**, at the bottom of the document window. This will select the cell so you can change the vertical alignment attribute tag by using the Quick Tag Editor.

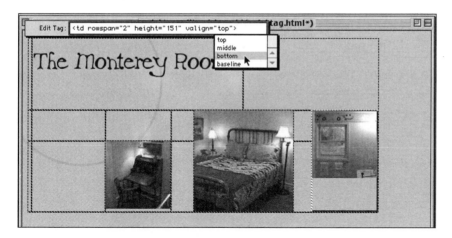

6. Press **Cmd+T** (Mac) or **Ctrl+T** (Windows) to access the **Quick Tag Editor**. (You could also choose **Modify > Quick Tag Editor**.)

7. The image should be aligned to the **bottom** of the cell, not the top. Click and drag to select the word **top** in the **Quick Tag Editor**. Be careful to select just the word, and not the quotation marks that surround it.

8. Delete the word "**top**," then double-click on the word "**bottom**," from the small pop-up menu this displays. This will change the VALIGN (vertical alignment) attribute to bottom and move the image accordingly. Press **Return** or **Enter** to accept your changes.

The Quick Tag Editor is a great tool if you want quick access to the HTML code. As you just saw, you can make changes to the HTML code without ever leaving the visual environment, which is very cool!

9. Save your changes and close this file.

5. _____Clean Up HTML

There might be times when you have to work with HTML that was written by another person or in a program other than Dreamweaver. This may not be the best HTML code you have ever seen and might need to be cleaned up a little. Dreamweaver has a command called **Clean Up HTML** that will automatically remove empty tags, redundant nested tags, non-Dreamweaver HTML comments, Dreamweaver HTML comments, nested font tags, and any tag you specify. This exercise will show you how to use this feature.

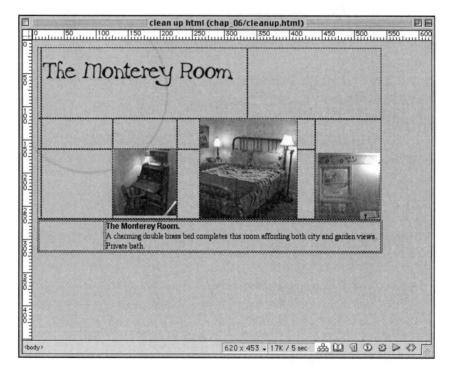

1. Open the **cleanup.html** file located inside the **chap_06** folder. While this page may look normal, it does have several things that need to be fixed. You will learn what needs to be fixed and how to fix it in this exercise.

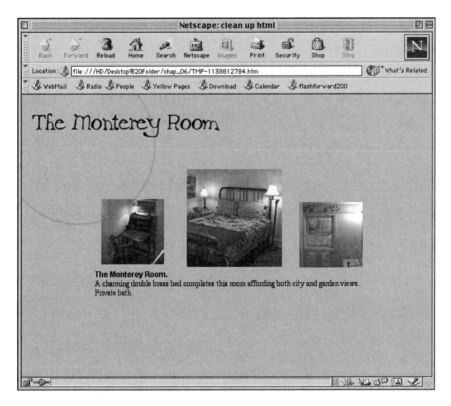

2. Press **F12** to preview this page in a browser. Everything looks fine, except that the words "**Private bath**" are blinking. That's because the `<blink>` tag was applied to that text. **Note:** The `<blink>` tag will not display in Version 5 of Microsoft Internet Explorer.

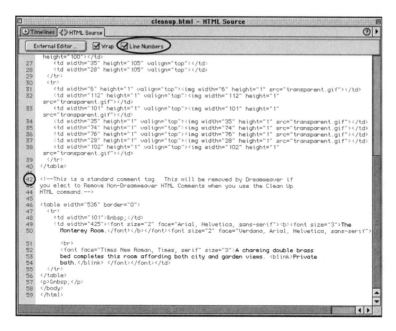

3. Return to Dreamweaver. Press **F10** to open the HTML Source window. Look at line **42** (scroll down, if necessary). If you can't see any line numbers, make sure there is a check in the **Line Numbers** checkbox at the top of the window.

A standard Comment Tag has been added on lines 42-44. While these don't take up that much room, you might want to remove them from documents you inherit. This is one of the things you will remove using the Clean Up HTML command.

```
45
46  <table width="536" border="0">
47   <tr>
48    <td width="101"> </td>
49    <td width="425"><font size="2" face="Arial, Helvetica, sans-serif"><b><font size="3">The
50    Monterey Room.</font></b></font><font size="2" face="Verdana, Arial, Helvetica, sans-se
51
52    <br>
53    <font face="Times New Roman, Times, serif" size="3">A charming double brass
54    bed completes this room affording both city and garden views. <blink>Private
      bath.</blink> </font></font></td>
```

4. Next, scroll down to line **50**. Notice that there is a nested <font> tag on that line. While this won't typically cause any problems when your page is displayed, it's a good idea to get rid of tags like these.

```
50    Monterey Room.</font></b></font><font size="2" face="Verdana, Arial, Helvetica, sans-se
51
52    <br>
53    <font face="Times New Roman, Times, serif" size="3">A charming double brass
54    bed completes this room affording both city and garden views. <blink>Private
      bath.</blink> </font></font></td>
55   </tr>
56  </table>
57  <p> </p>
58  </body>
59  </html>
```

5. Finally, scroll down to line **53**. Notice the <blink> tag that is surrounding the words "**Private bath.**" This is what's causing the words to blink on and off. This effect, while sometimes appealing at first, can get very annoying after a few seconds. You will remove this as well.

6. Close the HTML Source window.

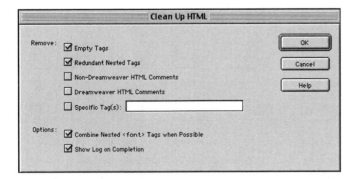

7. Select **Commands > Clean Up HTML**. This will open the Clean Up HTML window. This is where you can specify what parts of the HTML you want to clean up.

8. Click on the **Non-Dreamweaver HTML Comments** checkbox to put a check there. This will make sure that the comment tag you looked at in the HTML code will be removed.

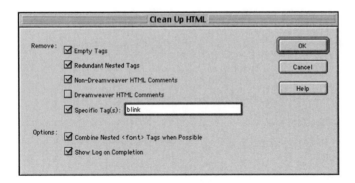

9. Click on the **Specific Tag(s)** checkbox to put a check there. Type **blink** in the text field to the right of the checkbox. This will ensure that the annoying <blink> tag at the bottom of the page is also removed. **Tip:** Be careful to type just the word **blink**, and not the greater than and less than marks that surround it. Click **OK**.

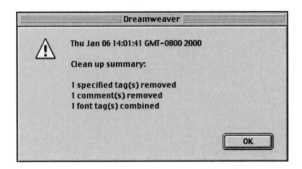

10. Dreamweaver will now analyze the HTML code in your document and clean up the HTML based on the selections you made. It will also produce a window with a brief summary of what actions were performed. Click **OK**.

11. Open the HTML Source window again by pressing **F10**. Scroll down and look for the comment tag, nested font tag, or the <blink> tag. They have all been removed. As you can imagine, the **Clean Up HTML** can be a very useful tool, especially when you get a file that was not written properly.

12. Close and save this file.

Clean Up HTML Selections

The chart below outlines the different selections available under the Clean Up HTML command and what each of them does:

Clean Up HTML	
Selection	**Purpose**
Remove: Empty Tags	This will remove any tags that have no content between them. For example, `<i></i>` would be removed because there is nothing between the two tags.
Remove: Redundant Nested Tags	This will remove tags that are redundant and not needed. For example, `<b>This<b>` is a `<b>redundant<b>` `<b>tag</b>`, has two redundant `<b>` tags that would be removed because they are not needed.
Remove: Non-Dreamweaver HTML Comments	This will remove any comment tags that are not specific to Dreamweaver, but will not remove comments that are native to Dreamweaver. `<!– #EndEditable "image" –>` for example, would not be removed, because it is used native to Dreamweaver to designate the end of an editable area of a template.
Remove: Dreamweaver HTML Comments	This will remove all HTML comments that are native to Dreamweaver. However, it will not remove standard HTML comments.
Remove: Specific Tag(s):	This lets you remove specific tags that you specify in the text field. For example, you could remove all of the `<blink>` tags in a document, or any other tag that you specify.
Options: Combine Nested `<font>` Tags When Possible	This will try to combine nested tags when they control the same block of text.
Options: Show Log on Completion	This will cause a small window to appear after this command has been applied. The window will summarize how the HTML was modified.

6. _____Clean Up Word HTML

Dreamweaver lets you import HTML files that were saved in Microsoft Word. This is a nice feature, because more and more business professionals are using Word to author Web pages. However, Microsoft Word has a reputation for generating a lot of unnecessary HTML code. Fortunately, the **Clean Up Word HTML** command will help you remove this extra code to ensure that your pages are written in the most appropriate and concise manner. This exercise will walk you through the process of using the Clean Up Word HTML command.

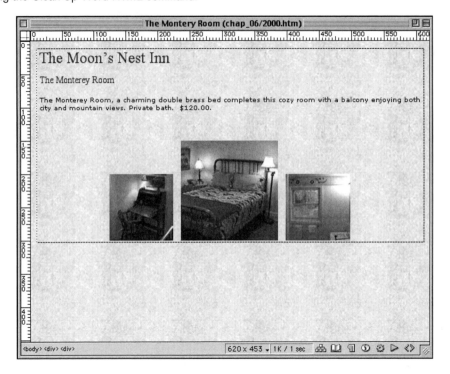

1. Open the **2000.htm** file located inside the **chap_06** folder. This file was created in Microsoft Word 2000 on a Windows machine.

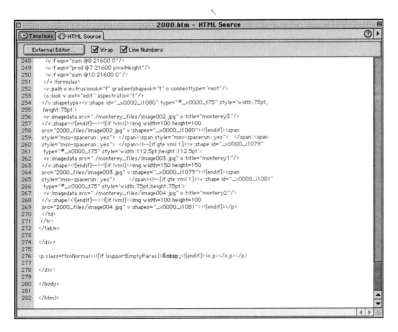

2. Open the HTML Source window by pressing **F10**. Scroll down to the bottom of the window. This page has more than 275 lines of HTML code. That's an awful lot to create this very simple page.

3. Press **F10** again to close the HTML Source window.

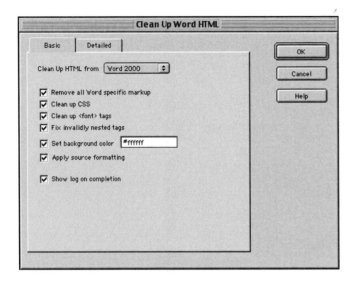

4. Select **Commands > Clean Up Word HTML**. This will open the Clean Up Word HTML window. It might take a few seconds for this window to appear. Dreamweaver is trying to detect which version of Word the file was created with.

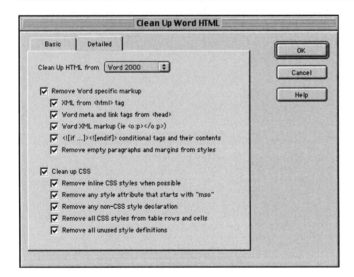

5. Click on the **Detailed** tab at the top of the screen. This will display the more advanced options you can control with this command. Unless you are really comfortable with XML and CSS, we suggest you leave these values at their default settings. Click **OK**.

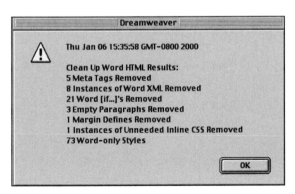

Summary Screen on Macintosh

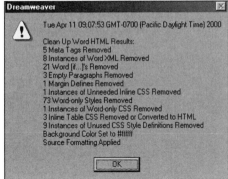

Summary Screen on Windows

6. A window will appear, summarizing the modifications that were made to the page. There will be some slight differences between the Mac and Windows summaries. When you are finished reviewing this information, click **OK**.

7. Press **F10** to open the HTML Source window. You should see significantly less HTML code now. The HTML was reduced from more than 275 lines down to 37 (Mac) and 35 (Windows). Now, that's something you'll want to show all your friends!

8. Close and save this file.

That's all for now. If you were intimidated by editing HTML before you read this chapter, we hope you are more at ease with it now.

7.

Typography

Creating and Formatting Text	Font Lists	Aligning Text
Use of <PRE> Tag	Ordered, Unordered, and Definition Lists
Color Schemes	Formatting Text in Tables	Repeat Last Action
Character Entities	Blockquotes and Non-Breaking Spaces

chap_7

Dreamweaver 3
H•O•T CD-ROM

Most professional typographers cringe when they look at Web pages because type that appears on the Web, for lack of a better expression, sucks. It sucks for many reasons. It sucks because Web browsers default to Times Roman, and most sites use the default font. It sucks because type appears differently on Macs, Win-dows, and UNIX platforms. It sucks because browsers rely on whichever fonts are installed in the end-users' systems, so you can't freely use any font you want. It sucks mostly because your choices for formatting type are limited, and that's guaranteed to frustrate the best of us.

Aside from all that, Dreamweaver gives you many hooks and handles into making the best of this sucky situation. This chapter will cover how to set font styles (such as **bold**, *italics*, and <u>underlined</u>), font sizes, font colors, and font faces (such as Times Roman, Helvetica, Arial, etc.). It will also cover making lists such as bullet lists, definition lists, and unordered lists. If you haven't heard those terms before, they, too, will be explained here. In the end, your Web-based type education should be quite complete!

A Word about FONT FACE

The **FONT FACE** element in HTML allows you to specify a typeface other than the end-user's default font. You can apply the attribute in Dreamweaver by creating **Font Sets**, which are described in the first exercise. The caveat is that the typeface must be installed in your end-user's system, or the browser will not be able to display it. It is therefore helpful to know which fonts ship in the systems of Macintosh and Windows machines. Below is a chart that lists them for you.

Default System 8.6 Macintosh	Default Windows 98 Fonts
Arial	Arial
Arial Black	**Arial Black**
CAPITALS	Arial Narrow
Charcoal	**Arial Rounded MT Bold**
Chicago	Book Antiqua
Comic Sans MS	Bookman Old Style
Courier	Century Gothic
Courier New	Copperplate Gothic
Gadget	Comic Sans
Geneva	Courier
Georgia	**Courier New**
Helvetica	**Franklin Gothic Medium**
Impact	Garamond
Minion Web	GOUDY STOUT
Monaco	Harlow Solid Italic
Monotype.com	Helvetica
New York	Helvetica Narrow
Palatino	Impact
Sand	LUCINDA CONSOLE
Techno	Lucinda Handwriting
Textile	Lucinda Sans
Times	Lucinda Sans Unicode
Times New Roman	MATTISSE
Trebuchet MS	Matura MT Script
Verdana	New Century Schoolbook
	News Gothic MT
	OCR A Extended
	Palatino
	STENCIL
	Tahoma
	Tempus Sans
	Times New Roman
	Trebuchet MS
	TW CEN MT
	Verdana
	ZapfChancery

Default System 8.6 Macintosh   *Default Windows 98 Fonts*

Note | HTML Default Text Size

It might come as a surprise that HTML text uses different sizing conventions than traditional print type sizes. Actually, all HTML text has a default size of 3, with a total range from 1 to 7. If you have no idea what default size of 3 looks like, see the picture below.

To change HTML text to a size other than the default of 3, you can either specify a number from 1 through 7, or + or −1 through + or -7 relative to the BASEFONT size (which is 3). For example, if you want your HTML text to be size 6, specify the font size to be 6 or +3. Either setting produces an HTML type at size 6. Some browsers let you set the BASEFONT for a page by using BASEFONT size = "4". You can specify any size you want, using one of the several above-mentioned methods.

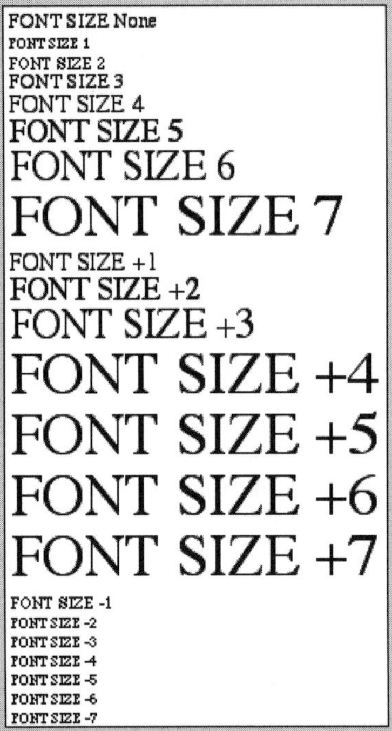

```
FONT SIZE None
FONT SIZE 1
FONT SIZE 2
FONT SIZE 3
FONT SIZE 4
FONT SIZE 5
FONT SIZE 6
FONT SIZE 7

FONT SIZE +1
FONT SIZE +2
FONT SIZE +3
FONT SIZE +4
FONT SIZE +5
FONT SIZE +6
FONT SIZE +7

FONT SIZE -1
FONT SIZE -2
FONT SIZE -3
FONT SIZE -4
FONT SIZE -5
FONT SIZE -6
FONT SIZE -7
```

Above is a handy list of the FONT SIZE *settings in Dreamweaver. The top example,* **None**, *is the equivalent of* FONT SIZE *3. Notice how the type does not look different in* FONT SIZE *+4 through +7, or* FONT SIZE *-2 through -7? There is no difference between these settings.*

I. _____ **Creating and Formatting HTML Text**

In this exercise you will learn how to add HTML text to a Web page. You will also learn how to format this text by modifying the typeface, size, style, and other attributes. As you will see, creating and formatting HTML text with Dreamweaver 3 is just as easy as working with any word processing application.

I. Copy **chap_07** to your hard drive. Define your site for Chapter 7 using the **chap_07** folder as the Local Root Folder. If you need a refresher on this process, visit Chapter 3, *"Site Control."*

2. Open the **text1.html** file.

3. Type **About the Inn** and press **Return** or **Enter.**

4. Type **Our Rooms** and press **Return** or **Enter.**

5. Type **Guest Services** and press **Return** or **Enter.**

6. Type **Reservations** and press **Return** or **Enter.**

```
☐ ▤                                    Untitled Document (chap_07/text1.html*)
About the Inn
Our Rooms
Guest Services
Reservations
```

7. Select the words "**About the Inn**."

8. In the Properties Inspector, choose the **Font List** pop-up menu and select the **Verdana, Arial, Helvetica, sans-serif** option. This will change your text to Verdana if you have that font installed; if you do not, Dreamweaver will display the next font in the list.

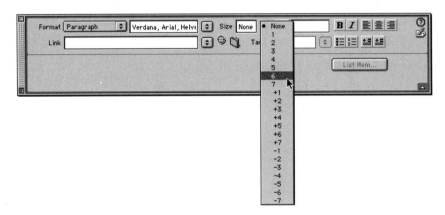

9. With "**About the Inn**" still selected, in the Properties Inspector, choose the **Size** pop-up menu and select **6**. This will change the size of your type.

10. Go to the **Size** pop-up menu again and select **+3**. Notice how the type size stays at 6. That's because all HTML text has a basefont size of 3, from which you add or subtract to make your type larger or smaller.

11. Select the words "**Our Rooms**."

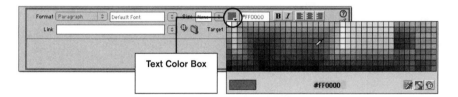

Text Color Box

12. From the Properties Inspector, choose the **Text Color Box**. Select a bright red color. Your text color is now red. This setting will override any text color that you might have specified under **Modify > Page Properties....**

13. Select the words "**Guest Services**."

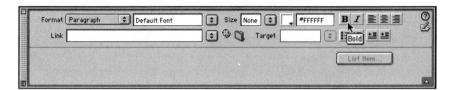

14. In the Properties Inspector, click the **Bold** button. This will make the selected text bold.

15. In the Properties Inspector, click the **Italic** button. This will make the selected text italic.

16. Select the word "**Reservations**."

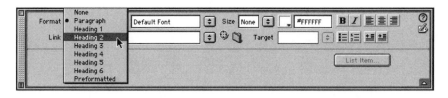

17. From the **Format** pop-up menu, select **Heading 2**. For more information about headings, see the tip on the next page.

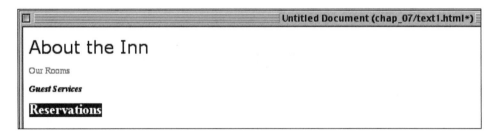

At the end of this exercise your page should look like this.

18. Save and close the file.

Tip | Headings

HTML text can also be formatted using Heading tags. The tags look like this: <H1>. They range from 1 to 6 and change the size of the HTML text. Here's a tricky thing that you might want to remember: The smaller the number next to the H, the bigger the text will be. For example, <H1> will produce the largest text, while <H6> will produce the smallest text. Generally, the (<H1>–<H6>) tags insert a line break before and after the text without requiring additional code. Heading tags can be useful for formatting large text. The image on the left shows the range of Heading tags in a browser.

Why might you use a Heading tag instead of a FONT SIZE element? If your Web page is accessed by an end user that is sight-impaired, he or she might not "see" your Web page, but will instead have a reading device "read" it aloud. Heading tags can be "read" by HTML readers as headlines, whereas large type is given the same emphasis as body copy. You might not imagine that your site has much of a sight-impaired audience, and perhaps do not think this information need apply to your site-design strategy. Many Web-design and HTML authorities, ourselves included, believe there will come a day where the Federal Disabilities Act will apply to Web pages and all of us will have to give consideration to our sight-impaired audience. Our advice is to use Heading tags instead of large font sizes for headlines.

2. _____Font Lists

In this exercise you will learn how to add and modify the **Font Lists** that come with Dreamweaver 3. By specifying a font (or fonts) using the Font Lists, you ensure that the HTML text on your page is viewed as you intended. You will learn how to modify what typefaces are in the existing Font Lists and how to create your own custom Font List. This knowledge will let you break out of the Times Roman mold a little bit, which is a welcome accomplishment in the bland Web-type landscape we all see every day. At the end of this exercise is a helpful note, explaining just how a Font List works.

1. Open **text2.html**.

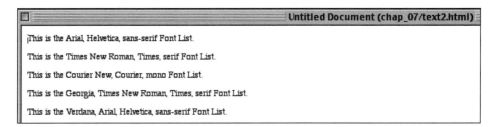

2. Select the words "**This is the Arial, Helvetica, sans-serif Font List.**"

3. From the **Font List** pop-up menu in the Properties Inspector, choose **Arial, Helvetica, sans-serif**. This will change your text to Arial if you have that font installed; if you do not, it will go to the next font in the list.

```
┌──────────────────────────────────────────────────────────────────────────┐
│ ▣                                        Untitled Document (chap_07/text2.html*) │
├──────────────────────────────────────────────────────────────────────────┤
│ This is the Arial, Helvetica, sans-serif Font List.                        │
│ This is the Times New Roman, Times, serif Font List.                       │
│ This is the Courier New, Courier, mono Font List.                          │
│ This is the Georgia, Times New Roman, Times, serif Font List.              │
│ This is the Verdana, Arial, Helvetica, sans-serif Font List.               │
│                                                                            │
└──────────────────────────────────────────────────────────────────────────┘
```

4. Select the words **"This is the Times New Roman, Times, serif Font List."**

5. From the **Font List** pop-up menu, choose **Times New Roman, Times, serif**. This will change your text to Times New Roman if you have that font installed; if you do not, it will go to the next font in the list.

6. Select the words **"This is the Courier New, Courier, mono Font List."**

7. From the **Font List** pop-up menu, choose **Courier New, Courier, mono**. This will change your text to Courier New if you have that font installed; if you do not, it will go to the next font.

8. Select the words **"This is the Georgia, Times New Roman, Times, serif Font List."**

9. From the **Font List** pop-up menu, choose **Georgia, Times New Roman, Times, serif**. This will change your text to Georgia if you have that font installed; if you do not, it will go to the next font.

10. Select the words **"This is the Verdana, Arial, Helvetica, sans-serif Font List."**

11. From the **Font List** pop-up menu, choose **Verdana, Arial, Helvetica, sans-serif**. This will change your text to Verdana if you have that font installed; if you do not, it will go to the next font.

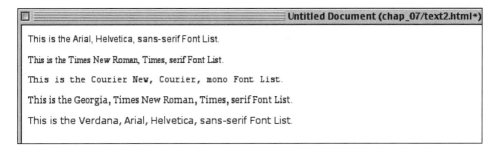

This is the Arial, Helvetica, sans-serif Font List.

This is the Times New Roman, Times, serif Font List.

This is the Courier New, Courier, mono Font List.

This is the Georgia, Times New Roman, Times, serif Font List.

This is the Verdana, Arial, Helvetica, sans-serif Font List.

This is what your page should look like now.

12. Click off the text to deselect it, and hit **Return** or **Enter**. Below the last sentence on the page, type **This is my very own Font List.**.

13. From the **Font List** pop-up menu, choose **Edit Font List...**.

Note | How Font Lists Work

Font Lists are a very useful way of ensuring that the HTML text on your Web page is viewed the way you intended. A Web browser will search for each font in the list until it finds one that is installed on the end-user's system. Once it finds a font in the list, it will use that font to display the HTML text on your Web page. For example, if your Font List were Arial, Helvetica, sans-serif, the browser would try to use Arial first to display text. If the end user did not have Arial installed, the browser would then try to use Helvetica. If it could not find Helvetica, it would then use the first sans-serif font it found. The goal of Font Lists is to create sets of fonts that have similar structure and characteristics, so that there is minimal change from viewer to viewer.

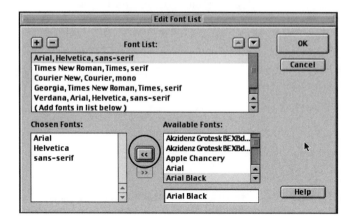

14. In the **Edit Font List** dialog box that will appear, select **Arial, Helvetica, sans-serif** from the **Font List:** option. Select **Arial** under **Chosen Fonts:**, then click the **>>** button to remove Arial from this Font List. Select **Arial Black**, under the **Available Fonts:** option.

15. Click the **<<** button in the **Edit Font List** dialog box to add this to the current Font List. You have just modified the order in which the fonts will be used for this Font List.

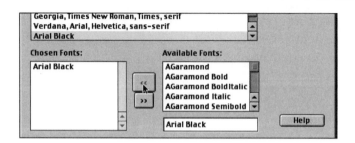

16. Select **(Add fonts in list below)** from the bottom of the **Font List:** option.

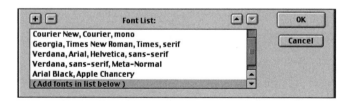

17. Select **Arial Black** under **Available Fonts:** and press the **<<** button to add this to your list.

18. Select **Verdana** under **Available Fonts:** and press the ≪ button to add this to your list.

19. Click **OK** to add your new list to the Font List.

20. In the **text2.html** file, select the words "**This is my very own Font List.**"

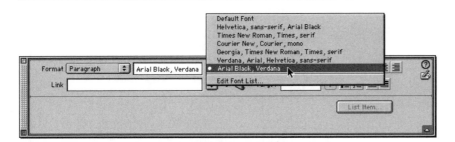

21. From the **Font List** pop-up menu, choose **Arial Black, Verdana**. This will change your text to Arial Black if you have that font installed; if you do not, it will go to Verdana.

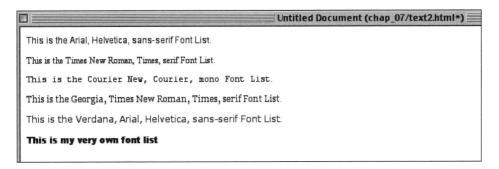

This is what your screen should look like now. This exercise gives you an example of how these Font Lists will display on your computer system. What you see might appear differently on other people's browsers, because they might have different fonts installed in their systems than you do.

22. Save and close the file.

Note | Type Size: Mac versus Windows

Unfortunately for all of us well-intentioned Web publishers, HTML type appears much larger on Windows than it does on the Mac. While they both display images at 72 dpi (dots per inch), Windows displays type at 96 dpi while the Mac displays it at 72 dpi. This deceptively small technical difference results in much larger type on Windows.

Macintosh

Untitled Document (chap_07/text2.html*)

This is the Arial, Helvetica, sans-serif Font List.

This is the Times New Roman, Times, serif Font List.

This is the Courier New, Courier, mono Font List.

This is the Georgia, Times New Roman, Times, serif Font List.

This is the Verdana, Arial, Helvetica, sans-serif Font List.

This is my very own font list

Windows

Untitled Document [Untitled-1*] - Dreamweaver

File Edit View Insert Modify Text Commands Site Window Help

This is the Arial. Helvetica, sans-serif Font List.

This is the Times New Roman, Times, serif Font List.

This is the Courier New, Courier, mono Font List.

This is the Verdana, Arial, Helvetica, sans-serif Font List.

This is my very own font list.

The images above illustrate the difference in size between the two platforms. Pretty scary, huh? There is no solution to this, except to turn to **Style Sheets** (see Chapter 10, *"Cascading Style Sheets"*) to size your text by using pixels, but that only works on 4.0 version and later browsers.

To compensate, we often make type smaller at -1 or -2 on our Macs, but it only results in a more appealing Windows version, and a less appealing Mac version. Ugh! The theory is that there are more Windows users than Mac users, so we've taken the tack to make the type on our pages look acceptable on Windows, and slightly small on Macs.

One other solution to the size difference issue is to use images of text instead of HTML text. Because images display at 72 dpi on either Mac or Windows, the type will look identical on either platform. The downside is that images are larger in file size than HTML text, and are not searchable by search engines. It's always one gotcha or another, right?

3. _____**Aligning Text**

In this exercise you will learn how to align text on the page. Unfortunately, HTML does not give you much control aligning text. You have three basic options – **Left Align**, **Center Align**, and **Right Align**. You do have some extra options when you align text next to images, which you will also explore in this exercise.

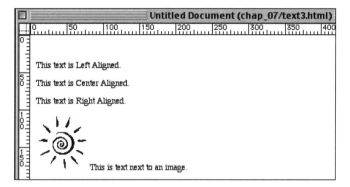

1. Open **text3.html**. Notice that the three lines of text at the top are left aligned. This is the default alignment setting for text.

2. Select the words "**This text is Center Aligned.**"

3. In the Properties Inspector, click the **Align Center** button. This will center your text on the page. **Note:** The centering of the text is relative to the size of the browser window.

4. Select the words "**This text is Right Aligned.**"

5. In the Properties Inspector, click the **Align Right** button. This will place your text on the right edge of the page.

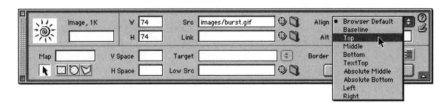

6. Click the **burst.gif** image. Notice when you select an image to align with type, you have different alignment options available in the Properties Inspector.

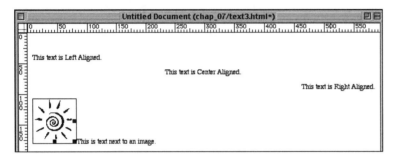

7. In the Properties Inspector, choose the **Align** pop-up menu and select the **Top** option. Notice that the text moves to the top of the image.

8. Save and close the file.

Aligning Text and Images

Dreamweaver offers many alignment options for text and images. Below is a chart defining all the alignment terms, so now you will know what you are requesting when you select one:

Dreamweaver Alignment Features	
Alignment	**Description**
Browser Default	Varies between browsers, but usually uses the Baseline option.
Baseline	Aligns text to the bottom of the image.
Bottom	Aligns text to the bottom of the image.
Absolute Bottom	Aligns text, including descenders (i.e., j), to the bottom of the image.
Top	Aligns the tallest character to the top of the image.
Text Top	Aligns the tallest character to the top of the image.
Middle	Aligns the baseline of the text to the middle of the image.
Absolute Middle	Aligns the middle of the text to the middle of the image.
Left	Left-aligns the image and wraps text to the right.
Right	Right-aligns the image and wraps text to the left.

4. _____Using the <PRE> Tag

HTML text is kind of weird in that it only allows you to insert a single space between characters. If you wanted to insert more than one space, you could use the <PRE> tag, which stands for "preformatted." This exercise will show off the <PRE> tag, and another use for a **Tracing Image**, with which you will be made more familiar in Chapter 8, _"Layout."_

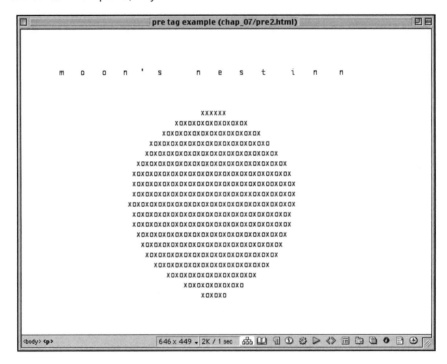

1. Open **pre2.html**. Notice the unusual formatting of the text?

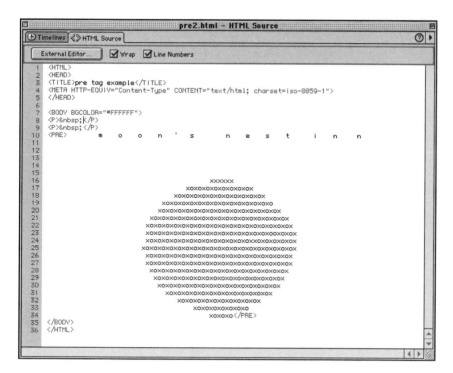

2. Press **F10** to view the HTML. Hey, what's going on here? It almost looks identical to the page in the document window, does it not? You have just discovered the wonders of the <PRE> tag, which allows for more spaces than any other text-formatting tag.

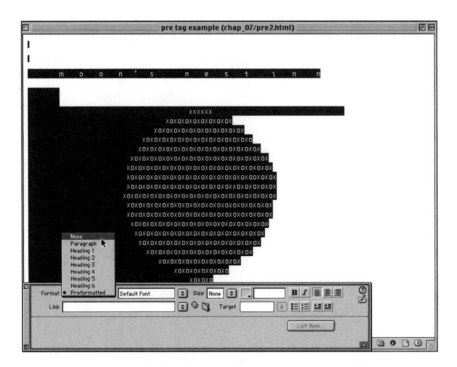

3. Press **F10** again, to make the HTML palette disappear so you can see the document window more easily. Select all the text on the screen via **Cmd+A** (Mac) or **Ctrl+A** (Windows) and change the **Properties Inspector's Format** pop-up menu to **None**. See all the text collapse to the left-hand side? There is no tag like the <PRE> tag — it's the only tag in HTML that allows you to put any number of spaces between text characters without retagging.

---

4. Close this page. In the following exercise, you will create this same page.

---

5. Want to try this on your own? Choose **File > New** (Mac) and **File > New Window** (Windows) to make a new blank page. Save it as **pre3.html** into the **chap_07** folder. We realize it might seem strange to save an empty document, but Dreamweaver kicks up quite a fuss if you do not save files before you start adding content.

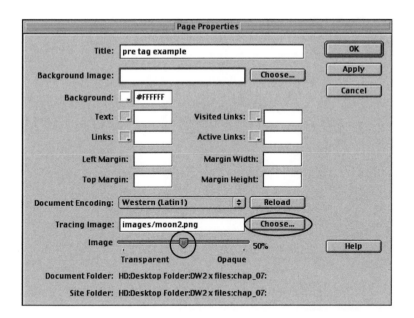

6. Choose **Modify > Page Properties…** to access the **Page Properties** dialog box. The shortcut is **Cmd+J** (Mac) and **Ctrl+J** (Windows). Enter the **Title: pre tag example**. To the right of the **Tracing Image:** field click **Choose…** and load **moon2.png**, located in the **images** folder. Change the **Image Transparency slider** to **50%**, halfway between **Transparent** and **Opaque**.

---

7. Click **OK** to return to the document you created in Step 5.

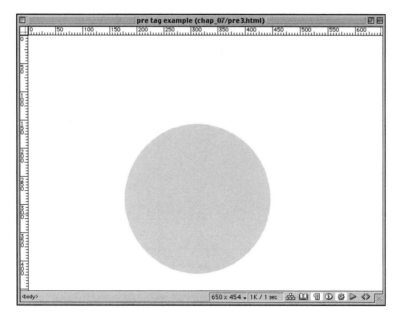

*The **Tracing Image** of the circle shape should appear in your page.*

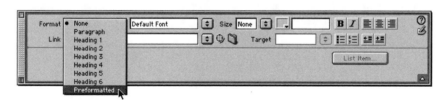

8. In the Properties Inspector, change the **Format** option to **Preformatted**.

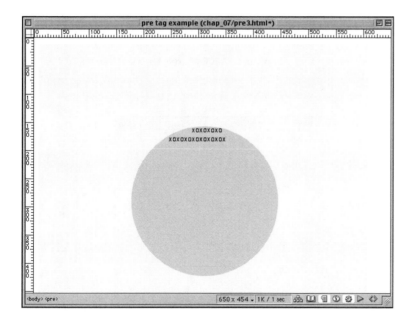

9. Press **Shift-Return** several times to move your cursor down the page. Use the spacebar to move to where the circle is and start typing **x's** and **o's** to follow the contour of the shape. The Tracing Image will act as a Template guide for the circle, and the **Preformatted** option accepts all the spaces in the document. **Note:** You must use Shift-Return. Pressing Return will not move your cursor down the page when you are working with Preformatted text.

---

10. Press **F12** to preview in your browser. You won't see the Tracing Image, but you will see your x's and o's.

---

11. Return to Dreamweaver and save and close this document.

---

5. _____**Ordered, Unordered, and Definition Lists**

In this exercise you will learn how to create a variety of lists – an **Ordered List**, an **Unordered List**, and a **Definition List**. These are HTML terms that refer to whether the list is formatted with a bullet, an indent, or Roman numerals. These lists can be generated from existing text or from scratch.

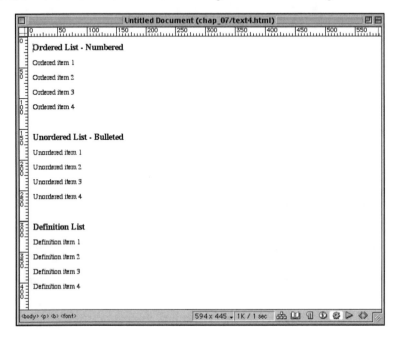

1. Open **text4.html**.

---

2. Select the four lines of text under the **Ordered List - Numbered** section (**Ordered item 1**, **Ordered item 2**, **Ordered item 3**, **Ordered item 4**).

---

3. Choose **Text > List > Ordered List**.

```
Ordered List - Numbered

   1. Ordered item 1
   2. Ordered item 2
   3. Ordered item 3
   4. Ordered item 4
```

This is what an Ordered List looks like.

---

4. Select the four lines of text under the **Unordered List - Bulleted** section (**Unordered item 1, Unordered item 2, Unordered item 3, Unordered item 4**).

---

5. Choose **Text > List > Unordered List**.

```
Unordered List - Bulleted

   • Unordered item 1
   • Unordered item 2
   • Unordered item 3
   • Unordered item 4
```

This is what an Unordered List looks like.

---

6. Select the four lines of text under the **Definition List** section (**Definition item 1, Definition item 2, Definition item 3, Definition item 4**).

---

7. Choose **Text > List > Definition List**.

```
Definition List

Definition item 1
     Definition item 2
Definition item 3
     Definition item 4
```

This is what a Definition List looks like.

---

8. Save the file and close it. You'll find that knowing how to set up these different types of lists will come in very handy as you create your own Web pages and sites.

---

6. _____ Color Schemes

Color Schemes are preset groups of colors that Dreamweaver provides for your background, text, links, active links, and visited links colors. You can apply a Color Scheme to a page at any time. They are useful when you are not sure which colors to use. Why is this exercise in the "Type" section? Because Color Schemes affect the color of type and links on your page, that's why!

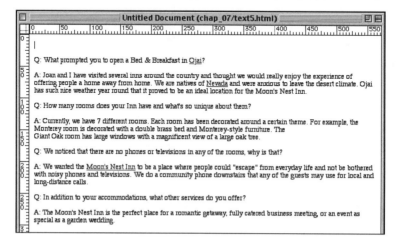

1. Open **text5.html**.

2. Choose **Commands > Set Color Scheme….**

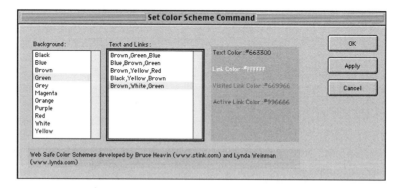

3. In the **Set Color Scheme Command** dialog box, select **Green** under the **Background:** option. Select **Brown, White, Green** under the **Text and Links:** option. Click **OK**.

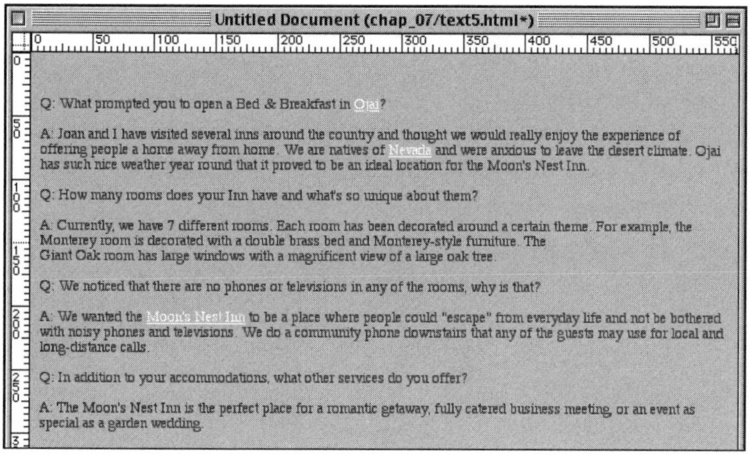

This is what the page looks like with the Color Scheme applied. If you do not like it, go ahead and choose another!

---

4. Choose **Commands > Set Color Scheme…** again. Pick a different combination of colors and click **Apply**. Knock yourself out! (In other words, enjoy yourself.)

---

5. When you're done having fun with colors, click **OK** and save and close the file.

Note | Can I Create My Own Color Schemes?

One question our students always ask is, "Can I create my own color schemes?" Well, the answer is yes and no. You can't do it through this dialog box; however, you can do it by using Templates, and we will show you how in Chapter 11, *"Templates/Libraries."* We think it would be great if you could do it from the **Set Color Scheme Command** dialog box – maybe someday… ;-).

Formatting Text in Tables

In this exercise you will learn to change a **Table's** type, style, color, alignment, and more. In the old days, which weren't so long ago, you would have had to edit each individual cell, one at a time, and it could have taken hours to edit a large Table. Not any more! With Dreamweaver 3, you can do it with a few deft clicks and drags. Praise the Dreamweaver engineers who figured this one out!

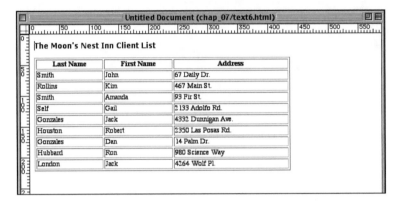

1. Open **text6.html**.

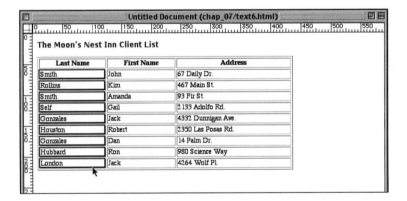

2. Highlight cell 1 in row 2 ("**Smith**") and drag down to the last cell in the column ("**London**").

3. In the Properties Inspector, choose the **Font List** pop-up menu and select the **Verdana, Arial, Helvetica, sans-serif** option. All the text in the selected column will update before your eyes. If you've ever hand-coded this sort of thing, you will be gasping in delight right now.

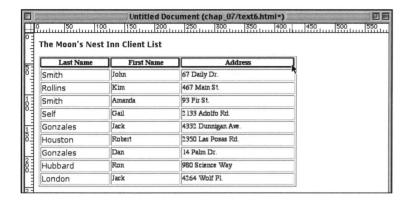

4. Highlight cell 1 in row 1 ("**Last Name**") and drag across to cell 3 ("**Address**").

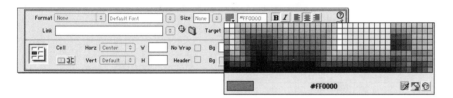

5. Using the **Properties Inspector's Color Box**, change the text color to a bright red.

6. Press **F10** to see the HTML. Look at all those FONT tags! Aren't you glad you didn't have to insert each one by hand? Press **F10** again to close the **HTML** palette.

7. Save the file and leave it open for the next exercise.

8. _____Repeat Last Action

Often you want to apply the same formatting to different blocks of text on your page. This is pretty easy to do if the words are adjacent. But what can you do when the words are in different places on the page? Well, Dreamweaver 3 has a new feature that will let you replay the last action you completed. This exercise will show you how to use that feature to format text easily and quickly.

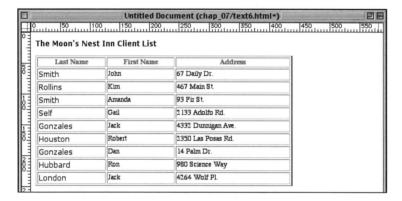

1. Make sure you have **text6.html** open from the previous exercise.

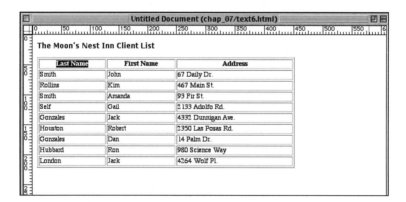

2. Select the text "**Last Name**" in the upper-left cell of the Table.

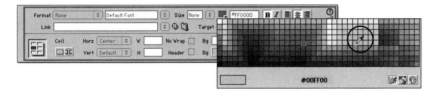

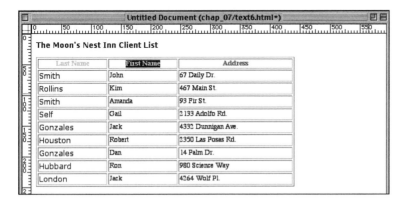

3. In the Properties Inspector, click the **Text Color Box** and select a bright green. This will change the color of the selected text to green.

4. Select the words "**First Name**" in the cell to the right of "**Last Name.**"

5. Choose **Edit > Repeat Font Color**. This will repeat the last step you completed, which in this instance was applying green to text.

6. Select the word "**Address**" in the cell to the right of "**First Name.**"

7. Choose **Edit > Repeat Font Color**. This will repeat the last step you completed, which in this instance was applying green to text.

8. In the second row, select the words "**67 Daily Dr.**"

9. Using the Properties Inspector, click the **Italics** button to format the selected text with italics.

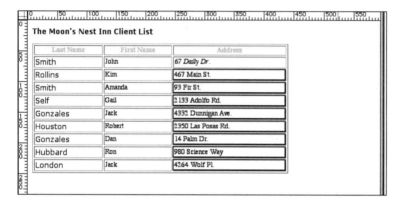

10. Click in the cell underneath ("**467 Main St.**") and drag down to the bottom of the column. This will select multiple blocks of text inside the Table.

11. Choose **Edit > Repeat Apply Italic**. This will apply the italics to all of the text you have selected. Try formatting some more text and using this feature to repeat your actions.

12. When you are finished, save and close this file. You won't need it for the rest of this chapter.

Tip | Repeat Last Action

You might have noticed that the **Repeat** menu command changes as you perform different tasks. In the first example, it said **Repeat Font Color,** and in the second example it said **Repeat Apply Italic.** This type of dynamic menu change is a good example of what is possible in Dreamweaver 3, because the application is written in JavaScript, XML, and HTML, which make this kind of functionality easy to implement. The menu has been created to give you feedback so you know what action you are going to repeat. This subtle addition makes this feature much easier to use.

9. Character Entities

Character Entities are text elements such as the © **Copyright** symbol, ® **Registered** symbol, and the ™ **Trademark** symbol. These symbols are very common and can be found on most Web pages. Inserting these symbols on your pages used to be quite a bear. Luckily, Dreamweaver 3 comes with a **Characters Object** palette, which lets you easily add several of the most frequently used character entities! This exercise will show you how to use this new feature.

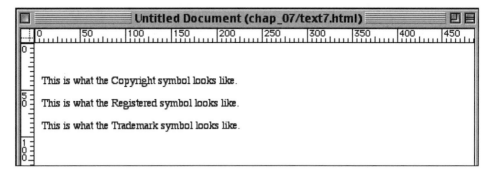

1. Open **text7.html** and click to the left of the capital "**C**" in "**Copyright.**"

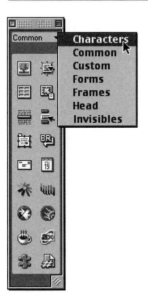

2. Open the Characters Object palette by clicking the arrow at the top of the **Objects** palette and choosing **Characters** from the pop-up menu.

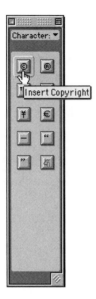

3. Click the **Insert Copyright** icon. This will insert the Copyright symbol where your cursor is placed.

4. Click to the left of the capital "R" in "**Registered**."

5. Click the **Insert Registered Trademark** icon. This will insert the Registered Trademark symbol where your cursor is placed.

6. Click to the left of the capital "T" in " Trademark."

7. Click the **Insert Trademark** icon. This will insert the Trademark symbol where your cursor is placed.

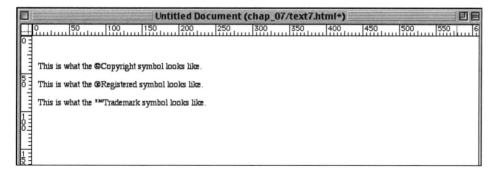

This is what your page should look like when you are finished.

8. Save and close the file.

Macintosh and Windows Character Entities

The chart below outlines some of the more frequently used **character entities**, their Macintosh and Windows keyboard shortcuts, and the HTML code for each. **Note:** If you are using Windows, you must use the keypad (not the keyboard) to enter the numbers or this will not work.

Character Entities in Dreamweaver			
Entity	**Macintosh**	**Windows**	**HTML**
©	Option+G	Alt+0169	&copy;
®	Option+R	Alt+0174	&reg;
™	Option+2	Alt+0153	&#153;

IO._____**Blockquotes and Non-Breaking Spaces**

On the surface, it looks like you have rather limited control over HTML text. How much can you really do with left, center, and right alignment? What if you want to indent a margin or something really wild like that? You can use the <BLOCKQUOTE> tag, that's what! This handy tag allows you to indent your text from both sides of the page, which can be very useful when you're setting up outlines and quotations.

In this exercise, you will learn how to use the <BLOCKQUOTE> tag to indent and align text on the page. You will also learn about the **Non-Breaking Space** tag, and the difference between a **Line Break** tag and a **Paragraph Break** tag. So, roll up those sleeves and get started now, before you faint from too many exercises in this chapter!

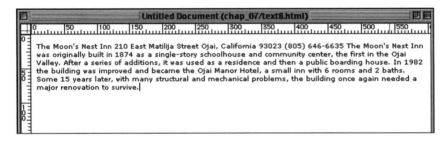

1. Open **text8.html**.

---

2. Click to the right of the word "**Inn**" in the first line, (the first time it appears).

---

3. Press **Shift+Return** (Mac) or **Shift+Enter** (Windows). This will insert a line break, which will force the text to the very next line.

---

4. Click to the right of the word "**Street**" in the second line.

---

5. Press **Shift+Return** (Mac) or **Shift+Enter** (Windows).

---

6. Click to the right of the last number "**5**" in the third line.

---

7. Press **Return** (Mac) or **Enter** (Windows). This will insert a paragraph break and insert a blank line between the two bodies of text.

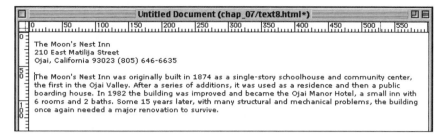

This is what your page should look like at this point.

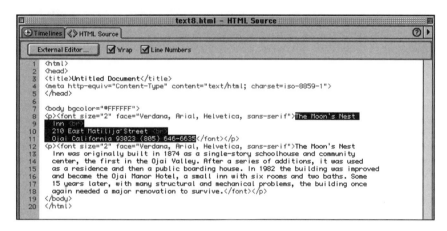

8. Press **F10** to see the HTML code. Notice the <br> and <p> tags! The <br> tag will insert a line break, taking your cursor to the next line. The <p> tag will insert a Paragraph Break, taking your cursor down two lines.

9. Press **F10** to close the **HTML** palette. Select the entire second paragraph by clicking and dragging over it.

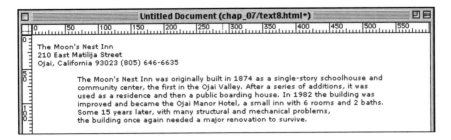

10. Choose **Text > Indent**. Choose it again. Notice that each time you choose this command your text is indented from both sides. **Warning:** This is very cool, but press **F12** and preview in a browser. Now, stretch the browser screen and then squish it. Yup, things start to fall apart on some browsers. There is nothing you can do about that, except to put all this text in a **fixed-percentage Table**, which you will learn to do in Chapter 9, *"Tables."* Close your browser window and return to Dreamweaver.

---

11. With the text still selected in the Dreamweaver document, select **Text > Outdent**. The text will be outdented on both sides of the page.

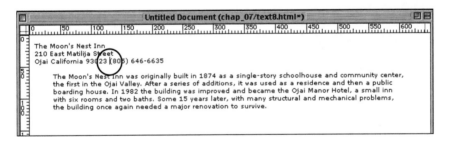

---

12. Click to the left of the first parenthesis in the telephone number at the top.

---

13. Press the **spacebar**. Nothing happens, right? That's because HTML only allows for one space between characters. Do not worry, you're going to learn the work-around for this next.

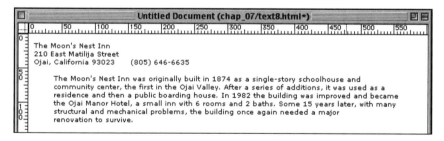

14. Press **Option+Spacebar** (Mac) or **Ctrl+Shift+Spacebar** (Windows) to insert a **non-breaking space**. This tag lets you insert as many spaces between text as you want. The image above shows what your page should look like after adding five non-breaking spaces. Check this out in the HTML palette (**F10**).

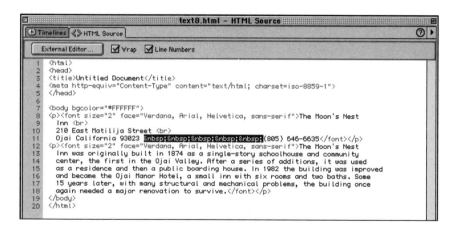

This is what the HTML for the page should look like. Notice the ** ** *code for each of the non-breaking spaces you added.*

15. Save and close the file. Take a nap, or go to the next chapter ;-).

8.

Layout

| Tracing Images | Layers |

| Converting Layers to Tables |

| Converting Tables to Layers |

| Using Margin Tags |

chap_8

Dreamweaver 3
H•O•T CD-ROM

In traditional layout programs, such as Adobe PageMaker and QuarkXPress, most people take it for granted that they can move blocks of text and images around almost anywhere on the screen. Unfortunately, standard HTML doesn't have any tags to easily position elements. This has caused considerable frustration among Web-page designers. There is good news – Dreamweaver has built-in functions that give you the freedom of absolute positioning while still conforming to strict HTML guidelines!

This chapter will cover Dreamweaver's key features that allow you to position elements anywhere on your Web page – **Tracing Images**, **Layers**, and **Convert Layers to Tables**.

Tracing Images, Layers, and Tables

What is a Tracing Image? Let's say that you have been in Photoshop, Fireworks, Illustrator, or any drawing or painting program of your choice, and you've mocked up a wonderful Web page. Don't you just wish you could take that mock-up and put it up on the Web? Dreamweaver's Tracing Image option allows you to place any GIF, JPEG, or PNG into a Tracing Layer on your page, which can then be used as an alignment reference for your HTML elements.

So far, you have been putting artwork and text directly on your page. With that method, you can right-, left-, or center-align elements, and that's the end of the story. This frustrates most people because it would be a lot nicer if you could stick that artwork or text anywhere you wanted on the page and have it stay there. Layers are your saviors, as they can be positioned freely on your page! Rather than simply placing artwork and text on a page, as you have been doing so far, you can put your content into Layers and move it anywhere you want.

If Layers are so flexible and let you move your images and text around so easily, why doesn't everyone use them? There's a little problem. They are not backward compatible with older browsers. If you're targeting an audience who uses a 3.0 browser or earlier, or an AOL browser, Layers aren't going to work for you. But there's more good news. Once you've designed a freeform layout using Layers, Dreamweaver allows you to then convert your Layers to HTML Tables so that the Web page is compatible with older versions of Netscape and Explorer. Tables were originally developed to insert data into HTML pages; however, many people use them for layout by turning off the borders and making them invisible. This trick allows you to use Tables as you would a grid in page layout. You can put images and text into an invisible Table, and the rows and columns and cells hold the objects in place. The bummer about Tables is that they're not intuitive to work with, and the code for creating them can get quite complex. Besides, when you are designing, it's best to be able to change your mind and nudge something up, down, left, or right at whim. You can do that easily with Layers.

Dreamweaver again offers a great solution. You can go back and forth freely between converting Layers to Tables and Tables to Layers so that you can really fine-tune your layout without worrying about writing complex code. With Dreamweaver, you can finally focus more of your energy on design, and less on HTML work-arounds for layout. Life is good!

I. _____**Applying a Tracing Image**

In this exercise, you will learn how to apply a Tracing Image to your Web page, as well as how to change its transparency and position on the page. You'll work with a Tracing Image that was supplied on the **H•O•T CD-ROM**. If you were to create your own Tracing Image, you would create a mock-up of your Web page in a graphics application of your choice, such as Photoshop, Fireworks, Illustrator, or whatever, and save it as a GIF, JPEG, or PNG. You would then specify this mock-up as a Tracing Image, so that you could use it in Dreamweaver as your guide to re-create your page design.

A Tracing Image is visible only in Dreamweaver. Visitors to your site cannot see it. Keep in mind that when you are viewing the Tracing Image in Dreamweaver while building your page, you cannot see the background image or background color that you are setting, unless you decrease the Tracing Image transparency setting.

1. Copy **chap_08** to your hard drive. Define your site for Chapter 8 using the **chap_08** folder as the Local Root Folder. If you need a refresher on this process, visit Exercise 1 in Chapter 3, *"Site Control."*

2. Open **index.html**. This page is blank, but it won't be for long! Choose **Modify > Page Properties...** The shortcut keys for this are **Cmd+J** (Mac) and **Ctrl+J** (Windows).

3. Click **Choose...** (Mac) or **Browse...** (Windows) next to the **Tracing Image** option.

4. Browse to **tracingimage.jpg** inside the **images** folder and click **Choose**.

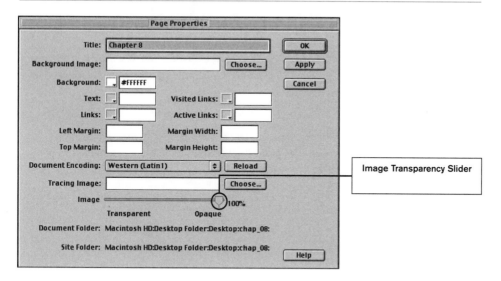

5. For this exercise, make sure the Image **Transparency Slider** is at **100%**. This will enable your **Tracing Image** to be visible when you insert it.

6. Click **Choose** and then **OK** in the **Page Properties** dialog box.

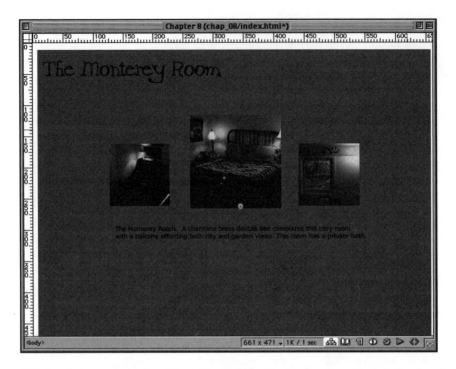

*This is what your page should look like with the Tracing Image applied. It was inserted at 100%
opacity in the **Page Properties** dialog box, which makes it opaque. **Note:** The white border you see
to the left of the Tracing Image is an offset created by Dreamweaver to emulate a Web browser. An
explanation of this feature is supplied on the next page.*

---

7. Press **F12** to preview this page in a Web browser (if you have not defined a browser yet, this
is explained in Chapter 2, *"Interface"*). When you do this, notice that the page appears as a blank
screen. This is supposed to happen! The Tracing Image only appears in Dreamweaver, and it won't be
visible to your end user.

Note | **Browser Offset**

The white space you see above and to the left of the Tracing Image is the result of an offset that Dreamweaver created. You can control this offset by choosing **View > Image > Adjust Position...**.

Why would Dreamweaver introduce such an offset? The program is emulating what would happen in a Web browser. For some dumb reason, browsers do not display foreground images flush top and left, but that's exactly how they display background images – flush top and left. This means that any image in the foreground (meaning it is not a background image) will always be displayed in the browser with this offset. Dreamweaver allows you to get rid of the offset; however, the offset is intentionally there to show you how the foreground artwork will align in a Web browser.

Dreamweaver offsets Tracing Images from the top-left corner to emulate an offset that exists in Web browsers. You can get rid of this offset if you like. We usually leave the offset alone, because it represents what will happen in a browser, anyway.

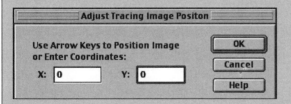

*You can use the **Adjust Tracing Image Position** dialog box to fix the offset. To bring up this dialog box, choose **View > Tracing Image > Adjust Position...** and enter **X: 0** and **Y: 0**.*

8. Return to Dreamweaver and choose **Modify > Page Properties...** to access the Tracing Image settings again.

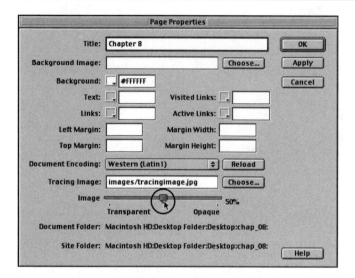

9. Drag the Image **Transparency Slider** down to **50%** and click **OK**.

Warning | Tracing Image Dilemma

Occasionally Dreamweaver will not allow you to insert a Tracing Image when your Image **Transparency Slider** is set to **50%**. You can troubleshoot this problem by dragging the slider up or down the scale in any direction.

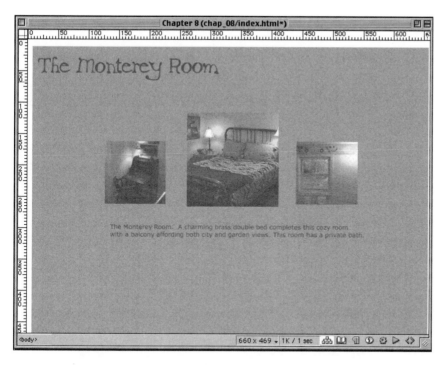

With the opacity reduced, it's much easier to use the Tracing Image as a guide rather than compet-
ing with foreground images and text.

10. Choose **File > Save** and leave this file open for the next exercise, in which you'll add images to match this layout.

Tracing Images, Background Colors, and Images

Once you apply a Tracing Image to your page, it will hide the background color and background images while you are editing the document inside Dreamweaver. However, if you view the page that contains the Tracing Image from a browser, the background color and/or background image will be visible and the Tracing Image will not. In other words, Tracing Images are only visible to you while you're working in Dreamweaver. This is a good thing, because you don't want people seeing your blueprint, you want them to see the final results.

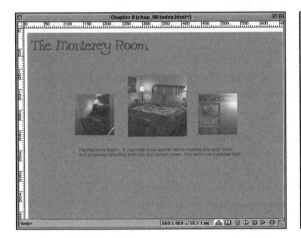

The Tracing Image is an internal function of Dreamweaver to help you follow a preconceived layout. When you preview the file on the left in a browser, it remains empty because there is no placed artwork yet.

Tracing Images, Layers, and Tables

The following chart outlines the concepts behind Tracing Images, Layers, and Tables, which you will learn about in the following exercise:

Tracing Images, Layers, and Tables Defined	
Item	**Definition**
Tracing Image	Consider this the blueprint you follow to build your pages.
Layer	This is where you put your text and images so you can move them around freely. The downside to using Layers is that they only work on 4.0 browsers and above.
Table	Tables work on almost all browsers, from version 2.0 and above. **Tables** can hold images and text in place, but they are not intuitive when it comes to design. It's ultimately the best of both worlds to design with **Layers** and convert to **Tables**.

2. _____Adding Layers

In this exercise, you will learn how to create Layers on your page and insert images and text inside them. Then – presto, you'll be able to move everything around. Ahh, the beauty of Layers!

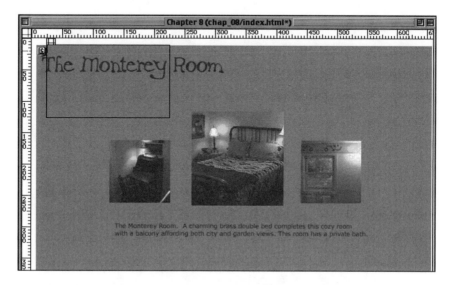

1. With **index.html** still open from the last exercise, choose **Insert > Layer**. This will insert an empty Layer in your document, in the form of a rectangle on the top left of your screen.

Layer Selection
Handle

Resizing
Handles

2. Click the white **Layer Selection Handle**. This will cause eight resizing handles to appear around the Layer.

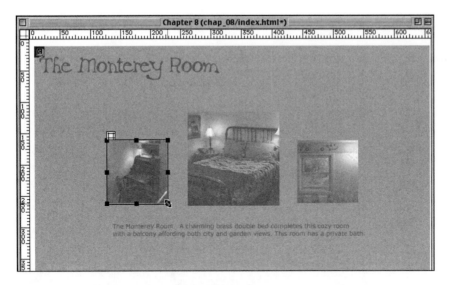

3. Using the **Layer Selection Handle**, move the Layer so its upper-left corner aligns with the photo of the desk that is visible in the Tracing Image. Using the bottom-right resizing handle, resize the Layer so that it fits around the edge of the desk image.

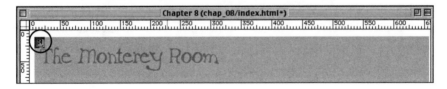

*Notice the yellow thingie in the upper-left corner? It's called an **Invisible Element** in Dreamweaver. If you deselect the Layer, by clicking outside its boundaries, you'll see that the Invisible Element is deselected as well. For more on Invisible Elements, see the note later in this chapter.*

4. Click inside the Layer. You should see a blinking I-beam cursor inside the Layer.

5. Choose **Insert > Image**.

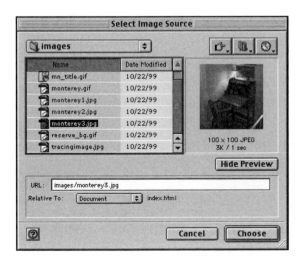

6. Browse to **monterey3.jpg** inside the **images** folder. Click **Choose**.

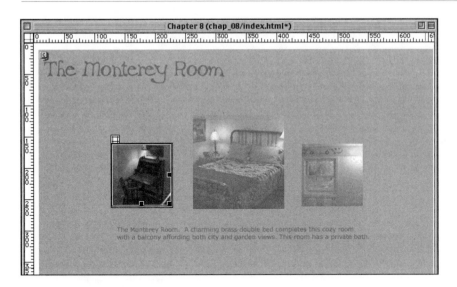

*An image is now inside the Layer. Notice how this image is darker, while the Tracing Image is screened back? That's because you set the Tracing Image's opacity to **50%** in the last exercise. This makes it easy to decipher between the layout and the final artwork, doesn't it?*

Warning | Invisible Element Markers

When you create a Layer in Dreamweaver, a small yellow icon appears at the top of your page. This is referred to as an Invisible Element marker. Each time you create a Layer, a yellow marker will be inserted. By selecting these markers, you can easily select the associated Layers.

You will see these markers in the **index.html** document after you have completed Exercise 2. If you find that these markers get in your way, choose **View > Invisible Elements** to hide/show them all. You can turn off **Invisible Elements** permanently if you want, by choosing **Edit > Preferences... > Invisible Elements**.

*This is what an **Invisible Element** marker looks like in Dreamweaver.*

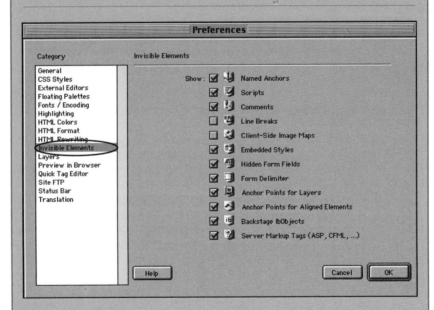

*We rarely use Invisible Elements and prefer to turn them off. You can turn them on or off permanently in Dreamweaver's **Preferences**, under **Edit**.*

7. In the **Common Objects** palette, click the **Draw Layer** object. If you have a different Objects palette visible, click on the small arrow at the top and select **Common** to switch back to the **Common Objects** palette.

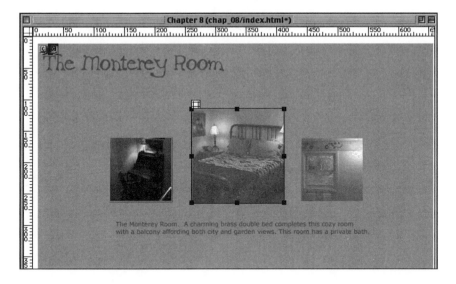

8. With this tool selected, draw a Layer around the large center image of the bed.

You've just inserted a Layer by using the Objects palette instead of the Insert menu. Either way works fine, and you have now been exposed to both.

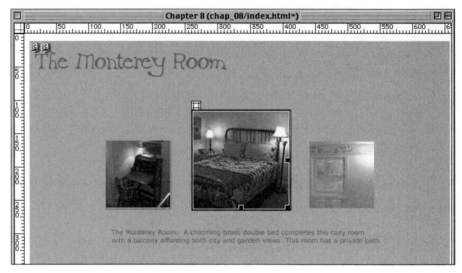

9. Click inside this Layer and click the **Insert Image** object in the **Objects** palette.

---

10. Browse to **monterey1.jpg** inside the **images** folder. Click **Choose**.

---

11. Add another Layer around the small image of the window. You can use either the **Objects** palette or the **Insert** menu to accomplish this.

---

12. Choose **Insert > Image** and browse to **monterey2.jpg** inside the **images** folder. Click **Choose**.

---

13. Add another Layer around the words "**The Monterey Room**" at the upper-left corner of the page.

---

14. Click inside the Layer around the words "**The Monterey Room**," then choose **Insert > Image** and browse to **monterey.gif** inside the **images** folder. Click **Choose**. If you have trouble aligning the image, select it by using the selection handle and use the arrow keys on your keyboard to nudge it into place.

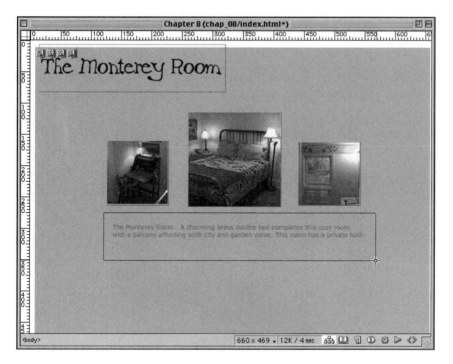

15. So far you have inserted images into Layers. Inserting text is just as simple. Add another Layer around the two lines of text at the bottom of the screen.

16. Click inside the Layer and type **The Monterey Room. A charming brass double bed completes this cozy room with a balcony affording both city and mountain views. This room has a private bath.**. For the purpose of this exercise, don't worry about matching the type of the original layout. If you need a refresher on type, revisit Chapter 7, *"Typography."*

17. Press **F12** to preview this page in a browser. When you are finished, return to Dreamweaver and save the file. Leave the file open for the next exercise.

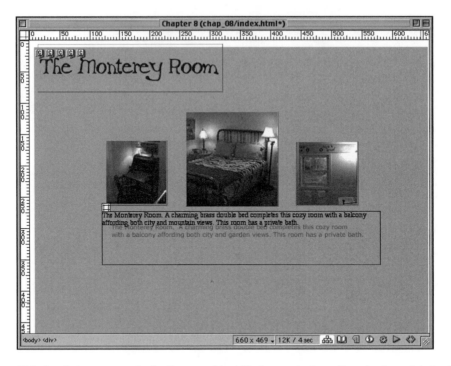

*This is what your page looks like now. Most likely your text won't perfectly match the Tracing Image.
That's all right – the Tracing Image is there only as a guide.*

 Movie | tracing.mov

To learn more about using Tracing Images, check out **tracing.mov** located in the **movies** folder on
the Dreamweaver 3 **H•O•T CD-ROM**.

3. _____Converting Layers to Tables

You've just positioned artwork precisely to match a specific layout. As you may recall from the introduction to this chapter, Layers only display on version 4.0+ browsers. People using earlier browsers will see the content of the Layers all jumbled up along the left side of your page, which, of course, is not cool at all! We're guessing that you want the luxury of freely positioning artwork with Layers, but still want people with older browsers to view your site. This exercise will show you how to convert Layers to standard HTML Tables so anybody can see your perfect layout, no matter their browser.

1. With **index.html** still open from the last exercise, choose **Modify > Layout Mode > Convert Layers to Table...**. The shortcut key is **Shift+Cmd+F6** (Mac) or **Shift+Ctrl+F6** (Windows). The **Convert Layers to Table** dialog box will open.

2. Click **Table Layout: Most Accurate**. Check the **Prevent Layer Overlaps** checkbox. This setting is required because Layers can overlap, but Tables cannot. Leave the **Use Transparent GIFs** option selected. This will ensure your Table doesn't collapse in some browsers. Click **OK**.

Note: *When you convert your Layers to Tables, by default Dreamweaver will set the Table borders to 0, shown above in the Properties Inspector. Why? You do not want to advertise that you are using Tables. The 0 gives you an invisible border, creating the illusion of floating background images and text on your Web page.*

You can access the Table properties by clicking anywhere in the Table, and then selecting the **<table>** *tag at the bottom of the document. The Properties Inspector will reveal the different Table settings.*

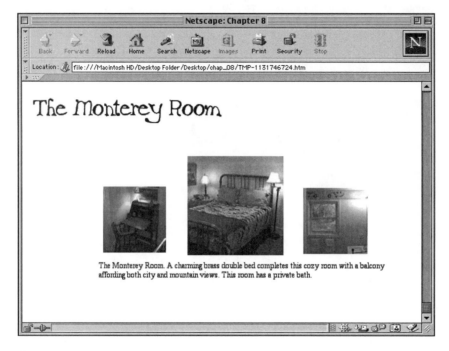

The Monterey Room. A charming brass double bed completes this cozy room with a balcony affording both city and mountain views. This room has a private bath.

3. Preview the results in a browser by clicking **F12**. Notice that in the browser you can't tell whether Layers or Tables were used. Converting Layers to Tables affects the compatibility of the HTML document, not the appearance.

4. Return to Dreamweaver. Save the file and leave it open for the next exercise.

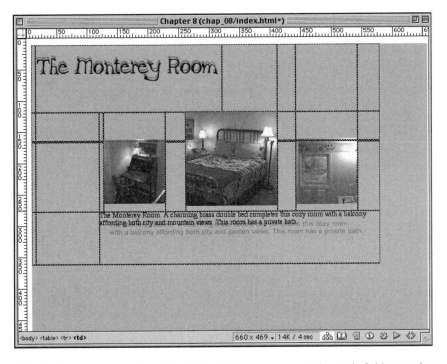

This is what your page should look like in Dreamweaver at the end of this exercise.

Convert Layers to Table Options

The **Convert Layers to Table** dialog box has several options to help you control how your Layers are converted. The chart below explains how these features work:

Convert Layers to Table Options	
Option	**Desciption**
Most Accurate	This default option creates a **Table** cell for each Layer and creates all the cells necessary to maintain the Layer structure. The term cell refers to one of the rectangles within a **Table**. More information about **Tables** and cells can be found in Chapter 9, *"Tables."*
Smallest: Collapse Empty Cells	This option sets the edges of the **Layers** to align if they are within a certain pixel range. This typically results in fewer columns and rows. This can be a good thing, because fewer columns and rows equate to faster downloading; or it can be a bad thing, because it can potentially disrupt your layout's appearance. We recommend experimenting to see which suits your needs best.
Use Transparent GIFs	This option inserts transparent GIFs in each of the empty cells. This helps maintain the **Table** structure across browsers. **Tables** can collapse in some browsers if they don't contain content, and transparent GIFs can fill in as content, though they are invisible.
Center on Page	This option centers the **Table** on the page.
Prevent Layer Overlaps	Table cells cannot overlap. This option prevents you from overlapping your **Layers** by warning you about which **Layers**, if any, overlap.
Show Layer Palette	This opens the **Layers** palette, which allows you to rename or reorder your **Layers**. This exercise didn't require that you view the **Layers** palette, but you'll get a chance to learn about this in Chapter 16, *"DHTML."*
Show Grid	If it's not already visible, this will turn on the grid for the page.
Snap To Grid	This snaps the **Layer** to the nearest snapping point on the grid. This can be useful for aligning objects.

4. _____Converting Tables to Layers

In Chapter 9, *"Tables,"* you'll learn how to create Tables in Dreamweaver. In the meantime, you will have to trust us when we tell you that creating Tables for layout purposes is a lot less easy than using Layers. Dreamweaver gives you the freedom to control your layout and browser compatibility by converting Layers to Tables. This powerful feature can be reversed as well, allowing you to convert Tables back to Layers. If you've ever hand-coded HTML Tables, you will no longer have to fuss with editing individual cells and rows of Tables because you can go freely between Layers and Tables. This back-and-forth control is extremely useful, and once you get the hang of it, it will save you countless hours modifying the layout of your pages.

In this exercise, you will convert the Table version of your page back to Layers, modify the layout, and then convert it back to Tables for browser compatibility. You will turn the Tracing Image off and be encouraged to modify the page's layout however you want. When you are finished, you should definitely appreciate how powerful these features are in helping you create and modify the layout of your pages.

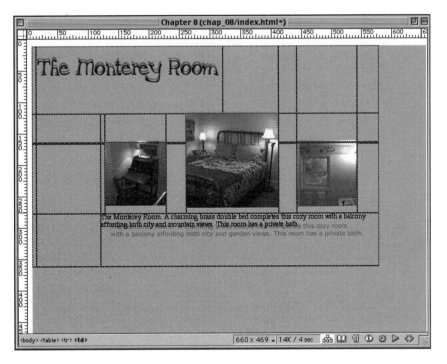

1. With **index.html** still open from the last exercise, choose **Modify > Layout Mode > Convert Tables to Layers....** The shortcut keys for this are **Cmd+F6** (Mac) and **Ctrl+F6** (Windows). The **Convert Tables to Layers** dialog box will open.

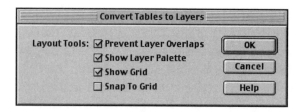

2. Remove the check in the **Snap To Grid** checkbox. This option will force your Layers to snap to a guide, sometimes causing unwanted shifting of page elements. We prefer to not use this option. Make sure that your settings are like those shown above and click **OK**.

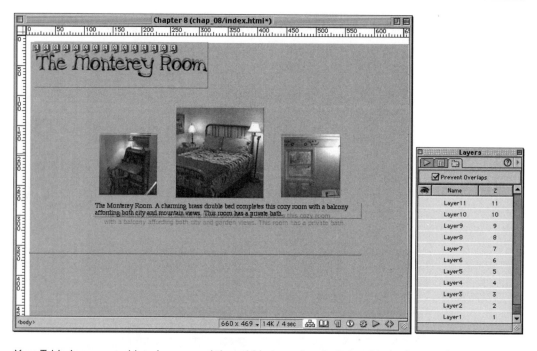

*Your Table is converted into Layers, and the grid is turned on to help with the layout of your page. If you want to change the layout, you'll find that it's much easier to do so with Layers than with Tables! If the grid bothers you, turn it off by choosing **View > Grid > Show**.*

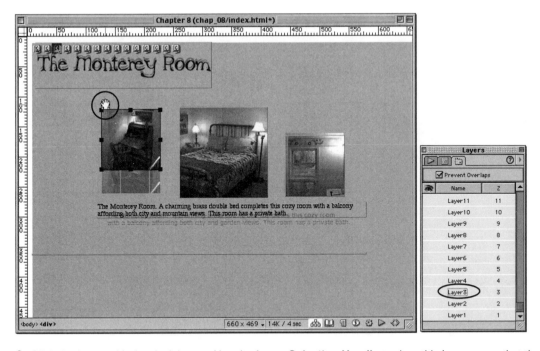

3. Click the Layer with the desk image. Use the **Layer Selection Handle** to drag this Layer up so that the top of it aligns with the top of the bed image.

Note: When you click and drag the desk image, that Layer becomes highlighted in the Layers palette.

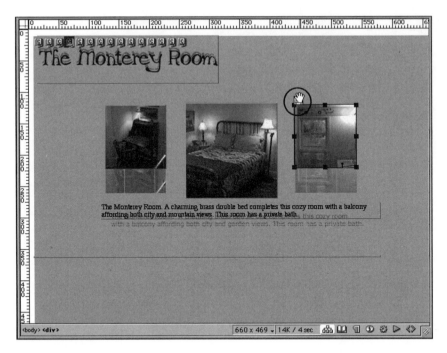

4. Select the Layer with the image of the window. Use the **Layer Selection Handle** to drag this Layer up so that top of it aligns with the top of the image of the bed.

5. Choose **Modify > Layout Mode> Convert Layers to Table....** Click **OK**.

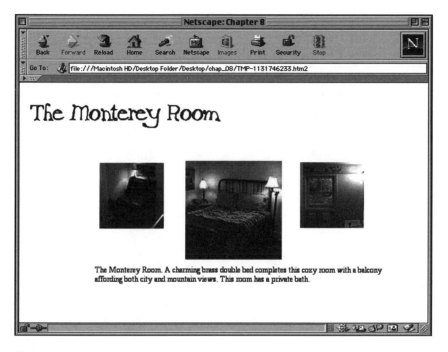

6. Press **F12** to preview the file in a browser.

---

7. Save and, finally, close the file.

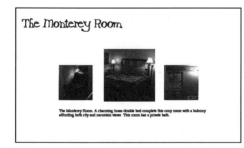
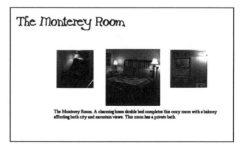

You can start to see how easy it is to change the layout of your pages by converting back and forth between Layers and Tables. On the left is the original page and on the right is the new page, with the artwork aligned with the top of the center image.

---

5. _____Using Margin Tags

Standard HTML has always produced an offset between the way foreground and background images are displayed, and this made it impossible to perfectly register a foreground image element to the background. However, both Explorer and Netscape introduced MARGIN tags in the version 4.0 browsers and above. This exercise shows you how to specify MARGIN settings in Dreamweaver that will remove the offset in Netscape and Explorer version 4.0 and above.

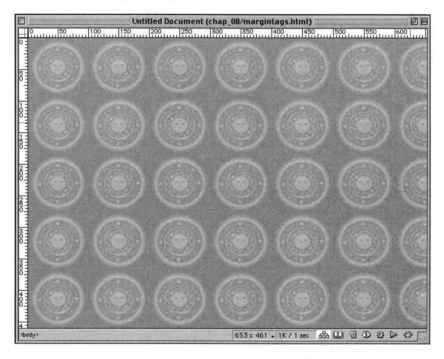

1. Open **margintags.html** located inside the **chap_08** folder. This page already contains a background image.

2. Click the **Insert Image** object in the **Common Objects** palette.

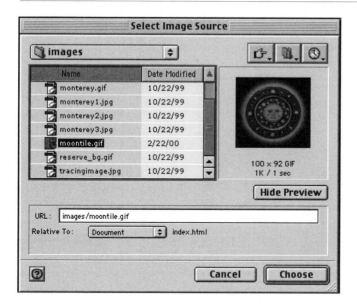

3. Browse to **moontile.gif** inside the **images** folder and click **Choose**. Since this image is the exact same size as the background image, it will help to demonstrate how to perfectly align foreground and background images.

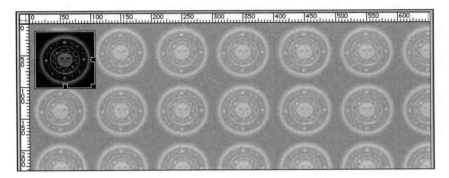

When the image is inserted, you can see a gap from the left edge of the document and the top of the document. In some designs, this can be really annoying. You'll fix this next.

Browser-Specific Margin Tags

It's important to know that specific tags work only in Netscape, while others only work in Explorer. Just to be safe, we recommend that you use both tags, to ensure that your page displays without an offset in either browser. The chart below outlines which tags work in which specific browser.

Browser-Specific Margin Tags	
Browser	**Tag**
Netscape Navigator 4.0 or later	MARGIN WIDTH MARGIN HEIGHT
Internet Explorer 4.0 or later	LEFT MARGIN TOP MARGIN

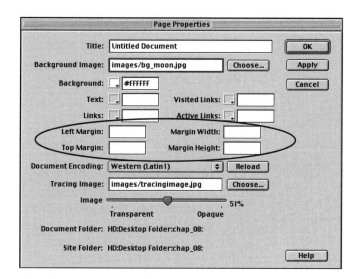

4. Choose **Modify > Page Properties....** This will open the **Page Properties** dialog box.

5. Type **0** for the **Left Margin**, **Top Margin**, **Margin Width**, and **Margin Height** options. This will eliminate the offset on the browser and align the foreground image perfectly with the background image. Click **OK**.

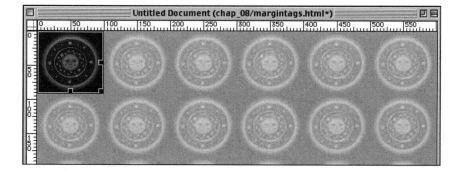

This is what your page should look like when you are finished.

6. Save and close this file.

You finished yet another chapter... congratulations, you might want to take a short break before moving onto Chapter 9, *"Tables."*

9.
Tables

| Creating, Sorting, and Modifying a Table |
| Using Tables to Align Images and Text |
| Assembling Seamless Images |
| Combining Pixels and Percentages |
| Inserting Tabular Data |

chap_9

Dreamweaver 3
H•O•T CD-ROM

HTML Tables were introduced back in Netscape 1.2 as a way to deal with charts and data. Tables are commonly used in financial or database spreadsheets and are defined by columns and rows. The HTML engineers who created Tables for the Web did not predict that developers would one day use Tables to align images, not just for displaying text and numbers. This chapter focuses on both uses for Tables: a formatting device for data, and a layout device for custom positioning of images.

This chapter shows you how to create custom Tables, insert rows and columns, come up with color schemes, and handle formatting and sorting tasks. You will also learn how to use Tables to align and position images. Tables are a critical item in your Web-design toolbox, and Dreamweaver gives you great control and techniques for mastering them.

What Is a Table?

A Table, as you will learn in this chapter, is a highly versatile feature in HTML. It can be useful for organizing data or positioning images. What does a Table look like under the hood of Dreamweaver? It is comprised of a combination of HTML tags.

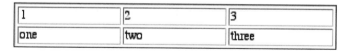

A Table in the browser.

```
8   <table width="300" border="1">
9     <tr>
10      <td>1</td>
11      <td>2</td>
12      <td>3</td>
13    </tr>
14    <tr>
15      <td>one</td>
16      <td>two</td>
17      <td>three</td>
18    </tr>
19  </table>
```

*Here's the HTML for the Table above. Tables always begin with a table tag. The width and border elements are attributes of the table tag. <tr> stands for **Table Row**, and <td> stands for **Table Data**.*

Anatomy of a Table			
	column		
row	– – – – – – – – – →		
			cell
	↓		

A Table contains rows, columns, and cells. If these terms are unfamiliar to you, this diagram should help.

I. _____Changing the Border of a Table

This first exercise helps you build your Table-formatting skills on a premade Table. It also alerts you to a common HTML problem relating to empty Table cells. You see, even if a Table cell is empty, you've got to put something in it to hold the Table formatting. That "something" can be a single-pixel transparent GIF. You'll learn how to add this in a few moments, once you get going with this exercise.

1. Copy **chap_09** to your hard drive. Define your site for Chapter 9 using the **chap_09** folder as the **Local Root Folder**. If you need a refresher on this process, visit Exercise 1 in Chapter 3, *"Site Control."*

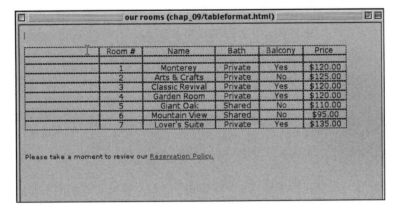

2. Open **tableformat.html**. The dotted lines that you see around each cell are just **formatting guides**, and will not show up inside the browser.

3. Click **F12** to preview this file in your Web browser. Notice how the dotted lines don't appear in the browser? Dreamweaver uses a default setting of 1 for Table borders. In this file, that setting was changed to **0** in order to make the formatting guides disappear. Next you'll learn how to control the weight of the lines with the **border** property.

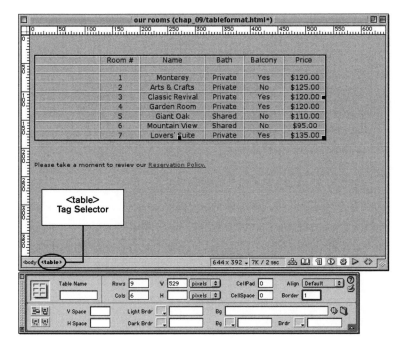

4. Return to Dreamweaver and select the entire Table. You can do this by using the **Tag Selector** at the bottom left of the document window. Click your mouse anywhere inside the Table. You should see the word **<table>** appear as a Tag Selector. Click the **<table>** element in the Tag Selector and the entire table should become selected.

5. With the Table selected, in the Properties Inspector enter **Border: 1**.

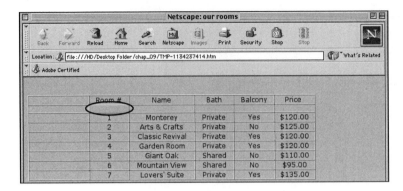

6. Click **F12** to preview the results. See how the border value affected the appearance? This is one of the many controls that you have over the appearance of Tables.

*Note: Netscape displays the cell underneath "**Room #**" in a different way than the other Table cells. In every other row there is content, but the row without content looks different because it is empty.*

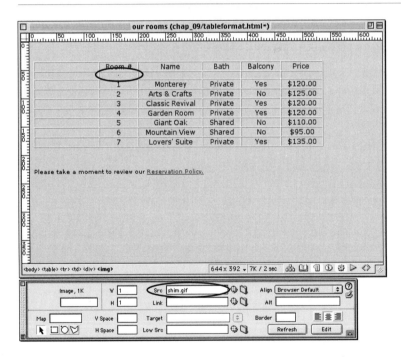

7. In Dreamweaver, click inside the cell below the "**Room #**" cell (column 2, row 2). Choose **Insert > Image**, browse to **shim.gif** located inside the **chap_09** folder, and click **Choose**. Be careful to deselect the image after you insert it. If you hit **Return** or **Enter** with it selected, it will disappear!

*The file that you just inserted (**shim.gif**), contains a single-pixel transparent GIF, which is invisible to your end user. By placing it inside the empty Table cell, you fool the browser into thinking there is content, even though your audience will never see that content. The sole purpose of inserting the graphic is to fix the appearance of the empty Table cell.*

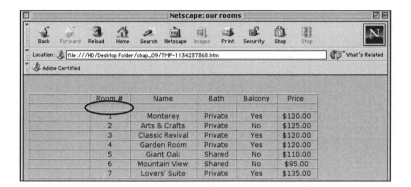

8. Choose **File > Save** to save the changes to the border. Click **F12** to preview the results. See, no more funky pixels, Mom! The empty cell looks like every other cell, which is just the way it should look! Return to Dreamweaver and leave this document open for Exercise 2.

Note | What Is a Transparent GIF?

The GIF file format supports a feature called transparency, which is a term for a mask. Transparency makes it possible to specify areas in a GIF graphic to disappear in a Web browser. A single-pixel transparent GIF is a graphic that only contains a single pixel that has been instructed to disappear. You can create transparent GIF files in Fireworks, Photoshop, ImageReady, or a host of other graphics applications. Methods for making them vary in each program, so consult the user manual of whichever graphics application you own. If you like, you can store the file **shim.gif** for Web projects other than this book, and that way you will always have a single-pixel transparent GIF on hand. **Note:** Shim is a term used in carpentry to hold things in place. You may name your single-pixel transparent GIF anything you like. Shim was just a name we chose.

2. _____Sorting the Table

Dreamweaver is the first HTML editor we've seen that has the ability to sort the content of Tables both alphabetically and numerically. Before this feature existed, if you wanted to sort a Table, you had to copy and paste each row or column manually. Thankfully, sorting Table content in Dreamweaver is only a simple dialog box away.

1. The document **tableformat.html** should still be open. If not, go ahead and open it again.

2. Make sure that the Table is selected and choose **Commands > Sort Table…**. The **Sort Table** dialog box will open.

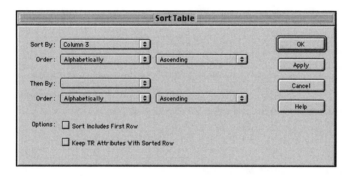

3. Change the settings to **Sort By: Column 3, Order: Alphabetically Ascending**. Click **OK**.

Room #	Name	Bath	Balcony	Price
2	Arts & Crafts	Private	No	$125.00
3	Classic Revival	Private	Yes	$120.00
4	Garden Room	Private	Yes	$120.00
5	Giant Oak	Shared	No	$110.00
7	Lovers' Suite	Private	Yes	$135.00
1	Monterey	Private	Yes	$120.00
6	Mountain View	Shared	No	$95.00

Notice that the file has been sorted differently than when you first opened it? The third column is now in alphabetical order. You can arrange Table contents through this kind of command. Try doing this manually, and you'll really appreciate this feature!

4. Save the file and keep it open for the next exercise.

The Sort Table Dialog Box

The **Sort Table** dialog box has a variety of options to help you modify the appearance of Tables. See the chart below for an explanation of all its features:

Sorting Features	
Feature	**Definition**
Sort By	Use this option to select which column or row you would like to sort.
Order	Use these two pull-down menus to choose **Alphabetically** or **Numerically** and **Ascending** or **Descending**.
Then By	Use this option to sort multiple columns in your Table.
Options: Sort Includes First Row	If this box is checked, the first row in your Table will be sorted. This option is off by default because most often the first row is used as a header for the Table.
Options: Keep TR Attributes With Sorted Row	If this box is checked and a row is moved around due to sorting, all the attributes for that row will also move (i.e. color, font, etc.). **<tr>** stands for **Table Row** in HTML.

Changing the Color Scheme

Now that you know how to change the order of a Table's text, the time has come to work on color formatting. This next exercise will show off Dreamweaver's color-picking features for Tables. Dreamweaver offers a variety of ways to get the job done. When it comes to coloring your Tables, you may use Dreamweaver's automatic color features or set whatever custom colors you desire.

1. With **tableformat.html** still open from the last exercise, make sure that the Table is selected. Choose **Commands > Format Table...** to open the **Format Table** dialog box.

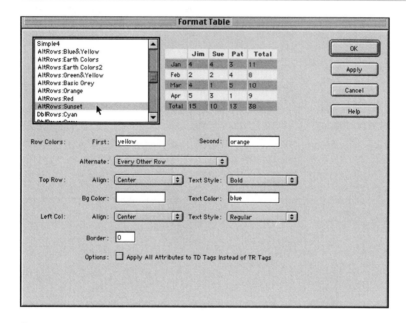

2. Scroll through the list of choices and try clicking some of them. See how the representation of the Table in the middle changes colors? These color combinations are part of Dreamweaver and can be applied to any Table. Select **AltRows: Sunset** and click **OK**.

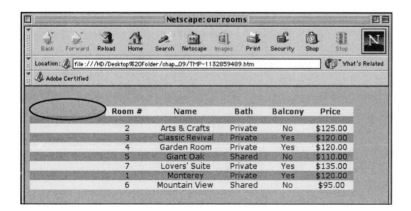

3. Click **F12** to preview the results. Notice how, in Netscape on the Macintosh, the top-left row is missing color information? You can correct this by once again inserting **shim.gif** in the offending cell.

4. Return to Dreamweaver. Click inside the top left cell. Choose **Insert > Image**, browse to **shim.gif**, and click **Choose**. There's that teeny single pixel again, so teeny yet so capable, because when you preview in your browser, the mistake is corrected.

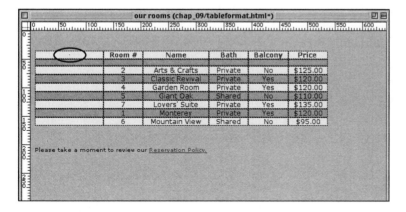

5. Click **F12** to preview the results. The Table should appear as it does in the above image, nice and colorful all the way to its top-left corner.

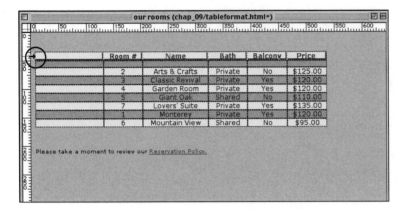

6. Return to Dreamweaver. Select the top row by positioning your mouse in the left-hand corner of the row — until it becomes an arrow — and click once, to select the whole row.

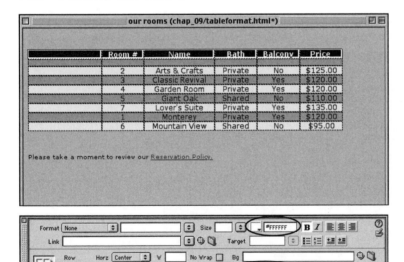

7. With the top row selected, go to the Properties Inspector. Change the **Text** color and **Bg** color (**Bg** as in background), as shown above. You can enter the values, or click the color well to the left of the values, to select colors from the built-in Dreamweaver color box.

8. Save your changes and close this document. Congrats, you've just combined automatic color features and custom color settings in one Table.

Note | An Alternative to Transparent GIFs

This exercise shows you how to insert transparent GIF files to correct empty Table cells, but there is another way to do this as well. If you change your Objects palette to show Invisibles, you can insert a non-breaking space <nbsp> tag into an empty cell, and then the Table will render correctly.

The advantage to transparent GIF files is the fact that their WIDTH and HEIGHT attributes can be stretched to move Table cells around (as you will learn first-hand in Exercise 5). If all you want to do is insert content, and you don't care about changing the shape of an empty Table cell, insert <nbsp> and it will work just as well as a single-pixel transparent GIF.

Creating and Modifying a Table

This exercise will show you how to create your own Table from scratch and how to modify it. You will learn to work with a combination of the **Insert Table** object, the **Modify > Table** menu, and the Properties Inspector. You won't be building a finished page yet. Instead, you'll have a chance to explore many of the different Table options first.

1. If an Untitled Document isn't already open, choose **File > New** (Mac) or **File > Window** (Windows). Save this file into the **chap_09** folder and name it **firsttable.html**. Choose **Modify > Page Properties**. The shortcut keys for this are **Cmd+J** (Mac) and **Ctrl+J** (Windows).

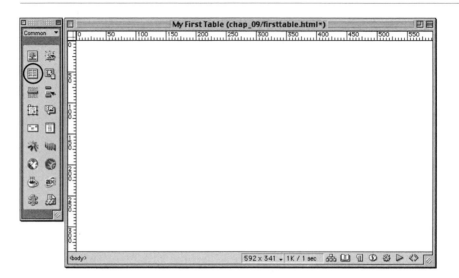

2. Enter **Title: My First Table**. Click **OK**. Click the **Insert Table** object in the **Common Objects** palette or choose **Insert > Table**. The **Insert Table** dialog box will appear.

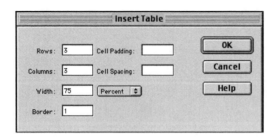

3. Make sure your settings match the settings above, then click **OK**.

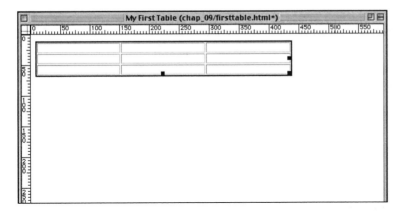

*The **Insert Table** dialog box's default settings result in a Table that is three rows high and three columns wide.*

4. Select the left column, by clicking your mouse inside the top-left cell and dragging down to the bottom row while leaving the mouse depressed.

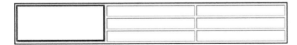

5. Choose **Modify > Table > Merge Cells**. This will result in a Table with three columns, with the left column using only one cell and the other two columns containing three rows of cells.

6. Select the middle row, by clicking your mouse inside the left-middle cell, and dragging over to the right-middle cell while leaving your mouse depressed.

7. In the Properties Inspector, click the **Merge Cells** button. This achieves the same effect as the **Modify** menu did in Step 5. As with many things in Dreamweaver, there are multiple ways to accomplish the same task. We prefer to use the Properties Inspector to merge cells, though you may prefer to use the **Modify** menu method.

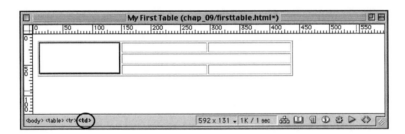

8. Just as you can merge cells in rows and columns, you can also add and delete entire rows and columns. However, selecting rows and columns can be tricky at times. For example, to select the column on the far left, you will find that you can no longer click and drag inside it because now it is only a single cell. Instead, put your cursor inside the cell and click the **<td>** element on the **Tag Selector** at the bottom of the document (**<td>** stands for **Table Data**).

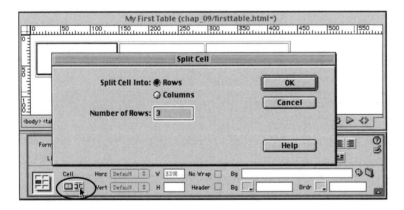

9. In the Properties Inspector, click the **Split Cell** button. This brings up the **Split Cell** dialog box. Enter **3**, if it's not already entered, and make sure the **Rows** radio button is selected, then click **OK**.

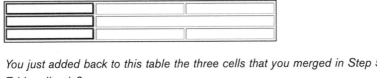

You just added back to this table the three cells that you merged in Step 5. See how flexible this Table editor is?

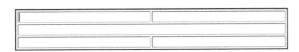

10. To delete the left column completely, select it again and choose **Edit > Cut**. The shortcut keys for this are **Cmd+X** (Mac) and **Ctrl+X** (Windows). You can delete rows or columns by selecting them and cutting them out at any time. **Note:** Sometimes, and we're not sure why, **Cut** will not work, but hitting your **Delete** key will.

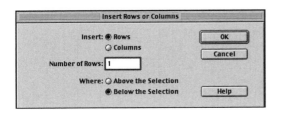

11. Add a new row by clicking inside the upper-right cell and choosing **Modify > Table > Insert Rows or Columns....** Select **Insert: Rows, Number of Rows: 1** and **Where: Below the Selection**. Click **OK**.

12. Here are the results of that action. You could have inserted **Above the Selection** instead or chosen **Columns** instead. Dreamweaver offers a lot of flexibility when it comes to formatting Tables, which you'll likely find useful for the variety of Table tasks which will arise over the course of your future Web-design projects. Save and close the file.

Note | **Contextual Table Menus**

Time and again, Dreamweaver lets you accomplish the same task in many different ways. For example, Exercise 4 showed you how to merge and split cells using the **Modify > Table** menu or the Properties Inspector. Wouldn't you know there is a third way? You could select the column as you did in Step 8 and **Ctrl+Click** (Mac) or use your right mouse button (Windows) to access the **Contextual** menu, which in this case is a handy list of everything you'd ever want to do to a Table.

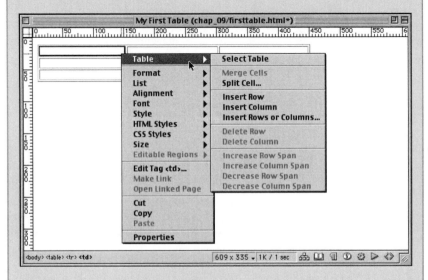

*In yet another case of Dreamweaver putting everything you need right at your fingertips, this comprehensive menu pops up via **Ctrl+Click** (Mac) or the right mouse button (Windows). You can use any of three ways to access this same information (Properties Inspector, Modify menu, or contextual menu), depending on your preference.*

5. _____Aligning Images and Text with Tables

Many people use Tables to align images and text because Tables offer the ability to position artwork freely on a page. This next exercise will show you how to work with a page layout and modify the alignment through adjusting the height and width of Table rows and columns.

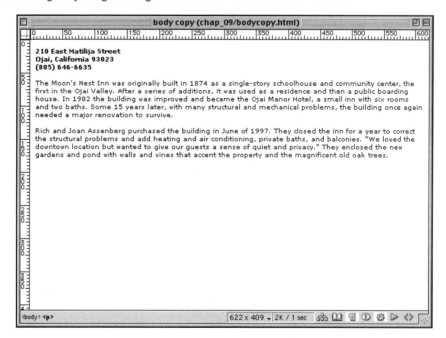

1. Open **bodycopy.html**. Click **F12**. This is a text file that has no Table formatting. See how the width of the text within the document extends to the width of the browser? This is default alignment behavior, and the problem with it is that it can create very wide layouts on large monitors.

Most design experts agree that column widths should be limited in order to make reading text easier. In order to create a narrower column, you will need to learn how to create a table with fixed pixels.

2. Return to Dreamweaver. Create a new document by choosing **File > New** (Mac) or **File New Window** (Windows). Save this file into the **chap_09** folder and name it **align.html**.

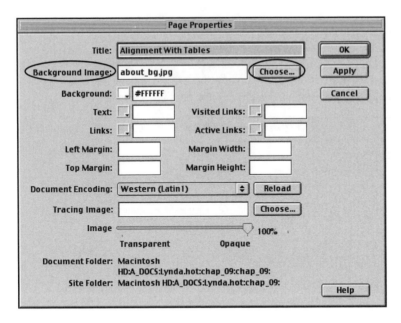

3. Choose **Modify > Page Properties** and enter **Title: Alignment With Tables**. Click **Choose...** to the right of the **Background Image:** field and browse to **about_bg.jpg**. Click **Choose**. You will be returned to the **Page Properties** dialog box. Click **OK**.

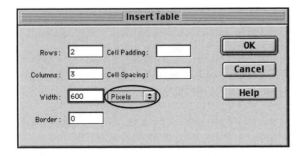

4. Now that you have placed a background image, choose **Insert > Table** and change the settings to **Rows: 2**, **Columns: 3**, **Width: 600 Pixels** (make sure you change this to **Pixels**, not Percent), **Border: 0**. Click **OK**.

Note | Fixed Pixels Versus Percentages in Tables

Values can be created using two types of Tables: percentages or pixels. So far, this chapter has worked with percentage-based Tables. A percentage-based Table will stretch with the width of the browser, meaning that its size will vary depending on the shape of the browser window. If you specify that a Table uses a width of 75%, for example, the Table will stretch to fill three-fourths of the horizontal space regardless of the browser window size. This can be a great thing in some cases, but not in others. When you want to restrict the size of a Table, regardless of the browser window size, pixel-based Tables are the way to go. When you want the table to stretch to the size of the browser window, percentage-based Tables are best. To complicate matters, it's possible to nest a pixel-based Table inside a percentage-based Table or vice versa. By the time you've finished the exercises in this chapter, you will have some concrete examples as to why and when to choose which type of Table, and how to combine the two for more complex Table formatting.

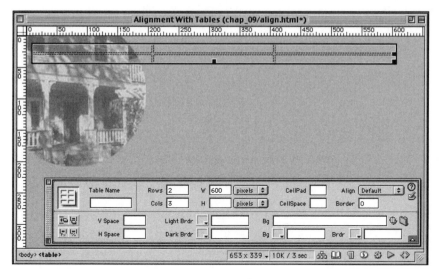

The result of those settings should look like this. You're laying the framework for a fixed-pixel Table that is suitable for aligning objects.

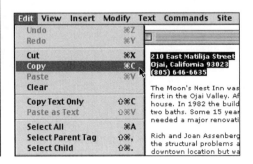

5. Choose **Window > bodycopy.html** (located at the bottom of the **Window** menu, which lists all the open documents). If for some reason **bodycopy.html** is not open, go ahead and open it from the Site window (**F5**).

---

6. Select and copy just the text that contains the address information.

7. Choose **Window > align.html** to bring forth the other open document. Click inside **column 2, row 1** and paste. You could also go back and forth between these two documents by clicking them on the screen if you have a large enough monitor.

---

8. Switch back to the **bodycopy.html** document by choosing **Window > bodycopy.html**. Select and copy the first paragraph. Switch back to the document with the Table in it by choosing **Window > align.html**. Click inside **column 2, row 2** and paste.

9. Switch between the two documents, using the **Window** menu, to copy and paste the second paragraph into column 3, row 2 of the Table, as shown above. Close **bodycopy.html**. You're finished with copying and pasting.

Notice that column 2, row 2 does not align with column 3, row 2? This is an example of default Table formatting, which vertically centers the text in a Table cell unless otherwise instructed. In order to fix this, you'll need to adjust the Table-alignment settings. The next step will show you how.

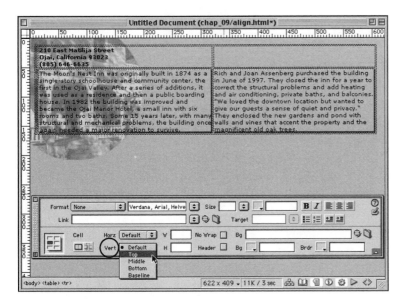

10. Select the entire second row by clicking inside the first column on the left and dragging your mouse across all the columns in the second row. Change the **Properties Inspector Vert** setting to **Top**. As you can see, this corrects the irregular alignment, but it also collapses the empty cell on the far left.

Empty cells in Dreamweaver and in browsers are certainly problematic, aren't they? The only solution is to insert a transparent GIF again, which you'll do in the following step.

11. If your rulers aren't visible, choose **View > Rulers > Show**. The visible ruler helps you see the page's pixel dimensions.

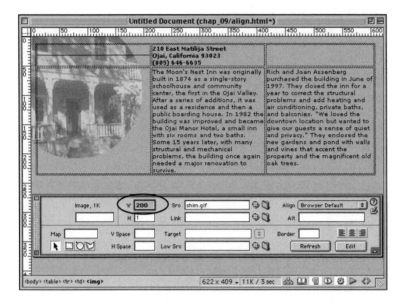

12. Click inside the collapsed top-left cell. Choose **Insert > Image**, and browse to **shim.gif**, then click **Choose**. The **shim.gif** will be selected, and you should see its settings inside the Properties Inspector. **Hint:** If the **shim.gif** accidentally gets deselected, click inside its Table cell and select the **<img>** element in the **Tag Selector** to reselect it. In the Properties Inspector enter **W: 200**. This should stretch the single-pixel GIF to hold the left-hand cell's dimension open.

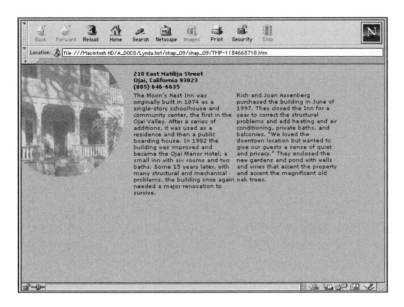

13. Press **F12** to preview the results. This layout is starting to look good, but the space between the Table cells feels a little cramped, doesn't it?

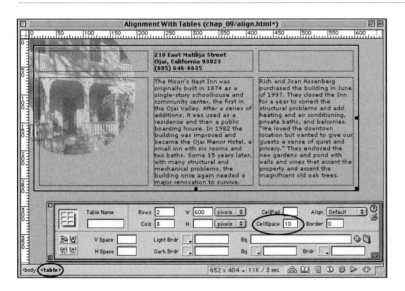

14. Return to Dreamweaver and select the Table by clicking anywhere inside it and choosing the <table> element inside the **Tag Selector**. In the Properties Inspector, enter **CellSpace 10**. As you will see, CellSpace controls the amount of space between cells. Click **F12** to preview the results.

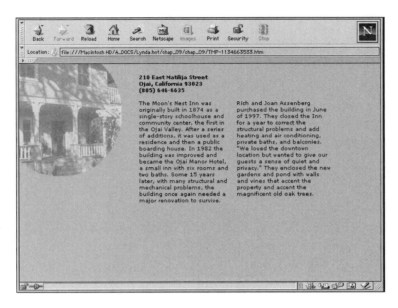

*Here are the results of changing the CellSpace attribute. Want to experiment further with this file? Try changing the dimensions of the **shim.gif** or the CellSpace or **CellPad** settings. You are in total control over the alignment of this page. By leaving the rulers turned on, you can get a better idea of what values to enter into the settings.*

15. Save and close all the open documents before you begin the next exercise.

Note | Using Rulers

Rulers in Dreamweaver are helpful for getting a sense of scale. You can access rulers by choosing **View > Rulers > Show**.

Note | CellPad Versus CellSpace

Using **CellPad** and **CellSpace** settings alters the amount of space between Table cells. CellPad adds room inside the Table cell, whereas CellSpace adds to the border width. When used with Table borders set to **0**, CellSpace and/or CellPad achieve the identical result, by interjecting more space between the data and the edge of each cell.

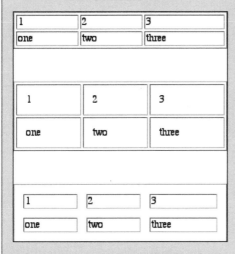

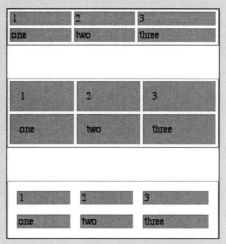

The top Table uses neither CellPad nor CellSpace, the middle Table uses a Cell-Pad setting of **10**, and the bottom Table uses a CellSpace setting of **10**.

With colored Table cells, the differences between CellPad (middle) and Cell-Space (bottom) are more noticeable.

6. _____Percentage-Based Table Alignment

In the last exercise, you worked with a Table that was fixed at 600 pixels. When you want to control your alignment precisely, fixed pixels are the way to go. There's another way to achieve alignment with Tables that is based on percentages. This next exercise will use percentage-based Tables to ensure that the page elements will be centered on any size browser window.

1. Create a new document and save it into the **chap_09** folder and name it **center.html**.

2. Choose **Modify > Page Properties** and enter **Title: Centered Page**. Click **OK**.

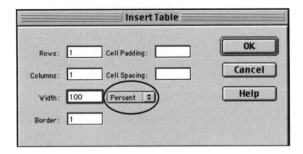

3. Choose **Insert > Table** and change the settings to **Rows: 1, Columns: 1, Width: 100 Percent, Border: 1**. For this exercise to work, it's imperative that the Width be set to Percent and not Pixels. Click **OK**.

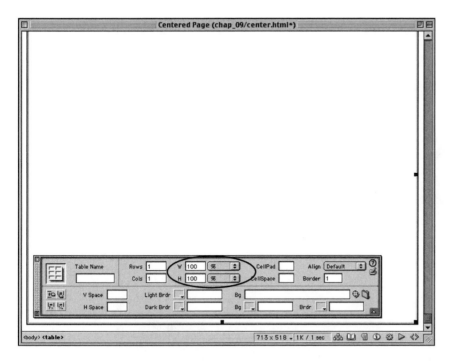

4. The Properties Inspector's width setting (**W**) should already be set to **100%**. Select the **<table>** tag at the bottom of the document and change the Properties Inspector's height setting (**H**) to **100%**. Press **F12** to preview this page in a browser.

*Note: When you press **F12** to preview this page right now, you can move the browser window size around and you'll see the Table stretch. What's happening? You specified that the width and height of this Table would fill 100% of the browser's shape, regardless of its size. This is critical to the success of this exercise, because you are now going to align an image to this table, and the image will be aligned in relationship to the size of the browser, regardless of its shape.*

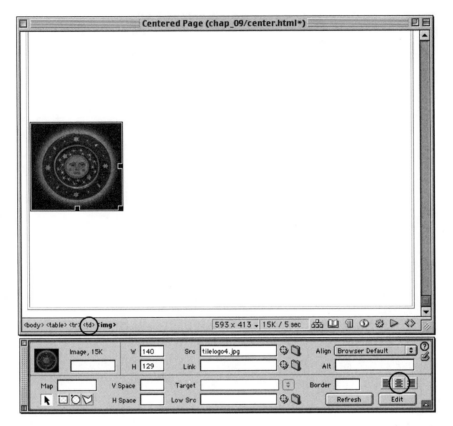

5. Return to Dreamweaver. Click inside the giant Table cell or select the **<td>** (**T**able **D**ata) element in the **Tag Selector**. Choose **Insert > Image**, browse to **tilelogo4.jpg**, and click **Choose**.

6. Make sure you have the image selected, and then in the Properties Inspector click the **Align Center** button. The image will pop into the center of the large table.

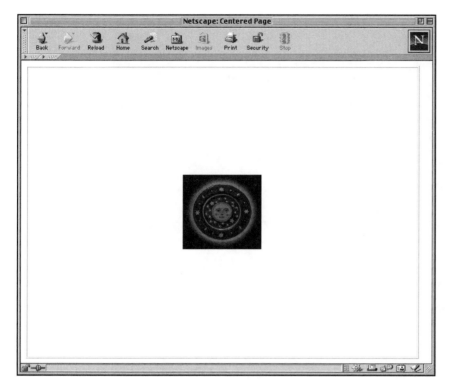

7. Click **F12** to preview and try stretching the browser to different positions. No matter how you set the browser window, this image will always be perfectly centered!

This is the power of percentage-based Table alignment. You could center an image to a pixel-based table, but because the Table wouldn't stretch to the size of the browser window, the image would center to the Table's shape, not the browser's shape.

8. To finish the effect, return to Dreamweaver. Select the Table by clicking inside it and highlighting the **<table> Tag Selector**. Change the Properties Inspector to the Table setting **Border: 0**. This will turn off the border.

9. Choose **Modify > Page Properties**, enter **Background: #000033**, and click **OK**.

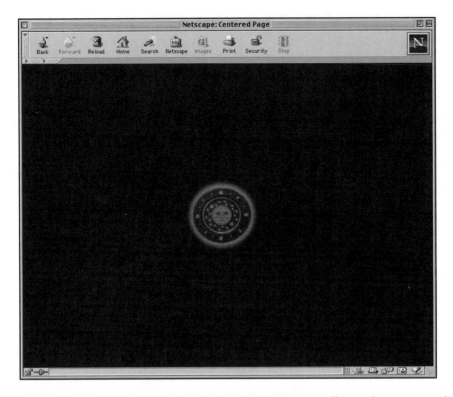

10. Click **F12** to see the results. People who view this page will never know you used a Table, yet the image will always be centered.

What's so great about hiding the Table from viewers? Because you've just created a layout that is centered regardless of the size or shape of the browser window, and people who view this page won't be distracted by a Table border at the edge of the browser screen.

11. Return to Dreamweaver. Save and close this file.

Seamless Image Assembly

If you've looked around the Web much, you've probably noticed that Tables are sometimes used to assemble multiple images so that they look like a single image. Why would anyone want to do this? Tables can ensure that artwork stays aligned and grouped, whereas HTML without Tables can be subject to movement depending on the size of the browser window. This exercise will show you how to reassemble multiple images into a pixel-based Table so that they won't be misaligned.

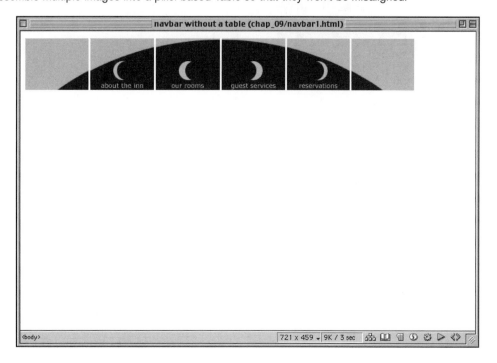

1. Open **navbar1.html**. Notice the gaps between each of the images? This can be the result of putting images next to each other without a Table.

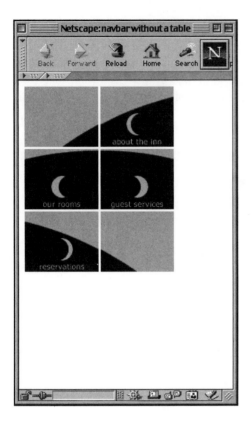

2. Press **F12** to preview this document, then make your browser window smaller. Notice how the row of images gets disrupted? By placing them inside a Table, they will become grouped, and won't be able to move around like this.

3. Return to Dreamweaver. Click each image once (don't double-click!), and you'll see its dimensions inside the Properties Inspector. You have six images, which are 100 pixels wide each. If you add that number together, it's 600. That's important, because you will be creating a 600-pixel-wide Table in order to assemble these as one seamless-looking image.

4. Position your cursor after the last image and hit the **Return** or **Enter** key, so your insertion cursor appears below the images on the screen and on the left.

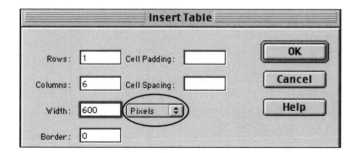

5. Choose **Insert > Table** and change the settings to **Rows: 1**, **Columns: 6**, **Width: 600 Pixels** (not Percent!), **Border: 0**. Click **OK**.

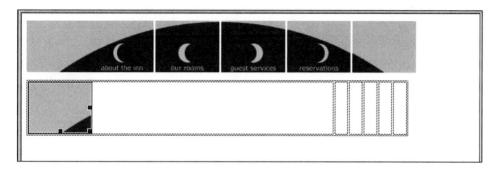

6. Click inside the far-left bottom cell, and choose **Insert > Image**. Browse to **navbar1.gif** and click **Choose**. The Table format is messed up, but the image is now inside the appropriate cell.

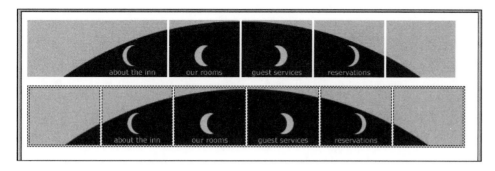

7. Once you insert all the other images into the appropriate cells, the Table should appear like this. The names of the files, from left to right, are: **navbar1.gif**, **navbar2.gif**, **navbar3.gif**, **navbar4.gif**, **navbar5.gif**, and **navbar6.gif**.

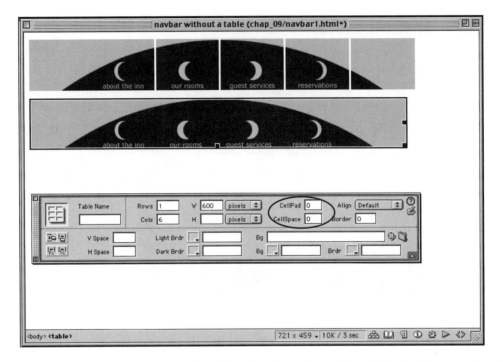

8. To get rid of the gaps between the cells, select the entire table by clicking inside any cell and selecting the **<table> Tag Selector**. Once you've selected it, change the Properties Inspector setting to read **CellPad 0** and **CellSpace 0**. The table will come together seamlessly.

9. Press **F12** to preview your seamless Table. Now that is what a navigation bar ought to look like!

10. Save this file and leave it open for the next exercise.

8. _____Combining Pixels and Percentages

This next exercise will show you how to combine a pixel-accurate Table, like the one you just created in Exercise 7, with a percentage-based Table like you created in Exercise 6. Why would this be important? Let's say that you had a navigation bar, like the one you just built, that you wanted to be center justified regardless of whether it was seen on a small or large monitor. Combining the last two techniques lets you do just that.

1. Create a new document and save it into the **chap_09** folder and name it **navbar2.html**.

---

2. Choose **Insert > Table** and change the settings to **Rows: 1, Columns: 1, Width: 100 Percent** (not Pixels!), **Border: 0**. Click **OK**. With the Table selected, change the **Properties Inspector's** height (**H**) to **100 Pixels**. By using percent for width and pixels for height, the Table will always be horizontally centered on the page.

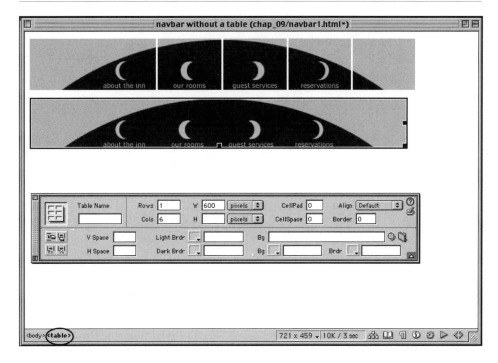

3. Return to **navbar1.html** (use the **Window** menu and look at the bottom to locate it) and select the bottom Table. Remember that you can click anywhere in the Table to access the Tag Selector in order to select it. With the Table selected, choose **Edit > Copy**.

---

4. Now switch over to **navbar2.html** and click inside the centered Table. Choose **Edit > Paste**.

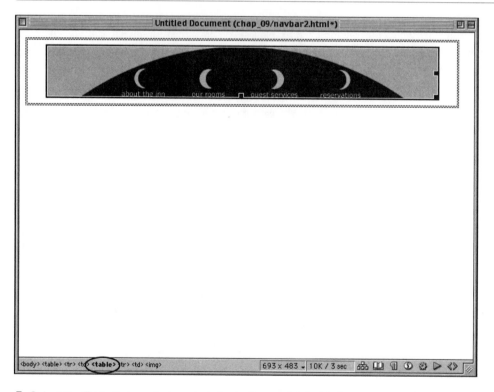

5. Select the Table that you just pasted. Again, if you click inside it you can use the **<table>** Tag Selector to select it. Notice there are two **<table>** tags in the Tag Selector now. This happens because you've got one Table nested inside another.

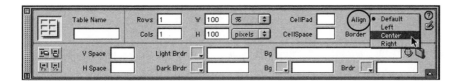

6. With the nested (navigation bar) Table selected, change the Properties Inspector **Align** setting to **Center**.

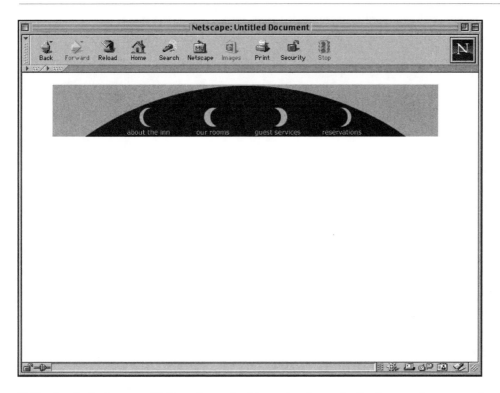

7. Preview in the browser (**F12**), and you should see that the navigation bar remains centered regardless of how wide you drag your browser window out. Congratulations again, you've just made a nested Table using a combination of pixels and percentages. Sounds impressive, but even better than that – it's useful!

8. Return to Dreamweaver. Save and close the **navbar1.html** and **navbar2.html** files.

9._____Inserting Tab-Delimited Data

As you just learned, creating Tables from scratch can be quite a chore. So anything that helps streamline the process is a dream. Dreamweaver 3 gives you the ability to easily insert tab- and space-delimited text. This is great for people who use Excel and other office applications, because now it's simple to get that data into Dreamweaver. This exercise will show you how to import a delimited text file.

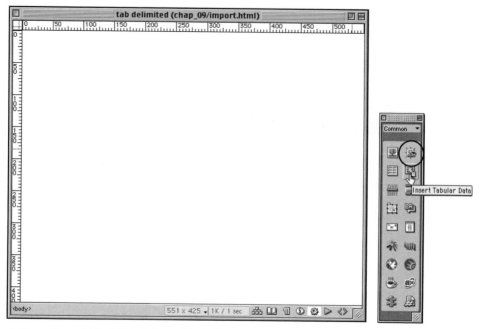

1. Open **import.html**. This is just a blank file that we created for you. Click the **Insert Tabular Data** object in the **Common Objects** palette to open the **Insert Tabular Data** dialog box.

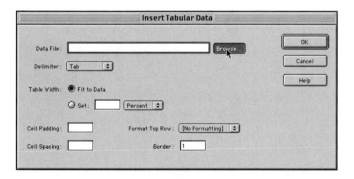

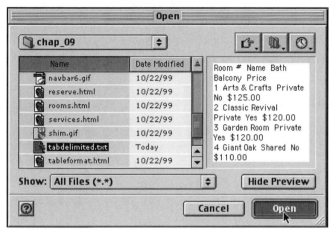

2. Click **Browse...** and navigate to **tabdelimited.txt** located inside the **chap_09** folder. Click **Open** to select that file.

Insert Tabular Data Settings

You won't be changing most of the default settings in this exercise, but you should know what those options mean. Here's a handy chart that explains what you can do in the Insert Tabular Data Settings dialog box.

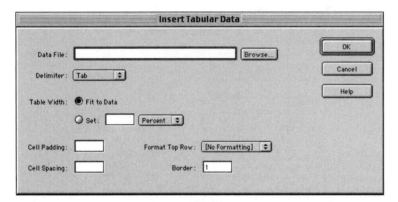

Insert Tabular Data Settings	
Setting	**Function**
Data File:	Use this option to browse to the delimited file on your hard drive.
Delimiter	This option specifies the type of **Delimiter** used in the imported file. It's important that you select the correct one, tab or space.
Table Width:	This option will create a Table large enough to fit the data in the imported file.
Table Width: Set	This option lets you specify how wide to make the Table that holds the imported data. You can choose either percent or pixel widths.
Cell Padding	Controls the **CellPad** value for the Table that holds the imported data.
Cell Spacing	Controls the **CellSpace** value for the Table that holds the imported data.
Format Top Row	You can apply a number of different formatting options to the first row of data in your Table.
Border	Controls the Table's border width.

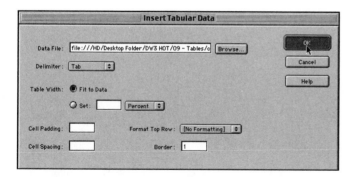

3. Leave the rest of the settings at their default settings. Click **OK**. This will import the data into Dreamweaver inside a custom Table.

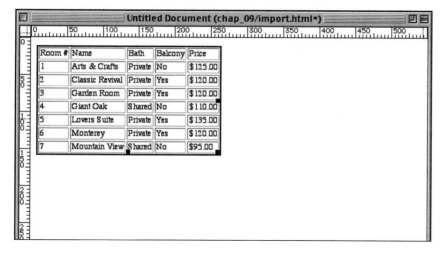

This is what your page should look like at this point.

4. Save and close this file when you are finished. Yes, another chapter accomplished! Congratulations.

10.

Cascading Style Sheets

| Redefining the Style of HTML Tags |
| Making Classes | Using Selectors |
| Linking to a Style Sheet |
| Converting Style Sheets to HTML |

chap_10

Dreamweaver 3
H•O•T CD-ROM

CSS, **C**ascading **S**tyle **S**heets offer a more flexible and accurate way to define the appearance of your text and formatting than standard HTML. If, for example, you wanted all the text in your document to be blue and all the headlines to be green, with standard HTML you would have to go through the elements on the page one by one and assign those colors to the text. Using **Style Sheets**, you can redefine all the body elements in the entire document to turn blue with just one instruction, and then perform the same single step for the headlines to turn green.

The Style Sheets specification also offers more control over type than standard HTML. With Styles, you can specify the amount of space between lines of type (also called the **Line Height** in Dreamweaver), the size of the type in pixels instead of points, and specific fonts for specific page elements. Anyone yearning for more control over typography is going to be drawn to using Styles, as opposed to the type attributes discussed in Chater 7, *"Typography."*

There is a dark side to Styles, however. It is only supported by Netscape 4.0, 4.7, and Explorer 4 and 5. If someone looked at your Styles-based page with an older browser, they would not see any formatting whatsoever beyond the default colors, sizes, fonts, and positions. Of course, Dreamweaver has a great solution to this. It's the only program we know of that can convert Styles to HTML tags automatically. Dreamweaver offers the best of both worlds – it allows you to design with Styles and convert to backward compatible HTML. Ya gotta love it!

This chapter offers exercises in setting up Styles and Style Sheets. Style Sheets are collections of rules that define the Styles of a document. You will get a chance to redefine the Styles of HTML tags, create custom Style **Classes**, which can be repeatedly applied to tags, link to an external Style Sheet, and convert everything you did to HTML.

Many Web developers think highly of Style Sheets, yet they do not use them as often as you would think. Until the support for them is more consistent, using Style Sheets is a challenging decision you will have to make. You may want to create two versions of documents – one with Style Sheets and one without. Using a Dreamweaver behavior, you could deliver the Style Sheet version to the people with current browsers and an HTML page to those who have older browsers. This chapter will show you how to do this, too.

_____Redefining HTML Styles with Style Sheets

As you'll soon learn, there are multiple ways to implement Styles in Dreamweaver. In this exercise, you'll learn how to assign font attributes – such as color and size – by redefining HTML tags, using the Styles feature.

> **1.** Copy **chap_10** to your hard drive. Define your site for Chapter 10 using the **chap_10** folder as the Local Root Folder. If you need a refresher on this process, visit Exercise 1 in Chapter 3, *"Site Control."*

> **2.** Open **interview.html**.

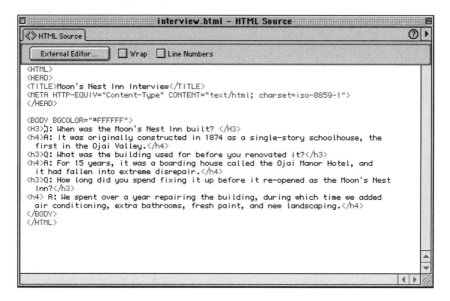

```
interview.html - HTML Source

<>HTML Source                                              (?) ▶

    External Editor...    ☐ Wrap   ☐ Line Numbers

<HTML>
<HEAD>
<TITLE>Moon's Nest Inn Interview</TITLE>
<META HTTP-EQUIV="Content-Type" CONTENT="text/html; charset=iso-8859-1">
</HEAD>

<BODY BGCOLOR="#FFFFFF">
<H3>Q: When was the Moon's Nest Inn built? </H3>
<h4>A: It was originally constructed in 1874 as a single-story schoolhouse, the
    first in the Ojai Valley.</h4>
<h3>Q: What was the building used for before you renovated it?</h3>
<h4>A: For 15 years, it was a boarding house called the Ojai Manor Hotel, and
    it had fallen into extreme disrepair.</h4>
<h3>Q: How long did you spend fixing it up before it re-opened as the Moon's Nest
    Inn?</h3>
<h4> A: We spent over a year repairing the building, during which time we added
    air conditioning, extra bathrooms, fresh paint, and new landscaping.</h4>
</BODY>
</HTML>
```

> **3.** Press **F10** to look at the HTML code for this document. Notice that it uses a combination of <h3> and <h4> tags as delineators between the formatting of the interview questions? Press **F10** to toggle off the **HTML** palette.

4. Make sure your **CSS Styles** palette is open. If it is not, choose **Window > CSS Styles** (**F7**). From the pop-up menu on its upper-right corner, choose **New...**. The **New Style** dialog box will open.

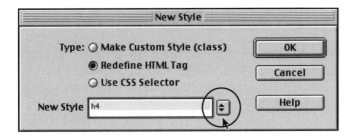

5. Click **Redefine HTML Tag**, then click the arrow next to the text box and select <h4> as the **New Style**. Click **OK**. A **Style Definition** dialog box will open.

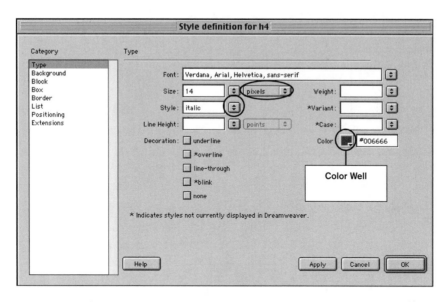

6. Select **Font: Verdana, Arial, Helvetica, sans-serif** and **Size: 14** pixels. Make sure you change the setting from points to pixels. **Tip:** You can click the arrows to select these. Choose **Style: italic.** Change **Color:** to a light blue by pressing down on the **Color Well,** (shown above) and selecting your own color, or by typing in the value **#006666.** Click **OK.**

*Note: For the Font setting, we prefer to use pixels rather than points, because this results in better consistency between the Mac and Windows platforms. Unfortunately, as discussed in Chapter 7, "Typography," Windows renders type at **96 dpi**, while Macs render type at **72 dpi**. Setting the type to pixels eliminates this problem, but only for 4.0+ browsers.*

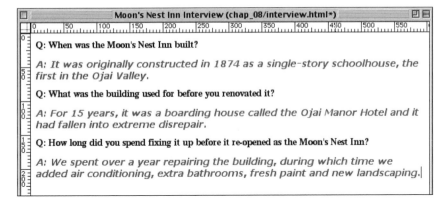

This is what the results of your labor should look like so far.

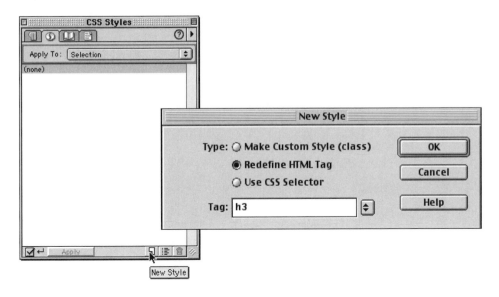

7. At the bottom of the **CSS Styles** palette, click the **New Style** icon. This will open the **New Style** dialog box.

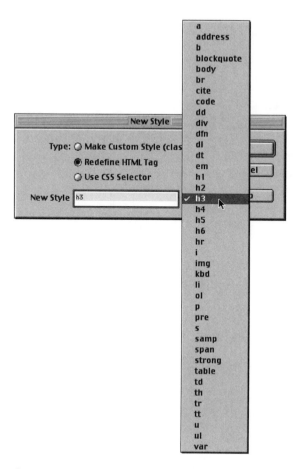

8. Click **Redefine HTML Tag** (if it isn't already selected) and use the arrow next to the **New Syle** box to select <h3>, if necessary. Click **OK**. This will open another **Style Definition** dialog box.

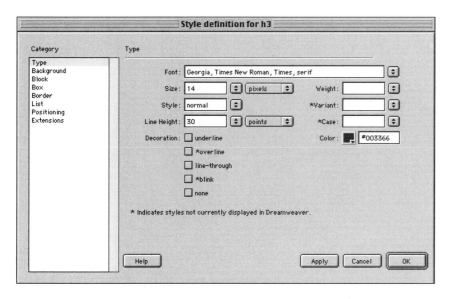

9. Select **Font: Georgia, Times New Roman, Times, serif** and **Size: 14**. Remember to change points to pixels. Select **Style: normal**, and enter **Line Height: 30 points**. Click **Apply**. Notice how the space between the lines of type just increased? Ya just can't do that in vanilla HTML, folks! Change **Color:** to a dark blue by using the **Color Well** or by typing in the value **#003366**, as shown above. Click **OK**.

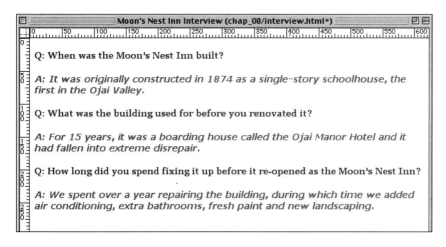

Your screen should look something like this.

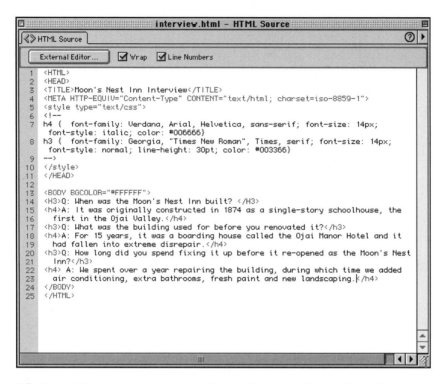

```
                    interview.html – HTML Source
HTML Source                                                        ?

   External Editor...      ☑ Wrap    ☑ Line Numbers

 1    <HTML>
 2    <HEAD>
 3    <TITLE>Moon's Nest Inn Interview</TITLE>
 4    <META HTTP-EQUIV="Content-Type" CONTENT="text/html; charset=iso-8859-1">
 5    <style type="text/css">
 6    <!--
 7    h4 {  font-family: Verdana, Arial, Helvetica, sans-serif; font-size: 14px;
          font-style: italic; color: #006666}
 8    h3 {  font-family: Georgia, "Times New Roman", Times, serif; font-size: 14px;
          font-style: normal; line-height: 30pt; color: #003366}
 9    -->
10    </style>
11    </HEAD>
12
13    <BODY BGCOLOR="#FFFFFF">
14    <H3>Q: When was the Moon's Nest Inn built? </H3>
15    <h4>A: It was originally constructed in 1874 as a single-story schoolhouse, the
16       first in the Ojai Valley.</h4>
17    <h3>Q: What was the building used for before you renovated it?</h3>
18    <h4>A: For 15 years, it was a boarding house called the Ojai Manor Hotel and it
19       had fallen into extreme disrepair.</h4>
20    <h3>Q: How long did you spend fixing it up before it re-opened as the Moon's Nest
21       Inn?</h3>
22    <h4> A: We spent over a year repairing the building, during which time we added
23       air conditioning, extra bathrooms, fresh paint and new landscaping.</h4>
24    </BODY>
25    </HTML>
```

10. Press **F10** to check out the code. Notice all the Style Sheet information that was added to the <head> of the document? Pretty darn cool of Dreamweaver to write all of that for you, wasn't it? Save and close this document.

*We encourage you to click the **Open Style Sheet...** icon, at the bottom of the **CSS Styles** palette, and to select either <h3> or <h4> then click **Edit...**. Make some changes and try some other settings. Knock yourself out, have some fun! When you're finished, close the document. Whether you save your changes is up to you, because this book won't require using the file again.*

So what was the point of all this, you might ask? Styles offer a different method for formatting your documents. They ensure consistency and can save a lot of time by formatting global changes. As you will soon see, redefining HTML is just one way in which to apply Styles. The next exercises will show you how to make changes that are local (that apply to individual text characters or words instead of entire tags).

2. _____Defining a Custom Class

You just learned to redefine the default formatting of an HTML tag with Style Sheets. Now it's time to move on to make your own custom Class. A Style Sheet Class is a set of specifications that can be applied to any tag on the page. Why would you use a Class instead of redefining the formatting of an HTML tag, like you did in the last exercise? Perhaps there's a set of Styles, like a particular color and text size, that you would like to apply randomly without it being automatically applied to every instance of a particular HTML tag. For example, maybe you don't want all the <h3> tags to automatically be green, and perhaps you want some <h4> tags to be green, as well. Rather than redefining an existing HTML tag like you did in the last exercise, a Class is a way to apply the same Style to different tags on your page. In other words, a Class can be applied to any tag at any time. If this sounds confusing, try the exercise and it will likely make more sense.

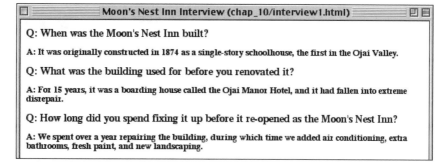

1. Open **interview1.html**. It should look like the file in Exercise 1, because at this point it is identical. It is very important that it does not contain any Style Sheet information as of yet!

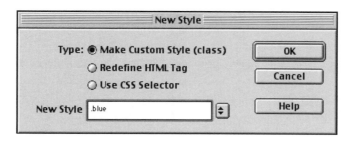

2. Make sure your **CSS Styles** palette is open. If it is not, choose **Window > CSS Styles** (**F7**). Click the **New Style** icon to open the **New Style** dialog box. Click **Make Custom Style (class)** and enter **New Style .blue**. Make sure you put a period before the word **blue**. All classes have this period. Click **OK**. This will open a **Style Definition** dialog box.

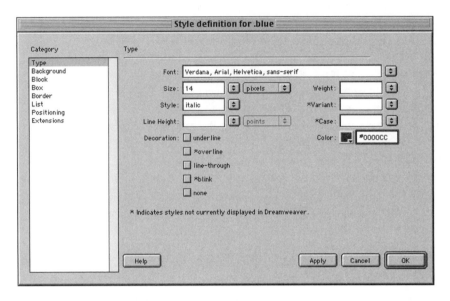

3. Fill out the **Style Definition** for **.blue** dialog box however you like, but make sure to set **Color:** to a blue! **Note:** Clicking **Apply** will have no effect in this instance, because you aren't redefining an existing tag. Therefore, click **OK** once you're finished, because you can always re-edit the Class. You will return to the **Edit Style Sheet** dialog box. Don't click **Done** just yet, you're not done creating Styles!

Note | Internal, Inline, and External Style Sheets

There are three types of **Style Sheets: Internal, Inline, and External**. In Exercise 1, you created an Internal Style Sheet that was applied to all the <h3> and <h4> tags in the document. An Internal Style Sheet is global to the entire document, yet it is limited to whatever document it is contained within. In Exercise 2, you created an Inline Style Sheet when you defined a **Custom Class**. Inline Styles may be applied selectively to elements within a document. Remember how in Exercise 2 you applied Styles to specific lines of text, individual words or characters? This is called an Inline Style Sheet because it doesn't apply to the entire page. An External Style Sheet is an external document to which you can link. For example, we could take a regular HTML page and link it to an External Style Sheet and it would take on all the Style properties of that document. This chapter will teach you how to make Styles in all three of these ways. You'll find that any of these three choices will be appropriate at different times.

Your **CSS Styles** palette should now contain the word *"blue"* in it. **Note:** It won't contain a period here in front of the word *"blue,"* even though you needed to specify one. Why? Beats us! It's just an interface inconsistency.

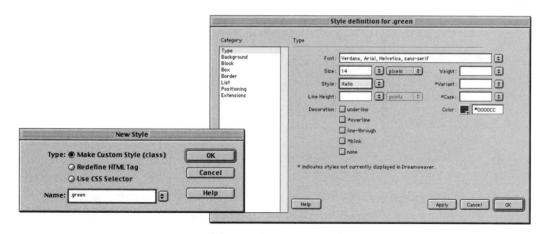

4. Create a **Class**, **Name: .green** by following Steps 2 and 3 and setting **Color:** to green. We don't want to be nags, but remember to put that period in front of the class name **.green**! Click **OK**. You may now click **Done** in the **Edit Style Sheet** dialog box.

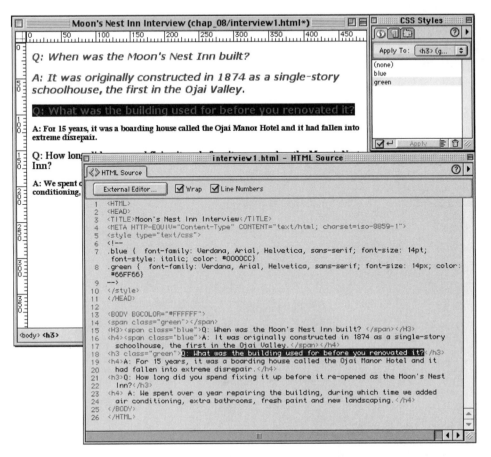

5. Select a line of type on your page, and click the **Class** named **green** inside the **CSS Styles** palette. If you leave the **HTML Source** window open, as shown above, you can watch Dreamweaver construct the Style code before your eyes. Classes can be applied to lines of text, or even individual words or characters. Go ahead and select different bits of type on your page and click the Classes named **blue** and **green** to see what happens. Congrats! You've just created Classes and applied them to a document.

6. Save and close the document.

Using Selectors to Group Tags

In the last two exercises you learned how to apply Styles to redefine a tag, and how to use Styles Custom Classes on selective text. What if you want to apply a single Style to multiple HTML tags? Let's say you wanted to reformat both the <h3> and <h4> tags at the same time? **Selectors** are the answer, as they allow you to apply Styles to multiple HTML tags at once.

1. Open **interview3.html**.

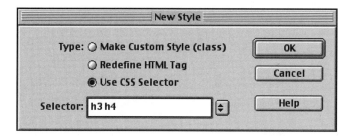

2. Make sure your **CSS Styles** palette is open. If it is not, choose **Window > CSS Styles** (**F7**). Click the **New Style** icon at the bottom of the **CSS Styles** palette. The **New Style** dialog box will open.

3. Click **Use CSS Selector**. Enter **h3 h4** in the **Selector:** field to select tags <h3> and <h4>. Note that there is a space between the two tags. **Warning:** Do not try to enter commas between these values; they will not work! Click **OK**. A **Style Definition** dialog box will open.

4. Set **Color:** to a blue and click **OK**.

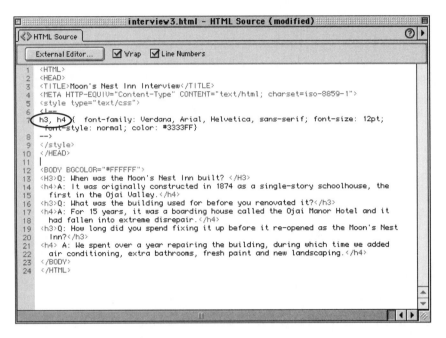

5. Press **F10** to view the code. Insert a comma between "**h3**"and "**h4**," as shown above. Dreamweaver doesn't support this feature, so you have to go right into the code to make it work.

While we wish Dreamweaver did directly support a Selector in this fashion, it is commendable that you can edit the code directly and Dreamweaver will still honor it. Many other HTML editors won't let you enter code that the editor doesn't generate.

6. Press **F10** to close the **HTML Source** window. The text will turn blue!

7. Save and close the file.

This exercise showed how you can apply a single Style to two HTML tags by using a Selector. Pretty tricky stuff.

Affecting Links with Selectors

The default appearance of a link in standard HTML is that it is formatted with an underline. One reason people use Style Sheets is to turn off the underlines of links. We're not sure if we think this is a good idea or not because many people rely on the visual cue of underlined text to know that it is truly a link. Regardless, some of you may want to do it anyway, so this exercise will show you how. Not only that, you'll get to use the CSS Selector feature again! Woo hoo!

1. Open **interviewlink.html**. As you can see by the underlined text, this document contains a link.

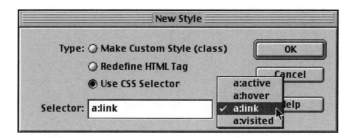

2. Make sure your **CSS Styles** palette is open. If it is not, choose **Window > CSS Styles** (**F7**). Click the **New Style** icon at the bottom of the **CSS Styles** palette. The **New Style** dialog box will open. Click **Use CSS Selector** and select **a:link**. This allows you to define the <a> (anchor) tag's link properties. Click **OK**. A **Style Definition** dialog box will open.

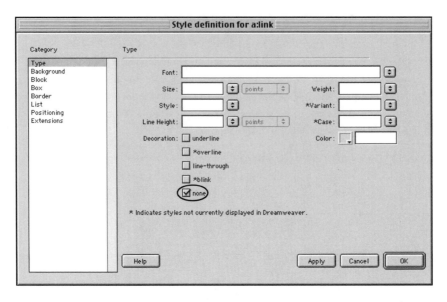

3. Check **Decoration: none** and click **OK**. You will be returned to the document window. The term Decoration refers to how the link is displayed. In this case, because an underline is not wanted, the Decoration is set to **none**. Notice that nothing looks different on your page. That is because this feature does not preview in Dreamweaver; it must instead be viewed inside a browser.

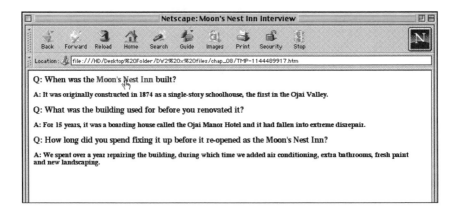

4. Press **F12**, and you'll see that the link is there, but it isn't underlined.

Note: This can only be seen from a 4.0+ browser. If you have an earlier browser, you will not be able to see it even though you created it. Such is life in the not-so-fair world of never-ending browser incompatibility.

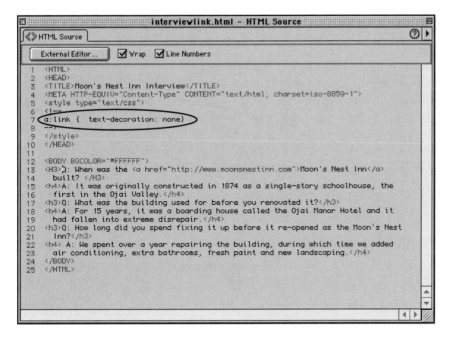

5. Return to Dreamweaver and press **F10** to view the HTML code. Notice the Style Selector information was added! We don't know about you, but we sure like that we don't have to hand-code this sort of thing.

6. Save and close this file.

Note | **Changing the Appearance of Links with Selectors**

You might have noticed that the pop-up menu for **CSS Selectors** had four entries: **a:active**, **a:hover**, **a:link**, and **a:visited**. Exercise 4 showed you how **a:link** affected the attributes for links, but what do the other entries stand for? The selection **a:active** affects the **Active Link**, which is the appearance when the mouse is depressed on a link. The selection **a:hover** affects the appearance of the link when your mouse rolls over it. You could, for example, have the text color change upon rollover. Note that **a:hover** is only honored by Explorer, not Netscape. The **a:visited** selection alters the appearance of a **Visited Link**, or, in plain English, a link that has already been clicked.

Redefine HTML, Custom Class, or Selector?

Now that you've learned to create Styles based on redefining HTML, a Custom Class, and a Selector, here is a handy chart that helps to explain when to use which type of Style:

Creating Styles in Dreamweaver	
When to Use?	**For What Purpose?**
Redefine HTML Tag	Use when you want to change the appearance of content based on a certain tag. For example, everything with an <h1> tag could be made to look consistent.
Create a Custom Class	Use when you want to change the appearance of your document, but not have it dependent on a tag. Use also when you want to make certain words a particular color — regardless of whether they are in the headline or the body copy.
Selector	A Selector can change the appearance of multiple HTML tags all at once. Use this when you want to make appearance changes based on tags, but on more than one tag at a time. Dreamweaver also includes the **a:Selectors** as a way to change the appearance of linked text (turning off the underline, for example).

5. —————————————————Linking to a Style Sheet

You might not have realized this, but so far you've been creating Internal Style Sheets. Internal Style Sheets apply only to the document in which they reside. It's also possible to create External Style Sheets, so different pages in your Web site can all share the same set of Style Sheet information. In the linked Style Sheet scenario, the Style information is in the external document, and it is only referenced by the internal document. External Style Sheets are very powerful, because you can base all the Style information in one document, and if you make a change you only have to change it there, instead of in each individual document that references it. This exercise will show you how to create an External Style Sheet, and then how to link to it once it's created.

1. Choose **File > New** (Mac) or **File New Window** (Windows) and save the empty document as **style.html**.

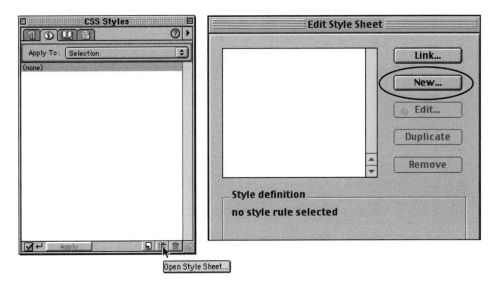

2. At the bottom of your **CSS Styles** palette, click the **Open Style Sheet...** icon. The **Edit Style Sheet** dialog box will open. Click **New...**. The **New Style** dialog box will open.

3. Click **Redefine HTML Tag** and select **New Style: body** (it might pop up automatically). Click **OK**. A **Style Definition** dialog box will open.

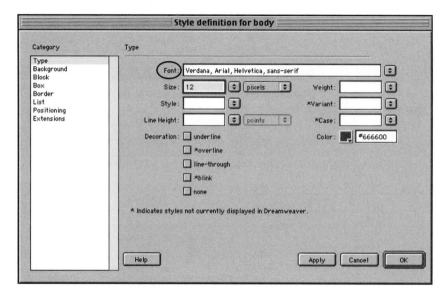

4. Select **Font: Verdana, Arial, Helvetica, sans-serif, Size: 12 pixels,** and **Color: green**. Click **OK**.

5. In the **Edit Style Sheet** dialog box, click **New...** again. You're going to add another Style to this External Style Sheet.

6. Click **Use CSS Selector** and select **a:link**, then click **OK**. This will open another **Style Definition** dialog box.

 Movie | **externalcss.mov**

To learn more about external CSS, check out **externalcss.mov** located in the **movies** folder on the Dreamweaver 3 **H•O•T CD-ROM**.

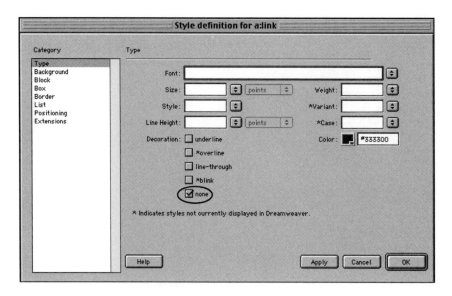

7. Check **Decoration: none**, because an underline is not wanted. Click **OK**. Click **Done** in the **Edit Style Sheet** dialog box.

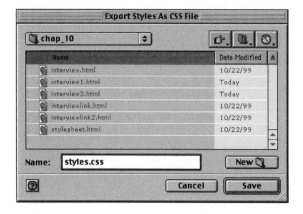

8. Choose **File > Export > Export CSS Styles....** Name the file **styles.css**. In the future, if you decide to create your own Style Sheets, you could name this file anything you like (as long as it's all lowercase and has no spaces), but you always have to give it a **.css** extension instead of an **.html** extension for it to work properly. Click **Save**.

9. Close the **style.html** document and do not save the changes. The **Style Sheet** information was saved when you chose to **Export CSS Styles....**

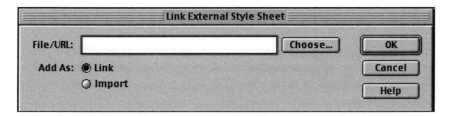

10. Open **interviewlink2.html**. In the **CSS Styles** palette, click the **Open Style Sheet...** icon. Click on **Link....** In the **Link External Style Sheet** dialog box make sure **Add As:** has the **Link** radio button selected.

11. Click **Choose...** (Mac) or **Browse...** (Windows). Navigate to **styles.css**, which you should have saved inside the **chap_10** folder, and click **Choose.** You will be returned to the **Link External Style Sheet** dialog box. Click **OK**.

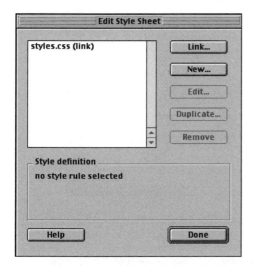

12. You should see **styles.css (link)** listed inside the **Edit Style Sheet** dialog box. Click **Done**.

13. The type on your screen should look green. Press **F12** to preview in a browser. The links should not be underlined. Save and close your document. You could link numerous documents to the **.css** file if you wanted to. This completes your education for the day in External Style Sheet linking.

6. _____From CSS to HTML

Now that you've successfully created Internal, Inline, and External Style Sheets, you ought to be feeling pretty proud. You may be feeling so good, in fact, that you might have forgotten that Style Sheets still aren't widely supported by browsers. What's a conscientious Web designer to do? Dreamweaver has a great solution – you can convert the CSS to HTML! The only caveat is that HTML doesn't support certain things, such as links with no underlines, or font sizes in pixels. Bear with us for a moment, and you'll see where we're going with all this.

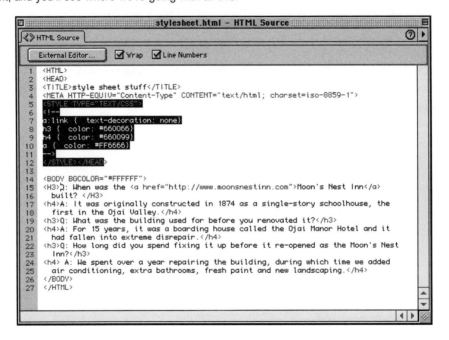

1. Open **stylesheet.html**. Press **F10**, and you'll see Style Sheet code in the document.

2. Choose **File > Convert > 3.0 Browser Compatible....** The **Convert to 3.0 Browser Compatible** dialog box will open.

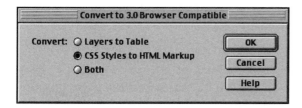

3. Click **CSS Styles to HTML Markup** and click **OK**. This creates a new Untitled Document.

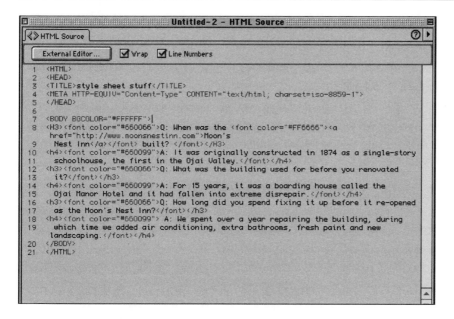

4. Return to the **HTML Source** window to look at the HTML. Look, Ma, no Styles information, just HTML code! Press **F10** to close the **HTML Source** window.

5. Save this file as **stylesheet2.html**. You should now have two documents in your **chap_10** folder, **stylesheet.html** and **stylesheet2.html**.

Why did Dreamweaver create another document for you? Because you might want to have two pages on hand: one to deliver to your 4.0+ browser audience, and another for your audience that can't see the Style Sheets.

6. Close both files.

As you can see, Cascading Style Sheets can be very useful. Now that you have finished these exercises, you should be much more comfortable working with them.

II.

Templates/Libraries

| Creating and Modifying Templates |

| Setting Up Templates So Others Can Use Them |

| Locking Template Content |

| Creating and Modifying Library Items |

chap_11

Dreamweaver 3
H•O•T CD-ROM

Two of the biggest challenges that face Web designers are making pages look consistent, and updating changes throughout a site. **Templates** and **Library Items** can help you meet both challenges successfully, because they make it easy to create consistent pages and page elements and to automatically update multiple pages when changes are made.

Templates are useful for entire page designs. They can lock in colors, fonts, tables, or images, while leaving other parts of the document editable. When you create a Template, you use it by requesting a copy of it. Instead of creating a new Untitled Document, you request a new page based on a Template that you have designed.

Library Items are useful for page-design elements, such as a navigation bar or copyright notice. They are little pieces of HTML or text that can be dropped anywhere within a page. You will soon learn the differences between these two Dreamweaver 3 features by following the hands-on exercises in this chapter.

Tip | Templates and Library Folders

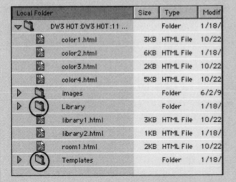

You might have noticed that there were two folders inside the **chap_11** folder, called **Templates** and **Library**. Dreamweaver automatically creates these folders for you on any site that uses Templates or Library Items. If you do not use Templates or Library Items, Dreamweaver will not put these folders in your directory structure. These folders (**Templates** and **Library**) do not need to be uploaded to your Web site if you publish it to the WWW. They are for internal purposes only. If Dreamweaver sees that these folders are present in your directory structure, it knows to insert any new Templates or Library Items that you create into each folder (**Templates** or **Library**) without you having to do so.

Note | Templates, Library Items, and HTML

Dreamweaver's Template format (**.dwt**) and Library format (**.lbi**) are internal file-naming conventions only. These files do not mean anything to other HTML editors, nor are they meant to be viewed on the Web inside a browser. Templates and Library Items are used internally by Dreamweaver, and function only in Dreamweaver. If you base an HTML page on a Template or use Library Items in it, it will appear as a normal page in the browser, the same as any other HTML page. It will be regarded differently in Dreamweaver only, in that it will be updated if the original Template or Library Items are changed.

Templates in Action

The best way to understand Templates in Dreamweaver is to observe them in action. For this first exercise, you will modify an existing Template, which will show you how quickly they can update across multiple pages in your site. You will also see how, with just a few clicks, you can use Templates to change your color scheme across several pages.

1. Copy **chap_11** to your hard drive. Define your site for Chapter 11 using the **chap_11** folder as the Local Root Folder. If you need a refresher on this process, visit Exercise 1 in Chapter 3, *"Site Control."*

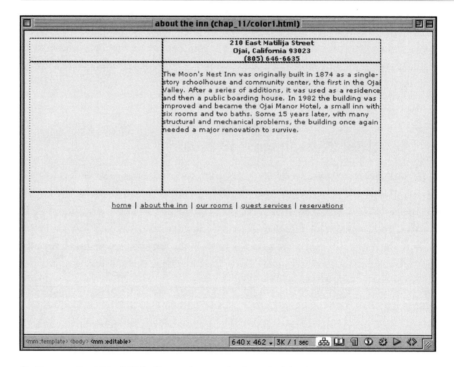

2. Open **color1.html**. This file, and several others inside the **chap_11** folder, including **color2.html**, **color3.html**, and **color4.html**, have a color scheme Template called **summer** already applied to them. If you want, go ahead and open these other files and notice that they all share the same color scheme.

3. When you are working with Templates in Dreamweaver, you will typically want to have the **Templates** palette open. Choose **Window > Templates** to open it.

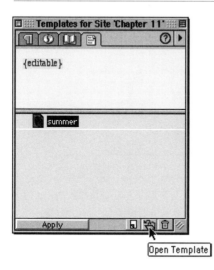

4. Highlight the Template called **summer** in the **Templates** palette, and then click the **Open Template** icon at the bottom of the palette. This will open the Template so you can start editing, or modifying it. **Tip:** As an alternative, you could simply double-click the Template to open it.

It's easy to tell when you are editing a Template because the title bar will display **<<Template>>**, *the Template file name, and a* **.dwt** *extension.*

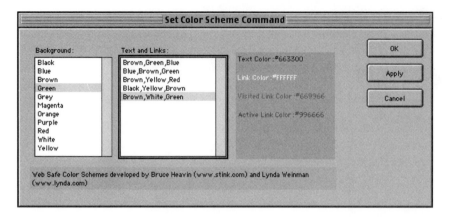

5. To change the color scheme of this Template, you will use some of the preset color schemes that ship with Dreamweaver. Choose **Commands > Set Color Scheme…**. This will open a **Set Color Scheme Command** dialog box. **Select Background: Green** and **Text and Links: Brown, White, Green**. Click **OK**.

6. Close the **summer.dwt** Template and save your changes when prompted.

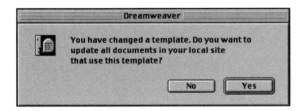

7. Once you close and save the modified Template, you will be notified that you have modified a Template and asked if you want to update all the files in your site that use this Template. Because you want to apply the new color scheme to all four pages, click **Yes**. If you are presented with the **Update Template Files** dialog box, click **Update**.

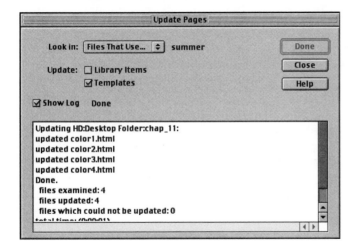

8. Once you click **Yes** or **Update**, Dreamweaver will scan your site to determine if any files are using this Template. If it locates any files that are, it will update them. In this case, there are four such files. A dialog box will list which files were updated. Once you are finished reviewing this screen, click **Close**.

*Note: If you have **color1.html** open while performing this operation, the **Color Scheme** will be updated, but if you close the file and don't save changes you'll lose them. Make sure you save your changes when you close any open files.*

Note | Modifying and Saving Templates

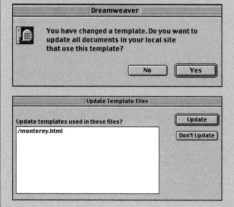

As you modify and save Templates, one of the two dialog boxes on the left will prompt you to update the files in your site that are using that Template. While the dialog boxes look very different, they both do the same thing.

Each asks if you would like to update the files in your site that use the Template you have modified. If you click **Yes** or **Update**, the files will be updated automatically. If you click **No** or **Don't Update**, the files will not be updated. So don't be alarmed if you get one or the other as you go through this chapter.

The dialog box on the top will appear the first time you make a modification to a Template. Any additional changes to that Template will cause the dialog box on the bottom to appear.

Tip | Templates and Page Properties

Once a Template has been applied to a page, you can no longer edit any of the Page Properties options, with the exception of the page title. Therefore, the only way to change the color scheme is by opening and editing the Template itself, as you just did in Exercise 1.

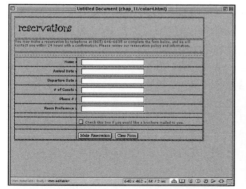

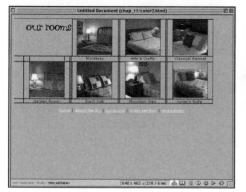

9. Open **color2.html**, **color3.html**, and **color4.html**, and you will see that each now has the new color scheme.

Imagine how much time this could save you if you had hundreds or thousands of pages that share the same color scheme?

Working with Templates is an excellent technique to ensure design consistency. The only caveat is that you must work from a Template file to begin with. How do you do that? Check out the next exercise to find out.

10. Close all the files. You will learn how to make a Template from scratch in the next exercise.

2. Creating a New Template

In this next exercise, you are going to create a new Template from an existing document and then make parts of your Template editable, and other parts non-editable. Once you have this skill under your belt, you will understand Templates' capabilities and limitations much more clearly.

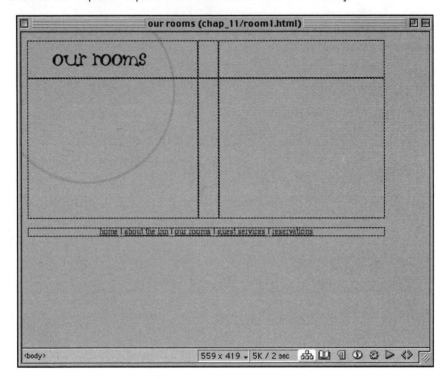

1. Open **room1.html**. This document was created for you, but the following steps would also work on a document of your own creation.

Once you have created the basic layout of your document, the next step is to save it as a Template.

2. Choose **File > Save As Template....**

3. When the **Save As Template** dialog box opens, make sure this Template is named **room1**. Dreamweaver 3 will automatically enter the name of the HTML file in the **Save As:** field. You can see that your other Template, **summer**, is already listed in this box. Click **Save**.

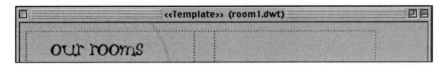

Again, you know that you are now working with a Template because the title bar displays
<<Template>> and the file name with a .dwt extension.

Now that you have created your Template, you need to decide which areas you want to be able
to modify and which areas you want to lock. By default, the entire document is designated as non-
editable. This means that if you were to close the file now, it would be impossible for anyone to
modify it later.

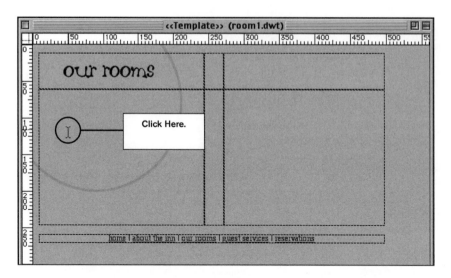

4. Click inside the large cell directly under the image "**our rooms**." Choose **Modify > Templates > New Editable Region...**, to designate this area as an editable region so that you or other members of your design team can enter the description of the room here.

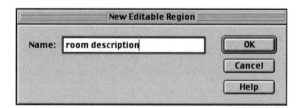

5. When the **New Editable Region** dialog box appears, enter **room description** and click **OK**.

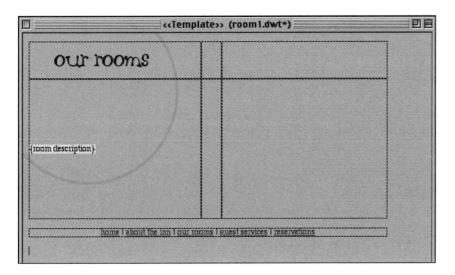

*Notice that the name you entered appears in that cell, surrounded by curly braces. This indicates that this area of the Template is editable − it will let you or other members of your team enter information inside this cell. By naming this region "**room description**," you can help others know what information should be entered there.*

---

6. Click inside the large cell on the far right. Choose **Modify > Templates > New Editable Region...** when the **New Editable Region** dialog box appears, type **room image** and click **OK**.

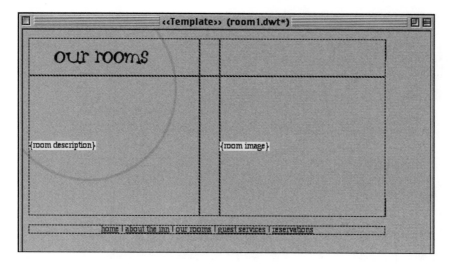

This is what your Template should look like at this point.

---

7. Now that you have designated the necessary areas as editable, go ahead and close this file. When prompted, make sure that you save your changes.

Congratulations, you have just created a custom Template. Next, you will create a new page based on your newly created Template.

---

8. Choose **File > New from Template....**

9. Highlight **room1** in the list and click **Select**. This will create a new document based on the **room1**Template.

---

10. Choose **File > Save As...** and save the file as **montereyroom.html** into your **chap_11** folder.

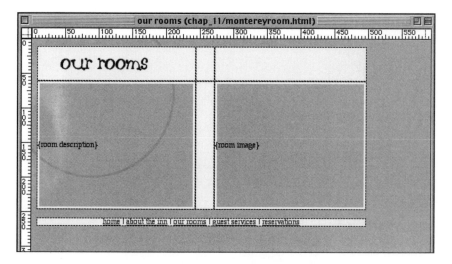

This is what the page will look like with a Template applied to it. The highlighted areas are non-editable. The two areas you designated as editable are not highlighted and are ready to be edited.

Tip | I Don't See Any Highlighting!

If you don't see any highlighting on your screen, make sure that you have the **View > Invisible Elements** option enabled. If you disable this feature, you will not see any highlighting. You can choose **View > Invisible Elements** to disable/enable this feature.

Tip | Highlighting Preferences

You can modify your document's highlighting colors in Dreamweaver's **Preferences** section. By choosing **Edit > Preferences...** and then selecting Highlighting under **Category**, you can set the highlighting colors to any color you want.

---

11. Highlight the text "**room description**" and its surrounding curly braces, press **Delete** to make sure the text and curly braces disappear, and type **The Monterey Room. A charming brass double bed completes this cozy room with a balcony affording both city and mountain views. This room has a private bath.**.

12. Highlight the text "**room image**" on the right and its surrounding curly braces, then press **Delete** to make sure the text and curly braces disappear. Click the **Insert Image** object in the **Common Objects** palette.

---

13. Browse to the **images** folder inside the **chap_11** folder to locate **monterey1.jpg**. Click **Choose**. This will insert the image into this editable region.

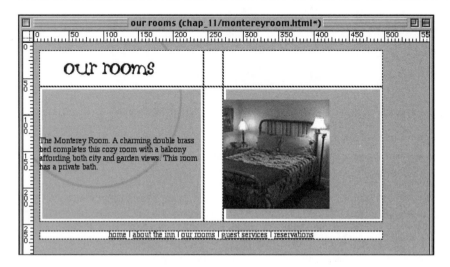

14. Save and keep this file open. You'll be using it in the next exercise.

> ### Tip | Detaching a Template
>
> There may come a time when you want to modify sections of a page that has a Template applied to it. Because some areas are locked, this is impossible to do with the Template still applied to the page. By choosing **Modify > Templates > Detach from Template**, you can detach the Template from the page and make the entire document editable.

3. _____**Modifying a Template**

Now that that you have created your first Template, you are ready to learn how to update it. In this exercise, you are going to change the alignment of the text and image in your layout, causing the text and the image to move to the center. Then, all you have to do is sit back and watch Dreamweaver update all the pages in your site that use this Template!

1. Make sure that **montereyroom.html** from the previous exercise is open. Before you can modify a Template, you must open it from the **Templates** palette. Double-click the **room1** Template in the **Templates** palette to open that Template.

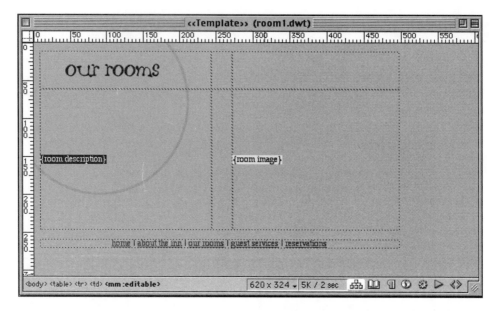

2. The actual Template file will be open for you to edit. Highlight the text "**room description**."

3. In the Properties Inspector, click the **Horz** pop-up menu and choose **Center**. This will move the text to the center of the cell.

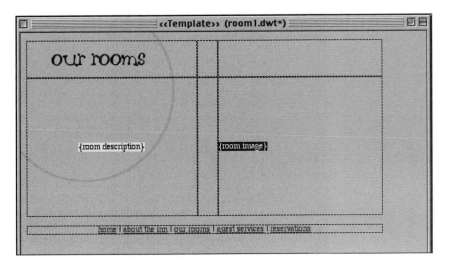

4. Highlight the text "**room image.**"

---

5. Again, from the Properties Inspector's **Horz pop-up** menu, choose **Center**. This will move the text to the center of the cell, which will also center any images that are inserted into this cell.

---

6. Go ahead and close this Template file. When prompted, make sure that you save your changes. A dialog box will appear, asking if you wish to update the files in your site which use this Template. Click **Yes**. If you are presented with the **Update Template Files** dialog box, click **Update**. Any files using this Template will update (in this case, **montereyroom. html** file), and a dialog box will list which files were updated. Click **Close**.

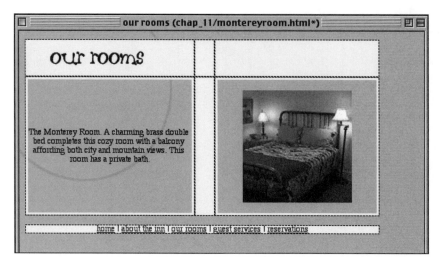

This is what **montereyroom.html** will look like with the revised Template applied to it.

Note: Templates used in this fashion are only helpful if the pages share the same layout and the same editable-region names.

7. Save and close all open files and move on to the next exercise.

Warning | **Template Beware!**

Once a Template has been applied to a page, you can no longer edit any information in the <HEAD> tag. This means you can't add any JavaScript, Styles, Behaviors, or anything else that would be contained within a <HEAD> tag. If you do need to add this type of code to a page that is based on a Template, you need to break the Template by choosing **Modify > Templates > Detach from Template**. This would remove the page's link to the original Template and allow you to edit anything within the <HEAD> element. The downside to this, of course, is that if you made changes to the Template, this unlinked copy would not be able to refer to it.

Library Items in Action

Library Items and Templates are somewhat similar in function. Both are used to apply changes to multiple pages with ease. The difference is that Templates affect the entire page design, while Library Items are used for individual page elements. You are going to start this section by working with an existing Library Item. This will demonstrate just how cool these things are and how much time they can save you!

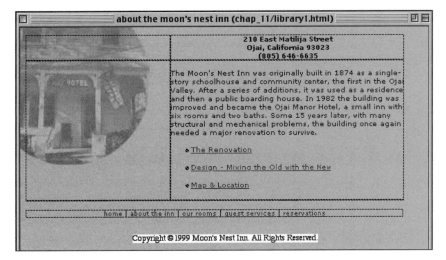

1. Open **library1.html**. At the bottom of this page, you will see a copyright notice that is highlighted in yellow. The yellow highlight is an indication that this text is a Library Item.

---

2. In order to modify the Library Item, you need to open the **Library** palette. Choose **Window > Library (F6)**, if it's not already open with the **Templates** palette. You will see that one Library Item already exists. This is what you will modify.

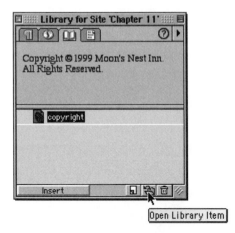

3. Highlight the **copyright Library Item** and click the **Open Library Item** icon in the **Library** palette.

Just as with Templates, it's easy to tell when you are editing Library Items. The title bar displays
<<Library Item>> and the file name with an .lbi extension.

4. Highlight the text "**1999**" and type **2000**. Of course, that is assuming your computer survived the Y2K catastrophe. Yeah right, what catastrophe!? ;-)

5. Close this file. If you are prompted, make sure to save your changes.

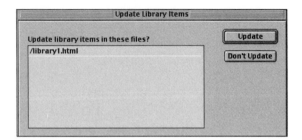

6. When you are asked to update the pages in your site that use this Library Item, click **Yes**. If you get the **Update Library Items** dialog box, click **Update**.

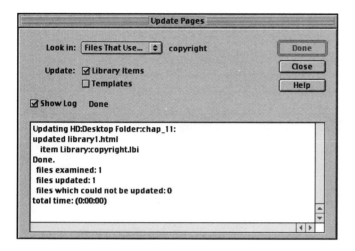

7. The **Update Pages** dialog box will appear. Just like with Templates, this dialog box gives you all the details of how many and which files were updated in your site. Click **Close** when you are finished reviewing this screen.

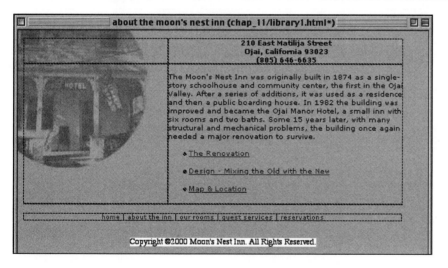

This is what your page should look like with the updated Library Item. Can you imagine how long it would take to update this text on a hundred pages? Library Items can offer incredible time savings.

8. Save your changes and close this file, you will not need it for the next exercise.

5. _____Creating a Library Item

Now that you understand how efficient Library Items can be, it's time to create your own. In this exercise, you will create a text navigation bar. You will then apply it to several pages by simply dragging it onto a page.

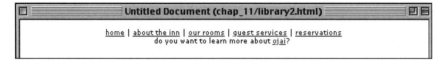

1. Open **library2.html**. This is a just a simple file with text navigation already created.

2. Make sure the **Library** palette is open. If it's not, choose **Window > Library** (**F6**).

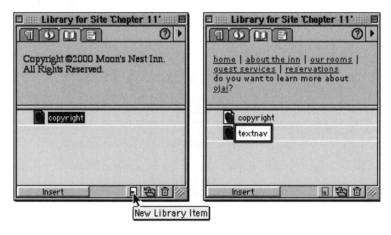

3. In the **library2.html** file, highlight both lines of text. In the **Library** palette, click the **New Library Item** icon. Your new Library Item will instantly appear in the palette. It needs a name, so type **textnav**.

4. Now that you have created your Library Item, you can apply it to a page. Create a new blank document by choosing **File > New**. Then choose **File > Save** and save this file inside the **chap_11** folder as **mypage1.html**.

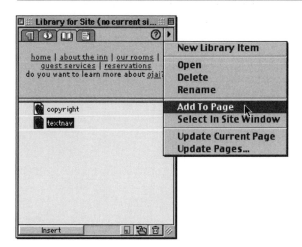

5. In the **Library** palette, highlight the **textnav Library Item** and choose **Add To Page** from the **Library** palette's pop-up menu.

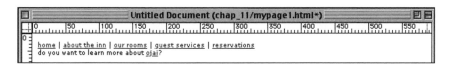

Pow! The Library Item is applied to the page. Notice that it did not retain the center alignment you had applied when it was created. You'll fix that next.

6. Click and drag to select both lines of text and then, in the Properties Inspector, click the **Center Align** button to center align both lines of text.

7. Save **mypage1.html** and leave it open. Leave **library2.html** open as well. You will be working with both files in the next exercise.

_____**Modifying a Library Item**

Now that you know how to create Library Items, you are going to modify the one you just created and then watch Dreamweaver quickly update your page. Can you imagine how joyous you would be if this were a change that needed to be made over hundreds or thousands of pages?

1. With **library2.html** open and **textnav** highlighted in the **Library** palette from the last exercise, click the **Open Library Item** icon. This will open the Library Item for editing.

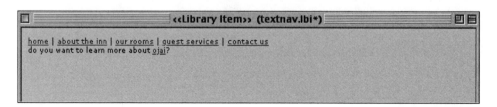

2. Highlight the word "**reservations**" and type **contact us**. This should replace the type but maintain the link.

3. Close this file, and when you are prompted make sure you save and update your changes. If you get the **Update Library Items** dialog box, click **Update**. Close the **Update Pages** dialog box when you are done reviewing it.

Check out what ***mypage1.html*** looks like now with the new Library Item applied to it.

4. Close all documents and save your changes.

You've just conquered making and modifying a Library Item. It's all very simple, once you know how. If you feel up to it, move on to the next chapter. If not, don't worry, it will be there tomorrow ;-).

12.

Frames

| The Pros and Cons of Frames | Saving Frames |
| Coloring Frames | Links and Targets | Adding a Background Image |
| Seamless Background Across Two Frames |
| Frames Objects Palette |

chap_12

Dreamweaver 3
H·O·T CD-ROM

So far in this book, you've learned to insert text, Tables, and images into individual HTML pages. The concept of **Frames** is a little more challenging since, in effect, a Frame is an HTML page inside another HTML page. Why would anyone want to put an HTML page inside another HTML page? So that one part of a page can update independently from another.

Let's say that you've created an image that belonged at the bottom of an HTML page. If your site contained 100 pages, and you wanted to put that same image at the bottom of all of them, you would need to insert that image 100 times into each of those 100 individual pages.

Frames allow you to reuse a single HTML page by nesting it inside another HTML document (otherwise known as a **Frameset**). This would make it possible to author that image at the bottom of an HTML page only once, but allow 100 other pages to load up beside it. If it sounds complex, it is. Frames have a high learning curve, but fortunately this chapter is here to walk you through every step of the way.

What Are Frames?

Lynda's husband Bruce, who also teaches classes at our training center, came up with this wonderful metaphor for teaching Frames. Imagine a TV dinner. You've got your peas and carrots, an entrée and, if you are really lucky, a dessert. Don't forget, though, about the tray that holds all these food items together! A Frameset, if you will, is the TV dinner tray that holds together multiple HTML documents.

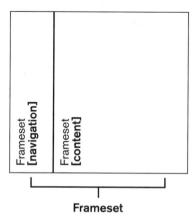

Frameset

If you were to build a Frameset that contained two Frames, a left Frame for your Web navigation element and a right Frame for your content, your audience would see only two Frames. What's hidden is that the audience would be working with three documents – a Frameset (think TV dinner tray) and two Frames (the content HTML page and the navigation HTML page). Every time you come to a page that contains Frames, it always includes a Frameset that holds the Frames in place. If this sounds confusing at all, welcome to Frames! Conceptually, they can be a bit of a brain twister.

We promise that the exercises in this chapter will help you unravel these concepts. You'll learn that Frames are controversial creatures, and that they are either loved or hated by most people. We'll do our best to fill you in on the pros and cons of using Frames, as well as a variety of techniques for using them effectively and creatively. In the end, you will have the honor of deciding if they are right or wrong for your site. Hey, we just teach this stuff!

Frames: A Love-or-Hate Proposition

First, a word from our sponsors (the venerable authors of this book). Frames are controversial — most people either love or hate them. You may want to consider the pros and cons before you use them in your site. Here are two charts to help you if you're weighing the decision to use or not use Frames:

Love Frames	
Pro	**Explanation**
Good Workflow	It's easier to update a single page than hundreds, right? If you put a navigation element (all your links) into a single Frame of a Frameset, and then your site's navigation changes, you only have to update that one page.
Fixed Navigation	The entire page doesn't have to reload each time a link is clicked, only sections of the page. This means that you can anchor a navigation page so it doesn't have to be reloaded with each new page click and always stays consistent throughout your site.
Special Effects	*Frames* let you do cool special effects, such as putting a single background into multiple **Frames** for aesthetic purposes. You'll learn this technique in this very chapter!

Hate Frames	
Con	**Explanation**
Confusing	If not well implemented, **Frames** can create confusing navigation for your audience. However, this chapter will teach you how to implement Frames well, of course!
Printing Hassles	It is not possible to print an entire **Frameset**. That would be like printing three or more HTML pages at once. Your end user can print individual **Frames**, but **Frames** are often transparent to the end user and this can prove challenging. Our suggestion? If you think people are going to print a page from your site, don't put it in a **Frameset**.
Bookmark Hassles	The only part of a framed page that can be bookmarked easily is the **Frameset**. Let's say you have 20 pages that load into a single **Frameset**. If one of your end users wanted to bookmark page 11, he/she would not be able to do so, since only the first page that loads into the **Frameset** could be bookmarked. We have no remedy for this problem, except to say that you should make it very clear how to get to the other 19 pages within that **Frameset**, by adding a simple navigation path on the first page.
Hidden Security Issues	At the **lynda.com** Web site, we once made the mistake of placing a secure order form into an insecure **Frameset**. Some of our customers complained because they couldn't see the lock symbol at the bottom left of their browser that ensures a page is secure. Although the order form page was in fact secure, we eventually took it out of the Frameset so our customers would see the lock symbol and feel more confident buying from us.
Too Boxy!	**Frames** divide an already small amount of screen real estate into smaller regions, which causes a boxy effect. You'll learn how to make **Framesets** without unsightly scrollbars and borders. That will help eliminate the ugly boxy effect.

I. _____Saving Your First Frameset

This chapter is going to build your Frame-making skills gradually. This first exercise will show you how to save a set of Frames properly. Sound simple? Unfortunately, Frames are much harder than anything you've learned so far. By taking you slowly through the process, our hope is that you'll get through these um… interesting hurdles without hitches.

1. Define your site for Chapter 12. Copy **chap_12** to your hard drive and press **F5** to define it. If you need a refresher on this process, revisit Exercise 1 in Chapter 3, *"Site Control."*

2. Start this exercise with a blank Untitled Document. If a blank Untitled Document is not already on your screen, choose **File > New** (Mac) or **File > New Window** (Windows). You may be surprised by the following advice, given our past warnings, but… don't save this just yet because saving now will cause Dreamweaver to believe that this is a single HTML page (which it is not!). You are going to divide this into a Frameset and Frames before you save.

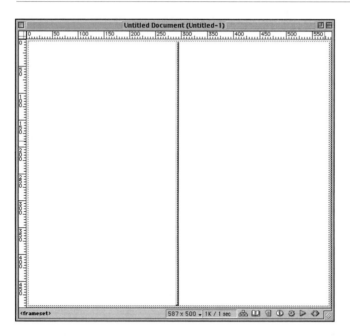

3. Choose **Modify > Frameset > Split Frame Left**. This puts a vertical Frame divider through your page. What's more, it switches you from looking at one page to looking at three: the **Frameset**, the **left Frame**, and the **right Frame**.

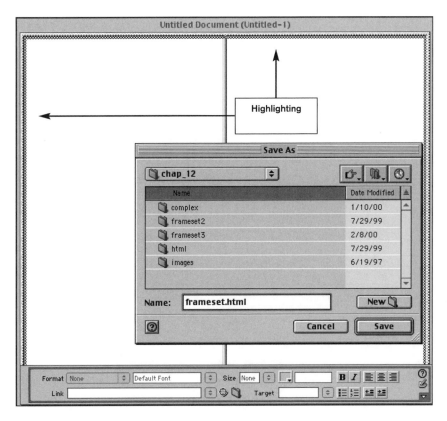

4. Learning to save a Frameset properly is a huge step toward making successful Frames. Choose **File > Save All** and don't click **Save** yet! Notice the highlighting around the periphery of the page? This is the ONLY visual feedback. Dreamweaver will give you that shows you what you are saving. What does that highlighting mean? That you're saving the entire Frameset (remember that good 'ol TV dinner tray metaphor?). Give this file the name **frameset.html**. Save it inside the **chap_12** folder.

Movie | saving_frames.mov

To learn more about saving Frames, check out **saving_frames.mov** located in the **movies** folder on the Dreamweaver 3 **H•O•T CD-ROM**.

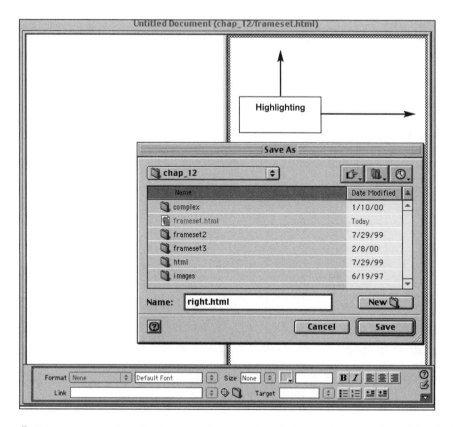

5. Dreamweaver automatically opens the **Save As** window again. Notice how it has highlighted the right Frame? Again, this is the ONLY visual feedback the program gives you to know which file you are about to save. Since it's on the right side, name this file **right.html**. Click **Save** again.

Warning | Saving Frames on the Macintosh

There is a known problem that sometimes occurs when you are saving the files on the Macintosh. The gray border, which indicates the section of the Frameset you are saving, doesn't appear around Frames against the right side of the screen. You should see the screen flash for a bit, the gray border might appear for a split second, then it will disappear. As far as we have determined, this is only a problem on the Macintosh and when you are saving Frames along the right side of the screen. You shouldn't have any problems saving the other sections of your Framesets.

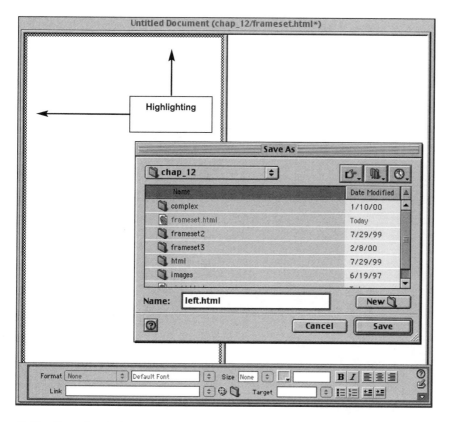

6. The **Save As** window appears once more, with the left side highlighted. This will prompt you again to notice which side you are saving. Since the highlight is on the left side, name this file **left.html**. When you click **Save**, the **Save As** window will disappear and you'll be done.

Note: *If you have any other unsaved documents open besides this Frameset, you will be prompted to save them too. You can click **Cancel** if you don't want to save the other open documents.*

*Even though you just saved this file, notice that it says Untitled Document at the top of the document window? What's up with that? As you learned in Chapter 4, "Basics," you've saved and named the HTML document, but have not assigned the Title yet. In order to assign the Title, follow the exact directions below, because you are juggling three HTML documents and you want to put the Title in the outermost page (**frameset.html**).*

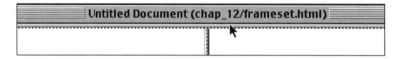

7. Click your mouse exactly where you see the cursor on this screen. This click ensures that Dream-weaver knows you want to access **frameset.html**, and not the **left.html** or **right.html** pages. Choose **Modify > Page Properties…** and give it the Title **My First Frameset**. When you click **OK**, that Unti-tled Document Title should be instantly replaced by your Title.

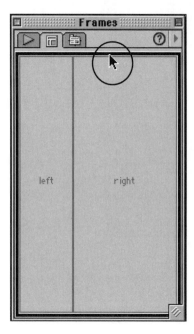

*If you are having trouble selecting **frameset.html** in the document window, you could try clicking on the outermost gray border in the **Frames** palette. It turns black when selected. Watch for the `<frameset>` tag in the **Tag** selector. If it appears, you've selected the Frameset properly.*

8. Choose **File > Save All** again. Notice that you didn't see all three files like you did when you chose **Save All** the first time? That's the way it works – once you define the initial Frameset and Frames, you can perform one simple **Save All** operation and be done. Leave this file open for Exercise 2.

*We personally never use **File > Save** when working with Frames because you can so easily save the wrong page and trip yourself up.*

Different Ways to Save Frames

This exercise taught you to save Frames by choosing **File > Save All**. There are a few different ways to save them besides this, but the way we already showed you is the best because of the visual feedback it offers on which Frame is being saved. All three ways are listed in the handy chart below.

Ways to Save Frames	
Option	**Explanation**
File > Save	To save a document inside a Frame, click the cursor in the Frame and use this method.
File > Save Frameset As **File > Save Frameset**	To save a Frameset file only, you may choose to use either of these methods.
File > Save All	To save all open files at once, use this method.

Note | No Frames!

Frames were introduced with Netscape 2.0 and Explorer 3.0. If anyone accesses your site with an older browser, they won't see your Frame content. Luckily for them and you, there's a way around this, the noframes tag. Whatever is inside this HTML tag is visible to end users who can't see Frames.

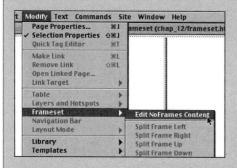

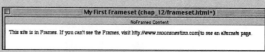

To insert a page into your Frameset that is visible with older browsers, choose **Modify > Frameset > Edit NoFrames Content**. A window will appear, and whatever you type into it will be viewed by end users who ordinarily wouldn't be able to see Frames. Some Web developers create a whole new page for these viewers, while others redirect them to another URL.

```
1    <html>
2    <head>
3    <title>My First Frameset</title>
4    <meta http-equiv="Content-Type" content="text/html; charset=iso-8859-1">
5    </head>
6
7    <frameset cols="301,301">
8      <frame src="left.html">
9      <frame src="right.html">
10   </frameset>
11   <noframes><body bgcolor="#FFFFFF">
12   This site is in Frames. If you can't see the Frames, visit http://www.moonsnestinn.com
13   to see an alternate page.
14   </body></noframes>
15   </html>
```

Here's the HTML for the frameset content. Notice how the noframes tag comes after the frameset tag? Dreamweaver writes the code automatically, and inserts whatever you specify into the HTML.

2. _____Coloring Frames

Creating Frames is challenging because you're manipulating multiple HTML documents in one Dreamweaver window. This exercise teaches you how to color two Frames independently. You'll also learn how to turn off the borders between them, which can help eliminate that boxy appearance that many people don't like about Frames.

1. You should still have **frameset.html** open from the last exercise. Click on the **left Frame** and make sure you see the text-insertion cursor blinking.

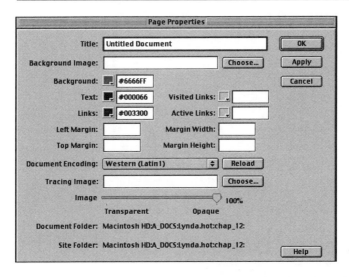

2. Choose **Modify > Page Properties... Cmd+J** (Mac) or **Ctrl+J** (Windows). Make the **Background:** a light blue color, the **Text:** a dark blue, and the **Links:** a dark green. Click **OK**. The left Frame should turn light blue.

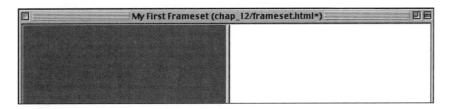

The left Frame should be light blue at this point.

3. In order to change the color for the right side, click in the right Frame and make sure you see the text-insertion cursor blinking. **Choose Modify > Page Properties...** yet again.

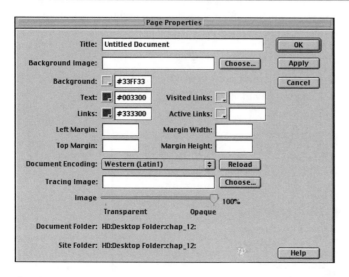

4. Make the **Background:** a light green, the **Text:** a dark green, and the **Links:** a dark yellow. Click **OK**.

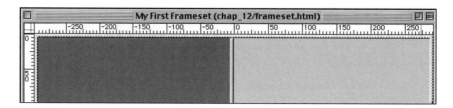

The left side of the document should be blue, and the right side green.

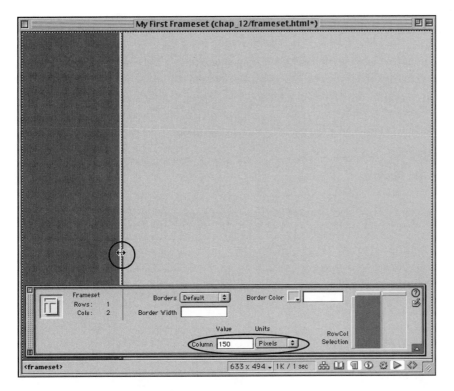

5. Click on the middle dividing **Frame** border and move it over to the left until the Properties Inspector reads **Column: 150 Pixels**. **Tip:** You can enter the value **150** into the **Column** setting instead of dragging, if you prefer. If the Properties Inspector's not visible, go to **Modify > Selection Properties**.

6. I don't know about you, but part of what I do not like about Frames is their boxy appearance. To turn off the border on the Frame divider, select **Borders: No**, and **Border Width: 0** in the Properties Inspector. Now the dividing border should be gone. Choose **File > Save All** and leave this document open for the next exercise.

3. _____Links and Targets

You've gotten through the hardest part of making a Frameset, but there's still more distance to go to the finish. This exercise will show you how to insert a link into the left side page of the Frameset. You've learned about making links, so much of this should be familiar. This exercise introduces a new concept, however – using a "target" – which allows you to specify which Frame the link will trigger in your Frameset. If you're wondering what we mean by that last sentence, read on.

1. Click inside the **left Frame** and make sure you see the blinking text-insertion cursor. Type the words **Our Rooms**.

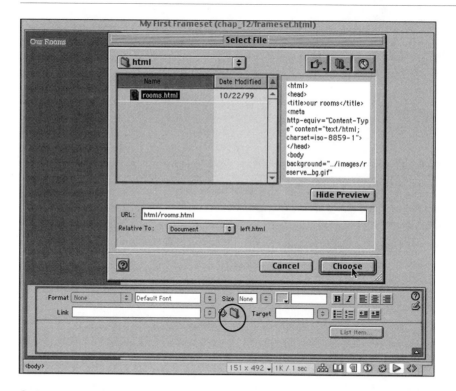

2. Select the words "**Our Rooms**" and click on the folder to the right of **Link** in the Properties Inspector. Browse to the **html** folder inside the **chap_12** folder and select **rooms.html**. Click **Choose**. "**Our Rooms**" should now appear as an underlined link.

3. You can't preview links in Dreamweaver, so press **F12** to preview in your browser. When prompted, click **Save**.

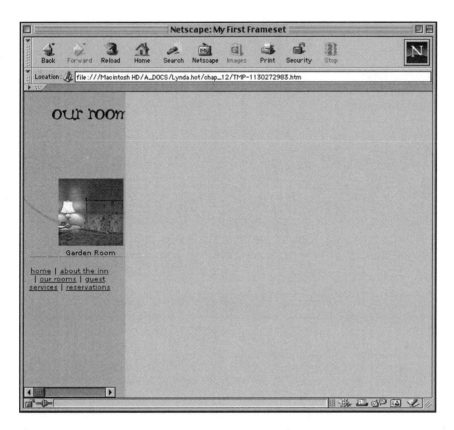

4. Once in the browser, go ahead and click the link "**Our Rooms**." You might be surprised that the "**our rooms**" page appears in the left Frame, the exact Frame where the link was in your Dream-weaver file! Just like in any other Web page, once you click on a link, it's replaced by the new page you just selected. However, in this situation, the narrow left Frame isn't where you want that linked page to appear. The left Frame should remain stationary, and the linked pages should open on the right. The way to make this happen is by setting up a target for the link.

If you'd prefer (as we do) that the link load in the larger right side of the Frameset, you must first name the two Frames. Giving a name to an element in HTML is something you haven't done yet, but you'll see that it is necessary in certain instances throughout the exercises in this book. In this situa-tion, you can't target the right Frame to receive the results of the link without first giving it a name.

*Note: You might be confused by the directive to give the Frame a name, because you've already saved all the documents with file names, **frameset.html**, **left.html**, and **right.html**. You also gave a Title, **My First Frameset**, to the **frameset.html** document. Giving a "name" to an element in HTML, in order to set custom targets in links, is something totally different, however.*

5. Return to Dreamweaver to fix the target problem. Choose **Window > Frames** to bring up the **Frames** palette. Notice that it reads "**(no name)**" on both the right and left sides? Click on the left side and it will become outlined with a dark line, as shown above.

6. The Properties Inspector should now display the setting for the **Frame Name** field. Enter **left**. You could name it anything you want. However, you should name it something meaningful because this name will appear in a menu later on and you'll want to easily remember what it meant.

7. Click on the right side of the Frames palette and look at the Properties Inspector again. This time there is no **Frame Name** because you haven't given the right side of the Frameset a name yet. Enter **right** into the **Frame Name** field. The Frames palette should now read **left** and **right** in faint letters. Leave the Frames palette open as you'll be needing it shortly.

8. Select the words "**Our Rooms**" in the left Frame. Click on the arrow next to the **Target** field to access the pop-up menu. Select **right** from the menu. The word "**right**" should pop into the **Target** field.

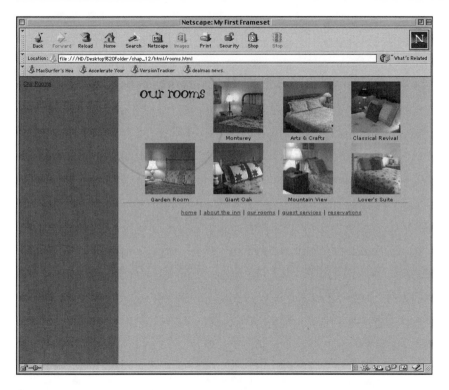

9. Press **F12** to preview the page again. Click on the link. When prompted, click **Save**. This time the results should appear on the right side. You've just set up your first target in your first Frameset. And you're on your way to mastering Frames, which is no small accomplishment!

10. Return to Dreamweaver and keep the files open for the next exercise.

Note | Target Names

A further explanation of **Target Names** is in order, because in the last exercise you used only the **Custom Target** feature.

When you access the pop-up menu for **Target**, you may wonder what do the terms **_blank**, **_parent**, **_self**, and **_top** mean? You created the targets right and left, and those names are in the menu because you added them. The other names, however, are part of the HTML specifications. Below you will find a chart that explains their meanings.

HTML Specifications for Target Names	
Target Name	**Significance**
_blank	Loads the link into a new browser window. This is the target to use if you want to keep someone inside your site, and show them another site at the same time. It opens a new browser window, so that two windows are on the screen at the same time — one containing your site, and the other containing the URL of the site you linked to.
_parent	Used when **Framesets** are nested, to send your end user to the parent of the nested **Framesets**. It's possible to put a **Frameset** inside another **Frameset**, but that's more advanced **Frameset** building than this book will cover. Frankly, we rarely use this target, because we rarely work with nested **Framesets**.
_self	Used when you want the results of the link to load in the same page that the link was in. That's default behavior of HTML anyway, so we never ever use this.
_top	Transports the end user from a **Frameset** to a single HTML page. This breaks the **Frames** and loads all of the results into a single page, in the same window. Use this target when you want to exit a **Frameset**.

Note | To Scroll or Not to Scroll?

We keep harping on the fact that Frames can look boxy, and you've already learned how to remedy this by turning off the Frameset border. What about scrollbars, which can also make a Frameset look boxed in? Scrollbars are necessary if your content is larger than the size of the Frame. You can turn scrollbars off completely or allow them to appear automatically, which is the Dreamweaver default. We suggest you leave the program at its defaults. If the content is big enough to warrant scrollbars, they'll appear.

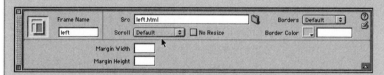

Scrollbars are set in the Properties Inspector.

*To access the Properties Inspector's **Frame Scroll** options, click on the right or left region of the Frames palette. Scrollbars are set independently for each Frame. It is not neccessary to do this at all unless you want to force scrollbars on or off via the **Scroll** option.*

Adding a Background Image

You've learned how to color the background of each Frame, but what about adding a **Background Image**? This is similar to coloring the background of each Frame, which you already did in Exercise 2. There can be unexpected alignment problems with this process, however, if the Frameset clips the Background Image on one of the Frames. In this exercise, you will learn how to set the left Frame to a specific size so that it doesn't cut off the Background Image unexpectedly.

1. Click inside the Frame named **left.html** and make sure you see the text-insertion cursor blinking to the right of the linked words "**Our Rooms**." Choose **Modify > Page Properties....**

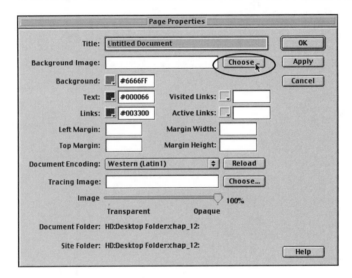

2. Click on the **Choose...** (Mac) or **Browse...** (Windows) button to the right of the **Background Image:** field to browse to the **images** folder, and select **bg_moon.jpg**. Click **Choose**, and then **OK**. The Background Image should appear in the left side of the Frameset.

3. Click inside the Frame named **right.html** and make sure you see the text-insertion cursor blinking, then choose **Modify > Page Properties....**

4. Click on the **Choose...** (Mac) or **Browse...** (Windows) button to the right of the **Background Image:** field to locate once again **bg_moon.jpg** in the **images** folder where you just were. Click **Choose**, and then **OK**. The Background Image should appear in the right side of the Frameset.

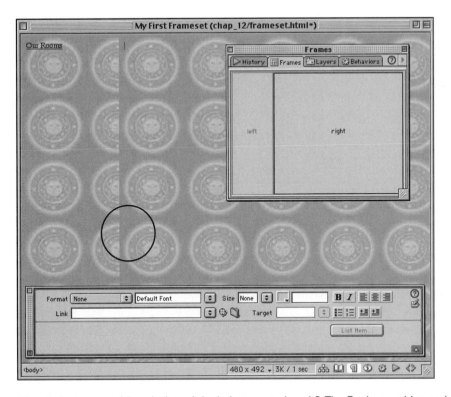

There's just one problem. It doesn't look that great, does it? The Background Image has been clipped by the size of the two Frames. To correct the problem, it's essential to know the dimensions of both the graphic and the Frameset. The following steps walk you through this process.

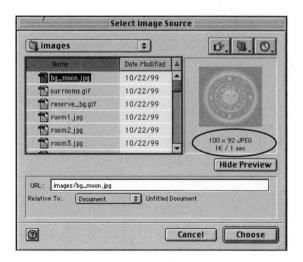

5. To establish the size of the Background Image, click on the **left.html** Frame again and make sure you see the blinking text-insertion cursor. Choose **Modify > Page Properties...** again. Click on the **Choose...** (Mac) or **Browse...** (Windows) button to the right of the **Background Image:** field to locate **bg_moon.jpg**. Notice that the dimensions **100 x 92** appear in the **Select Image Source** window? You now know that the width of the image is 100 pixels. Click **Cancel** twice to return to the document window.

Why Cancel? The sole purpose for doing this step was to read the dimensions of the graphic, not to actually reinsert the Background Image! Often we will insert an image just to learn more about its size or downloading speed, and then cancel out of the process once the information is gathered.

---

*Next, you'll want to make the left column of the Frameset match the column size of that Background Image. Because the Background Image is 100 pixels wide, you could make the **left.html** column 200 pixels wide, and it would tile twice perfectly. Question is, how do you get to the information about what size the left column is? Frankly, it's a bit tricky and takes some clicking around.*

6. In the **Frames** palette (if it's not visible, go to **Window > Frames**), click on the outer border of the palette. Your **Frames** palette might already look like this before you read this step. If so, click on the left side, and then click on the outer border again.

*Sometimes you have to toggle the outer border of the **Frames** palette on and off to get it to show the correct information settings in the Properties Inspector. What's the goal of doing this? Changing your Properties Inspector to show you the Frameset's column size.*

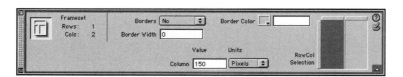

*The goal of clicking on the outer border of the **Frames** palette is to change your Properties Inspector so that it looks like this, which gives you access to the **Column Value**. See the **Column 150** setting? That shows the setting that you created way back in Exercise 2. You'll want to change this to accommodate the size of the Background Image in this exercise. The next steps will walk you through this process.*

 Movie | frames_settings.mov

To learn more about Frames, check out **frames_settings.mov** located in the **movies** folder on the Dreamweaver 3 **H•O•T CD-ROM**.

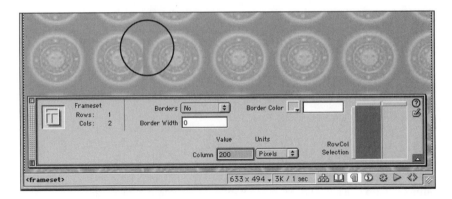

7. Enter the value **Column 200** into the Properties Inspector and press the **Return** or **Enter** key on your keyboard. The left column should have just shifted a bit to the right. Things still don't fit properly because there are more steps to follow.

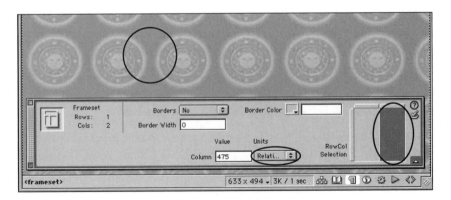

8. In the Properties Inspector, click on the right **Column** icon, at the right of the palette. Select **Units: Relative**. Bingo! The background image now tiles perfectly!

9. Select **File > Save All**. Close the file.

If the directions in Exercise 4 seemed odd and/or mysterious to you, it's because they are a little odd and mysterious! Perhaps this review will help: Clicking on the right side of the Properties Inspector's **Column** icon allowed you to change the settings for the right column. Choosing **Relative Units** makes HTML allocate to the right column whatever space is left over from the fixed-pixel left column. In Exercise 4, you wanted the left side to be fixed, but the right side to scale proportionately depending on how big the end-user's monitor is.

Tip | Specifying a Frame Size

The last exercise showed how to specify the left Frame to be 200 pixels wide. Here are step-by-step directions to access the Frame size settings.

1. Make sure the **Frames** palette is open (**Window > Frames**).

2. Next, click on the outer region of the Frames palette. **Tip:** You might have to click on an inner region and an outer region to jog the Properties Inspec-tor to show the correct setting.

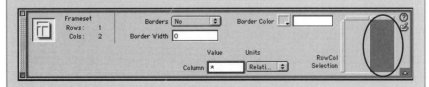

3. Click on the icon to the far right of the Properties Inspector to select the appropriate Frame. In this instance, it's the right one.

4. Enter the **Column Value** of your choice. You can select **Units** of either **Pixels**, **Percent**, or **Relative**. See the chart on the next page for a description of each.

Units

Below is a chart that defines the choices you have when specifying a Frame size in the Properties Inspector:

Frame Size Settings	
Units	**Function**
Pixels	Sets the size of the selected column or row at an absolute value. This option is the best choice for a **Frame** that should always be the same size, such as a navigation bar. If you set one of your **Frame** regions to **Pixels**, then all the other **Frames** will have to yield to that size. In other words, **Pixels** takes priority over all other settings.
Percent	Specifies that the current **Frame** take up a specified percentage of its **Frameset**. This causes **Frames** to dynamically resize according to the width or height the end-user's browser was opened to. If you mix **Pixels** and **Percent**, **Pixels** will be honored first.
Relative	Allocates space after **Frames** with **Units** set to **Pixels** and **Percent**. These **Frames** are designed to take up all the remaining space in the browser window.

Note | Frame Properties

What do the Frame settings mean in the Properties Inspector? On the following page you will find a chart to help you understand them.

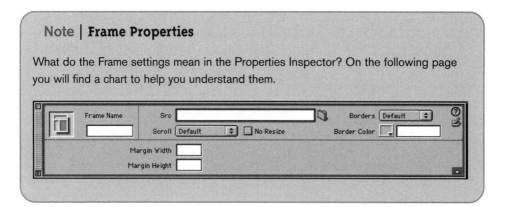

Frame Settings In Dreamweaver	
Setting	**Description**
Frame Name	Sets the name of the current **Frame** so you can use targets (remember _blank, _parent _self, and _top?) when setting up links. This name must be a single word or use underscores (my_name) or hyphens (my-name). Spaces are not allowed.
Src	Sets the source document for each **Frame**. Enter a file name or click the folder icon to browse to and select the file. You can also open a file in a **Frame** by clicking the cursor in the **Frame** inside the **document** window and choosing **File > Open in Frame…**.
Scroll	Determines whether scrollbars appear when there is not enough room to display the content of the current **Frame**. Most browsers default to **Auto**. This is a good thing, because you only want scrollbars if they are necessary. Scrollbars aren't pretty, but they are necessary when there's more content than the **Frameset** column size can display.
No Resize	Prevents a **Frame** from being resizable in browsers. **Tip:** If you turn the borders off in your **Frameset**, end users won't be able to resize them even if the **No Resize** option is left off.
Borders	Controls the border of the current **Frame**. The options are **Yes**, **No**, and **Default**. This choice overrides border settings defined for the **Frameset**. It's important to set the borders to No even if you've set them to **0**, because of differences between Netscape and Explorer. Netscape honors **0**, while Explorer honors **No**.
Border Color	Sets a **Border Color** for all borders adjacent to the current **Frame**. This setting overrides the **Border Color** of the **Framesets**. It's only supported on 4.0+ browsers, so if you choose to use it at all, we don't recommend that you make it an integral part of your design.
Margin Width	Sets in pixels the width of the left and right margins (the space between the **Frame** border and the content). The default is that the **Frame** border and content are aligned, so unless you want an offset, you don't need to adjust this setting.
Margin Height	Sets in pixels the height of the top and bottom margins (the space between the **Frame** border and the content). The default is that the **Frame** border and content are lined up, so unless you want an offset, you don't need to adjust this setting.

5. _____Seamless Background Across Two Frames

In the previous exercise, you learned to put the same background into two Frames and to set a Frameset's column width. Next, you'll repeat that same exercise with different artwork to show you some of the cool effects that you can apply to Framesets.

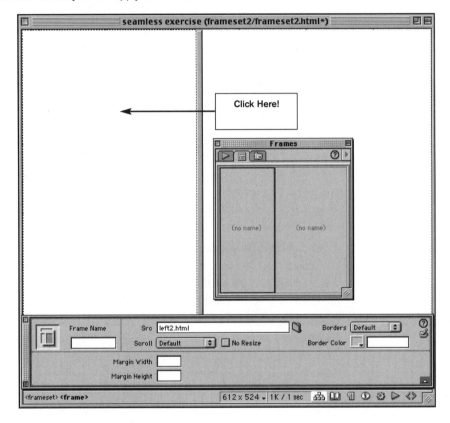

1. Open **frameset2.html** from the **frameset2** folder. This is similar to the document you made before, but a lot of the early steps are already completed. Click on the **left Frame**. Next, choose **Modify > Page Properties....**

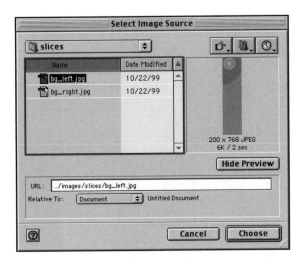

2. Click on the **Choose...** (Mac) or **Browse...** (Windows) button to the right of the **Background Image:** field and browse to the **images** folder and then the **slices** folder. Select **bg_left.jpg**. Notice that the dimensions appear in the **Image Preview** of the **Select Image Source** window and that the width of this image is 200 pixels. Click **Choose**, then **OK**.

---

3. Click on the **right Frame** of the Frameset and choose **Modify > Page Properties...**. Select **bg_right.jpg** (from the **slices** folder you'll find inside the **images** folder) as your Background Image. Notice that the dimensions appear in the **Image Preview** of the **Select Image Source** window and that this image is 824 pixels wide. Click **Choose**, then **OK**

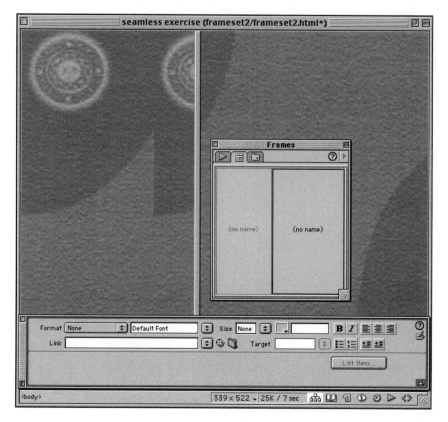

Your screen should look funky because you haven't set the Frameset's dimensions yet.

---

4. Make sure the **Frames** palette is open (**Window > Frames**), and click on the outer region (if you've forgotten how, check Exercise 4, Step 6) to make your Properties Inspector display the Frameset's dimensions. Click on the left side of the **Column** icon and select **Borders: No**. Then enter **Border: Width 0**, **Column Value: 200**, and **Units: Pixels**.

---

5. Next, click on the right side of the **Column** icon, and enter **Units: Relative**. Press **F12** to preview the results. When and if prompted to **Save**, click **OK**.

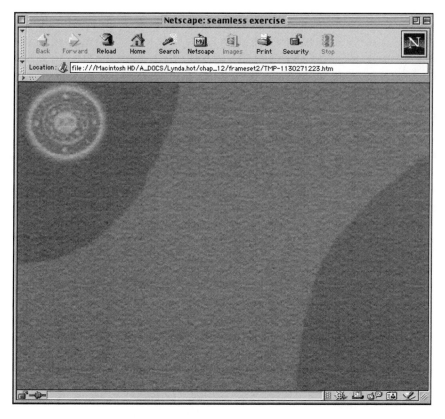

*If your screen looks like this, you did everything right! If it doesn't, go back and reread all the steps (especially the part about setting the right side to **Relative**!) It looks like a single page with a single background, does it not? If your audience hates the way Frames look, they should have no complaints with this little sleight of hand.*

6. _____Frames Objects Palette

The previous examples taught you a lot about the basics of Frames. Now that you have that knowledge under your belt and understand the concepts behind Frames, you will be able to fully understand the power of the **Frames Objects** palette. This new Dreamweaver 3 feature is a huge timesaver and a great way to get your Framesets started. This exercise will show you how to use the Frames Objects palette.

1. Open a new blank document.

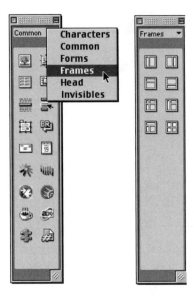

2. Click on the small black arrow at the top of the **Objects** palette. Select **Frames** from the pop-up list. This will change the icons on the Objects palette.

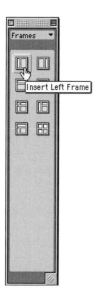

3. Click on the first icon in the top-left column. This will make Dreamweaver create a Frameset similar to the icon.

Note: This step is an alternative method to Step 3 in Exercise 1. You don't have to choose **Modify > Frameset Split Frame** *anymore if you use these handy objects on the Objects palette.*

Tip | **What Does the Blue and White Mean?**

You might have noticed that the icons in the Frames Objects palette are colored in blue and white. This has significant meaning: it tells you how the different areas have been specified with regard to size. The blue areas are set to a relative size, and the white areas have been set to an exact pixel size.

What you spent several steps establishing in Exercise 4 by setting the Frames to be either relative or pixel-based is accomplished automatically by using one of these Frames Objects from the Objects palette. This is a huge improvement in Dreamweaver 3. Don't hate us for making you go through all those steps in Exercise 4 though. As teachers, we decided it was good for your education to appreciate the new Frames features in Dreamweaver by learning how to do it manually and painfully first. Sorry 'bout 'dat, but not really. Just think, "no pain, no gain." ;-)

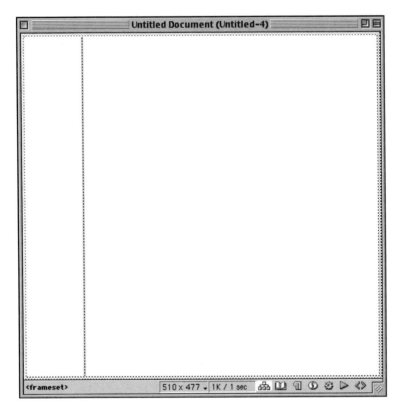

This is what your page should look like at this point. Notice that since these files have not been saved yet, your page remains blank.

---

4. Select **File > Save All** to save each part of your new Frameset. This works just like the procedure you learned in Exercise 1.

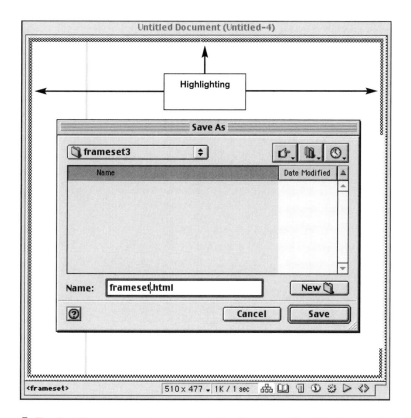

5. The first file you are going to save is the **Frameset** file. This file contains all of the information on how the entire structure of the page is set up. Notice the highlighting around the entire screen? This is the only feedback Dreamweaver offers to let you know you are saving the Frameset. Save this file as **frameset.html** inside the **frameset3** folder.

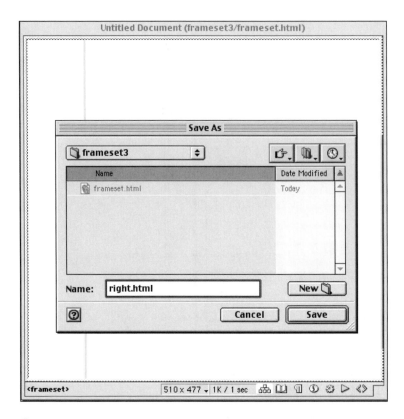

6. The next file you are going to save is the right Frame of your Frameset. Save this file as **right.html** inside the **frameset3** folder. Notice the highlighting on the right of the screen? This is the visual cue to let you know you are saving the right Frame.

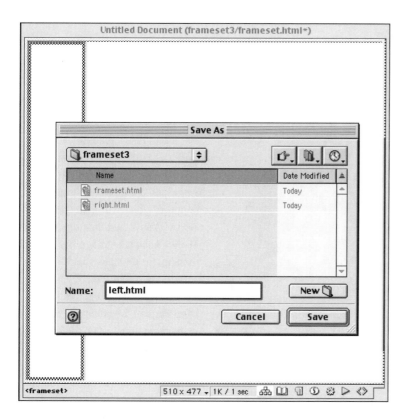

7. The next file you are going to save is the left Frame of your Frameset. Notice the highlighting on the left of your screen? This is the cue that lets you know you're about to save the left Frame of this Frameset. Save this file as **left.html** inside the **frameset3** folder.

8. As you can see, using a Frames Object from the Objects palette is a pretty simple way to create a Frameset. But you still need a working knowledge of Framesets, so that's why we chose to wait until the end of this chapter to show you this option. Now that you know it's here, use it!

9. Close this file. You are done working with it.

Phew, this was a long chapter. Take a quick break, and then it's time to move on to the next chapter.

13.
Rollovers

| Creating a Simple Rollover | Animated Rollovers! |
| Creating Pointer Rollovers | Creating Multiple-Event Rollovers |
| Inserting a Navigation Bar Rollover |
| Inserting a Simple Rollover from Fireworks 3 |

chap_13

Dreamweaver 3
H•O•T CD-ROM

One of the key challenges in Web development is to invent artwork that clearly communicates how to navigate through your site. **Rollover** graphics, which change when the end-user's mouse goes over them, are great for adding visual cues that ensure your audience knows an image has special meaning, for example, that it is a link. Rollovers are also great if you have limited space (which is true of all Web pages!), because you can put extra information within the changing graphic. For example, we could make a button that says "Services," and when a visitor to our site places his or her mouse over the word, it could change to list the services we offer, such as training, consulting, videos, books, lectures, etc.

Rollovers have been used for years in multi-media presentations as an effective device to indicate that an image is a button or is linked to other documents. What you might not realize is that rollovers are a relatively new addition to the Web, because standard HTML doesn't offer this feature. Instead, rollovers are written in a widely used scripting language, invented by Netscape, called JavaScript.

Dreamweaver automatically writes JavaScript rollovers for you without you ever having to write the scripts or even understand how they are constructed. This is great news, because a lot of people, ourselves included, don't know how to write JavaScript from scratch. Alternately, we have trained many developers who do know how to write JavaScript by hand, but enjoy Dreamweaver for its rollover capabilities because it can literally save days of programming work. For this reason, Dreamweaver's rollover features are helpful to both the non-programmer and the programmer.

Rollover Rules

While this book provides many exercises that teach you how to implement rollovers, it is our hope that you'll move beyond the exercises to create your own custom rollover graphics once you get the hang of this feature. If you plan to make your own rollovers from scratch, you should be aware of a few important concepts.

Rollovers require a minimum of two graphics – an "off" state and an "on" state. Because this is a book on Dreamweaver, it doesn't cover how to make the graphic component of rollovers. You would need an imaging program, such as Fireworks, Photoshop, or ImageReady, to make the images.

If you are going to make your own rollover graphics in an image editor, one important rule to understand is that the graphics for the "off" state and "on" state for each of your rollover images must be the same size in dimensions, or you risk that they will look distorted. JavaScript requires **WIDTH** and **HEIGHT** information, which Dreamweaver will add for you automatically. If you have two different-sized pieces of artwork, the JavaScript will scale both to the same width and height, causing distortion. For this reason, all the images that are provided in this chapter's exercises share the same dimensions.

I. _____Creating a Simple Rollover

This first exercise will show you how to create a simple rollover. These types of rollovers involve two pieces of artwork. The first graphic appears on the screen initially, and the second appears when the mouse "rolls over" it. In JavaScript terminology, this is called a swap image. But you will not be writing any JavaScript from scratch, because Dreamweaver makes creating a simple rollover easier than many other operations you've already learned.

1. Define your site for Chapter 13. If you need a refresher on this process, revisit Exercise 1 in Chapter 3, _"Site Control."_

Before the mouse moves over the star in the Web browser.

After the mouse moves over the star in the Web browser.

2. Open **basicrollfinal.html** in the **html** folder. Move your mouse over the star. Nothing happens, right? Press **F12** to preview the page. When you move your mouse over it in your Web browser, it changes to a yellow star. You can only view a rollover inside a browser because Dreamweaver cannot preview such an effect. Return to Dreamweaver and close the file. You'll get to build this same file from scratch in the following steps.

3. Choose **File > New** (Mac) or **File > New Window** (Windows) to create a new Untitled Document. It is always a good practice to save a file before you begin working with it, because Dreamweaver will give you error messages if you don't. Choose **File > Save As...** and name this file **simpleroll.html**. Save it in the **html** folder.

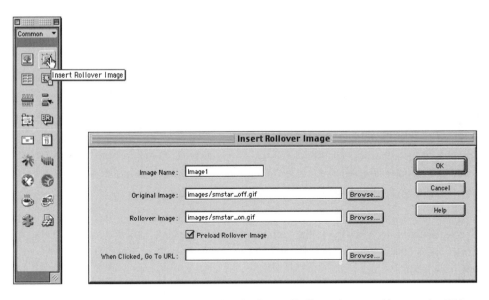

4. Choose **Insert > Rollover Image** or click the **Insert Rollover Image** object on the Objects palette. If the Objects palette is not visible, go to **Window > Objects**.

5. The **Insert Rollover Image** dialog box will appear. For the **Original Image**, click **Browse...** to select **smstar_off.gif** located inside the **images** folder. For the **Rollover Image**, click **Browse...** to select **smstar_on.gif** located inside the same folder. Make sure your dialog box looks just like the one above and click **OK**.

Movie | rollover_list.mov

To see this exercise in action, check out **rollover_list.mov** located in the **movies** folder on the Dreamweaver 3 **H•O•T CD-ROM**.

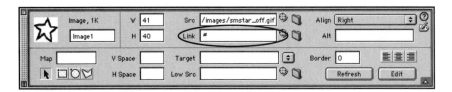

*With the image selected, notice the hash mark (**#**) inside the **Link** area of the Properties Inspector? Dreamweaver inserted this symbol in order to create a link even though you didn't specify one. Why? Because a link is necessary for the JavaScript rollover to work. Putting a hash mark in the **Link** area inserts a stand-in link that doesn't link to anything. It simply acts as a placeholder so that you can still click it and see the rollover.*

6. In the Properties Inspector, click the **folder** icon to the right of the **Link** field, and browse to select **rooms.html** located in the **chap_13** folder. Press **F12** to preview the rollover. Click the star and voilà, **rooms.html** will appear!

7. Return to Dreamweaver and save and close the document.

Note | JavaScript and Java: Separated at Birth?

You might wonder if JavaScript bears any relation to the popular programming language Java, developed by Sun Microsystems. Only in name. Netscape licensed the name from Sun in hopes that the Web community would embrace the scripting language more quickly if it had a recognizable name. Ironically, since then, JavaScript has become more widely embraced than Java, and has taken on a life and following all of its own.

One important distinction between JavaScript and Java is that the code for JavaScript is placed inside your HTML pages, while Java is compiled as a separate program, meaning that you can't see the code for it inside an HTML page. This means that you can see JavaScript code inside HTML documents if you view the source code, while the code within a Java applet is hidden. This has made JavaScript immensely popular among Web authors, as many people were able to teach themselves the language by looking at other people's Web-page source and by copying, pasting, and experimenting.

2. _____Animated Rollovers!

This next exercise uses the same technique as Exercise 1, only instead of two static images, the rollover image is an animated GIF. You'll be putting the rollover graphics inside a table to ensure that they don't move around once they're in place. Working with animated rollovers may look complicated, but it's just as easy as the last exercise you completed.

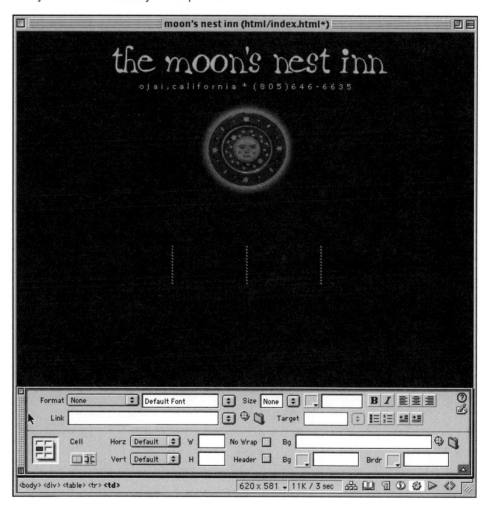

1. Open **index.html** located in the **html** folder. Notice the empty Table where the navigation elements belong? This is where you're going to insert rollovers for each button. Click inside **Cell A** (row 1, column 1) and click the **Insert Rollover Image** object on the **Objects** palette.

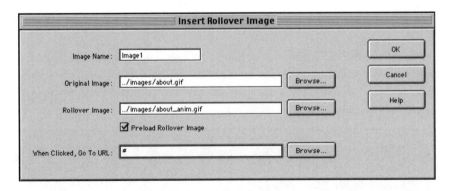

2. The **Insert Rollover Image** dialog box will appear. For the **Original Image**, click **Browse...** to select **about.gif** located in the **images** folder. For the **Rollover Image**, click **Browse...** to select **about_anim.gif** located in the same folder. Click **OK**.

Notice that the Table got all smooshed up after you inserted the image? You'll fix that shortly, so don't worry about it just yet.

 Movie | **smooshed_table.mov**

To see a movie of how to insert these rollovers into the Table, check out **smooshed_table.mov** located in the **movies** folder on the Dreamweaver 3 **H•O•T CD-ROM**.

3. Unfortunately, you can't preview the results of what you just did in Dreamweaver, so press **F12** to view it in a browser. Move your mouse over the **about the inn** image. Notice that the rollover state is an animated GIF? Dreamweaver treats the animated GIF as it would any other GIF, yet the result when previewed in a browser is different than a rollover created from two static GIFs. This technique produces a simple, novel effect.

4. Return to Dreamweaver and click to the right of the **about the inn (about.gif)** graphic to make sure it is deselected. Press **Tab** to insert your cursor in the next cell, which is now scrunched up with the other cells on the right-hand side of the Table.

5. Once your cursor is in **Cell B** (row 1, column 2), click the **Insert Rollover Image** object on the Objects palette. For the **Original Image**, click **Browse...** to select **rooms.gif** located in the **images** folder. For the **Rollover Image**, click **Browse...** to select **rooms_anim.gif** located in the same folder. Click **OK**.

6. Click to the right of the **our rooms (rooms.gif)** image to deselect it. Press **Tab** to insert your cursor in **Cell C** (row 1, column 3), then click the **Insert Rollover Image** object on the Objects palette. For the **Original Image**, click **Browse...** to select **services.gif** located in the **images** folder. For the **Rollover Image**, click **Browse...** to select **services_anim.gif** located in the same folder. Click **OK**.

7. Click to the right of the **guest services (services.gif)** image to deselect it. Press **Tab** to insert your cursor in **Cell D** (row 1, column 4) and click the **Insert Rollover** Image object on the Objects palette. For the **Original Image**, click **Browse...** to select **reservations.gif** located in the **images** folder. For the **Rollover Image**, click **Browse...** to select **reservations_anim.gif** located in the same folder. Click **OK**.

8. Press **F12** to preview the results. We hope you agree that this was simple to execute and impressive upon completion. Return to Dreamweaver, then save and close your document.

Warning | **Animated GIF Rollovers and Preload**

The previous exercise used animated GIF files for one of the rollover states. Dreamweaver regards these files no differently than static GIFs. If you make your own animated GIF files in an image editor and use them in Dreamweaver as rollover states, there's a problem that we would like to warn you about.

Insert Rollover Image		
Image Name :	Image1	
Original Image :	file :///HD/Desktop Folder /DW2 x files/chap_11 /	Browse...
Rollover Image :	file :///HD/Desktop Folder /DW2 x files/chap_11 /	Browse...
☑ Preload Rollover Image		
When Clicked , Go To URL :		Browse...

Notice that Dreamweaver automatically checks the **Preload Rollover Image** checkbox in the **Insert Rollover Image** dialog box? What does that mean, exactly? The browser is being instructed to wait until all the graphics for the rollover have been downloaded before the rollover functions.

Animated GIFs can be set to play once, any number of times (2x, 3x, etc.) or loop indefinitely. If when you create your animated GIF files you set them to loop indefinitely, then leaving the Preload Rollover Image box checked will work just fine, as it did here. However, if you have your animated GIF play only one time, it will play when it's preloaded and by the time your end user looks at your rollover it will no longer animate! The rule of thumb is this: leave Preload Rollover Image on for looping GIFs, and uncheck Preload Rollover Image if your GIF is set to play only one time.

3. _____Creating Pointer Rollovers

This next exercise shows you how to create pointer rollovers. Pointer rollovers reuse one piece of artwork (in this example, the star) which follows the mouse as you move over each word. This type of rollover involves making a Table to hold all the artwork in place. You'll also get to use the **Behaviors** feature, instead of the **Insert Rollover Image** object from the Objects palette. Are you feeling macho, or what?

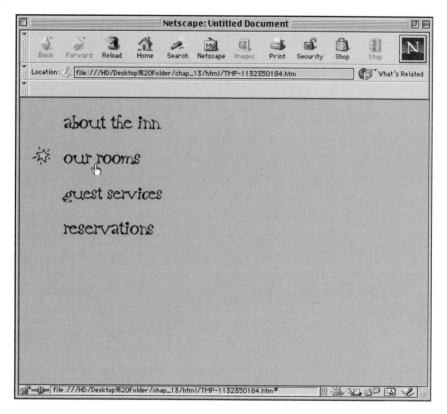

1. View the finished file first. Open **pointerfinal.html** located in the **html** folder and press **F12** to preview it inside a browser. Return to Dreamweaver and close the file. You're going to re-create it from scratch.

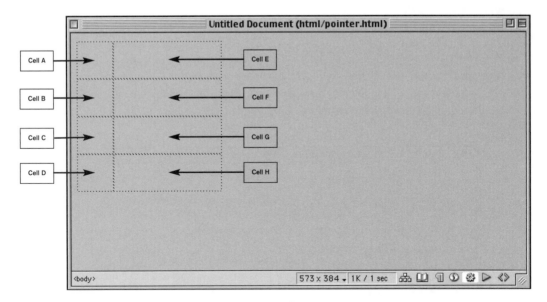

2. Open **pointer.html** in the **html** folder, which already contains an empty Table with four rows and two columns. You could have created this Table from scratch, but we just wanted to help you get to programming the rollovers faster.

3. Click inside **Cell A** and choose **Insert > Image**. Select **blank_p.gif** from the **images** folder, then click **Choose**. The object of the first part of this exercise is to insert the same **blank_p.gif** image in every location that the pointer will appear. Why? Because rollovers require two images, the original state and the rollover state. In this instance, the original state looks like nothing, because it is a transparent GIF, which lets the background color show through.

4. Repeat this process three times, inserting the same **blank_p.gif** file inside **Cells B**, **C**, and **D**.

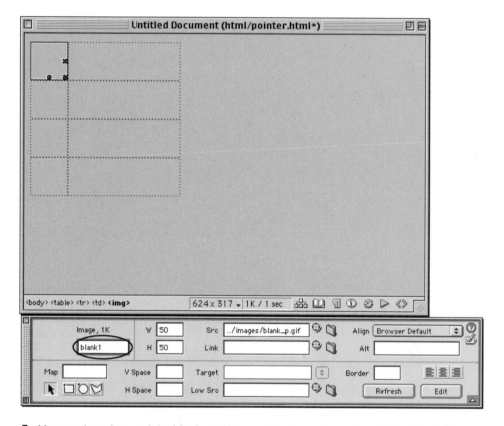

5. After you have inserted the **blank_p.gif** image into these four cells, click inside **Cell A**, as shown above. Inside the Properties Inspector, give it the name **blank1**. It is essential that you assign a unique name to each image by selecting each instance of **blank_p.gif** and naming it respectively **blank1**, **blank2**, **blank3**, **blank4**. Make sure to highlight the appropriate **blank_p.gif** image when naming each graphic.

*Note: In Exercise 1, Dreamweaver gave the rollovers names automatically. When you use the **Swap Image Behavior**, you have to manually give each image a unique name, or the Behavior will not work. Be aware that names in Dreamweaver (or HTML) cannot contain any spaces.*

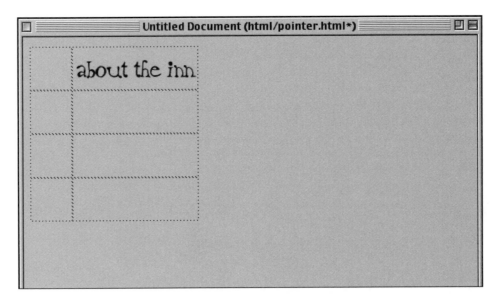

6. Click **Cell E** and choose **Insert > Image**, then browse to **about_p.gif** located in the **images** folder and click **Choose**.

7. With **about_p.gif** selected, enter the name **about** inside the Properties Inspector.

Note: Naming each image is essential to working with rollovers in Dreamweaver. This is because JavaScript requires a unique name for each source graphic in order to perform rollover functions. For this reason, you will need to add a unique name for every image that you insert into this Table.

8. Click **Cell F** and choose **Insert > Image**, then browse to **ourrooms_p.gif** located in the **images** folder and click **Choose**.

9. While **ourrooms_p.gif** is selected, enter the name **rooms** inside the Properties Inspector.

10. Click **Cell G** and choose **Insert > Image**, then browse to **reservations_p.gif** located in the **images** folder and click **Choose**.

---

11. While **reservations_p.gif** is selected, enter the name **reservations** inside the Properties Inspector.

---

12. Click **Cell H** and choose **Insert > Image**, then browse to **services_p.gif** located in the **images** folder and click **Choose**.

---

13. While **services_p.gif** is selected, enter the name **services** inside the Properties Inspector.

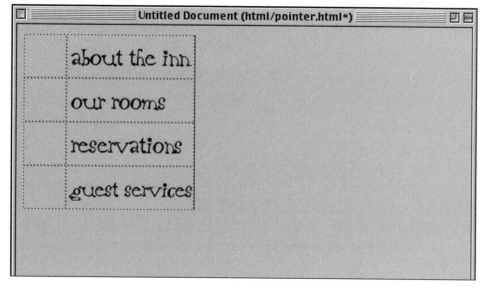

*This is what **pointer.html** should look like at this point in the exercise.*

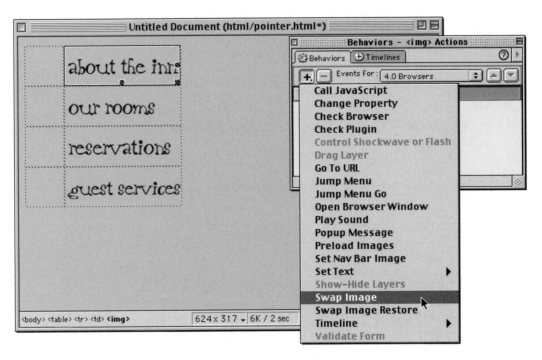

14. Click **about_p.gif** (**about the inn**) to select it. Open the **Behaviors** palette (if it isn't already open) by selecting **Window > Behaviors** or using the shortcut key (**F8**).

15. With **about_p.gif** (**about the inn**) selected, click the plus sign above the **Events** column and select **Swap Image** from the pop-up menu.

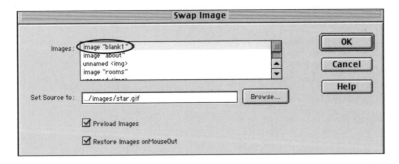

16. In the **Swap Image** dialog box that will open, make sure the "**blank1**" image name is highlighted at the top. Click **Browse...** and select **star.gif** located in the **images** folder. Click **Choose**. Back in the **Swap Image** dialog box, click **OK**.

17. Next, select **ourrooms_p.gif (our rooms)** and click the **plus** sign, in the Behaviors palette, to select **Swap Image**. Select image "**blank2**" from the **Images:** list and click **Browse...** to locate **star.gif**. Click **Choose**. Back in the **Swap Image** dialog box, click **OK**.

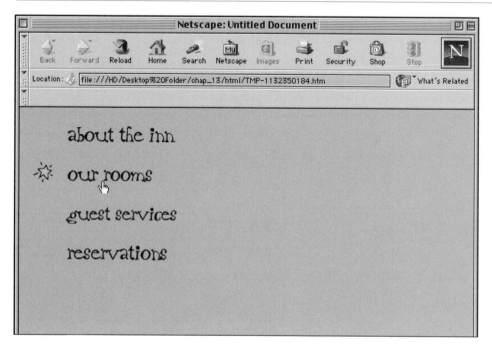

18. Repeat this process for **reservations_p.gif**, selecting image "**blank3**," and **services_p.gif**, selecting image "**blank4**."

19. Press **F12** to preview in your browser. What you see should look just like the **pointerfinal.html** document you opened and previewed at the beginning of this exercise. To make yourself feel really good, return to Dreamweaver and press **F10** to view the code. Hey, you didn't have to write any of that! Press **F10** to close the **HTML** palette. Save and close the file, to move on to the next exercise.

This exercise demonstrated the benefit of using a Table to hold together multiple graphics. It also reinforced the fact that you need two images for a rollover – the original state and the rollover state. In this instance, the original was a blank image. When you program rollovers from the Behaviors palette, you also must give them a name, which you did several times in this exercise!

4. _____Creating Multiple-Event Rollovers

A multiple-event rollover uses more than two pieces of artwork in the Swap Image Behavior. In this example, three different pieces of artwork change for every rollover. If that sounds complicated, it is! Assembling this type of rollover can be tedious, but not nearly as tedious as writing all the HTML and JavaScript from scratch.

1. Open **multiple_final.html** located in the **html** folder, and preview this finished exercise in your browser. Roll your mouse over each item in the list and watch the rooms change. This is a very impressive type of rollover, and you (yes you!) are going to know how to do it as soon as you follow along. Close this file.

 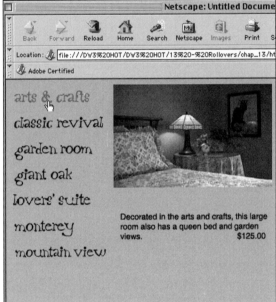

The image on the left shows the page before the rollover. The image to the right shows the page when the mouse rolls over a name on the list, the name turns red and a photograph and description appear at the same time.

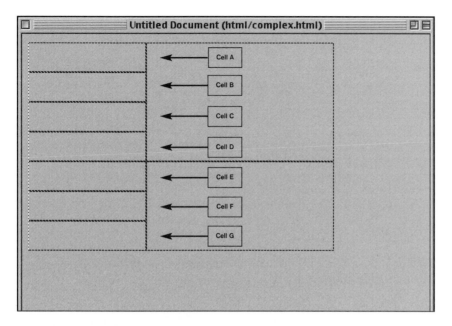

2. Open **complex.html** located in the **html** folder. Because this chapter covers rollovers, not Tables, we figured we'd, again, provide you with a Table. You learned to make a Table like this in Chapter 9, *"Tables."*

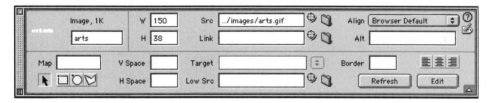

3. Click inside **Cell A** (row 1, column 1) and choose **Insert > Image** to browse to **arts.gif** located in the **images** folder, then click **Choose**. In the Properties Inspector, name the image **arts**.

4. Click inside **Cell B** (row 2, column 1) and choose **Insert > Image** to browse to **classic.gif** located in the **images** folder, then click **Choose**. In the Properties Inspector, name the image **classic**.

5. Click inside **Cell C** (row 3, column 1) and choose **Insert > Image** to browse to **garden.gif** located in the **images** folder, then click **Choose**. In the Properties Inspector, name the image **garden**.

6. Click inside **Cell D** (row 4, column 1) and choose **Insert > Image** to browse to **giant.gif** located in the **images** folder, then click **Choose**. In the Properties Inspector, name the image **giant**.

7. Click inside **Cell E** (row 5, column 1) and choose **Insert > Image** to browse to **lovers.gif** located in the **images** folder, then click **Choose**. In the Properties Inspector, name the image **lovers**.

8. Click inside **Cell F** (row 6, column 1) and choose **Insert > Image** to browse to **monterey.gif** located in the **images** folder, then click **Choose**. In the Properties Inspector, name the image **monterey**.

9. Click inside **Cell G** (row 7, column 1) and choose **Insert > Image** to browse to **mountain.gif** located in the **images** folder, then click **Choose**. In the Properties Inspector, name the image **mountain**.

10. Click in the **top cell** (row 1, column 2) and choose **Insert > Image** to browse to **blank1.gif** located in the **images** folder, then click **Choose**. In the Properties Inspector, name the image **blank1**.

11. Click in the **bottom cell** (row 2, column 2) and choose **Insert > Image** to browse to **blank2.gif** located in the **images** folder, then click **Choose**. In the Properties Inspector, name the image **blank2**.

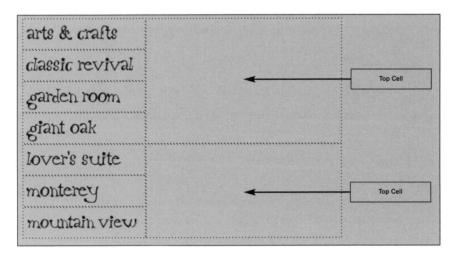

This is what your page should look like now.

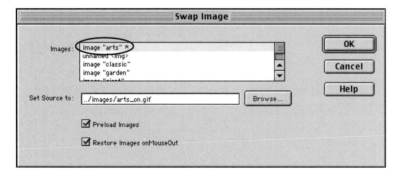

12. Select the image in **Cell A** (row 1, column 1). With the image selected, click the plus sign in the **Behaviors** palette to select **Swap Image**. If the **Behaviors** palette is not open, press **F8** to open it. In the **Swap Image** dialog box that will open, notice that "**arts**" is selected in the **Images:** list. Be sure not to click **OK** until we say so.

13. Click **Browse...** to **Set Source to: arts_on.gif**, then click **Choose**. This sets the rollover for the graphic **arts & crafts (arts.gif)** to turn red when you move your mouse over it. Don't click **OK** yet!

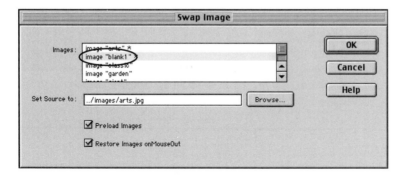

14. Select "**blank1**" from the same **Images:** list. Click **Browse...** again to **Set Source to: arts.jpg**, then click **Choose**. You just instructed the Behavior to swap the **blank1 (blank1.gif)** artwork to the picture of the **arts & crafts hotel room (arts.jpg)**. Don't click **OK** yet!

*The rollover now triggers two Behaviors: the lettering for **arts & crafts** has been instructed to turn red, and an image of the room will appear when the mouse moves over the original image.*

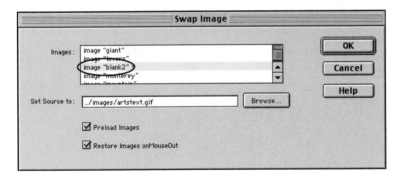

15. Scroll down the **Images:** list to select "**blank2**". Click **Browse...** again to **Set Source** to: **arts-text.gif**, then click **Choose**. You may now finally click **OK** to end this process.

16. Press **F12** and test your first rollover! Move your mouse over the words "**arts & crafts.**" The lettering should turn red and a picture of the room should appear to the upper right, with its description below. You've just set the rollover for **arts & crafts.**

There are only six more items on the list to go.

 Movie | **swap_image.mov**

This isn't the most intuitive operation in the universe, so don't kick yourself if you don't get it right the first time. If it didn't work, please view the movie **swap_image.mov**, located in the **movies** folder on the Dreamweaver 3 **H•O•T CD-ROM**.

Swap Image At A Glance		
Cell	**Images**	**Set Source To**
B (row 2, column 1)	classic.gif	classic_on.gif
	blank1	classic.jpg
	blank2	classictext.gif
C (row 3, column 1)	garden.gif	garden_on.gif
	blank1	garden.jpg
	blank2	gardentext.gif
D (row 4, column 1)	giant.gif	giant_on.gif
	blank1	giant.jpg
	blank2	gianttext.gif
E (row 5, column 1)	lovers.gif	lovers_on.gif
	blank1	lovers.jpg
	blank2	loverstext.gif
F (row 6, column 1)	monterey.gif	monterey_on.gif
	blank1	monterey.jpg
	blank2	montereytext.gif
G (row 7, column 1)	mountain.gif	mountain_on.gif
	blank1	mountain.jpg
	blank2	mountaintext.gif

17. Return to Dreamweaver and repeat this process for the other images. Start by selecting the image in **Cell B** and clicking the plus sign in the **Behaviors** palette, to select **Swap Image**. When you're done, press **F12** to preview your work in a browser, then close the file and move on to the next exercise. The chart above shows which files go where.

5. _____**Inserting a Navigation Bar Rollover**

So far, you have created simple rollovers, animated rollovers, and multiple-event rollovers. You have one more to create before you finish this chapter – the Navigation Bar rollover. This is a new type of rollover that Dreamweaver allows you to make with little programming effort. A navigation bar-style rollover allows each button to display four **states: up**, **over**, **down**, and **over while down**. Instead of working with two images for each rollover, this type of rollover requires that you work with four, one for each separate state. This might sound intimidating, but Dreamweaver's new **Insert Navigation Bar** feature makes it much easier than you might imagine.

1. To view a sample of what you are about to create, open **navbar_final.html** located in the **html** folder. Press **F12** to preview this page in a browser. Move your mouse over the images and click a few as well. Notice there are more than two rollover states? This is what you'll learn to build in this exercise. Pretty neat-o!

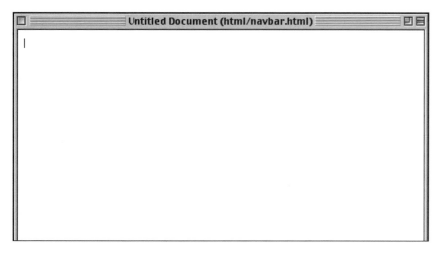

2. Return to Dreamweaver. Close **navbar_final.html** and open **navbar.html** located in the **html** folder. This is simply a blank file that has been saved for you already. You are going to use it as a starting point to create your own navigation bar.

3. Click the **Insert Navigation Bar** object in the Objects palette. As an alternative, you could select **Insert > Navigation Bar**. Either way is fine and will open the **Insert Navigation Bar** dialog box (and a big dialog box it is at that!).

Different Rollover States

Keeping track of the different types of rollover states can be a little tricky. Heck, we have a hard enough time keeping track of our car keys, not to mention rollover states. So, we have included the chart below to help you with this task:

Rollover States	
State	**What It Does**
Up	The graphic that appears on the Web page when it is loaded. This is also referred to as the "static" or "off" state.
Over	The graphic that appears when the end-user's mouse moves over the image. Most often, this image will revert back to the **Up** state when the mouse is moved off of the image. This is sometimes referred to as the "on" state.
Down	The graphic that will appear after the end user has clicked on the **Over** state. This state will not change again until the end-user's mouse moves over this image or clicks on another image.
Over While Down	Not used very often, this appears when the end-user's mouse moves over the **Down** state. It works just like the **Over** state, except that it works on the **Down** state only.

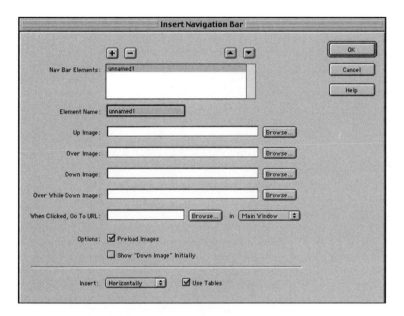

This is what the **Insert Navigation Bar** dialog box looks like by default.

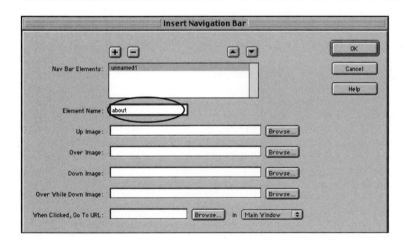

4. Enter **Element Name: about**. This assigns a name to the first rollover image in this navigation bar. Each element (rollover) must have a unique name. We suggest you name them in relationship to their function on the page. The first button will access the **About the Inn** page, so you will name this first element **about**.

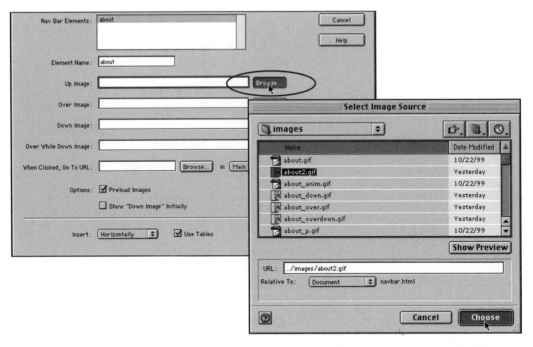

5. Click **Browse...** next to **Up Image:**. Browse to the **images** folder and select **about2.gif**. Click **Choose** to select this image. You've just specified the image for the Up state of the rollover.

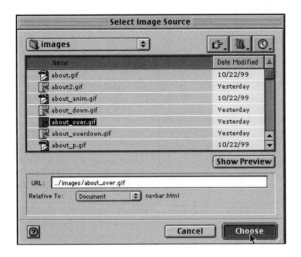

6. Click **Browse...** next to **Over Image:**. Browse to the **images** folder and select **about_over.gif**. Click **Choose** to select this image. You've just specified the image for the Over state of the rollover.

7. Click **Browse…** next to **Down Image:**. Browse to the **images** folder and select **about_down.gif**. Click **Choose** to select this image. You've just specified the image for the Down state of the rollover.

8. Click **Browse…** next to **Over While Down Image:**. Browse to the **images** folder and select **about_overdown.gif**. Click **Choose** to select this image. You've just specified the image for the Over While Down state of the rollover.

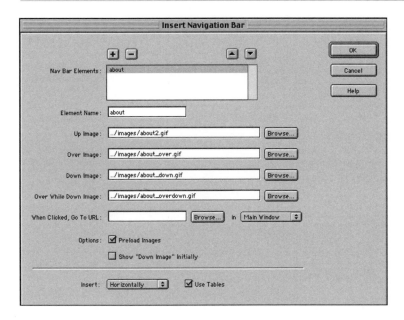

This is what your screen should look like at this point in the exercise.

Now that you have added the first rollover button in your navigation, it's time to add the next one. By the end of this exercise, this will all be second nature to you!

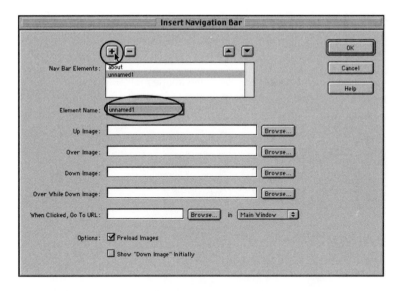

9. Click the plus sign at the top of the dialog box. You will see that a new unnamed element is added. This will let you add the second rollover image to the navigation bar.

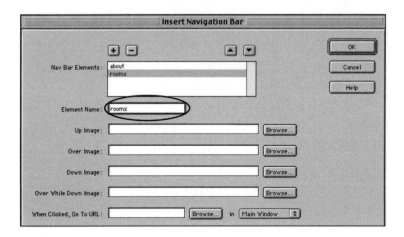

10. Enter **Element Name: rooms**. This will assign a name to the second rollover image in this navigation bar. Remember, each element must have a unique name.

11. Click **Browse...** next to **Up Image:**. Browse to the **images** folder and select **rooms2.gif**. Click **Choose** to select this image. This option lets you specify the image for the **Up** state of the rollover for the second element in the navigation bar.

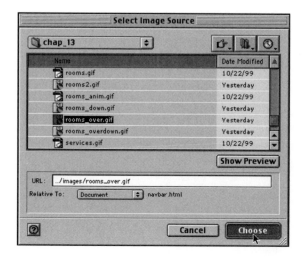

12. Click **Browse...** next to **Over Image:**. Browse to the **images** folder and select **rooms_over.gif**. Click **Choose** to select this image. This option lets you specify the Over state of the second rollover.

13. Click **Browse...** next to **Down Image:**. Browse to the **images** folder and select **rooms_down.gif**. Click **Choose** to select this image. This option lets you specify the Down state of the second rollover.

14. Click **Browse...** next to **Over While Down Image:**. Browse to the **images** folder and select **rooms_overdown.gif**. Click **Choose** to select this image. This option lets you specify the Over While Down state of the second rollover.

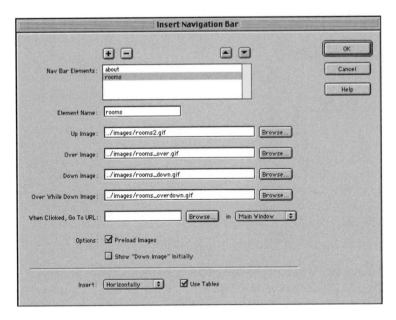

This is what your dialog box should look like with the second rollover settings.

Adding Elements to the Navigation Bar

Element	State	File
guest	Up	guest2.gif
	Over	guest_over.gif
	Down	guest_down.gif
	Over While Down	guest_overdown.gif
reserve	Up	reserve2.gif
	Over	reserve_over.gif
	Down	reserve_down.gif
	Over While Down	reserve_overdown.gif

15. Now that you know how to add new elements to the navigation bar, go ahead and add two more 4-state buttons, using the chart above.

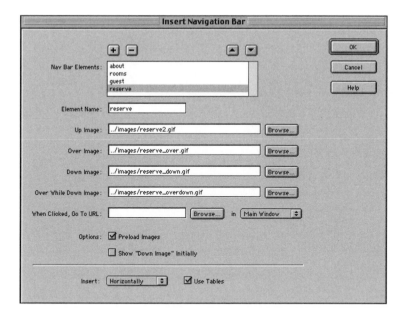

This is what the dialog box should look like when you are finished.

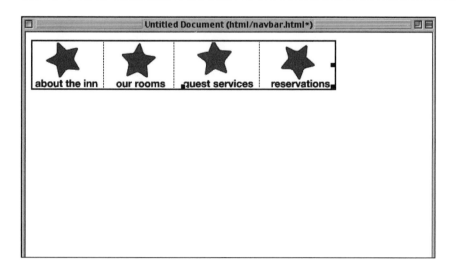

16. After you have added the fourth element, click **OK**. Dreamweaver will automatically create a Table, insert the images you specified, and create all of the complex JavaScript necessary for the rollovers to function. It does all of this in about two seconds. We dare any JavaScript programmer to compete with this time!

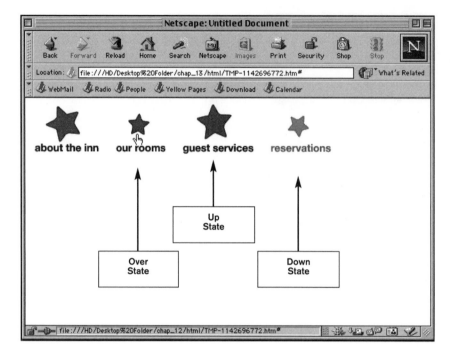

Here you can see three of the four possible states in the Navigation Bar. If you move your mouse over the Down state, you will see the fourth.

---

17. Go ahead and press **F12** to preview your navigation bar in a browser. Make sure you roll over each of the images, click them, and then roll over them again to see the four different states of each.

---

18. Return to Dreamweaver. Save and close the file.

---

6. _____**Inserting a Simple Rollover from Fireworks**

Like peanut butter and jelly, Dreamweaver and Fireworks were made to go together. But once you've created your rollovers in Fireworks, how in the heck do you get them into Dreamweaver and still have them work? Until now, this drove a lot of people crazy. Have you ever tried to copy and paste your rollovers from Fireworks into Dreamweaver, only to end up with a bunch of broken images and Java-Script? This exercise is going to introduce you to another new feature in Dreamweaver 3, that makes importing Fireworks HTML files as easy as clicking a button.

*Note: You do not need to have Fireworks 3 installed to complete this exercise. We have included the **exported Fireworks HTML** file on the **H•O•T CD-ROM**.*

> **1.** Open **fw_simple.html** located in the **html** folder of **chap_13**. This is simply a blank file that we created for you.

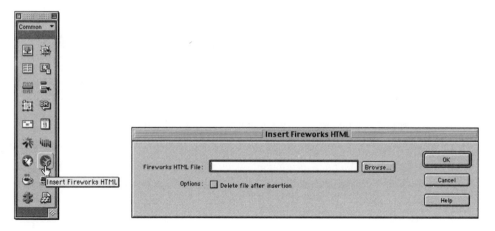

> **2.** Click the **Insert Fireworks HTML** object in the **Objects** palette. This will open the **Insert Fireworks HTML** dialog box.

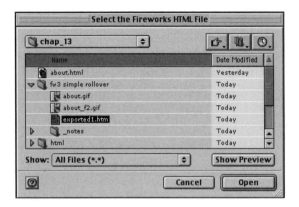

3. Click **Browse...** to select **exported1.htm** located in the **fw3 simple rollover** folder. Click **Choose**.

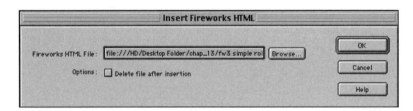

4. You'll be returned to the **Insert Fireworks HTML** dialog box. Click **OK**.

*Note: If you check the **Delete file after insertion** checkbox, the original HTML file that you selected will be deleted after it is inserted into your document. We recommend that you don't delete the file unless you are sure you don't want to import it into another page.*

Note | **Import from Outside Your Local Root Folder**

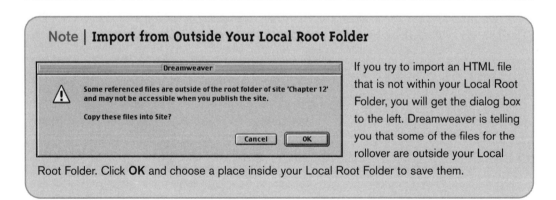

If you try to import an HTML file that is not within your Local Root Folder, you will get the dialog box to the left. Dreamweaver is telling you that some of the files for the rollover are outside your Local Root Folder. Click **OK** and choose a place inside your Local Root Folder to save them.

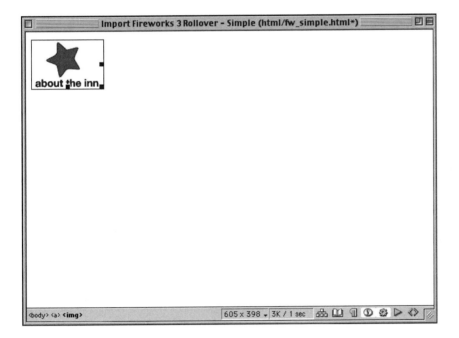

This is what your page should look like now.

---

5. Press **F12** to test your rollover. With the click of a few buttons, Dreamweaver imported the images, Table, and JavaScript.

---

6. Save and close the file.

That's all there is to it. If you haven't used previous versions of Dreamweaver, this feature may not impress you that much. But for us old-timers who had to struggle through the toils of copying and pasting images and JavaScript from Fireworks files, this is HUGE.

Wow, another chapter under your belt, congratulations. We know it was a lot of hard work, but you are well on your way to becoming a Dreamweaver expert.

I4.

Automation

| Using the History Palette for Undo/Redo |
| Copying and Pasting History |
| Applying HTML Styles |
| Creating Custom Keyboard Shortcuts |

chap_14

Dreamweaver 3
H·O·T CD-ROM

Web design and development seem to require an abundance of incredibly repetitive and boring tasks. Fortunately, Dreamweaver 3 has introduced a number of new features that can memorize certain actions and replay them in an automated fashion.

One such new feature is the **History** palette, which displays a list of all the steps you performed since you created or opened a file. This allows you to undo steps in a linear fashion and gives you more feedback about what stages a document went through during its development.

Another new feature is HTML Styles, which enables Dreamweaver to memorize HTML settings and apply multiple settings with a single click of a mouse. This is incredibly useful for automating the formatting of a document, since you won't need to keep setting the same HTML properties over and over and over.

Another new timesaver is the ability to customize keyboard shortcuts. While Dreamweaver ships with a default setup of menus, toolbars, etc., how many times have you wished there was a keyboard shortcut for a feature you use regularly? Good news! Now you can customize your keyboard shortcuts to save time.

This chapter will teach you how to use the **History** palette to **Undo/Redo** and to copy and paste information into other Documents. It will also show you how to create and modify HTML Styles and how to create your own custom keyboard shortcuts.

I. ———————————Using the History Palette for Undo/Redo

This first exercise will get you comfortable working with the **History** palette. You will learn how to use this palette to undo and redo functions. This method can be much easier than choosing **Undo** and/or **Redo** multiple times. Think of the History palette as the Undo and Redo commands on steroids.

1. Copy **chap_14** to your hard drive. Define your site for Chapter 14 using the **chap_14** folder as the Local Root Folder. If you need a refresher on this process, visit Exercise 1 in Chapter 3, "*Site Control.*"

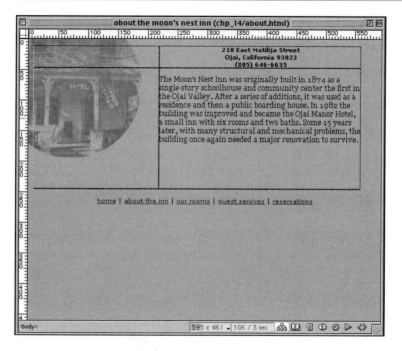

2. Open **about.html**. The large block of text in the middle of the screen would be easier to read in a different font, so you will change it.

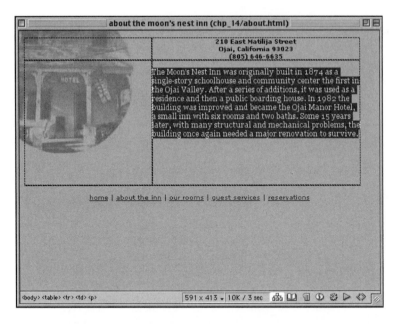

3. Click and drag so that the entire paragraph of text is highlighted.

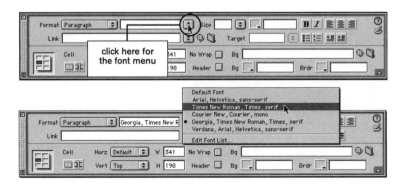

4. In the Properties Inspector, click the font pop-up menu and select **Times New Roman, Times, serif**. This will change the font that is used to display this text.

5. Make sure your **History** palette is open. If it is not, choose **Window > History** (**F9**).

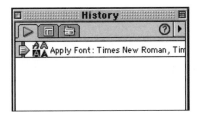

The History palette is displaying the change you made to the block of text in Step 4. As you continue to make additions/changes to your document, your steps will be displayed here.

6. With the block of text still selected, change the font to **Verdana, Arial, Helvetica, sans-serif**. Notice how the History palette recorded this step as well.

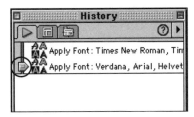

7. In the **History** palette, click and drag the **History Slider** up so that the first step is highlighted. This will undo the last formatting you applied to the text, working the same as the **Undo** command. Click and drag the **History Slider** down to the bottom of the list to reapply the text formatting.

*This is a nice way to step through the changes you have made to your document. It beats having to press **Cmd+Z** (Mac) or **Ctrl+Z** (Windows) because it gives you feedback about what change you are undoing.*

Note | The History Slider

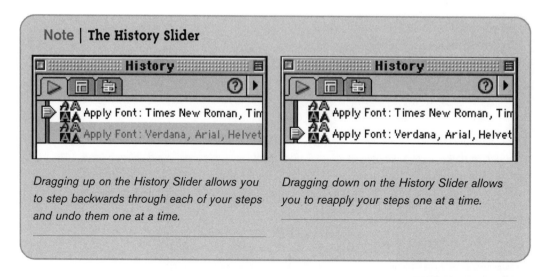

Dragging up on the History Slider allows you to step backwards through each of your steps and undo them one at a time.

Dragging down on the History Slider allows you to reapply your steps one at a time.

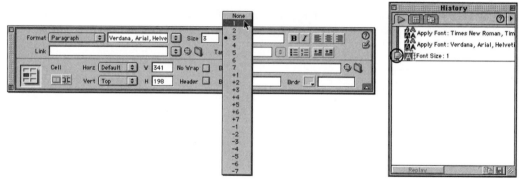

8. Again, with the block of text still selected, reduce the **Size** to **1**. This, too, will be recorded in the History palette.

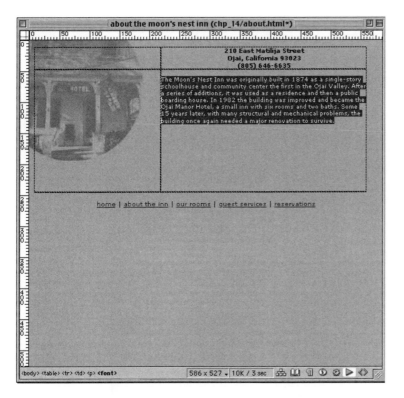

9. Choose **File > Save** to save the changes you have made to this document. When you are finished, leave this file open for the next exercise.

Note | Saving Files and Clearing the History Palette

The History palette is not cleared automatically when you save a file. This is great if you want to utilize it to make changes even after you have saved the document. However, if you close the file and reopen it, the history will be removed.

It is possible to clear the History palette at any time. For instance, if you want to save memory (RAM), clear the history by clicking the upper-right arrow of the History palette and choosing **Clear History** from the pop-up menu. This action cannot be undone, so be careful when using this option.

2. _____**Copying and Pasting History**

Now that you have a grasp of the basic functions of the History palette, you will learn how to utilize it to automate some of your workflow. In this exercise, you will learn how to copy and paste information from the History palette into another document. This allows you to easily replicate what you have done in one document inside another.

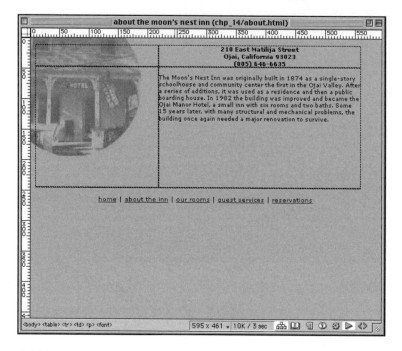

1. Make sure you have **about.html** open from the previous exercise.

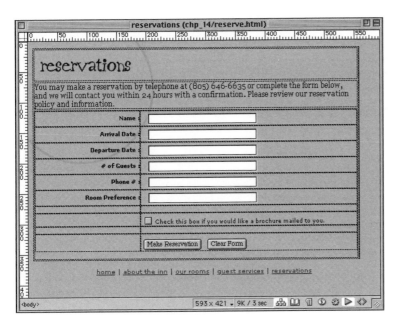

2. Open **reserve.html**. Notice that the text at the top of this page doesn't match the other text on the page, but don't worry, you'll fix that in a jiffy.

---

3. Choose **Window > about.html** to make it your current document.

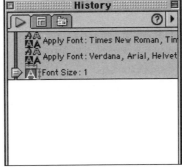

4. In the History palette, click the last entry. Next, press **Shift** and click the top entry in the palette. This will select all the steps in the History palette. You want to make sure that all are selected before you copy them.

5. Click the **Copy selected steps to the clipboard** icon at the bottom of the History palette. This will copy everything you have selected to the clipboard so that it can be pasted into the History palette of another document.

6. Choose **Window > reserve.html** to bring **reserve.html** forward and make it your current document.

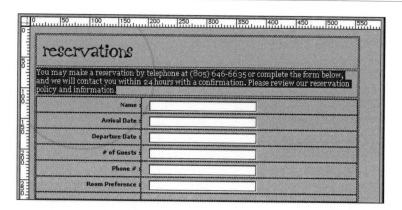

7. Select the block of text at the top of the **reserve.html** page by clicking and dragging.

You want to make sure that the selection represents everything you want reformatted when you paste the steps from the other document into the History palette.

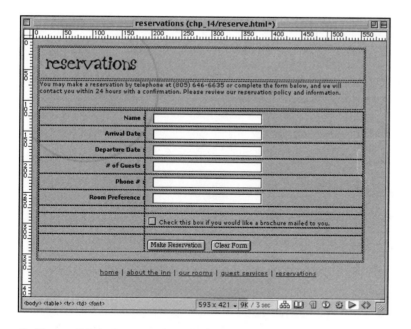

8. Choose **Edit > Paste**, or **Cmd+V** (Mac) or **Ctrl+V** (Windows). This will paste the three steps you copied from the History palette of **about.html** into this document. Notice that Dreamweaver just formatted the text you selected the same way it was formatted in **about.html**. This is because it followed the steps you copied from the History palette of **about.html**.

9. Save and close both documents. They will not be needed again for any exercises in this chapter.

Note | Paste Steps in the History Palette

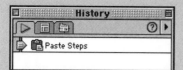

Any time you paste content from the History palette of one document into another, it will appear in the History palette as a single step, called **Paste Steps**. Regardless of how many steps you copied, they will always be pasted as one single entry in the History palette. In addition, pasted steps will have the **Paste** icon (a clipboard with a small piece of paper) next to them in the History palette.

3. _____ Applying HTML Styles

HTML Styles are a great way to quickly format text in a document. You can save specific text format-ting attributes and then apply them to any text on a page or within an entire site. Unlike Cascading Style Sheets, which require a 4.0+ browser, HTML Styles will work in earlier browsers, which makes them an attractive option. In this exercise, you will format some text and create an HTML Style based on that formatting. Then you will apply that formatting to other blocks of text on the same page. You will quickly begin to see how HTML Styles can help automate simple text formatting.

Note | The Library Folder and HTML Styles

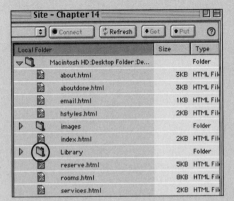

As you begin working with HTML Styles, you might notice a small addition to your Local Root Folder. When you create your first HTML Style, Dreamweaver automati-cally adds to your Local Root Folder a Library folder, inside which you will see a styles.xml file. All of your HTML Styles will be saved in that file. The file is impor-tant to Dreamweaver's internal workings, but it is not necessary to upload it when you publish your site to the WWW. The folder does not hurt anything by residing in your Site window. In fact, it is a needed element to ensure that HTML Styles will work properly.

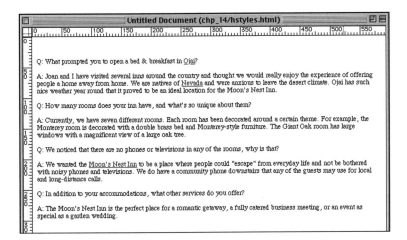

1. Open **hstyles.html**. This document contains a lot of text, and it provides a good example of when you might want to use HTML Styles to apply formatting across large amounts of text.

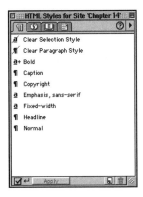

2. Make sure your **HTML Styles** palette is open. If not, choose **Window > HTML Styles**. The shortcut keys are **Cmd+F7** (Mac) or **Ctrl +F7** (Windows).

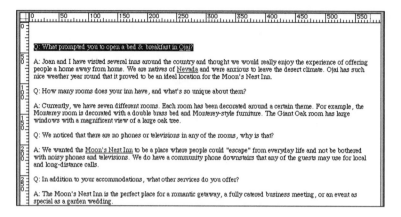

3. Click and drag to select the first line of text.

4. Using the Properties Inspector, change the font to **Verdana, Arial, Helvetica, sans-serif**, the **Size** to **4**, and the color to blue (any color of blue is fine).

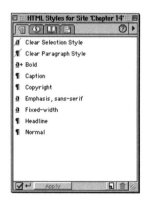

5. With your text still selected, click the **New Style** icon at the bottom of the **HTML Styles** palette. This will open the **Define HTML Style** dialog box, which allows you to define an HTML Style based on the selected text.

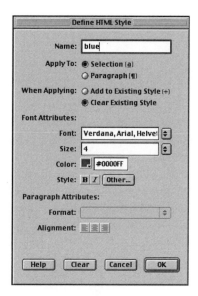

6. For **Name**, enter **blue**.

*Tip: We recommend that you name your HTML Styles relative to something that describes how they look. Because this text is formatted with a blue color, we named it **blue**.*

---

7. You can leave the rest of the options at their default values. Click **OK**. For an explanation of the options in the **Define HTML Style** dialog box, refer to the handy chart on page 405.

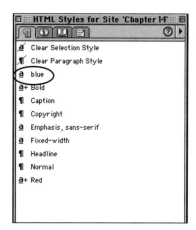

8. You should see your new style, **blue**, listed in the **HTML Styles** palette.

Note | Managing Your HTML Styles

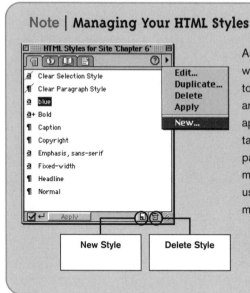

As you begin working with HTML Styles, you will no doubt want to go back and make changes to them. You might also want to delete ones that are no longer needed, make duplicates, and/or apply your styles. You can complete all of these tasks from the pop-up menu in the HTML Styles palette. This handy menu is your quickest path to managing your HTML Styles. In addition, you can use the **New Style** and **Delete Style** buttons to make quick changes.

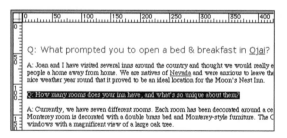

9. Select the third paragraph of text in the **hstyles.html** file by clicking and dragging.

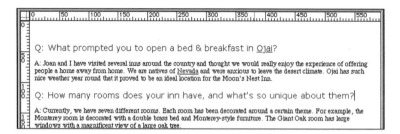

10. In the **HTML Styles** palette, click the **HTML Style** named **blue**. This will format the selected text using the HTML Style you previously defined. Now, that is what we call quick formatting ;-).

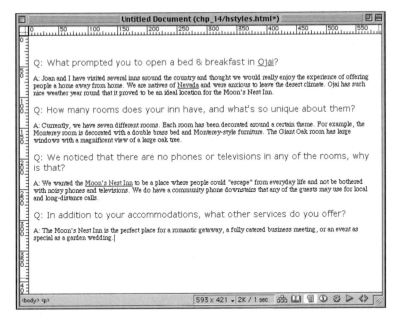

11. Go ahead and repeat this process for the fifth and seventh paragraphs. When you are finished, your page should look like the one above.

12. Now the only real way you are going to learn this is by doing it on your own. So, see if you can make another HTML Style and then apply that to the other paragraphs. Don't worry; if you get stuck, just refer to the beginning of this exercise.

13. When you are finished exploring this feature, save and close the file. It will not be needed for future exercises.

HTML Styles Options

Here is a quick definition for each of the options in the
Define HTML Style dialog box:

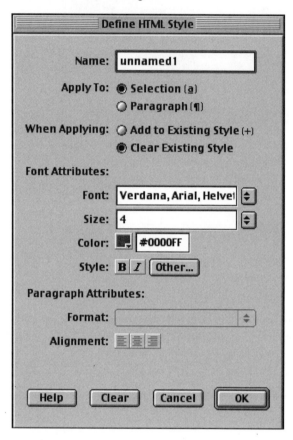

HTML Styles	
Option	**Description**
Name:	This is the name of your style that appears in the **HTML Styles** palette.
Apply To: Selection	With this option selected, the formatting will only be applied to the text you have selected.
Apply To: Paragraph	With this option selected, the formatting will be applied to everything within the paragraph <p> tag.
When Applying: Add to Clear Existing Style	With this option selected, the formatting will be added to any formatting that has already been applied to the selected text.
When Applying: Clear Existing Style	With this option selected, the formatting will replace any formatting that has already been applied to the selected text.
Font Attributes: Font:	This allows you to specify what font is used with the style.
Font Attributes: Size:	This allows you to specify what font size is used with the style.
Font Attributes: Color:	This allows you to specify what font color is used with the style. You can choose from the swatch or enter in a hexadecimal value.
Font Attributes: Style:	This allows you to specify which font styles (bold, italic, etc.) are used with the style. The **Other...** pop-up menu displays less frequently used options.
Paragraph Attributes: Format:	Only available if **Apply To: Paragraph** is selected, this lets you choose formatting options such as **Heading 1**, Paragraph, etc.
Paragraph Attributes: Alignment:	Only available if **Apply To: Paragraph** is selected, this lets you specify the alignment settings for the style.

Creating Custom Keyboard Shortcuts

This exercise will teach you how to create your own custom keyboard shortcuts. This is cool, because it lets you tailor Dreamweaver to the way that works best for you. In this exercise, you will assign a keyboard shortcut for the **Insert > Rollover Image** command. Why? Well, because it doesn't have one and is a commonly used item on many Web pages.

Note: This exercise requires that you have a text editor installed on your computer. You can use BBEdit (Mac) or Allaire HomeSite (Windows), which are included on the Dreamweaver 3 **H•O•T CD-ROM**. This is a very advanced exercise and assumes you know how to navigate through large documents, use a text editor, and make a backup of your files. If you aren't comfortable with these tasks, you may want to skip this exercise for now.

1. Quit Dreamweaver for now. This exercise will not work properly if Dreamweaver is open.

Dreamweaver Folder Locations	
Macintosh	**Windows**
Desktop:HD:Applications:	C:\Program Files\Macromedia\
Dreamweaver 3	Dreamweaver 3

2. Navigate your way to the **Dreamweaver** folder on your computer. This may be found in different places, depending on your platform. If you used the default installation settings, it's probably in one of the locations listed in the chart above.

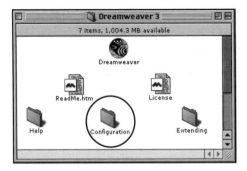

3. Double-click the **Configuration** folder.

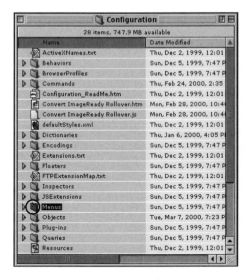

4. Once inside the **Configuration** folder, double-click the **Menus** folder.

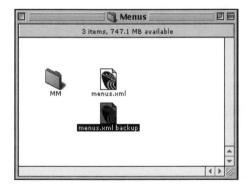

5. Inside the **Menus** folder, you will see a file titled **menus.xml**. Don't open this file yet!

Warning: *Make a backup of **menus.xml** before you get started. This is very important in case something weird happens and the file becomes corrupted.*

 Movie | **keyboard.shortcut.mov**

To learn more about custom keyboard shortcuts, check out **keyboard.shortcut.mov** located in the **movies** folder on the Dreamweaver 3 **H•O•T CD-ROM**.

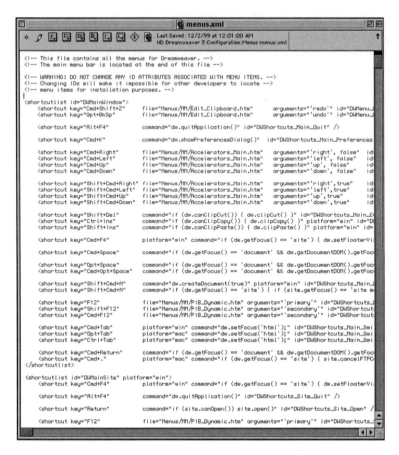

6. Open **menus.xml**. Do not use Dreamweaver or a word processor such as Microsoft Word to open the file. This is because word processors add proprietary formatting and HTML must be written in pure ASCII. You should use an ASCII text editor such as BBEdit (Mac) or Homesite (Windows). The file might be too large to open with SimpleText, WordPad, or NotePad, but you can try.

7. Scroll down until you see a line that reads `<menu name="_Insert" id="DWMenu_Insert">`. It is toward the bottom of the document.

Tip | Use the Find/Search Feature

Scrolling through documents with long text can be tedious. We have found it helpful to use the text editor's **Find/Search** feature. Almost every text editor has the ability to search and locate specific words. This can be very helpful when looking through documents with seemingly endless text, such as the **menus.xml** file. On the left is the **Find** Feature in BBEdit.

```
                                       menus.xml
   [toolbar icons]          Last Saved: 12/2/99 at 12:01:00 AM
                            HD:Dreamweaver 3:Configuration:Menus:menus.xml

        <menuitem name="_Pixels"                        enabled="dw.getFocus() == 'document'"
        <menuitem name="_Inches"                        enabled="dw.getFocus() == 'document'"
        <menuitem name="_Centimeters"                   enabled="dw.getFocus() == 'document'"
      </menu>
      <menu name="Gri_d" id="DWMenu_View_Grid">
        <menuitem name="_Show"          key="Cmd+Alt+Shift+G"   enabled="dw.getFocus() == 'document'"
        <menuitem name="S_nap To"       key="Cmd+Alt+G"         enabled="dw.getFocus() == 'document'"
        <menuitem name="S_ettings..."                           enabled="dw.getFocus() == 'document'"
      </menu>
      <menuitem name="_Prevent Layer Overlaps"          enabled="dw.getFocus() == 'document' && dw.getDocu
      <separator />
      <menu name="Tracing I_mage" id="DWMenu_View_TracingImage">
        <menuitem name="_Show"                  enabled="dw.getFocus() == 'document' && dw.getDocu
        <menuitem name="_Align with Selection"  enabled="dw.getFocus() == 'document' && dw.getDocu
        <menuitem name="Adjust _Position..."    enabled="dw.getFocus() == 'document' && dw.getDocu
        <menuitem name="_Reset Position"        enabled="dw.getFocus() == 'document' && dw.getDocu
        <separator />
        <menuitem name="_Load..."               enabled="dw.getFocus() == 'document' && dw.getDocu
      </menu>
      <menu name="Plugi_ns" id="DWMenu_View_Plugins">
        <menuitem name="_Play"          key="Cmd+Alt+P"     enabled="dw.getFocus() == 'document' && dw
        <menuitem name="_Stop"          key="Cmd+Alt+X"         enabled="dw.getFocus() == 'document' &&
        <separator />
        <menuitem name="Play _All"      key="Cmd+Alt+Shift+P"   enabled="dw.getFocus() == 'document'"
        <menuitem name="S_top All"      key="Cmd+Alt+Shift+X"       enabled="dw.getFocus() == 'documen
      </menu>
      <separator />
      <menuitem name="_Status Bar"                      enabled="dw.getFocus() == 'document'" command="dw.
    </menu>
    <menu name="_Insert" id="DWMenu_Insert">
      <menuitem name="_Image"         key="Cmd+Opt+I"     file="Image.htm"     id="DWMenu_Insert_Image" />
      <menuitem name="_Rollover Image"                    file="Rollover.htm"  id="DWMenu_Insert_RolloverImag
      <menuitem name="_Table"         key="Cmd+Opt+T"     file="Table.htm"     id="DWMenu_Insert_Table" />
      <menuitem name="T_abular Data"                      file="Tabular Data.htm"  id="DWMenu_Insert_TabularD
      <menuitem name="Hori_zontal Rule"                   file="HR.htm"        id="DWMenu_Insert_HR" />
      <menuitem name="Navi_gation Bar"                    file="Navigation Bar.htm"  id="DWMenu_Insert_NavBar
      <separator />
      <menuitem name="La_yer"                             enabled="dw.getFocus() == 'document' && dw.getDocu
      <menuitem name="_Form"                              file="Form.htm" id="DWMenu_Insert_Form" />
      <menu name="Form O_bject" id="DWMenu_Insert_FormObject">
```

8. Next, locate the line that reads `<menuitem name="_Rollover Image"`. This is the menu command for the **Rollover Image** option under the **Insert** menu.

9. Click to the right of the last quotation mark around the word **Image**. This is where you will insert the text to create the keyboard shortcut for this option.

```
        <separator />
        <menuitem name="_Status Bar"
</menu>
<menu name="_Insert" id="DWMenu_Insert">
        <menuitem name="_Image"        key="Cmd+Opt+I"
        <menuitem name="_Rollover Image"      key="Opt+R"
        <menuitem name="_Table"        key="Cmd+Opt+T"
        <menuitem name="T_abular Data"
        <menuitem name="Hori_zontal Rule"
        <menuitem name="Navi_gation Bar"
        <separator />
        <menuitem name="La_yer"
        <menuitem name="_Form"
```

10. Type **key="Opt+R"** to create the keyboard shortcut. If the keyboard shortcut you want to use is already in use, select something else. **Note:** The new menu item will appear as **Alt+R** in Windows even thought you edited the **XML** document to read **Opt+R**.

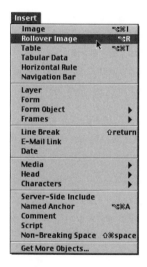

11. Save the changes you made and close the file. Open Dreamweaver and make sure you have a document open. Look in the **Insert** menu, and you should see your new keyboard shortcut listed to the right of the **Rollover Image** option. Try the custom keyboard shortcut you just created.

Congratulations, you have completed this chapter! Take a break or forge ahead. It's your call.

15.

Forms

| Working with Form Objects |
| Creating a Form | Creating a Jump Menu |

chap_15

Dreamweaver 3
H•O•T CD-ROM

Forms are one of the most important elements of a Web site, because they enable you to ask questions of your end user and receive answers. While Forms can be identical to those we're used to in the non-virtual world (think IRS, car insurance, or loan paperwork), they can also be used for more exciting things, such as voting, guestbooks, or e-commerce. In general, Forms-based pages are much more interactive than other types of HTML pages, because they can collect and report information to you.

There are two aspects to creating Forms: creating the **Form Objects** (Text Fields, Checkboxes, Submit Buttons, etc.) and making the Forms function properly. This chapter focuses on the creation of Form Objects, not on the programming required to make Forms transmit data to and from your server. Unfortunately, making the Forms operational involves programming that goes beyond the scope of Dreamweaver and this book. Forms might not sound like much fun, but they are at the heart of what makes the Web different from paper and publishing mediums of the past.

Form Objects

The objects you use to create a Form, in Dreamweaver, are referred to as Form Objects. These include Text Fields, Checkboxes, Images, Buttons, etc. You'll find all the Form Objects on the **Objects** palette. Instead of working with the Common Objects, as you have in most of the other chapters so far, this chapter will require that you set your Objects palette to Forms. This will display the Form Objects, as shown below.

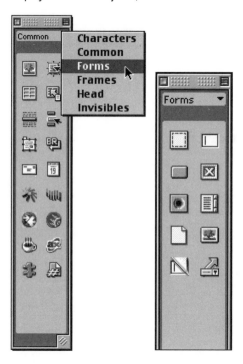

If the **Objects** palette is not visible, go to **Window > Objects**. In order to access the Form Objects, you need to change your Objects palette from its default setting (**Common**) to **Forms**. You do this by clicking on the arrow at the top of the Objects palette and selecting Forms from the pop-up menu.

Form Objects

The table below outlines the different Objects available from the **Form Objects** palette. As you become more familiar with Forms, you will not need this chart. Meanwhile, it should help you get a better inkling of what each of the Objects does:

	Form Objects in Dreamweaver	
Icon	**Name**	**Function**
	Insert Form	This is the very first step in creating a **Form**. This inserts the `<form>` tag into your document. If you do not place all your Objects inside the `<form>` tag, your **Form** will not work!
	Insert Text Field	Inserts a **Text Field Object** on your **Form**. You will use several of these in your **Form**. They can be set to contain single or multiple lines of data.
	Insert Button	Inserts a **Submit Button Object** (Dreamweaver default) on your **Form**. You can also make this a **Reset Button**, or set it to **None**.
	Insert Checkbox	Inserts a **Checkbox Object** on your **Form**. These Checkboxes are used to select an option on a **Form**.
	Insert Radio Button	Inserts a **Radio Button Object** on your **Form**. **Radio** buttons are used to select one item out of a list of available options.
	Insert List/Menu	Inserts a **List** or **Menu Object** on your **Form**. These two Objects (list or menu) allow you to make single or multiple selections in a small area of space.
	Insert File Field	Inserts a text box and button that lets the end user browse to a file on his or her hard drive, for uploading.
	Insert Image Field	Inserts an image into a **Form**, which the user can click on. This can be used to make graphic-based buttons.
	Insert Hidden Field	Stores information that does not need to be displayed but is necessary for processing the **Form** on the server
	Insert Jump Menu	Inserts a **Jump Menu** which allows the user to select an URL from the menu and then jump to that page.

Note | Making Forms Function with CGI

Dreamweaver gives you complete control over the layout of your Form and the creation of Form Objects, but that is just half the battle. Sending the information from the Form to your server or database requires more than HTML can do. In order to process Forms, it's necessary to use some type of additional scripting beyond HTML. While it is possible to process Form data through JavaScript or even Java, most Web developers agree that the most foolproof way to program Forms is through CGI, PHP, or ASP.

CGI stands for **C**ommon **G**ateway Interface. In essence, CGI is a protocol to send information to and from a Web server. CGI scripts can be written in a variety of programming languages, ranging from Perl, to C, to AppleScript. If that doesn't sound complicated enough for you, add that different types of CGI scripts work with different Web servers, ranging from UNIX to MacOS to WindowsNT.

Though it is complex, CGI is considered by most Web developers to be the most reliable method to work with Forms. If you have a Web site, chances are very high that your Internet service provider or Web administrator has existing CGI scripts that you can use. Because there are so many variables to CGI, and it is outside the scope of Dreamweaver, it will be up to you to coordinate obtaining the scripts and implementing the processing of your Forms.

Here are some online resources for CGI scripts:

Matt's Script Archives
http://www.worldwidemart.com/scripts/

Selena Sol's Public Domain CGI Scripts
http://www.extropia.com/

Free Code
http://www.freecode.com/

Working with Form Objects

Even if you are not going to be adding CGI scripts yourself, you still need to set up the layout of the Form Objects on the page. In this exercise, you will get hands-on experience with each of the various Form elements. You won't be adding any scripts because doing that would require another book, but you will get everything set up so that when you do want to add a CGI script, your pages will be ready!

1. Copy the contents of **chap_15** to your hard drive and press **F5** to define the site. If you need a refresher on this process, revisit Exercise 1 in Chapter 3, *"Site Control."*

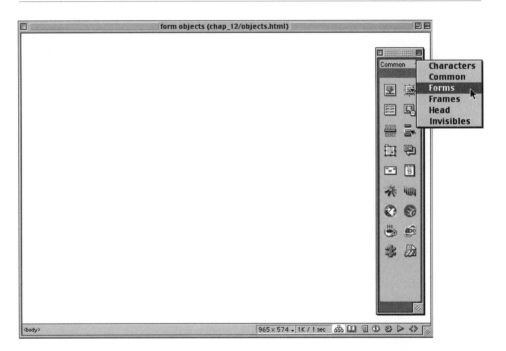

2. Open the **objects.html** file. It's just a blank page, but at least it has a page Title for you. ;-)

3. Make sure the **Form Objects** palette is visible. If it's not, click on the small black arrow at the top of the **Objects** palette and select **Forms** from the pop-up menu.

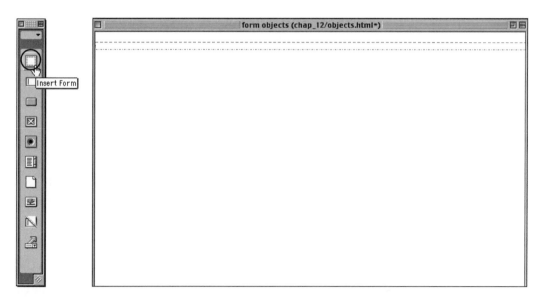

4. Click on the **Insert Form** object in the **Form Objects** palette. This will insert the `<form>` tag into your document. You should see red dashed lines on your page. If you do not see them, select **View > Invisible Elements**.

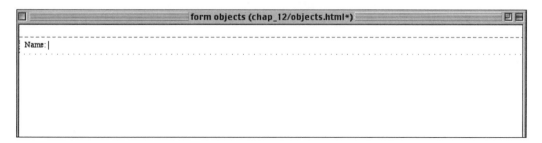

5. Position your cursor inside the red dashed lines, and type **Name:**. Press the spacebar once to create a single space.

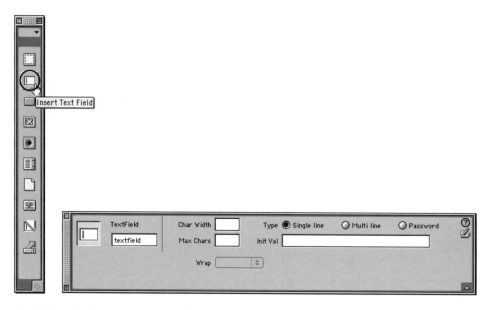

6. Click on the **Insert Text Field** object in the **Form Objects** palette. This will insert a blank text field onto your page. With the text field highlighted, notice that the Properties Inspector options change.

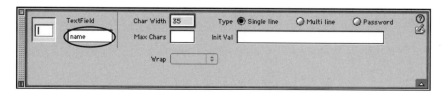

7. In the **TextField** setting in the Properties Inspector, replace the existing text with the word **name**. This will give a unique name to this text field. Enter **Char Width 35**. This sets the length of the text field. It does not limit the amount of text entered, just how much is visible. To limit the amount of text entered, you would enter a value for **Max Chars**.

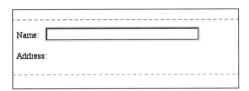

8. Click to the right of the text field in your document and press **Return** or **Enter**. Type **Address:** and press the spacebar to create one space.

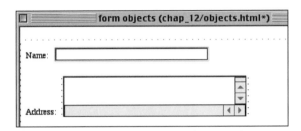

9. Click on the **Insert Text Field** object. This will insert another text field onto your page. In the Properties Inspector, enter the word address in the **TextField**. Choose **Type: Multi line** and set **Num Lines: 2**, then set **Char Width: 40**. You can see how the **Multi line** attribute works. This is great for larger areas of text when you don't know how much will be inserted.

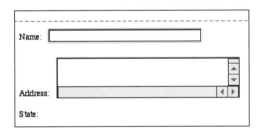

10. Click to the right of the **Multiline** text field and press **Return** or **Enter**. Type **State:** and insert one space by pressing the spacebar.

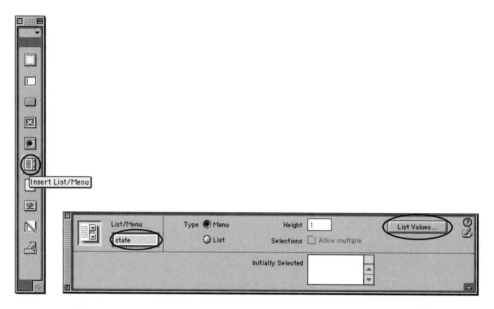

11. Click the **Insert List/Menu** object. By default, this will insert a **Menu Object** onto your Form. In the Properties Inspector, type **state** in the **List/Menu** field. Next, click the **List Values...** button.

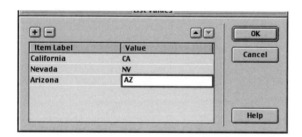

12. For the first **Item Label**, type **California**, and then press **Tab**. For the first **Value**, type **CA**, and then press **Tab**. Repeat this same process for **Nevada** and **Arizona**, using the information from the image above. This Form Object will give you a pull-down menu displaying the information in the **Item Label** column. The information in the **Value** column is what a CGI or JavaScript program would process with the Form. Click **OK**.

13. In the Properties Inspector, select **Initially Selected: California**. This determines what menu item is visible before the user clicks on the pull-down menu.

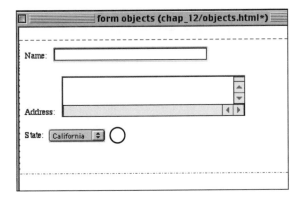

14. Click to the right of the **State** pull-down menu and press **Return** or **Enter**.

15. Click the **Insert Checkbox** object. This will insert a checkbox onto your page.

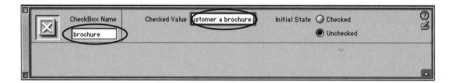

16. In the Properties Inspector, name the checkbox **brochure**. For the **Checked Value**, type **Send the customer a brochure**. The Checked Value information will appear next to the checkbox name when a CGI script processes the Form. This information is hidden from your end user, but it is useful to a programmer who is setting up the CGI because it tells him or her what the checkbox relates to.

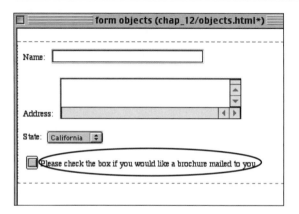

17. Click to the right of the checkbox and type **Please check the box if you would like a brochure mailed to you**. This will help end users, understand what information they are sending by checking this box. Press **Return** or **Enter**.

18. Click the **Insert Button** object. This will insert a **Submit** button onto your page, which is the default that Dreamweaver automatically inserts. Because you need to have a button to submit the Form, leave the other options at their default values.

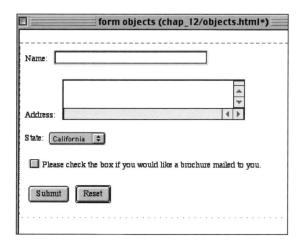

19. Click to the right of the **Submit** button. Click the **Insert Button** object again. This will insert another **Submit** button onto your page. In the Properties Inspector, change the **Action** to **Reset form**. This will create a button that clears the Form, just in case your end user makes a mistake and wants to start over. Change the **Button Name** to **Reset**.

---

20. Save your file. Press **F12** to preview your Form in a browser. Remember, the **Submit** button will not work because you did not attach any CGI scripts.

---

21. Return to Dreamweaver, save, and close the document.

The purpose of this exercise was to get you comfortable inserting different Form Objects and modifying some of their properties. To make a Form perform its functions, you would need to attach a CGI or other scripting program to it.

2. _____Creating a Form

This exercise is designed to help you become more familiar with creating a layout for your Forms. Forms can combine other HTML elements such as Background Images and Tables, and this exercise should get you comfortable with combining your new Form-creation skills with your existing Web-layout skills.

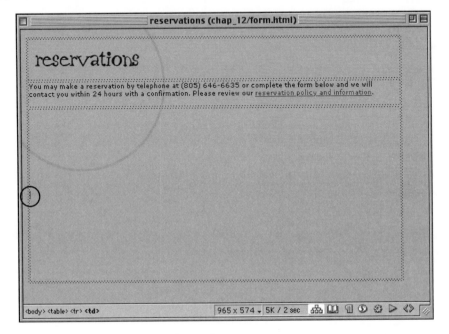

1. Open the **form.html** file. Notice that it already contains a Background Image, a graphic (reservations) and a Table. Click your cursor in the bottom cell of the Table.

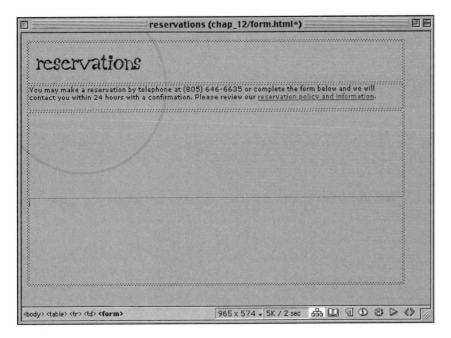

2. Click on the **Insert Form** object in the **Objects** palette. Red dashes should appear in the Table cell, indicating that you have inserted a `<form>` tag. If you don't see these red dashes, select **View > Invisible Elements**.

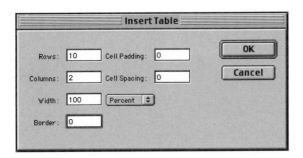

3. Select **Insert > Table**. (If you're used to clicking on the Table Object in the **Objects** palette, you would need to switch it back to **Common**. Otherwise, for convenience's sake, just use the **Insert** menu right now.) Change the settings to **Rows: 10**, **Cell Padding: 0**, **Columns: 2**, **Cell Spacing: 0**, **Width: 100 Percent**, and **Border: 0**. Click **OK**.

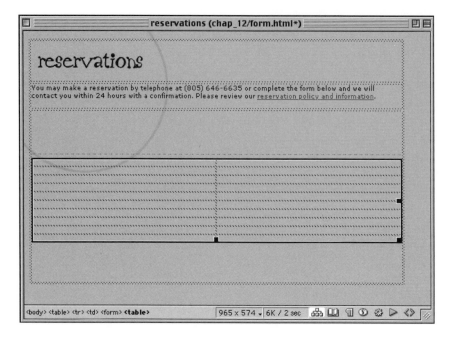

A Table will appear below the red dashes, as shown here.

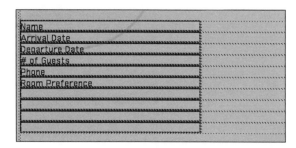

4. Click inside the first cell in column 1 and type **Name**. Click inside the second cell in column 1 and type **Arrival Date**. Click inside the third cell in column 1 and type **Departure Date**. Click inside the fourth cell in column 1 and type **# of Guests**. Click inside the fifth cell in column 1 and type **Phone**. Finally, click inside the sixth cell in column 1 and type **Room Preference**.

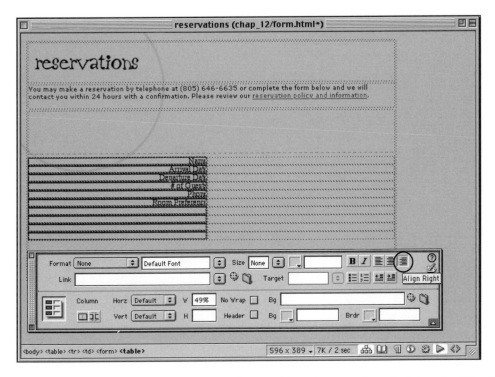

5. Click and drag to select all the cells in column 1. Once they are selected, click on the **Align Right** button in the Properties Inspector.

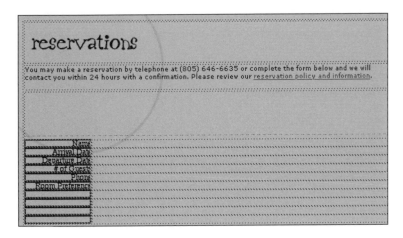

6. Click and drag on the middle divider between the two columns to move it over to the left.

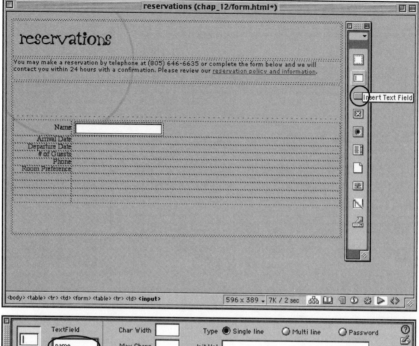

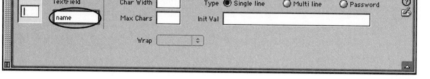

7. Next, you'll add some entry fields to the **Form**. Click inside column 2, row 1 and choose the **Insert Text Field** object in the **Objects** palette. In the Properties Inspector, name the **TextField name**.

---

8. Repeat this same process for the next five cells down. Make sure you give each text field a unique name that describes the associated column.

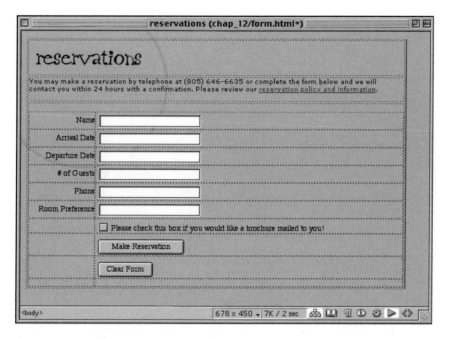

9. Position your cursor inside row 7 in column 2 and click. Next, click on the **Insert Checkbox** object in the **Objects** palette. In the Properties Inspector, change the **CheckBox Name** to **mail** and the **Checked Value** to **mail brochure to customer**. Click to the right of the checkbox that just appeared, and type **Please check this box if you would like a brochure mailed to you!** into the document.

---

10. Click in row 8 in column 2, then click the **Insert Button** object in the **Objects** palette. In the Properties Inspector, change the **Label** to **Make Reservation**. The **Action** should be set to **Submit form**.

---

11. Click in row 9 in column 2, then click the **Insert Button** object in the **Insert Objects** palette again. In the Properties Inspector, change the **Action** to **Reset Form**, the **Label** to **Clear Form**, and the **Name** to **Clear**.

Congratulations, you've just designed a a custom-formatted Form that utililized Form and Table elements. Go ahead and leave this file open for the next exercise. If you are brain-fried and want to quit, make sure you save your work!

3. _____Creating a Jump Menu

The **Menu** form element can be combined with JavaScript to create a fantastic navigation tool for your site. This can be very useful when you have a small amount of screen real estate in which to place a lot of navigation choices. This exercise will show you how to use Dreamweaver to create a **Jump Menu** on your page. The Jump Menu works really well as a navigation tool within Framesets.

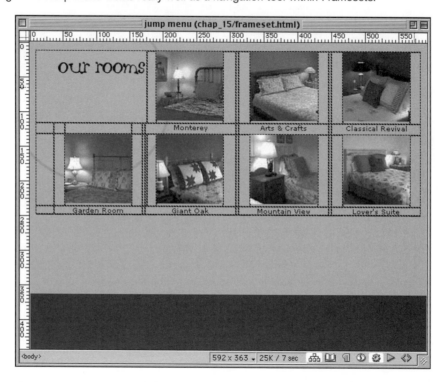

1. Open the **frameset.html** file located inside the **chap_15** folder. This is a simple Frameset that we created for you.

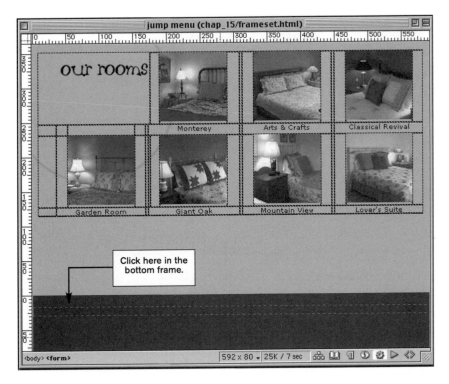

2. Click in the bottom frame. Select **Insert > Form**. This will insert the `<form>` tag into your document so that your Jump Menu will function properly.

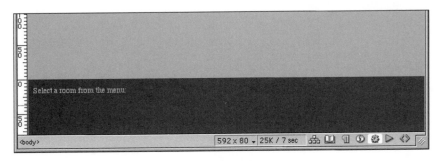

3. Type **Select a room from the menu:**. This text will help the user understand what the menu contains and what it's used for.

4. Select **Insert > Form Object > Jump Menu**. This will open the **Insert Jump Menu** window. As an alternative, you could have clicked on the **Insert Jump Menu** icon in the **Objects** palette.

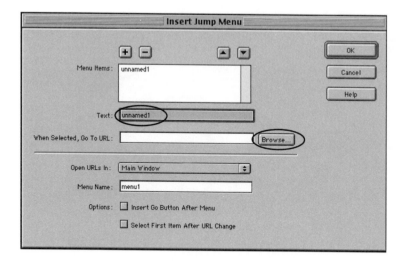

5. In the **Text:** field, type **Monterey**. This option sets the actual text that appears in the menu, when the user clicks on the menu. Press **Tab** to go to the next field.

6. Click on the **Browse...** button next to the **When Selected, Go To URL:** field. This lets you browse to the HTML file you want to jump to when this menu item is selected.

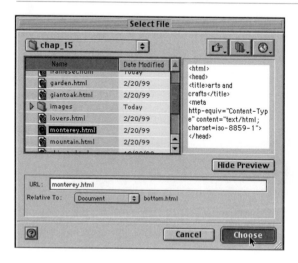

7. Navigate to the **monterey.html** file located inside the **chap_15** folder. Select it and click **Choose**.

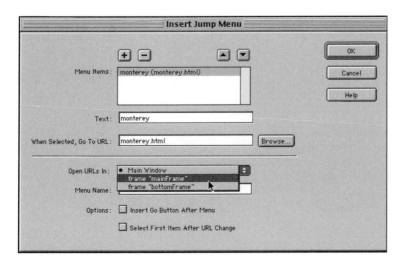

8. Click on the pop-up menu next to the **Open URLs In:** option and select **frame "mainFrame."** This option determines what frame the Web page will load into.

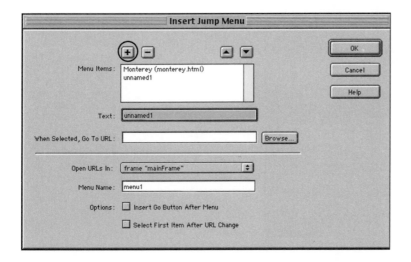

9. Click on the **plus** button at the top of the dialog box. This will allow you to add another item to your **Jump Menu**. This interface is very similar to the **Insert Navigation Bar** dialog box you learned about in Chapter 13, *"Rollovers."* It's nice to see the continuity in the interface; you gotta love it!

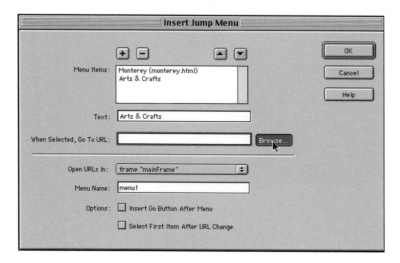

10. Enter **Arts & Crafts** for the **Text:** field. Click on the **Browse...** button next to the **When Selected, Go To URL:** option.

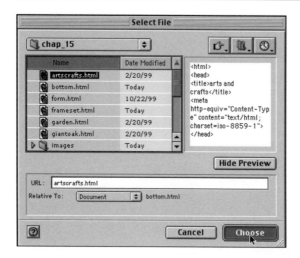

11. Browse to the **artscrafts.html** file located inside the **chap_15** folder. Select it and click **Choose**.

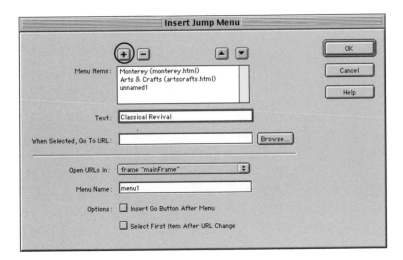

12. Click on the **plus** button at the top of the dialog box. This will allow you to add another item to your Jump Menu. Enter **Classic Revival** for the **Text:** field. Click on the **Browse...** button.

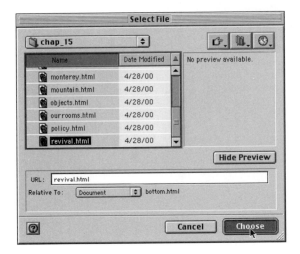

13. Browse to the **revival.html** file located inside the **chap_15** folder. Select it and click **Choose**.

14. You've just finished setting up your Jump Menu. Click **OK**.

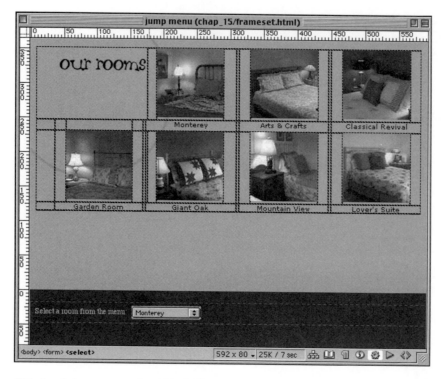

This is what your page should look like now.

15. Save your work. Press **F12** to preview your page in the default browser.

---

16. Click on the menu and select **Arts & Crafts**. This will jump you to the **artscrafts.html** page.

---

17. If you want, you can select the other two options from the menu to see them work.

---

18. Return to Dreamweaver and close the document.

Phew, another chapter under your belt. Move to the next chapter if you feel ready.

16.

DHTML

| Dragging Layers | Using the Timeline for Animation |
| Playing, Stopping, and Resetting the Timeline |

chap_16

Dreamweaver 3
H•O•T CD-ROM

The "D" at the beginning of DHTML stands for "dynamic," as in **D**ynamic **H**yper**T**ext **M**arkup Language. DHTML was introduced a couple of years ago to offer more dynamic content, such as animation and interactivity, than basic HTML gives. DHTML is not just one single item. It's a combination of technologies, such as HTML, JavaScript, Style Sheets, Absolute Positioning, Plug-Ins, and DOM. For a definition of these technologies, revisit Chapter 1, *"Background."*

Unfortunately, most of the content produced by using DHTML works only on current browsers, and fails on anything below a 4.0 browser. If you plan to use techniques presented in this chapter, it's best to put them on interior pages so visitors with older browsers can see your first page and important content. DHTML is usually reserved for entertainment-based sites, where games and/or dynamic presentations are expected and embraced. Alternatively, you could offer DHTML content only to those end users who can see it, by using the browser-detection techniques discussed in Chapter 17, *"Behaviors."*

This chapter introduces you to several DHTML techniques. Whether you use them or not will likely depend on what type of site you are designing. The exercises in this chapter were tested to work well in Microsoft Internet Explorer 4.5 and Netscape Navigator 4.7 for both the Macintosh and Windows operating systems. However, newer versions of both browsers seem to have less support for this type of DHTML. These exercises will not work well in Microsoft Internet Explorer 5.0 or Netscape Navigator 6 PR1. It's a shame; just know it's the browser and not you. ;-)

Warning | Prevent Overlaps

This chapter works with Layers, which you also worked with in Chapter 8, *"Layout."* Before you begin the exercises, open your **Layers** window (**F11**) and make sure that **Prevent Overlaps** is not checked. If this is left checked, the exercises in this chapter will fail.

When you are converting Layers to Tables as you did in Chapter 8, it's necessary to put a check in the Prevent Overlaps checkbox. That's because Table cells can't overlap, and the Layers information was being used to produce Tables.

In this chapter, however, you want the Layers to overlap, since you will be creating animations where objects fly on top of each other. It's easy to change this setting by simply unchecking the Prevent Overlaps setting in the Layers window.

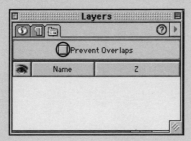

In order to successfully complete this chapter's exercises, make sure you do not have the Prevent Overlaps setting checked.

I. _____ Dragging Layers

When Lynda was in Dallas speaking at a Macromedia seminar, her husband Bruce sat and drew this little game for their daughter. We thought the example was delightful, though Lynda's daughter did complain that the monkey had no shoes! Regardless of her criticism, it's a fun example of what you can do with DHTML, and so it leads this chapter.

1 Define your site for Chapter 16. Copy the contents of **chap_16** to your hard drive and define it (**F5**). If you need a refresher on this process, revisit Exercise 1 in Chapter 3, _"Site Control."_

2. Open **dress_final.html** and press **F12** to preview it in a browser. Take any item and drag it onto the monkey. This game was created using Dreamweaver's **Drag Layer Behavior**, which you're about to learn. Return to Dreamweaver and close the file.

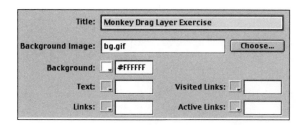

3. Choose **File > New** (Mac) or **File > New Window** (Windows) and then save the document as **monkey2.html** into the **chap_16** folder. Choose **Modify > Page Properties...** and enter the **Title: Monkey Drag Layer Exercise**. To the right of **Background Image:** click **Choose...** (Mac) or **Browse...** (Windows), and then browse to **bg.gif**. Click **OK**.

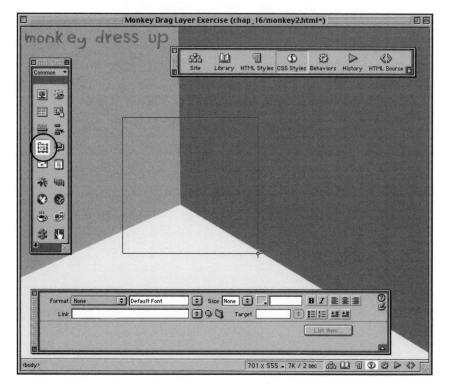

4. In the **Common Objects** palette, use the **Insert Draw Layer** object onto drag a Layer on the page.

5. Make sure the cursor is inside the Layer, and choose **Insert > Image**. Browse to **lilmonkey.gif**, and click **Select**.

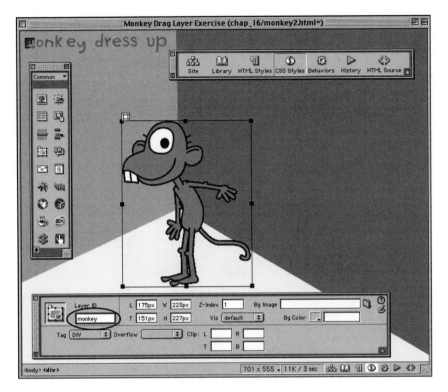

6. Click on the top handle of the Layer to select it. In the **Layer ID** area of the Properties Inspector, type the name **monkey**. It's best to name your Layer something that relates to the image.

Tip: Resizing each Layer to fit the dimensions of its artwork will help keep your work area clean.

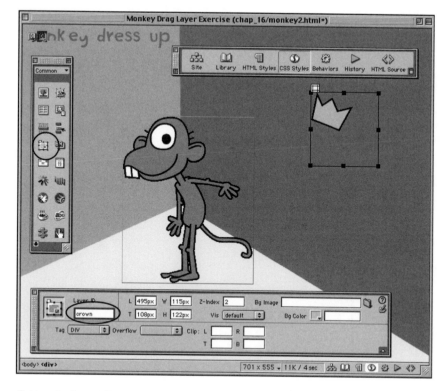

7. Use the **Insert Draw Layer** object again to drag another, smaller Layer on the page. With the cursor inside the Layer, choose **Insert > Image**. Browse to **crown.gif**, and click **Select**.

8. Now go ahead and select the Layer by its handle. Name it **crown** inside the **Layer ID** area of the Properties Inspector.

9. Using its handle, move the **crown** layer by on top of the monkey's head. **Tip:** Once the handle selects the Layer, you can use the arrow keys on your keyboard to nudge it into place.

10. Click on the image of the crown (not the **crown** layer) to select it. It's essential that the image is selected, not the Layer. This has to do with the fact that the JavaScript Behavior of the **Drag Layer** command must be attached to the `<img>` tag, not the `<layer>` tag.

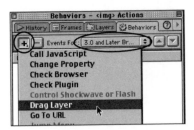

11. Open the **Behaviors** window (**Window > Behaviors** or **F8**), and select **Events For: 3.0 Browsers**. (By the way, even though the program claims this will work on 3.0 browsers, it will not work on all of them.) Click on the **plus sign** button and select **Drag Layer**.

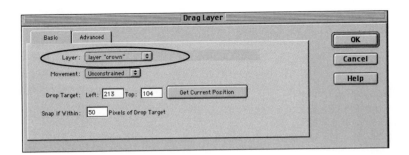

12. The **Drag Layer** dialog box will open. Switch to **Layer: layer "crown."** Leave the **Movement: Unconstrained**, and click on the **Get Current Position** button. This procedure will insert numbers into the **Drop Target** area. The program has just captured the exact position of the crown on the page. (**Note:** These numbers will vary because you might have positioned your monkey and crown differently than I did.) Leave **Snap if Within: 50 Pixels of Drop Target** and click **OK**.

13. Move the **crown** layer away from the monkey. **Note:** Wherever you place it is where it will appear in the browser. It's important to drag it away from the monkey so your end user can drag it back on!

14. Press **F12** to preview the results. Move the crown back onto the monkey.

15. See if you can complete the exercise with the rest of the dress-up artwork found in the **chap_16** folder. You'll probably be grateful that Bruce didn't make shoes, as it would be more objects to set up! When you're finished fooling around with this exercise, close the file to move on to the next exercise.

2. _____Using the Timeline for Animation

You've probably noticed the item **Timelines** in the Dreamweaver **Launcher** interface and wondered what it stood for. You'll finally get to find out with this exercise. This time, you'll use the same artwork, but instead of creating a drag-and-drop game, you'll create an animation of the clothes flying onto the l'il monkey's body. Even if this isn't the sort of content you think you'll be adding to your site, you'll still be learning the principles of Dreamweaver animation and have a smile on your face while doing so.

1. Open **dress_timeline1.html** in Dreamweaver, and press **F12** to preview it. This gives you the opportunity to see what you will build by completing this exercise.

2. Close **dress_timeline1.html**, and open **dress_timeline2.html**. This document has been partially built for you.

3. Make sure the **Timelines** window is open (**Window > Timelines** or **F9**). Using its handle, drag the Layer with the pants in it into **Channel 1**. It will appear inside the Timeline, as shown above.

4. When this dialog box appears, just click **OK**. This is merely an information window letting you know the different ways in which you can animate Layers.

 Movie | keyframe.mov

To learn more about using **keyframes**, check out **keyframe.mov** located in the **movies** folder on the Dreamweaver 3 **H•O•T CD-ROM**.

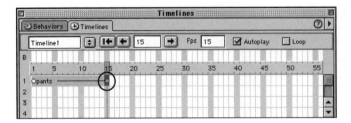

You will see two dots in the Timeline for the pants. These are called keyframes. (The term keyframe means an extreme point of movement.) The first keyframe establishes where the pants are at the beginning of the animation. The second one establishes where they will be at the end.

5. Right now, both keyframes are set to the same position, because you have not programmed any motion yet. Click on the second keyframe (the second dot) of the **pants** element in the Timeline. In this case, since both extremes (or keyframes) are set to the same position, nothing happens.

6. With the the second keyframe (the second dot) highlighted, use the Layer handle to move the pants to where they belong on the monkey. Make sure you are moving the entire Layer, not just the image. **Tip:** You can use the arrow keys to nudge the pants into place. **Note:** See the light gray line that appears on the screen, from the spot where the pants were originally to where you just moved them? This indicates that you set up the motion properly.

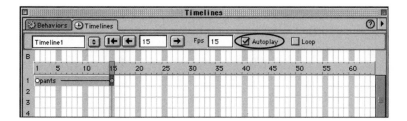

7. Make sure that the **Autoplay** checkbox is checked in the **Timelines** window. This tells Dreamweaver to play the animation once it is viewed from a browser.

8. Press **F12** to see the results of your labor. Unfortunately, you cannot preview animation from within Dreamweaver, only from a browser. You'll see that the pants now fly onto the body. The hat and T-shirt remain stationary, because you haven't programmed the animation of these yet. That's coming up next, so return to Dreamweaver.

9. Using its **Layer** handle, drag the hat into **Channel 2**. Now, click on its second keyframe (the second dot), and move the hat by its **Layer** handle to the top of the monkey's head.

10. Using its **Layer** handle, drag the T-shirt into **Channel 3**. Click on its second keyframe (the second dot), and move the T-shirt by its **Layer** handle to the monkey's torso.

11. Press **F12**, and voilà! You've got animation.

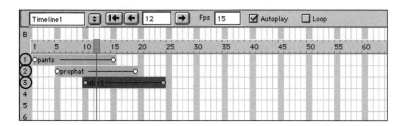

12. Return to Dreamweaver, and move the Layers in the Channels as shown above. Press **F12** to see the difference. You can adjust the timing of these Layers by moving them around on the Timeline. Also, you can extend the number of frames of any Layer by clicking on its second keyframe, then dragging it to the right. When you're done playing, save and close the document.

Note | Docking and Undocking Windows

The Dreamweaver Interface ships with a bunch of windows and palettes arranged in a way that made a lot of sense to the people who designed the program. Fortunately, if you want your windows and palettes arranged differently, you can customize your interface by docking and undocking windows in different combinations. This is a great feature because it allows you to combine just the windows you use most often.

Docking Windows

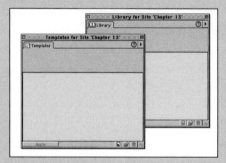 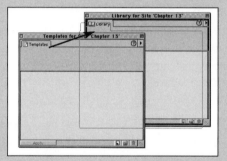

Click anywhere in the title bar of the window, and drag it toward the title bar of the window with which you want to combine it. Release the mouse button, and the two windows are combined!

Undocking Windows

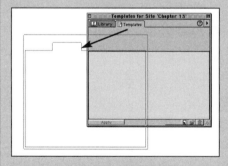 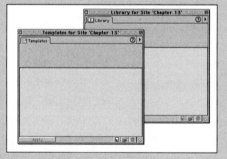

Click on one of the tabs, and drag outside the current window. This will give you a silhouette of the new window. Release the mouse button, and voilà, the two have been separated!

Tip | The Timeline Explained

The Timeline Inspector is used to control animation in Dreamweaver. In addition, it can control many other events and JavaScript Behaviors over time, such as specifying when music starts and stops, starting and stopping a slideshow presentation, etc. To understand all the Timeline features, see the image and chart below:

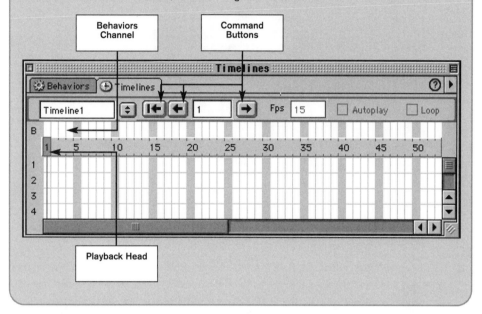

Behaviors Channel

Command Buttons

Playback Head

Dreamweaver Timeline Features

Feature	Explanation
Command Buttons	Three controls, **Rewind**, **Back**, and **Play**, let you control your Timeline.
Playback Head	Dragging the **Playback Head** allows you to preview your animation and move between frames.
Behaviors Channel	Shows any Behaviors that are attached to specific Frames.

Playing, Stopping, and Resetting the Timeline

Let's say you wanted some links you could click on to play, stop, and reset the Timeline. The next exercise shows you how to set this up.

1. Open **anim_button.html**, and press **F12** to preview it in the browser. Remember that you can't see this DHTML stuff from within Dreamweaver. Click on the link that says **GO** and watch the animation play. Click **STOP** and **RESET** to see them in action, too.

2. Return to Dreamweaver and close the file. Open **anim_button1.html**. This has been partially built for you, only you'll be adding the Behaviors. Highlight the text **GO**.

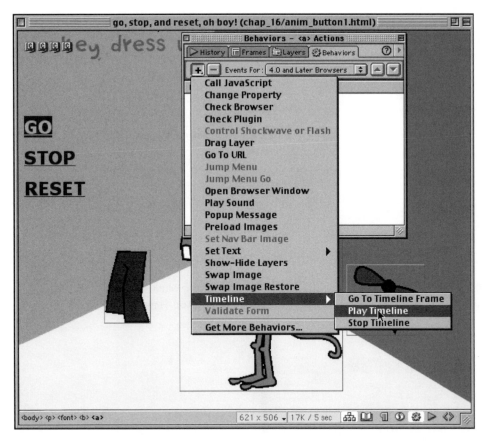

3. Make sure the **Behaviors** window is open, and select **Events For: 4.0 Browsers**. With **GO** selected, click on the **plus sign** in the Behaviors window, and choose **Timeline > Play Timeline**.

Note: In the Properties Inspector, you'll see that the word GO contains a link with a hash mark (#) in it. The hash mark sets up a link that doesn't go anywhere, which can be very useful. Many Behaviors have to be applied to links, but often you don't want a link to work, just to exist.

4. The **Play Timeline** dialog box will appear. It should be set to **Play Timeline: Timeline1**, so click **OK**.

5. Highlight the word **STOP**, click on the **plus sign** in the **Behaviors** window, and choose **Timeline >** **Stop Timeline**. The **Stop Timeline** dialog box will appear. Select **Stop Timeline: Timeline 1** (the only Timeline you have defined in this file). Click **OK**.

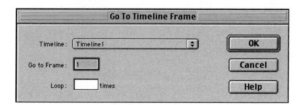

6. Highlight the word **RESET**, click on the **plus sign** in the **Behaviors** window, and choose **Timeline > Go To Timeline Frame**. Enter **Go to Frame: 1**, and click **OK**. This tells the **RESET** link to move the Timeline back to Frame 1.

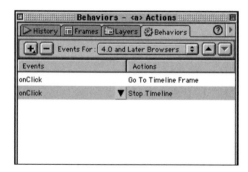

7. With **RESET** still highlighted, click on the **plus sign** in the **Behaviors** window again, and choose **Timeline > Stop Timeline**. The **Stop Timeline** dialog box will appear. Select **Stop Timeline: Timeline 1**. Click **OK**. This will add a second Behavior to the **RESET** link. As you can see, it is sometimes necessary to add more than one Behavior to a single link. Now, when the user clicks on the **RESET** link, it will go to Frame 1 and then stop the Timeline.

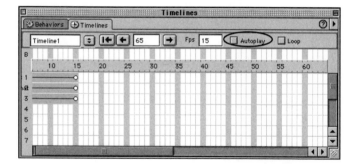

8. In the **Timelines** window, make sure you uncheck **Autoplay**. In this exercise, you want the links to control whether the animation plays or not, so Autoplay is no longer necessary.

9. Save your work, and press **F12** to see the fruits of your Timeline labor.

When you're finished, you can tell all your friends, family, and coworkers that you just made your first DHTML animation page! Don't forget to tell them where you learned it ;-).

17.

Behaviors

Macromedia Exchange	Check Browser
Set Text of Status Bar	Set Text of Text Field
Open New Browser Window	Installing the Extension Manager
Insert ImageReady HTML	Downloading from Macromedia Exhange

chap_17

Dreamweaver 3
H•O•T CD-ROM

Dreamweaver **Behaviors** are a set of JavaScript-based extensions that enable you to add extra interactivity to your pages. There are two components to Behaviors, the **Event** and the **Action**. Events are defined by a user's actions, for example, moving the mouse over an image. Actions, on the other hand, are blocks of prewritten JavaScript that are executed when the Event occurs. In the context of a rollover, when the Event is completed (the user's mouse moves over the graphic), the Action takes place (one image is swapped with another). While these terms Events and Actions might sound like Greek to you right now, once you see how easy Behaviors are to use, you'll find the learning curve to be remarkably low.

Before you go through the exercises in this chapter, you should be comfortable working with images, Tables, and forms. This chapter will show you how to use some of the Behaviors that ship with Dreamweaver right out of the box, and you'll learn how to work with the new **Set Text** Behaviors, how to do browser detection, and how to create some very complex navigation systems.

In addition to doing the exercises in this chapter, you might want to refer to Appendix B, *"Online Resources,"* for a list of Web sites that offer hundreds of free Behaviors. These sites are definitely worth checking out. For us, Behaviors junkies that we are, visiting these sites and looking through all the offerings is like being a kid in a candy store.

The Macromedia Exchange — Dreamweaver

http://www.macromedia.com/exchange/dreamweaver/

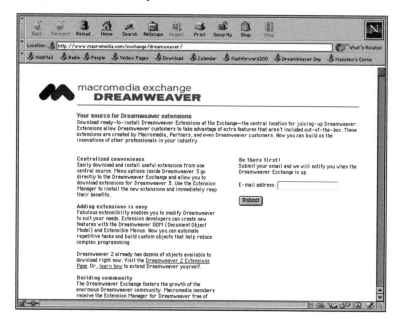

Macromedia has set up a new section of their Web site, designed to be a portal for Dreamweaver users, called the Macromedia Exchange – Dreamweaver. There you'll find hundreds of free extensions for Dreamweaver that can help you build new features into your Web site. Many of these are advanced features that normally would require the skills of a programmer to create. For example, extensions available from third parties can give you the ability to perform complex browser detection, password protect areas of your site, connect to back-end databases, etc.

The Macromedia site is not just for developers, but for any Dreamweaver user who wants to take Dreamweaver to the next level. If you are a developer, this is a great place to learn how to take advantage of the Dreamweaver DOM (**D**ocument **O**bject **M**odel). The DOM for Dreamweaver is a specification that enables increased levels of extensibility that standard HTML and JavaScript do not afford.

The Macromedia Exchange for Dreamweaver is also where you can download a free copy of the **Macromedia Extension Manager**. This indispensable add-on for Dreamweaver lets you easily (and painlessly) download, install, and manage your extensions. This is a must have for any serious Dreamweaver user, because it makes it easy for you to add new features to the program. As an added bonus to you, we have included a copy of the Extension Manager on the **H•O•T CD-ROM** in the **Software/Macromedia** folder.

_____**Creating a Check Browser Behavior**

As you start adding different features and technologies to your site, such as DHTML and JavaScript, you might want to make sure the people viewing your pages are using a browser that can see these features (4.0 browsers and above). This exercise will show you how to use the **Check Browser** Behavior to determine which browser and version the user has, and then redirect the user to another page. This is very useful if you want to create different versions of your site, one that works with 4.0 or later browsers and one that works with earlier browsers.

Note: In order to check the success of this exercise, it is required that you have both Netscape Navigator 3.0 and 4.0 installed on your computer. If you don't have both versions, and wish to complete this exercise, please install both of these browsers before continuing. We've included copies of Netscape Navigator 3.0 and 4.0 on the **H•O•T CD-ROM** in the **Software/Browsers** folder.

1. Define your site for Chapter 17. If you need a refresher, visit Exercise 1 in Chapter 3, _"Site Control."_ Browse to **checkbrowser.html** and open it. This file contains some text in a table. You will add the Check Browser Behavior to it.

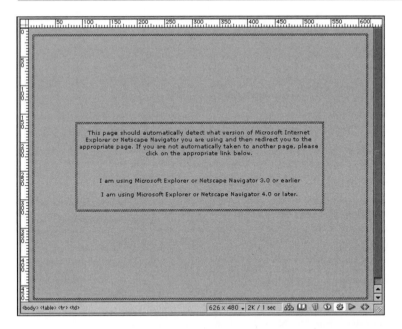

This is what **checkbrowser.html** looks like at the beginning of this exercise. It's a page with a table that has text in it. You'll add the Check Browser Behavior to it, which will determine which browser and version a user has, and then redirect the user to another page.

2. Click on the **<body>** tag in the **Tag Selector** at the bottom of the document window. You want to attach the Check Browser Behavior to the **<body>** tag of the document so that the behavior can run when the page is first loaded.

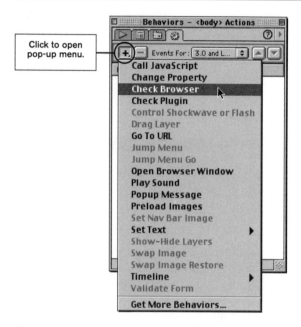

3. In the **Behaviors** palette (**Window > Behaviors** or **F8**), click the **plus** sign and choose **Check Browser** from the pop-up menu. This will open the **Check Browser** dialog box.

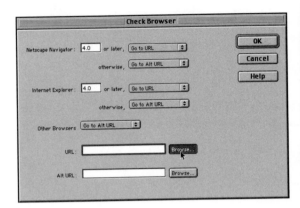
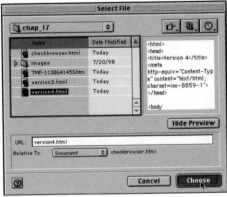

4. Click **Browse...** near the bottom next to **URL:**. Browse to **version4.html** in the **chap_17** folder and click **Choose**. This will be the page your end users will see if they are using Netscape or Explorer 4.0 or later. Don't click **OK** just yet.

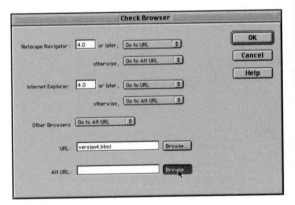
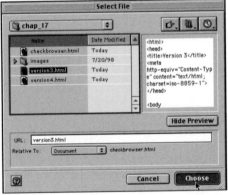

5. Click **Browse...** at the bottom next to **Alt URL:**. Browse to **version3.html** in the **chap_17** folder and click **Choose**. The **Alt URL** is the page your end users will see if they are using something other than Netscape or Explorer 4.0 (i.e., Netscape 3.0, Explorer 2.0, etc.).

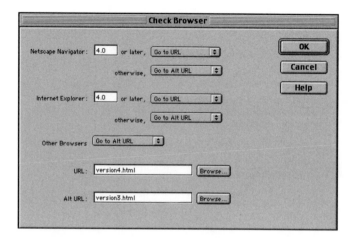

*This is what your **Check Browser** dialog box should look like at this point.*

6. Click **OK** to accept these settings. You won't detect any visual changes to your page, but a whole bunch of complex JavaScript was just added to it.

7. Notice that the Check Browser Behavior now appears in the **Behaviors** palette. Also, notice that its Event is automatically set to **onLoad**. This means that when the Web page is loaded, it will perform the Check Browser Behavior. Cool!

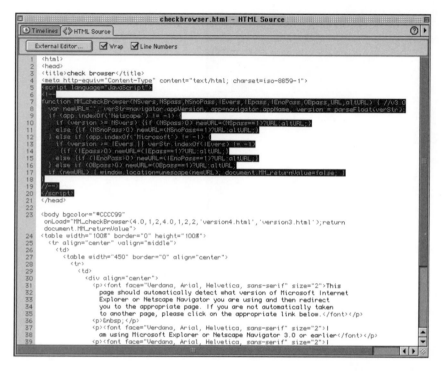

8. Press **F10** to open the **HTML Source** window. Notice all the JavaScript that was added to your page. Could you imagine having to create all of that code from scratch? Part of the power of Behaviors is that they shield you from such tedious tasks. Press **F10** again to close this window.

9. Choose **File > Save** to save the changes you made to **checkbrowser.html**.

Now that you've added the Check Browser Behavior to your page, you're ready to check your work by opening this page in both the Version 3 and Version 4 browsers. Will the correct version load? Stay tuned.

10. Launch Netscape 3.0. Select **File > Open File…**. Browse to the **chap_17** folder, select **check-browser.html**, and click **Open**. Notice that you are immediately taken to **version3.html**. Exit the Netscape 3.0 application.

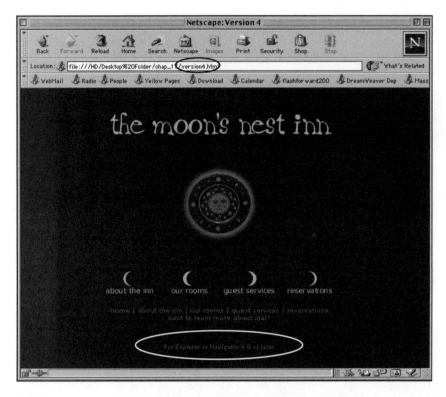

10. Launch Netscape 4.0. Select **File > Open > Page in Navigator...**. Browse to the **chap_17** folder, select **checkbrowser.html**, and click **Open**. Notice that you are immediately taken to **version4.html**. Exit the Netscape 4.0 application and return to Dreamweaver.

Warning | JavaScript Potential Problem

There's a potential problem with using this type of browser detection. Because this detection is constructed with JavaScript and users can disable JavaScript in their browser preferences, this script may not always work properly. As a safeguard against this, you'll finish this exercise by learning how to give the user an option to load the appropriate page by clicking a link. This will prevent anyone from being locked out of your site, which is a very good thing ;-).

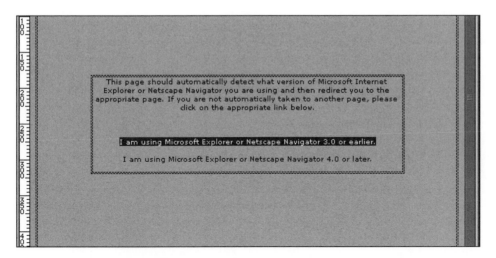

11. In the Dreamweaver **checkbrowser.html** document, click and drag to select the words **I am using Microsoft Explorer or Netscape Navigator 3.0 or earlier.**. Now, you'll use the Properties Inspector to make this text into a hyperlink to **version3.html**.

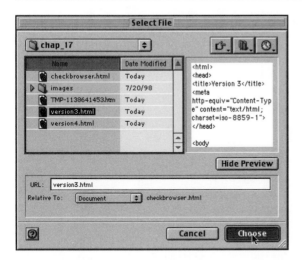

12. In the Properties Inspector (**Window > Properties** or **Cmd+F3**), click the **Browse for File** folder icon to the right of the **Link** field. Browse to **version3.html** and click **Choose**.

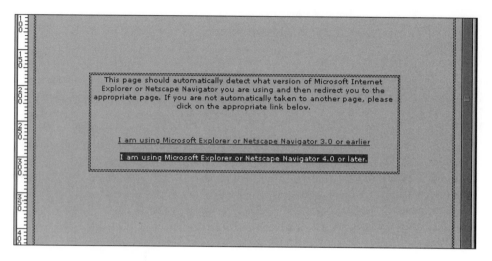

13. In the **checkbrowser.html** document, click and drag to select the text **I am using Microsoft Explorer or Netscape Navigator 4.0 or later.**.

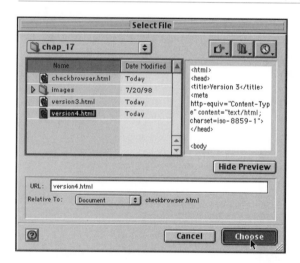

14. In the Properties Inspector, click the **Browse for File** folder icon again. This time, browse to **version4.html**. Click **Choose**.

Setting up these two links is a good idea, because if users don't have JavaScript turned on, they will still have a way to get into the site.

15. Choose **File > Save**, and close this file. You will not be working with it anymore.

2. —————————————————Creating a Set Text of Status Bar Behavior

The **Status Bar** is located at the bottom of a browser window and can display text in addition to what is on the Web page. Using the **Set Text of Status Bar** Behavior, you can display any text that you want in the Status Bar of the browser window. This is often used in conjunction with links, to provide additional detail about the destination page. This exercise will show you how to add the Set Text of Status Bar Behavior to a page.

This is what text looks like in a browser Status Bar.

1. Open **statustext.html**, located inside the **chap_17** folder. You will add the Set Text of Status Bar Behavior to several of the links on this page, to provide additional feedback to the user.

2. Click the **about the inn** image to select it. In the Properties Inspector (**Window > Properties** or **Cmd+F3**), notice that this image has a hash mark (**#**) in the **Link** field. This is referred to as a "nowhere" link. It's a link that goes, well..., nowhere. The only reason you need it is that certain Behaviors (such as the one you're about to add) must be attached to links.

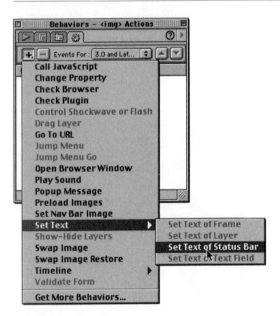

3. With the image still selected, in the **Behaviors** palette (**Window > Behaviors** or **F8**), click the **plus sign** to access the pop-up menu and choose **Set Text > Set Text of Status Bar**. This will open the **Set Text of Status Bar** dialog box.

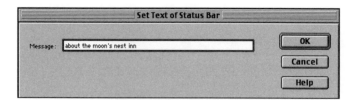

4. Enter **Message: about the moon's nest inn**. Click **OK**.

5. Notice that the **Set Text of Status Bar Behavior** now appears in the **Behaviors** palette with the **onMouseOver Event**.

6. Repeat this process for each of the other buttons, adding a short description for each of one.

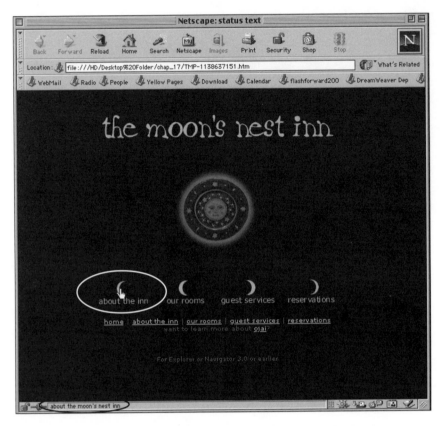

7. When you're finished, press **F12** to preview your page in a browser. Move your mouse over any of the four images and look at the text that is displayed in the browser window's Status Bar.

---

8. Return to Dreamweaver and choose **File > Save** to save your changes, then close this file. You won't need it any longer.

---

3. _____**Creating a Set Text of Text Field Behavior**

Earlier, in Chapter 15, *"Forms,"* you learned how to create **Forms**. This exercise will show you how to make content change dynamically as the user interacts with your Form, by using the Set Text of Text Field Behavior.

1. Open **reserve_done.html**. This is what your file will look like when you finish this exercise. Press **F12** to preview this in a browser.

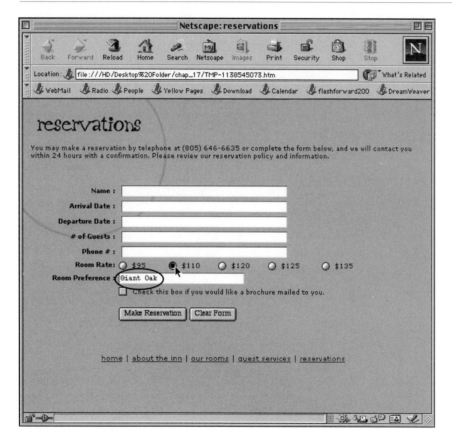

2. Click any of the **radio** buttons next to **Room Rate:**. Notice that text automatically appears in the **Room Preference:** text field. Close this file for now. You will create this effect in the following exercise.

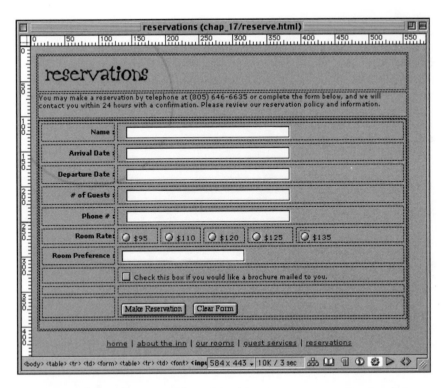

3. Return to Dreamweaver and open **reserve.html**, located inside the **chap_17** folder. This file consists of a Form that we created for you. You will learn how to use the Set Text of Text Field Behavior to dynamically update this Form as the user interacts with it.

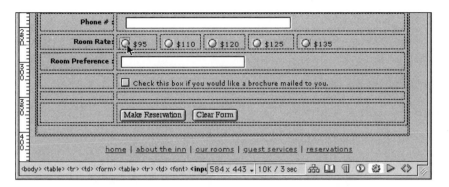

4. Click the **radio** button next to "**$95**." You are going to apply the Set Text of Text Field Behavior to this form element so that the **Room Preference:** text field will be automatically updated.

5. From the **Behaviors** palette (**Window > Behaviors** or **F8**), click the **plus sign** and choose **Set Text > Set Text of Text Field** from the pop-up menu. This will open the **Set Text of Text Field** dialog box.

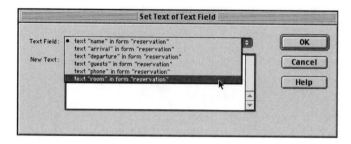

6. Click the **Text Field:** pop-up menu at the top and choose **text "room" in form "reservation."** Don't click **OK** just yet.

*The drop-down menu lists each of the **Form Objects** with the names that we gave them. As you can see, it's a good idea to use descriptive names that are relative to the information being requested. The **Text Field** option determines which text field in the **Reservation** form will automatically display the text.*

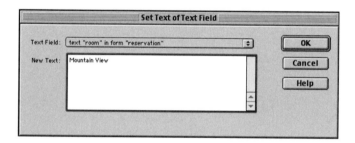

7. Enter **Mountain View** in the **New Text:** field. This is the text that will replace any text that is in the **Room Preference** text field of the Form when the user clicks the **$95** button. Click **OK**, and now you're ready to set up the next button.

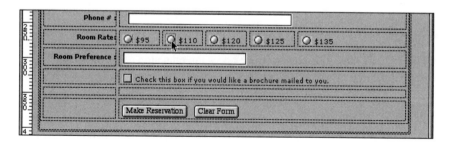

8. Click the **radio** button next to **$110**.

9. From the **Behaviors** palette, click the **plus sign** and choose **Set Text > Set Text of Text Field** from the pop-up menu. This will open the **Set Text of Text Field** dialog box.

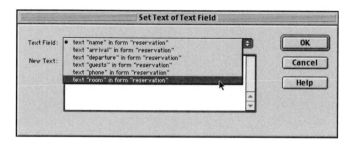

10. Click the **Text Field:** pop-up menu at the top and choose **text "room" in form "reservation."** Don't click **OK** just yet.

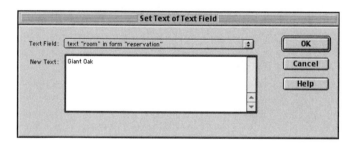

11. Enter **Giant Oak** in the **New Text:** field. This is the text that will replace any text that is in the **Room Preference** text field of the Form when the user clicks the "**$110**" button. Click **OK**.

Set Text of Text Field Behavior

Radio Button Text	New Text
⊙ $120	Garden or Monterey
⊙ $125	Arts & Crafts
⊙ $135	Classical Revival or Lovers' Suite

12. Using the chart above, add the Set Text of Text Field Behavior to the other three **radio** buttons.

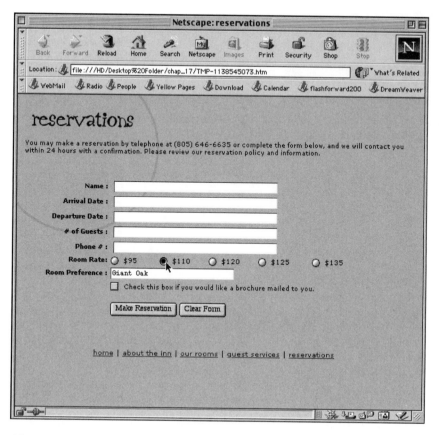

13. When you're finished, press **F12** to preview this page in your primary browser. Click each of the **radio** buttons and watch the text field below change automatically.

14. Return to Dreamweaver. Save and close this file. You will not need it for the remainder of the book.

4. _____Opening a New Browser Window

Let's face it, a Web page is pretty small. There are going to be times when you just can't cram everything onto a single page. So, what can you do? One option is to open the information in another window. In this next exercise, you will open a new browser window to display information that wouldn't fit comfortably on a single page.

1. Open **newwindow.html**, located inside the **chap_17** folder.

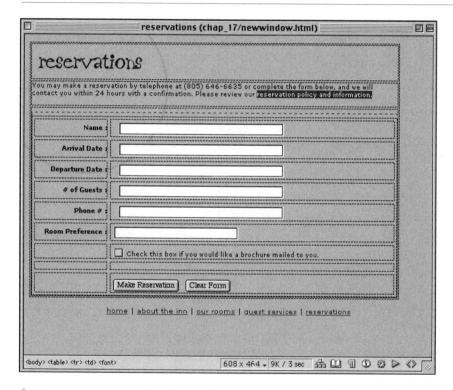

2. Click and drag to highlight the text "**reservation policy and information.**"

3. In the Properties Inspector (**Window > Properties** or **Cmd+F3**), enter a # mark in the **Link** field. You know what that's about from Exercise 2, right?

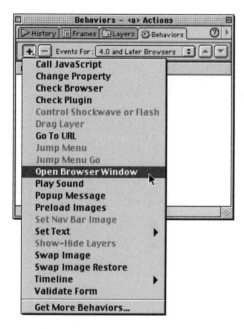

4. From the **Behaviors** palette (**Window > Behaviors** or **F8**), click the **plus** sign and choose **Open Browser Window** from the pop-up menu. This will open the **Open Browser Window** dialog box.

5. Click **Browse...** and browse to **policy.html**. Click **Choose**. This is the HTML file that will be displayed in your new window. The link can be an internal or external link.

Next, you'll specify the size of your new browser window.

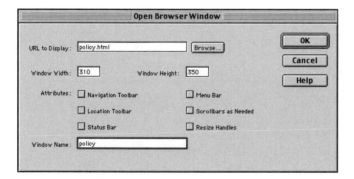

6. Back in the **Open Browser Window** dialog box, enter **Window Width: 310** and **Window Height: 350**. This will specify the pixel size of your window when it opens.

*We specified **310 x 350** pixels because those dimensions will fit the contents of **policy.html**, the page you are going to display in the second browser window. On other projects, you could specify any size that's appropriate to your second window's content. At the bottom of the window, type **policy** in the **Window Name:** field. Click **OK**.*

This is what the Behaviors palette should look like now.

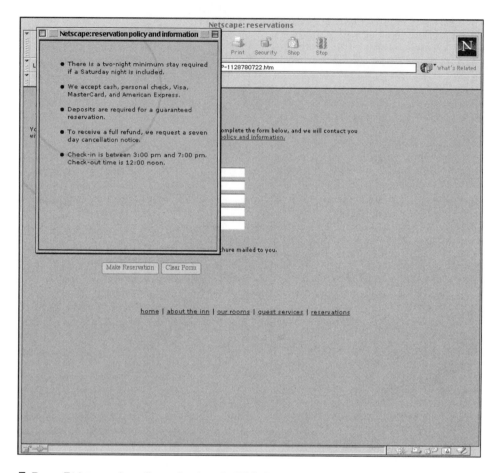

7. Press **F12** to preview all your hard work. Click the **reservation policy and information** link at the top of the page. Voilá! A new browser window will open, displaying **policy.html** in a window set to **310 x 350** pixels.

8. Return to Dreamweaver, and save and close the file.

5. _____Installing the Extension Manager

As we mentioned earlier, Macromedia recently released the Extension Manager for Dreamweaver, which enables you to easily install and manage all of the extensible features you add to Dreamweaver. This is such a great thing, because installing the extensible features was rather confusing for beginners and even some seasoned Dreamweaver users. Well, fear not, with the help of this handy new tool, Macro-media has placed all of these cool add-ons within your reach. This exercise will show you how to install the Macromedia Extension Manager for Dreamweaver.

1. If you have Dreamweaver open, Quit the application now. You don't want to have Dreamweaver open when you're installing the Extension Manager.

2. Open the appropriate Extension Manager folder on the **H•O•T CD-ROM**. Copy the Extension Manager installer to your hard drive, preferably to your desktop.

 Movie | **xman_win.mov**

The Extension Manager interface is different on Windows. To see the difference, view **xman_win.mov** located in the **movies** folder on the Dreamweaver 3 **H•O•T CD-ROM**.

3. Once you have the installer copied to your computer, double-click on the installer's icon to begin the installation program.

4. Click **Continue....**

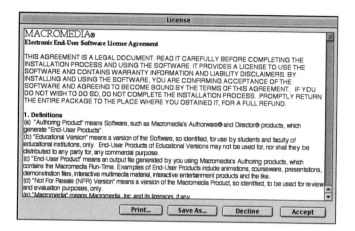

5. When you are ready, click **Accept**.

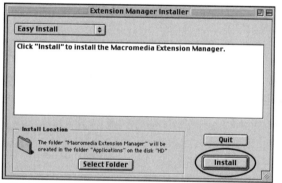
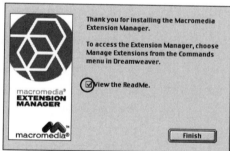

6. Select the specific folder where you'd like to install the Extension Manager. Because it is a separate application, you can install it into any folder on your hard drive. Click **Install**.

7. When the installation process is finished, you will see a screen like the one shown above right. Click **Finish**. If you leave the check in the **View the ReadMe.** checkbox, it will open a browser file with some extra information about the Extension Manager.

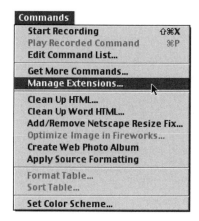

8. Launch Dreamweaver. To confirm that the Extension Manager is installed, select **Commands > Manage Extensions...**. This menu command will only be available if you have properly installed the Extension Manager.

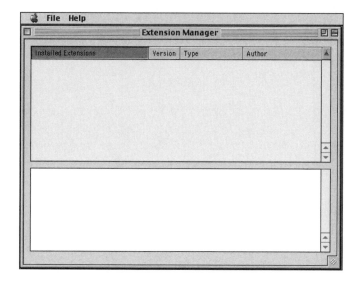

9. Selecting the **Manage Extensions...** menu item will launch the Extension Manager and open the interface. You will learn how to use the Extension Manager with the Macromedia Exchange – Dreamweaver site in the next exercise.

10. Quit the Extension Manager and return to Dreamweaver. You are now ready to move on to the next exercise, which will show you how to install an extension using the Extension Manager.

6. _____Inserting ImageReady HTML

Dreamweaver 3 added a great new feature for inserting Fireworks HTML; however, it only works with HTML files generated by Fireworks. We thought it would be great if there was a similar feature available for users of ImageReady. Well, since neither one of us knows how to program JavaScript (even though Garo is learning!), we decided to contact one of the best Dreamweaver developers for help. Massimo Foti, a top Dreamweaver developer, worked with us to develop a new extension that will insert ImageReady HTML in your Dreamweaver page. This is great news for ImageReady users. But wait, it gets even better. Not only will it insert ImageReady HTML into Dreamweaver, but it will convert the JavaScript to Dreamweaver JavaScript. What exactly does this mean? This means that you can now create rollovers in ImageReady, and edit the JavaScript in Dreamweaver.

This exercise will show you how to install the **Insert ImageReady HTML** extension, using the Dreamweaver Extension Manager. In addition, you will learn how to insert ImageReady HTML into your Dreamweaver page.

1. In Dreamweaver, select **Commands > Manage Extensions....** This will launch the Extension Manager, so you can install the **Insert ImageReady HTML** extension.

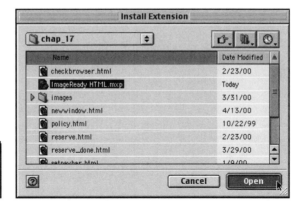

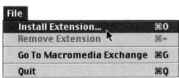

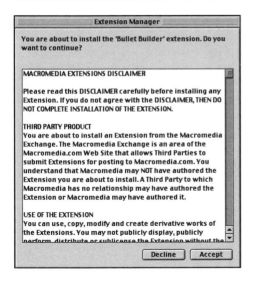

2. From the Extension Manager, select **File > Install Extension…**. Browse to the **chap_17** folder and locate the **ImageReady HTML.mxp** extension file. Highlight this file and click **Open**.

3. A disclaimer will appear for you to read. When you are finished, click **Accept** (assuming you agree with the terms). The installation of the **Insert ImageReady HTML** extension will proceed.

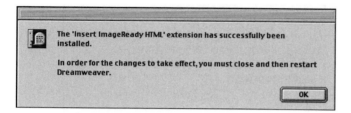

4. When it's finished, a dialog box like the one above will display, indicating that the installation was successful. Click **OK**.

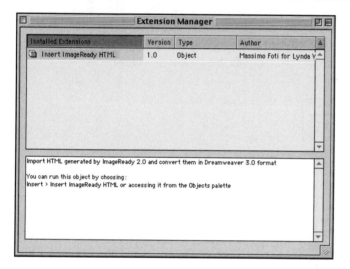

When the extension has been installed properly, it will be displayed in the Extension Manager window. If it is highlighted, a brief description will appear in the bottom portion of the window.

5. To exit the Extension Manager, select **File > Quit** (Mac) or **File > Exit** (Windows).

6. Once the extension has been installed properly, return to Dreamweaver.

7. Quit, and then re-launch Dreamweaver.

TIP: Each time you use the Extension Manager to install a new extension, you'll need to Quit and then re-launch Dreamweaver before you can use your new extension.

8. From Dreamweaver, select **File > New**. This will create a new blank document. Save this file inside the **chap_17** folder as **insertir.html**.

9. In the **Common Objects** palette, click on the **Insert ImageReady HTML** icon, the new object that was added to Dreamweaver when you installed the **Insert ImageReady HTML** extension. This will open the **ImageReady HTML** dialog box.

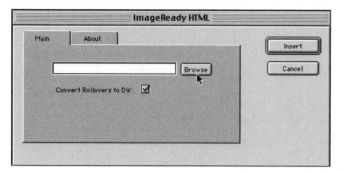

10. Click **Browse**. Locate the **irrollover.html** file inside the **irrollover** folder. This file was created in Adobe ImageReady 2 and contains a rollover button.

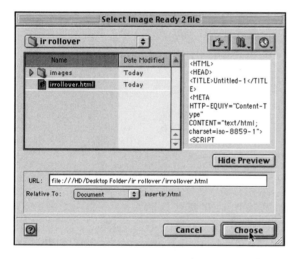

11. Once you locate the **irrollover.html** file, highlight it and click **Choose**, then click **Insert**.

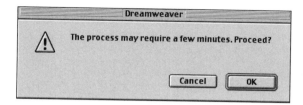

12. A dialog box will open, indicating it may take a few minutes to convert and import the file. Click **OK**.

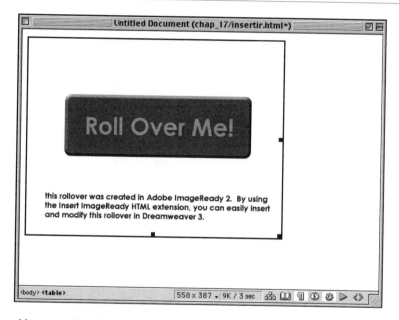

After you click **OK**, *the ImageReady HTML file will be converted and then imported into Dreamweaver. This is what your screen should look like now.*

13. Make sure your **Behaviors** palette is open. If it's not, select **Window > Behaviors** or **(F8)**.

14. Click on the "**Roll Over Me!**" image. In the **Behaviors** palette, notice that this was converted to a native Dreamweaver **Action**. Pretty slick, huh?

15. Press **F12** to preview this page in a browser. The rollover is not only written as a native Dreamweaver JavaScript rollover, but it works flawlessly as well.

16. Exit the browser and return to Dreamweaver.

7. _____Downloading from Macromedia Exchange

As we mentioned earlier, the Macromedia Exchange – Dreamweaver is a new site that Macromedia developed to serve as a repository for Dreamweaver extensions. It is literally a gold mine of widgets and add-ons to help you add life to your Web pages. In this exercise, you will learn how to download one of these cool extensions from the Exchange and install it, using the Extension Manager.

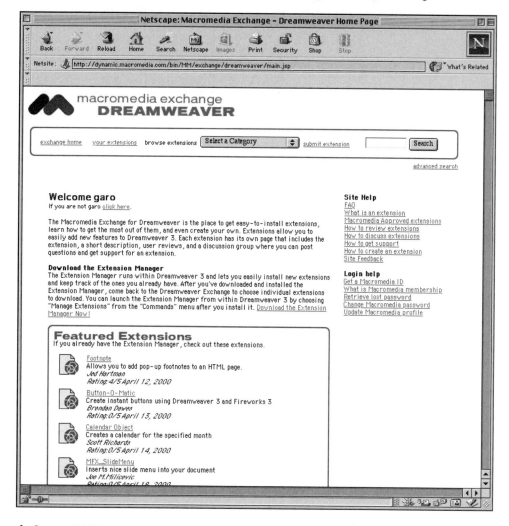

1. Open a Web browser and go to http://www.macromedia.com/exchange/dreamweaver/. This will take you to the new Macromedia Exchange – Dreamweaver Web site. If you have not created an account yet, you will need to do so before downloading any of the extensions.

> ### Note | Behaviors, Commands, and Objects
>
> As you start downloading extensions from the Exchange and other Web sites, it's important to know where to find a Behavior, Command, and/or Object. These are accessed from different places in the Dreamweaver interface. Behaviors are accessed from the **Behaviors** palette, Commands are accessed from the **Commands** menu, and Objects are stored in the **Objects** palette and accessed from the **Insert** menu. This little bit of information will help you find the extensions once they've been installed.

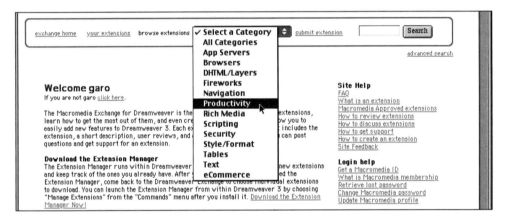

2. Click on the drop-down menu, at the top of the screen. As you can see, the extensions have been neatly organized into various groups for easy access. Select **Productivity**. This will take you to a page with extensions that relate directly to productivity.

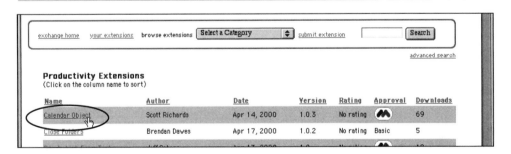

3. Notice that this page gives you a lot of useful information about each extension, such as author, date created, version, rating, approval, and number of downloads. Click on the **Calendar Object** link. This will take you to a page where you can download this extension.

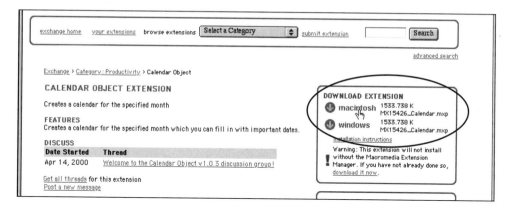

4. Under the **DOWNLOAD EXTENSION** section, click on the appropriate download link for the operating system you are using. For example, if you are using a Macintosh, click on the **macintosh** link. This will start the download process.

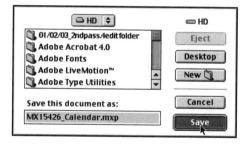

5. When you are prompted to save the extension, choose a location on your hard drive and click **Save**. Remember where you saved this file, because you'll need to access it later. You may want to store it in the same directory as the Dreamwever 3 application, so you'll know where it is in the future.

6. You're done with the Macromedia Exchange – Dreamweaver site for now, and you may log off before continuing with the exercise, if you wish.

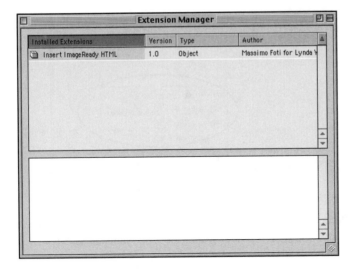

7. Select **Commands > Manage Extensions…**. This will launch the Extension Manager. As you did earlier, you will use this to install the extension you just downloaded.

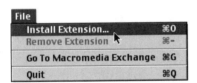

8. In the Extension Manager, select **File > Install Extension…**. This will open a dialog box so you can browse to the extension file you just downloaded. **Note:** All extension files you download should have an extension of **.mxp**.

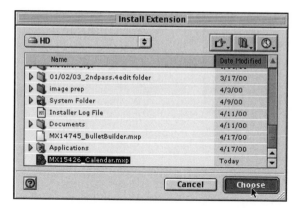

9. Locate the file on your hard drive and click **Choose**.

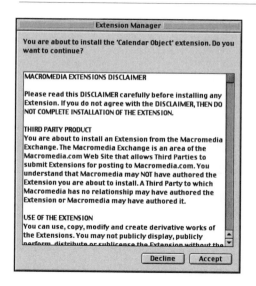

10. This is the same disclaimer you have seen before. Click **Accept**, and the installation will continue.

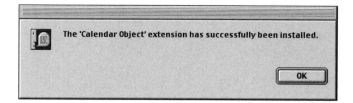

11. When the installation process is finished, the above dialog box will be displayed. Click **OK**.

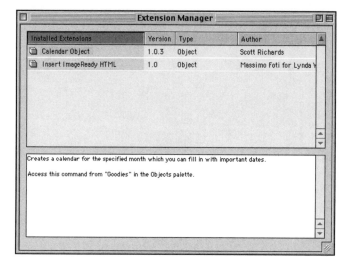

Once the installation is complete, your new extension will appear in the Extension Manager window.

12. Select **File > Quit** (Mac) or **File > Exit** (Windows) to exit the Extension Manager.

13. Return to Dreamweaver. Quit, and then relaunch so you can check out your new extension.

14. Return to Dreamweaver. From the Site window (**F5**), open the **calendar.html** file. This is nothing more than a blank file that we created for you.

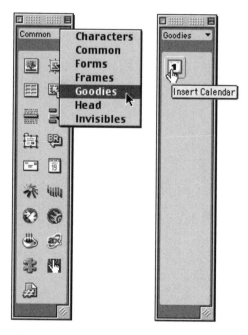

15. From the **Objects** palette, select **Goodies**. This is a new group that was added when you installed the **Calendar Object** extension; it's not part of the normal installation. Aren't you glad we told you that?

16. Click on the **Insert Calendar** icon in the **Goodies Object** palette. This will open the **Insert Calendar** dialog box.

> ### Tip | Extending Dreamweaver
>
> If you're well versed in JavaScript, you can learn to write your own custom extensions, and you'll find plenty of great resources on the Macromedia Exchange – Dreamweaver. If you want, you can download a PDF version of the Extensibility Manual from the Macromedia Web site and/or subscribe to their Extensibility newsgroup. Both are great resources for extensibility authors.

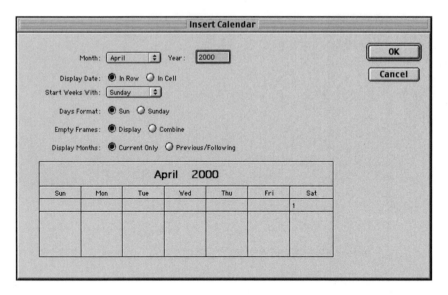

This extension, complete with this great interface, was designed by Scott Richards. Creating extensions requires a working knowledge of JavaScript and the Dreamweaver DOM.

17. If you want to modify some of the options, you can. Click **OK**.

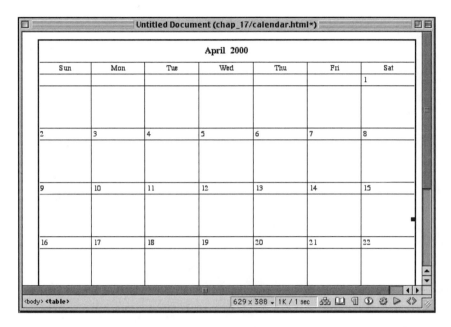

This is what the calendar looks like within Dreamweaver. Pretty slick, huh? Can you imagine having to create that Table and insert all the correct dates yourself? **Note:** *If you modified some of these options, your calendar may look different than this one.*

---

18. Save and close this file.

This is just one example of the many cool extensions you can download from the Macromedia Exchange. It is definitely one of those sites you should bookmark and check back with on a daily or weekly basis since new extensions are constantly being added.

If you have the energy, move on to the next chapter. If not, that's OK, don't worry, it will still be there when you are ready.

18.

Commands

| Color Schemes | Create Web Photo Album Command |

| Optimize Image in Fireworks Command |

| Mailto Command, using the History Palette |

chap_18

Dreamweaver 3
H•O•T CD-ROM

In Chapter 14, *"Automation,"* you learned how to automate your workflow using several techniques and features in Dreamweaver. Commands are another way to automate different actions in Dreamweaver. Commands are an internal Dreamweaver term that refers to the creation of a re-playable script or macro. Once you create a Command, it will appear in the Commands menu. If you are familiar with Photoshop, you might find Commands similar to Actions in that application.

This chapter focuses on two different approaches to Commands: creating your own custom Commands, or using one of the preexisting Commands that ships with Dreamweaver right out of the box, such as the **Set Color Scheme** Command. Dreamweaver also ships with two Commands that script actions between Dreamweaver and Fireworks, the **Create Web Photo Album** Command and the **Optimize Image in Fireworks** Command. (A demo version of Fireworks 3 is included in the **software** folder of the Dreamweaver 3 **H•O•T CD-ROM**).

This chapter includes hands-on exercises that show you how to use these Commands, and that demonstrate the power in scripting interaction between Dreamweaver and Fireworks. We will also show you how to build your own custom Command by copying steps from the **History** palette, which you used in earlier chapters.

Getting More Commands

It is possible to create Commands that are far more complicated than this chapter describes, such as scripting complex interactions between Dreamweaver and Fireworks. However, creating this type of Command requires very strong JavaScript skills, which are way beyond the scope of this book.

The good news is that the JavaScript jocks who can create more complicated custom Commands often distribute these from their own sites. There is actually a siz-able third-party market for Dreamweaver Commands. You'll find information below on the Macromedia Dreamweaver Support Center and a couple of the third-party sites we've found most useful. Make sure you also check out Appendix B, "*Online Resources*," for a listing of these sites. In addition, you can choose **Commands > Get More Commands...** to access Dreamweaver Exchange, the online community for extensibility developers.

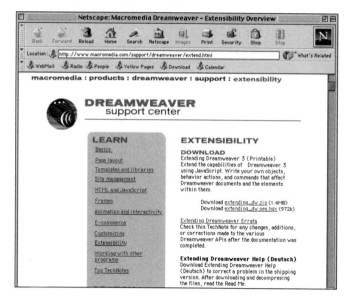

Dreamweaver Support Center

If you are proficient in HTML and JavaScript, the Macromedia site offers a great resource for developers who plan to create custom commands and other extensions to Dreamweaver. Macromedia has prepared a comprehensive document that gives detailed information on the extensive Dreamweaver API (**A**pplication **P**rogramming **I**nterface), which you can also download at the URL listed below. The API refers to the methods a programmer can use to make requests of the application.

http://www.macromedia.com/support/dreamweaver/extend.html

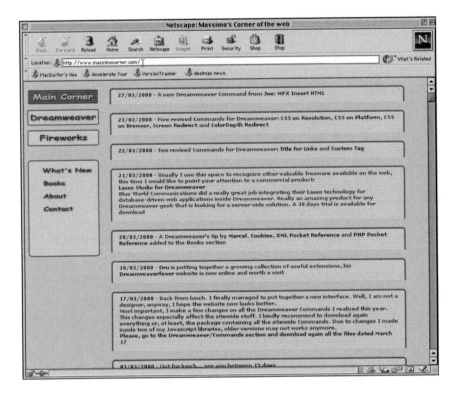

Massimo's Corner

Massimo's is a great site for getting some really useful Commands.

http://www.massimocorner.com

Dreamweaver Depot

One of the Web's largest repositories for Dreamweaver Behaviors, Commands, and Objects.

http://weblogs.userland.com/dreamweaver/commands/

I. _____Color Schemes

If you've ever developed Web pages on your own, there are a lot of intense decisions to make about the look and feel of your site. If you don't know which colors to pick, Dreamweaver has a helpful Command called Set Color Scheme, that will give you a variety of choices that are easy to change or experiment with. You'll learn how to use the Set Color Scheme Command in this exercise.

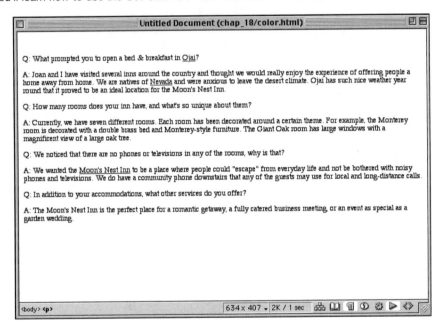

1. Define your site for Chapter 18. If you do not remember how to do this, revisit Exercise 1 in Chapter 3, _"Site Control."_ Open **color.html**. This file contains text and links that use the default color scheme.

2. Choose **Commands > Set Color Scheme....** The **Set Color Scheme Command** dialog box will open.

**Note:** If you don't like part of the color scheme in the Set Color Scheme Command, you can always go into Page Properties and change each option separately.

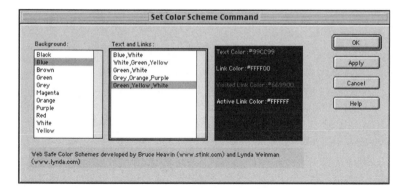

3. Select **Background: Blue** and **Text and Links: Green, Yellow, White**. Click **OK**.

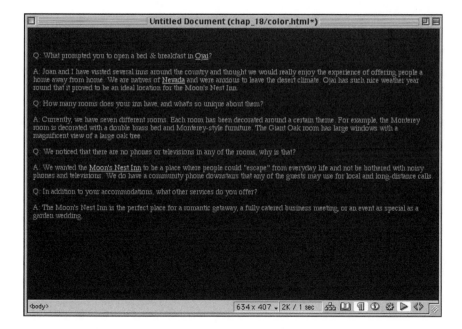

This is what the page looks like with the color scheme applied.

4. Choose **Commands > Set Color Scheme...** again. Experiment with a different combination of colors and click **Apply**. The preset color schemes are a great way to test different color variations.

5. When you're done playing with colors, save and close the file.

Create Web Photo Album Command

The Create Web Photo Album Command is a new feature in Dreamweaver 3 that automatically creates a complex Web site that displays your images. The Web Photo Album is great way for artists to display their work, for architects to show renderings to clients, for photographers to show proofs to clients, for families to share personal photos on the Web, and for other purposes too numerous to list here. All you need is a folder of images on your hard drive, and the Create Web Photo Album Command will convert them into an elaborate Web site, complete with thumbnails and larger images, and links to navigate between them. You'll be impressed by how easy it is to create this complex site with just a folder of images and the Dreamweaver Create Web Photo Album Command.

Note: Before completing this exercise, you must have Fireworks 3 installed on your computer. If you don't own a copy of Fireworks 3, don't worry. There is a free, 30-day trial demo copy in the **software** folder of the **H•O•T CD-ROM**.

1. Choose **File > New** to create a new blank document.

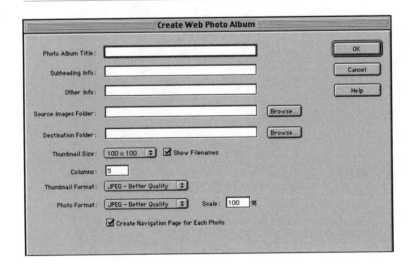

2. Choose **Commands > Create Web Photo Album**. This will open the **Create Web Photo Album** dialog box. If you don't have Fireworks installed yet, Dreamweaver will display a download Fireworks **trial** button.

3. Enter **Photo Album Title: The Moon's Nest Inn**. This text, along with the other information you enter on this page, will appear at the top of the home page of your completed Web Album site once you've completed this exercise.

4. Enter **Subheading Info: Ojai, California**. This text will appear immediately below the **Photo Album Title:** on your Web Album site.

5. Enter **Other Info: (805) 646-6635**. This text will appear immediately below the **Subheading Info:**.

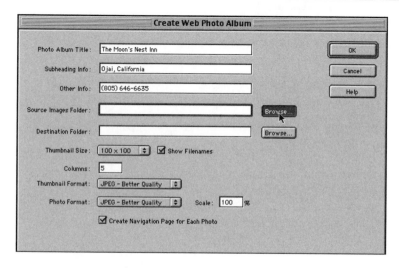

6. Click **Browse...** to the right of **Source Images Folder:** field. Browse to the **source images** folder inside the **chap_18** folder.

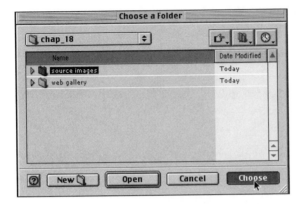

7. Click **Choose**. This option determines which folder contains the source files you want to use to create your Web Photo Album.

Tip: Web Photo Album can only process whole folders of images.

Tip | Web Photo Album Source Files

The source files for your Web Photo Album must be saved in either a .gif, .jpg, .jpeg, .png, .psd, .tif, or .tiff file format. The files must have the proper extension in order to be included in the Web Photo Album. If they are in another file format, you will get an error message that says no files exist in your source folder.

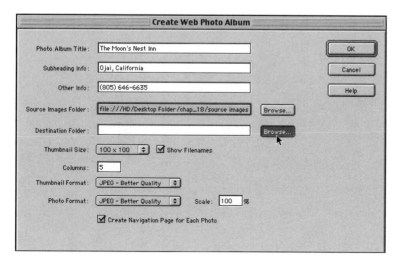

8. Click **Browse...** to the right of the **Destination Folder:** field. Navigate inside the **chap_18** folder to select the **web gallery** folder. This is an empty folder we made for you that will be the destination folder for the Web Photo Album once Dreamweaver is finished executing this Command.

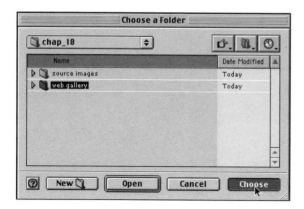

9. Click **Choose**.

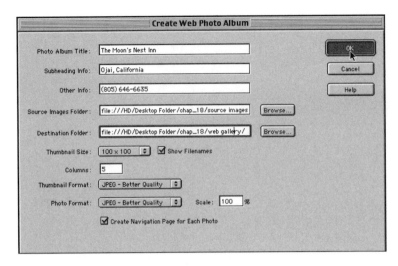

10. Inside the **Create Web Photo Album** dialog box, click **OK**. This will cause Fireworks to launch and start processing the images.

You will see a window like this while Fireworks is processing the images in your source folder.

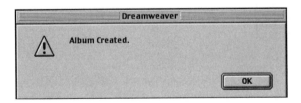

11. When Fireworks 3 is done processing the images, you will be returned to Dreamweaver, and you will see this dialog box. Click **OK**.

This is what your Dreamweaver page should look like after the Web Photo Album has been created.

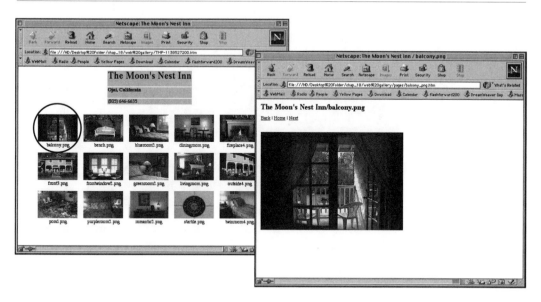

12. Press **F12** to preview your page in a browser. Click any of the images to see the larger version. Dreamweaver and Fireworks worked together to modify your images, create several Web pages, insert the images, and create links to all of the pages. It all happened in just a few seconds! Sweet.

3._____Optimize Image in Fireworks Command

In the previous exercise, you saw the power of Dreamweaver and Fireworks working together to create a Web Photo Album. This power is also available for editing single images in a document. The Optimize Image in Fireworks Command allows you to re-optimize an image without leaving Dreamweaver. This can save you a lot of time when you are trying to make your file sizes as small as possible.

Note: This exercise also requires that you have Fireworks 3 installed on your computer. If you don't own a copy of Fireworks 3, don't worry. There is a free, 30-day trial demo copy in the **software** folder of the **H•O•T CD-ROM**.

1. Open **optimize.html**, located inside the **chap_18** folder. This file contains a really large image, **monterey.jpg**, that is well over 80K. You are going to use the **Optimize Image in Fireworks** command to re-optimize this image right from Dreamweaver.

2. In the document window, click the image of the bed to select it.

3. Choose **Commands > Optimize Image in Fireworks…**. This will launch Fireworks, if you don't already have it open.

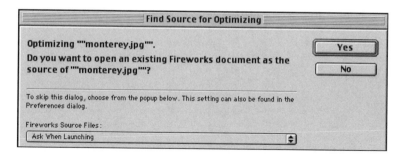

4. Fireworks will ask if you want to open an existing Fireworks document as the source of **monterey.jpg**. Click **Yes**. We have included a copy of the **monterey.png** source file for you to work with.

5. Browse to **monterey.png**, located inside the **images** folder, and click **Choose**.

Note | The Significance of PNG in Fireworks

What does it mean to click **Yes** or **No** in the **Find Source for Optimizing** dialog box? Fireworks uses the PNG file format as its native source format. A PNG that was generated by Fireworks includes proprietary information, such as vector, layer, effects, frames, and optimization settings. This type of PNG is also uncompressed, so it is a true master file, which is the best thing to start with when you plan to optimize for the Web. (If you are familiar with Photoshop, the same is true for a .psd file there.) If you save a GIF or JPEG from Fireworks and do not save the source PNG, you will not have an original uncompressed file to return to.

A simple guideline would be: if all you have is a GIF or JPEG, then click **No** in this dialog box; if you do possess a Fireworks PNG, then click **Yes**. Though it can be done, it's not a good idea to recompress an existing GIF or JPEG, because the image quality of your end result will not be as good.

6. If you get this dialog box, check the **Don't show again** checkbox, and then click **OK**. This is just advising you that you can increase the redraw speed by unchecking the **Preview** option, which means that the computer will draw the image faster on the screen as you make changes.

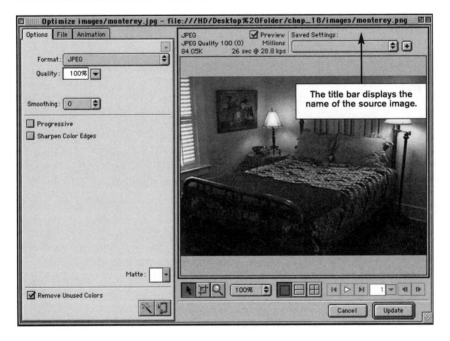

*The image will open inside Fireworks 3 in the **Optimize Images** dialog box. You can optimize this image just as if you had opened it in Fireworks 3 yourself.*

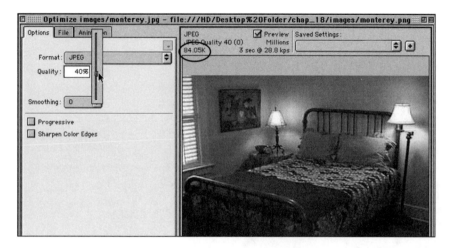

7. Notice that the image is over 80K. Click the **Quality Slider** and drag it down to **40%**.

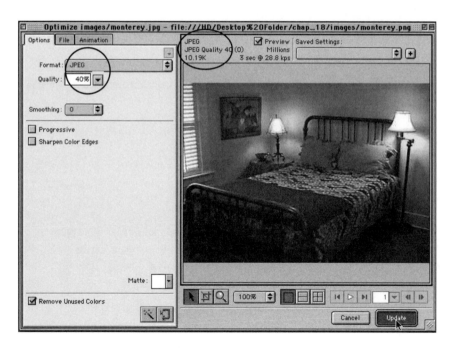

8. This will apply additional compression to the image and reduce its size to about 10K, an 800% reduction in file size! You can experiment with some of the other settings if you want. When you are happy with your changes, click **Update**.

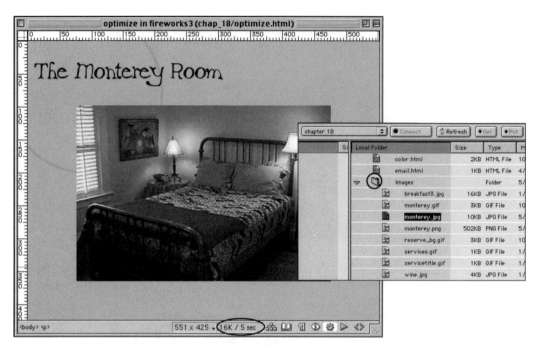

9. Fireworks will re-optimize and save a new .jpg file. You will then be returned to Dreamweaver and the new, much smaller image, will be inserted automatically inside your page. You can also look inside the **images** folder to see the smaller JPEG file.

10. Save your changes and close this file.

Tip | Refresh Problems

You might notice that the page size information at the bottom of your Dreamweaver document window does not update properly all of the time, especially after using the Optimize Image in Fireworks command. If that happens, you might have to save your work, quit and then restart Dreamweaver to see the lower page size.

4.————————————**Mailto Command, Using the History Palette**

This exercise will teach you how to create a custom Command that produces a **mailto:** link which can be added easily to other pages. A **mailto:** link is a link that allows a user to access a Web browser's email function. You'll learn to use the **History** palette to create this Command.

1. Open **email.html**, located inside the **chap_18** folder. This is just a blank file that has been saved for you.

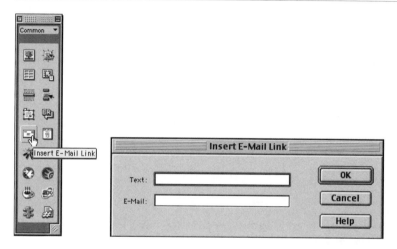

2. Click the Insert **E-Mail Link** object in the **Objects** palette (**Window > Objects** or **F2**). This will open the **Insert E-Mail Link** dialog box. If you have used this option before, you will see the last email address you entered inside the **E-Mail:** field.

3. Enter **Text: Send Us Email**. This is the text you want to appear on the page that will serve as a link. In some cases, you might want to type your email address here, so that it is more obvious to the user what will happen when he/she clicks the link.

4. Enter **E-Mail: email@moonsnestinn.com**. This is the email address where you want the email to be sent. Click **OK**.

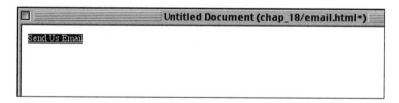

Your email link will appear on the page. You cannot test links inside Dreamweaver. To do that you must preview the page in a browser.

5. Make sure your **History** palette is open (**Window > History** or **F9**). Notice that it lists the **Insert E-Mail Link** you created.

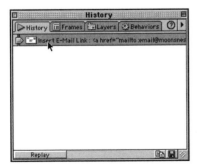

6. Click once in the **History** palette to select **Insert E-Mail Link:**. Selecting content from the **History** palette is the first step in creating Commands.

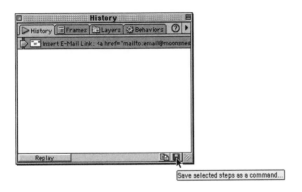

7. Click the **Save selected steps as a command...** icon at the bottom of the **History** palette. This will open the **Save As Command** dialog box.

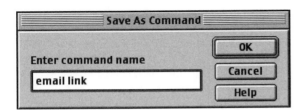

8. Type **email link** and click **OK**.

You've just created your first Command in Dreamweaver. Now it's time to try it out and see it in action.

9. Save and close this file. You won't need it for the rest of this chapter.

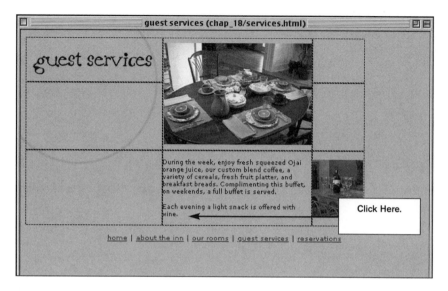

10. Open **services.html**, located inside the **chap_18** folder. Using the Command you just created, you will add an email link to the bottom of the page.

11. Click to the right of the period after the word "**wine**" at the bottom of the page, and press **Return** (Mac) or **Enter** (Windows). This will make some room so you can add the email link.

12. Choose **Commands > email link**. This will insert an email link onto your page. Is that cool or what? You can just begin to see how Commands can really help automate many of your tasks.

This is what your page should look like at the end of this exercise.

---

13. Save and close the file.

Note | Using the History Palette for Commands

Not everything you do in Dreamweaver can be saved as a Command. Most simple tasks can, but some mouse movements, such as clicking and dragging, can't be captured. In addition, actions across documents and in Frames can't be captured either. That's the bad news. The good news is that anytime you do something that can't be captured as a Command, a thin black line will appear across the History palette. Likewise, any menu command that can't be repeated will appear in the History palette with a red X next to it. Either way, the History palette provides you with great visuals so you know when something won't save as a Command.

Another chapter down the hatch. We hope you see the value in using Commands; they're a great way to automate complex tasks.

19.
Plug-Ins

| Linking to Sounds | Embedding Sounds |

| Inserting Flash Content | Inserting Director Content (Shockwave) |

| Inserting QuickTime Content |

chap_19

Dreamweaver 3
H•O•T CD-ROM

Hey, you're almost through the book! There's still another important feature of Dreamweaver to learn about, though – **Plug-Ins**. It's good to understand how to work with Plug-Ins because you may want to add exciting multimedia effects to your page, such as sound, Flash content, Director content (Shockwave), or QuickTime content. In this chapter, you'll learn how to add these effects in Dreamweaver via a variety of objects, and you'll learn how to set parameters in the Properties Inspector to control how and when your multimedia content will play.

Exciting as this sounds, it's also the area of Web development where the compatibility issues between browsers really get intense. Not everyone has the same Plug-Ins loaded, and some of the Plug-Ins work differently on Macs and Windows. Dreamweaver does a great job of letting you put this content on your site. It's the rest of the Web's limitations that you'll more likely have to struggle with!

Plug-Ins Require Viewer Participation

As you are working through these exercises, you might find yourself being directed to download Plug-Ins from the Internet or reassign them in your browser preferences. If this seems like a hassle, remember that you are asking your audience to do the same thing when you present Plug-In-based content to them!

URLs for Downloading Plug-Ins

Plug-Ins	URL
QuickTime	http://www.apple.com/quicktime
Flash	http://www.macromedia.com
Director	http://www.macromedia.com

I. _____Linking to Sounds

There are multiple ways to add sound to your page. In this first exercise, you will learn to add sound to your page by simply creating a link to a sound file. As you will see, there are some nuances to con-sider when you are working with sound files. For example, there is no standard format for sounds on the Web. Sounds are handled differently between browsers and operating systems (as if designing Web pages was not difficult enough). But have no fear! By the time you finish the hands-on exercises in this chapter, you'll have a much better understanding of sound on the Web.

1. Define your site for Chapter 19. Copy the contents of **chap_19** to your hard drive and press **F5** to define it. For a refresher on this process, revisit Exercise 1 in Chapter 3, *"Site Control."*

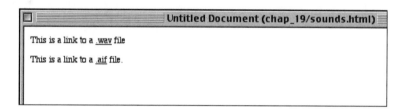

2. Open **sounds.html**. You will see two links at the top of the page. These two links point directly to two different sound files. The first link points to a .wav file, and the second link points to an .aif file.

3. Click on the .wav link at the top of the page. In the Properties Inspector, notice that this links to the **tell-me-about.wav** file. That's all there is to it. When the user clicks on this link in a Web browser, the sound will be played. You'll need to preview it in a browser in order to play it.

4. Click on the **.aif** link. Notice that this link points to the **sound.aif** file. Nothing too complicated about this so far. You are simply creating a link, but instead of pointing to an HTML document, you are pointing to a sound file.

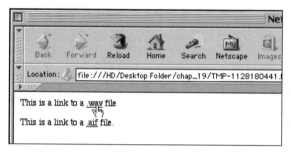

*When the page is previewed in Netscape Navigator 4.7 on the Mac, clicking on the **.wav** link should play the sound with the Netscape Audio player, the default setting. If you have QuickTime installed, it will play the sound with the QuickTime player.*

Tip | Different Sound Players

Both Netscape and Explorer let you choose what application or Plug-In will play audio files on Web pages. In fact, you can have different ones set for each type of audio format. For example, you might choose to have the QuickTime Plug-In play .aif and .wav files, and have the Flash Plug-In play .swf files. The point is, you have complete control over this by modifying your browser Preferences. You should check these settings if you experience any problems while trying to play sound files. For instructions on how to change these settings, refer to your browser's help feature.

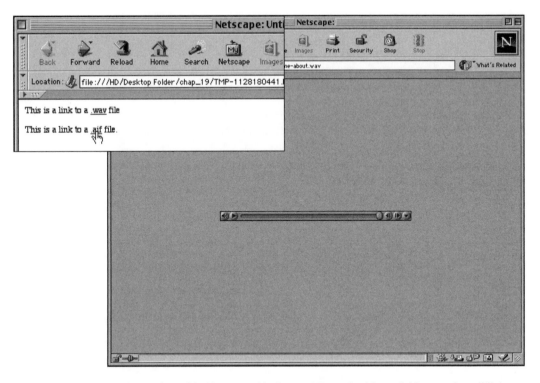

*When the same page is previewed in Netscape Navigator 4.7 on the Mac, clicking on the .aif link will launch the QuickTime Plug-In, if you have set the QuickTime Player as the audio player for all **.aif** files. You can do this in the Netscape **Preferences**, under **Applications**.*

---

5. Press **F12** to preview this page in a browser. Click on each one of the links. Clicking on the **.wav** link will play a sound of a man saying, "Tell me about your childhood." Clicking on the **.aif** link will play a beeping sound. You will have to use the **Back** button in the browser after clicking on the first link. Depending on how your browser Preferences are set up and what operating system you are using, clicking on the links might launch different audio players – or none at all!

---

6. Return to Dreamweaver and close the file.

Different Sound Formats

One of the problems of adding sound to your Web page is deciding which format you should use. Most Web publishers use either .aif or .wav files. These two formats are the native sound formats for the Mac and Windows operating systems, meaning that you will not have to rely on Plug-Ins, but it is a good idea to be familiar with the other formats that you might run into on the Web. The chart below gives you an idea of what's out there:

Sound Formats	
Extension	**Description**
.au	This format was one of the first introduced on the Internet and was designed for NeXT and Sun Unix systems.
.aiff/.aif	The .aif (**A**udio **I**nterchange **F**ormat) was developed by Apple and is also used on SGI machines. This is the main audio format for Macintosh computers.
.midi/.mid	The .midi (**M**usical **I**nstrument **D**igital **I**nterface) format was designed to translate how music is produced. MIDI files store just the sequencing information (notes, timing and voicing) required to play back a musical composition, rather than a recording of the composition itself, so these files are usually small, but playback quality is unpredictable.
.MP3	The .MP3 (**MP**EG-1 Audio Layer-**3**) format is the newest audio file format on the Web. It offers superior compression and great quality.
.ra/.ram	The .ra (**R**eal **A**udio) format was designed to offer streaming audio on the Internet.
.rmf	The .rmf (**R**ich **M**usic **F**ormat) was designed by Headspace and is used in the Beatnik Plug-In. This format offers good compression and quality.
.swa	The .swa (**S**hock**w**ave **A**udio) format was developed by Macromedia and is used in Flash.
.wav	The .wav (**Wav**e) audio format was developed by IBM and Microsoft. This is the main audio format for the Windows operating system. Wav files will play on Macs and other systems, as well.

2. _____**Embedding Sounds**

In addition to linking to a sound file, there is another, much better, approach to adding sound to your Web pages. You can choose to embed the sound so that it shows up inside your page, instead of linking to it (as in the last exercise). Embedding sounds gives you much more control over them, since they actually appear inside your HTML files, along with the other content. By modifying specific parameters, you can control when the sound plays and how it appears on the page, whether it loops (replays continuously) or not, and several other settings. So if you embed your sounds, you get more control, and hey, that's what most people want in life, right?

1. Open **embed.html** inside the **chap_19** folder. This is simply a blank file that we created for you.

2. Click on the **Insert Plugin** object on the **Objects** palette. Browse to the **chap_19** folder and highlight **sound.aif**. Click **Choose**. This will insert a small **Plug-In** icon on your page.

*In this instance, it does not matter where the sound file is placed physically on the page. If you had a page where you wanted the sound controllers (**play, stop,** and **rewind** buttons) to appear, you would simply position this element like any other image or text component of any page.*

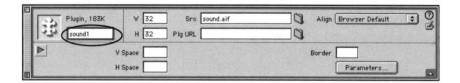

3. In the Properties Inspector, name this sound **sound1**.

4. Click on the **Parameters...** button. This will open the **Parameters** dialog box, which is where you would insert any of the parameters and values. There are some URLs listed at the end of this exercise that will give you more information about parameters and values.

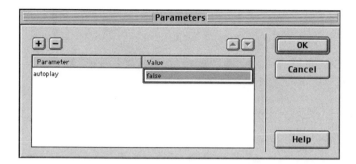

5. Under **Parameter** in the **Parameters** dialog box, type **autoplay**, then press **Tab**. Type **false**, and then click **OK**. This will prevent the sound file from automatically playing until the user clicks on the **play** button. This is a very useful parameter!

6. Press **F12** to preview your page in a browser. Click on the **play** button to hear the sound play. Here you can see that QuickTime is being used to play .aif files in Netscape Navigator 4.7 for the Macintosh. **Note:** If you get a broken image icon, you might have to download the Plug-In from http://www.apple.com/quicktime.

7. Return to Dreamweaver to save and close the file.

Note | What's a Parameter?

Most Plug-In content is controlled by a variety of parameters, which are different for each kind of Plug-In. A parameter is an option passed to the Plug-In which tells it how to behave. In this exercise, you learned how to set autoplay to be off. That setting was a parameter within the QuickTime specification.

This chapter covers sound, Flash, Shockwave, and QuickTime, but there are many other types of Plug-Ins on the Web as well. In order to learn what all the parameters are for a Plug-In, it's best to visit the site from which it can be dowloaded. Here's a list of sites with more information on Plug-In parameters from a variety of vendors.

LiveAudio Plug-In
http://developer.netscape.com/docs/manuals/js/client/jsguide/liveaud.htm

Apple's QuickTime Plug-In
http://www.apple.com/quicktime/authoring/embed2.html

Macromedia's Flash Plug-In
http://www.macromedia.com/support/flash/ts/documents/tag_attributes.htm

Macromedia's Shockwave Plug-In
http://www.macromedia.com/support/director/how/shock/objembed.html

Netscape's Plug-In Registry
http://www.home.netscape.com/plugins

Inserting Flash Content

Because both Dreamweaver and Flash are Macromedia products, it is not entirely surprising that Dreamweaver's support for Flash is superb. Instead of the generic **Insert Plugin** object that you used in the last exercise, Dreamweaver has an **Insert Flash** object all of its own.

1. Create a new document and save it as **flash.html** inside the **chap_19** folder.

2. Click on the **Insert Flash** object, and browse to **splash.swf**. Click **Choose**. This Flash piece was donated courtesy of Greg Penny of Flower Records (http://www.flowerrecords.com) and was designed by Richard Joffray (http://www.joffray.com).

3. Notice that the Properties Inspector has a play button? You should be able to play the content right in Dreamweaver, unlike DHTML or generic Plug-In content. Press **F12** to view the content in your browser, to check it again. It's that simple.

4. Return to Dreamweaver. Because Flash is vector-based, it can scale. Change both the **W** and **H** properties to **100%**, and press **F12** again. Now change the size of your browser. The content in your browser scales, too! This only happens if you set the width and height information to a percentage.

5. Save and close the file.

The next exercise will explain how to embed Shockwave content.

Note | What Is Flash?

Flash is a Macromedia software product that combines vector graphics, bitmap graphics, and sound to create dynamic content for the Web. Just as you can insert a graphic you created in another program into your Web page, you can author full-screen animation, sound, and interactivity within Flash, and add these features to your site without being dependent on HTML. Flash consists of both an authoring tool and a Plug-In. If you want to author Flash content, you will need the Flash application. If you want to view Flash content, you will need the Flash Plug-In installed in your browser. For more information, check out the Macromedia software Web site.

Macromedia's Flash
http://www.macromedia.com/software/flash/

Inserting Director (Shockwave) Content

Next, you'll get a chance to work with some Director (Shockwave) content. Once again, because this is a Macromedia product, you'll have the advantage of using an **Insert Shockwave** object instead of the generic **Insert Plugin** object.

1. Create a new document and save it as **director.html** inside the **chap_19** folder.

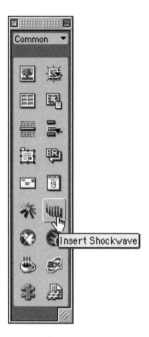

2. Click on the **Insert Shockwave** object, and browse to **leroy.dcr**. Click **Choose**.

3. Notice that the Properties Inspector has **W 32** and **H 32** as the dimensions? These are the default dimensions that you'll see in the Properties Inspector for Director or QuickTime content, because Dreamweaver can't automatically detect the size of these two formats. You'll need to plug in the correct dimensions to get this to work.

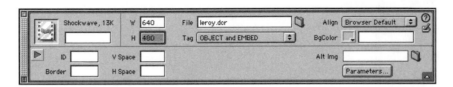

4. Enter the values **W 640** and **H 480**, and press **F12** to preview the content. How did we know that the width and height of the piece were **640 x 480**? Because Bruce, Lynda's husband, created it! Sadly, you must know the dimensions of the Shockwave piece before you enter the values, because Dream-weaver doesn't detect them for you.

Note | What Is Shockwave?

Shockwave is a Plug-In that allows a Web audience to view Macromedia Director content online. Macromedia Director, like Flash, is an authoring tool that supports better animation, sound and interactivity than HTML pages. The differences between Flash and Director relate to how the authoring tool is structured, how the interactivity is programmed, and how images are formatted for the Web.

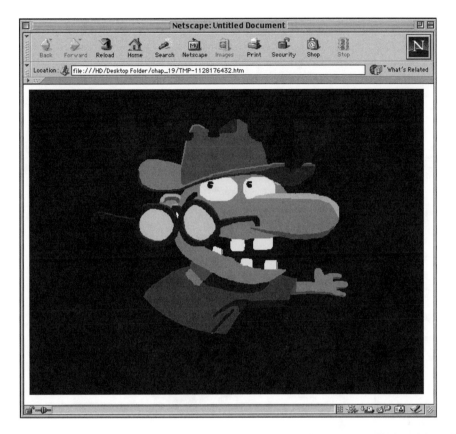

5. Try pulling Leroy's eyeglasses off. Lots of parts come off, so keep pulling on things. This is very similar to the drag-and-drop exercise you completed in Chapter 16, *"DHTML,"* only it was created in Macromedia Director.

---

6. Return to Dreamweaver. Save and close the file.

Time to move on to the next exercise, which shows how to insert a QuickTime movie.

5. _____Inserting a QuickTime Movie

QuickTime content is inserted in Dreamweaver using the **Insert Plugin** object. This exercise shows you how to embed the content and preview the results.

1. Create a new document and save it as **quicktime.html** inside the **chap_19** folder.

2. Click on the **Insert Plugin** object on the **Objects** palette, and browse to the file **testing.mov**. Click **Choose**.

3. Change the width and height information to **W 320**, **H 260** in the Properties Inspector. Note how Dreamweaver could detect the dimensions of a Flash movie, but not the dimensions of QuickTime or Director content?

It's important that you know the dimensions of the file before you embed it into Dream-weaver, so you can insert the correct values into the Properties Inspector. In this instance, the movie was **320 x 240**, but adding an extra 20 pixels makes room for the controller below the movie, as shown above.

4. Press **F12** to preview the movie in your browser. **Note:** If you get a broken image icon, you might have to download the Plug-In from http://www.apple.com/quicktime.

5. Return to Dreamweaver. Save and close the Dreamweaver file.

Note | What Is QuickTime?

QuickTime is a both a file format and a Plug-In that can present sound and movies. It is one of the most versatile file Plug-Ins on the Web, because it is able to play all the formats listed in the chart below this note.

QuickTime Versatility
QuickTime Supports:
AIF • AU • AVI • BMP • DV Stream • FLC
Image Sequence movie exporters • JPEG/ JFIF • MacPaint
MIDI • MP3 • Photoshop • PICT • Picture
PNG • QuickTime Image • QuickTime Movie
SGI • System 7 • Sound • Targa • Text • TIFF • WAV

20.

Getting It Online

| Free Web Hosting with GeoCities | Setting Up A GeoCities Account |
| Setting the FTP Preferences | Putting Files to the Web Server |
| File Synchronization |

chap_20

Dreamweaver 3
H•O•T CD-ROM

It's one thing to design a Web page, and it's an entirely different thing to get it online. One of the things we felt was missing from other books was concrete instructions covering how to access, upload and update files to a Web server. Until now, you were forced to struggle through this process on your own, which can prove frustrating. Well, fear not, we are here to walk you through the process of uploading your pages to a real live Web server. This means that you, your family, and friends will be able to see your creation on the Web.

This chapter will show you how to create a free Web hosting account with GeoCities and then use Dreamweaver to upload a Web site so that it can be viewed live, on the Internet. You do not have to sign up for the GeoCities account unless you want to follow along with the exercises. If you already have a Web hosting account, you can use that information to complete the following exercises. Either way, this chapter will show you how to set up your FTP preferences and upload your site, using Dreamweaver.

Free Web Hosting with GeoCities

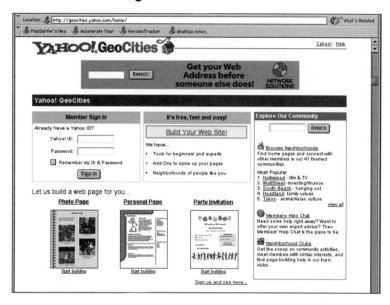

GeoCities: http://geocities.yahoo.com *is one of the many free Web host-ing services available on the Internet.*

There are several books that tell you how to upload your site, but we have never seen one that actually recommends a free hosting service and provides instructions about how to upload your files and test all of the FTP features of your HTML editor. Well, there is good news; this book is here to help with this essential missing link.

There are several services on the Web that offer free Web hosting. Of these free services, GeoCities is probably the most famous. GeoCities was one of the first Web services to offer free Web hosting to anyone that wanted to sign up. Within just a few minutes, you could have a place to upload your files to on the Web. GeoCities was recently acquired by Yahoo!, and continues to offer a great free service to the Web community.

You will be pleasantly surprised by how much you get for free. The GeoCities free Web host-ing package includes a lot of extras. All you need to complete the exercises in this chapter are the 15 megabytes of free disk space and FTP access that are provided with the free Web hosting account.

If you already have a hosting service of your own, feel free to try the same exercises that are offered for the free GeoCities account. For the FTP information, just substitute the info you've received from your own hosting service.

Signing Up with GeoCities

The first step in getting your free GeoCities Web site online involves filling out a form on their Web site. This exercise will show you what parts of the form need to be completed.

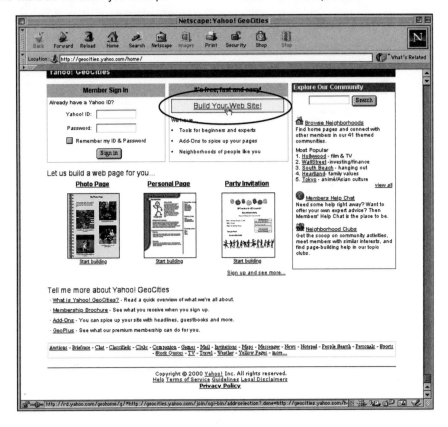

1. Launch your preferred Web browser and browse to the GeoCities home page at http://geocities.yahoo.com. Here you'll find a complete rundown on their services.

2. Click on the **Build Your Web Site!** link. This will take you to another Web page where you can choose to sign up for your own account.

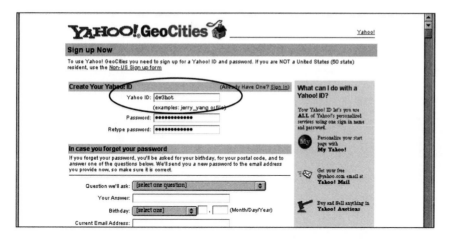

3. Complete all of the information requested on the form. Your **Yahoo! ID** will appear as part of your GeoCities URL. Our Yahoo! ID is **dw3hot**; therefore, our URL is http://www.geocities.com/dw3hot/.

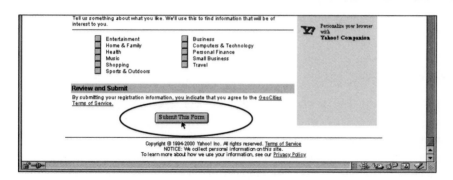

4. When you are finished entering your information, click the **Submit This Form** button at the bottom of the page. This will submit your information for processing.

5. On the **About Your Home Page** page, you'll answer a few questions about your Web site. For item **1**, enter a brief description for your site. For item **2**, choose a category that is appropriate for your site. Click **Submit**. This will finalize the activation process.

Note | Privacy Policies

Anytime you provide personal information about yourself on a Web site, you should be familiar with the recipient's privacy policy. Some sites gather personal information and then sell it to marketing companies. This can result in some extra and unsolicited emails in your inbox. If this is of serious concern to you, make sure you review GeoCities' Privacy Policy before you provide them with information. You can review their Privacy Policy at: http://docs.yahoo.com/info/privacy/.

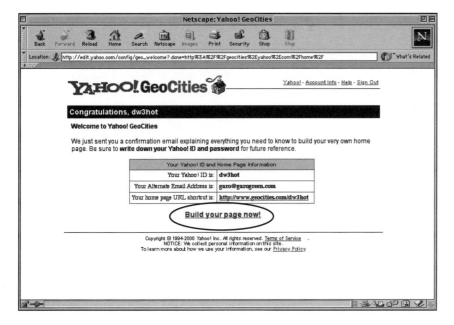

This is what your page should like when you have successfully registered with Yahoo!

---

6. When GeoCities has finished processing your application for free Web space, you'll be taken automatically to the **Welcome** page, where your Yahoo! ID, email address, and URL are confirmed. Click the **Build your page now!** link to complete the configuration of your Web site.

---

7. You should immediately receive a confirmation email (or two) that repeats your user info and URL, and provides more information on GeoCities Web services.

---

8. You are now ready to set up your **FTP Preferences** in Dreamweaver and begin uploading your site. Exit the browser; you will come back to it later after you have uploaded your site from Dreamweaver.

---

2. _____ Setting the FTP Preferences

In order for your site to be seen on the World Wide Web, your files need to be uploaded to a live Web server. Most Web developers and designers build pages on their hard drive (as you have done in this book) before transferring their files to a live Web server. In Dreamweaver, the files on your hard drive are referred to as local files, and the files on a live Web server are referred to as remote files. You can upload your files from Dreamweaver by using the Site Definitions FTP (**F**ile **T**ransfer **P**rotocol) settings.

The information that you need to fill out in the FTP settings of Dreamweaver will be contained in the email you receive from GeoCities, such as the FTP Host, Host Directory, Login (user name or ID), and Password. In this exercise, you will enter this necessary information into Dreamweaver's settings, so that you can upload your Web site to a Web server.

1. Copy **chap_20** to your hard drive. Define your site for Chapter 20 using the **chap_20** folder as the **Local Root Folder**. If you need a refresher on this process, visit Exercise 1 in Chapter 3, _"Site Control."_

2. In the **Define Sites** window, choose **Chapter 20** and click **Edit....**

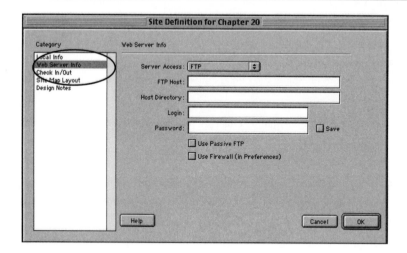

3. In the **Site Definition** dialog box, click on **Web Server Info** in the **Category** list, and then choose **FTP** from the **Server Access:** pop-up menu. This will give you access to the various FTP settings you will need to modify before you upload files to your site.

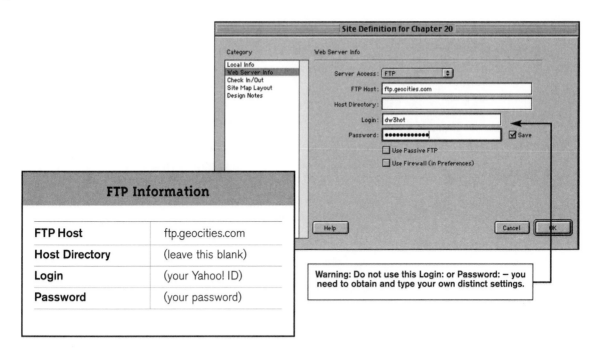

<table>
<tr><td colspan="2">FTP Information</td></tr>
</table>

FTP Host	ftp.geocities.com
Host Directory	(leave this blank)
Login	(your Yahoo! ID)
Password	(your password)

Warning: Do not use this Login: or Password: — you need to obtain and type your own distinct settings.

If you signed up for the free GeoCities account, your FTP information should be similar to the infor-mation above. You can get more information about these settings from the email that you receive from GeoCities. However, if you are using your own FTP service, you would enter that information instead.

4. Enter the information for the **Web Server Info** options as shown above.

5. Click **OK**. This will return you to the **Define Sites** window. Click **Done**.

What is FTP?

FTP stands for **F**ile **T**ransfer **P**rotocol. This term is usually associated with the process of uploading Web files to a live Web server. You will hear this term used as a noun ("I used an FTP program to upload my files"), and as a verb ("I am going to FTP all of my files now!").

It is important to note that you do not have to use Dreamweaver to exchange files with the remote server. You can use other FTP applications as well, such as Fetch (Mac) or WS_FTP (Windows). There are advantages to using Dreamweaver over these applications however, such as file synchronization and site management, and you'll learn about these advantages shortly.

Below you will find a handy chart that describes the FTP settings in Dreamweaver:

FTP Settings in Dreamweaver	
Setting	**Description**
FTP Host	This will typically be an address similar to the URL of your Web site. In some cases it may begin with an FTP prefix.
Host Directory	If you have a specific directory on the server where you are supposed to place your files, you would enter that here. This option is not always used.
Login	You will be given a user name or ID to access the remote server. It is important that you enter this information exactly as it is given to you, otherwise you will have problems connecting.
Password	In addition to a user name or ID, you will also be given a password to access the remote server. If you don't want to enter the password every time you connect to the remote server, place a check in the **Save** checkbox and then Dreamweaver will remember your password! By the way, the password entered here is just stored in a text file on your hard drive, so anyone can read it. Don't check this if security is a concern at your location.

3. _____Putting Files to the Web Server

Now that you have set up your FTP preferences, you are ready to use Dreamweaver to connect to a Web server and upload your files. Once you have completed this exercise, you will be able to see your Web site live on the Internet. Woo-hoo!

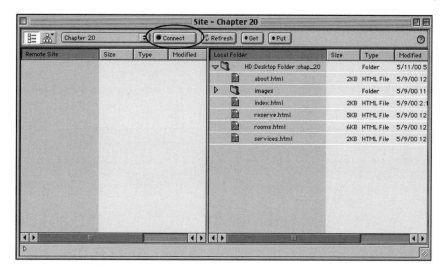

1. Before you try to upload your files to the Web server, make sure you have established a connection to the Internet. For most people, this simply involves connecting through an ISP with a modem.

2. Make sure your Site window is open; if not, press **F5**. Notice that the **Connect** button, at the top of the window, is no longer grayed out. Once you enter your FTP Preferences, you will have access to this feature.

3. Click **Connect**. This will connect Dreamweaver to your Web server. If you have not established a connection to the Internet with your modem/network, you will get an error message.

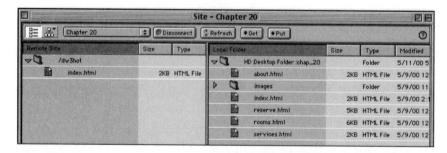

*After making a successful connection to the Web server, your Site window should look like this. The contents of the Web server are displayed in the left side of the window. The **index.html** file was put there automatically by GeoCities. You'll overwrite this with your own **index.html** in the next few steps.*

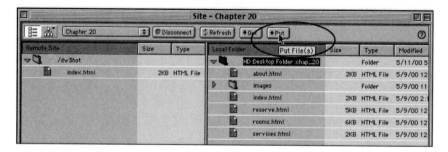

4. Scroll to the top of the **Local Folder** column and click on the Local Root Folder to select it. With the Local Root Folder selected, you are ready to upload your site. Click **Put**.

5. You will be prompted on whether you want to upload your entire Web site. Since this is the first time you are uploading your site, click **OK**.

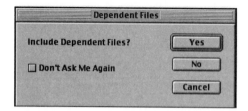

6. When you are prompted to include the dependent files, click **Yes**. This will ensure that all of the necessary files are uploaded to your Web server. Dreamweaver will now upload your files. You can sit back for a few minutes. This would be a great time to get some coffee. ;-)

Note | The Difference Between Getting and Putting

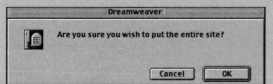

There are two different ways to transfer files between the local site and the remote site (Web server). The **Get** command will copy the selected files from the remote site to your local site. This process is referred to as downloading. In addition, if you are using the **Check-In** and **Check-Out** option, the Get command will copy the file to the local site as a Read-Only file, leaving the original on the Web server for others to download. The **Put** command will copy the selected files from the local site to the remote site. This process is referred to as uploading.

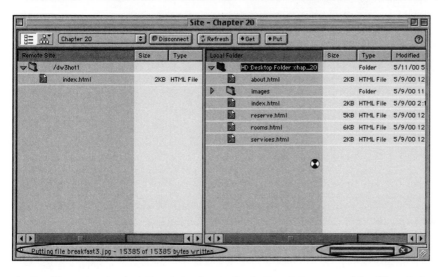

As the files are uploaded, the status bar in the bottom left corner of the Site window confirms that files are being uploaded. The progress bar, in the bottom right corner, displays the upload progress for individual files.

7. When you are prompted to overwrite the **index.html** file, click **Yes**. This will overwrite the default **index.html** that is already on the server. This file was created automatically when you set up your account with GeoCities; it is no longer needed.

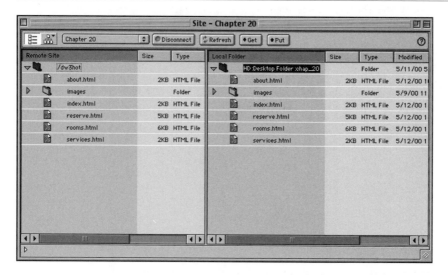

When Dreamweaver has finished uploading your files, the status bar will no longer display any upload status. **Note:** *If an error occurs during the transfer process, Dreamweaver maintains a log of FTP errors that you can review to help troubleshoot the problem. You can access this log by select-ing* **Site > FTP Log** *(Mac) or* **Window > FTP Log** *(Windows).*

8. Open a browser. Browse to the URL provided in the emails from GeoCities. Since we are using Garo's account, the URL will be http://www.geocities.com/dw3hot/. Of course, your URL will be different. Voilà, your Web site is live on the Web! Congratulations, make sure you show all your friends. ;-)

File Synchronization

Once you have your Web site uploaded, it's no longer necessary to upload the entire site. You only need to upload the pages that have been modified since the last upload. Dreamweaver has a great way of checking the modification dates of files and then downloading/uploading only the files that have changed. This process is called **File Synchronization**. Dreamweaver lets you specify which files you want to put onto or get from your remote server, and it will confirm which files have been updated after the synchronization process completes.

This exercise will have you revise a file, and then show you how to synchronize your local and remote files within Dreamweaver.

1. Make sure your Site window is open. If it's not, press **F5**.

---

2. In the **Local Folder** column, double-click the **index.html** file to open it. You are going to modify this file so you can see how file synchronization works.

3. At the bottom of the page, type **your name** next to "**This web page was created by:**"

---

4. Press **Shift+Return** (Mac) or **Shift+Enter** (Windows) to insert a line break and move your cursor to the next line.

Next, you'll add a feature to your page that displays when the page was last updated.

---

5. Type the words **last revised:**.

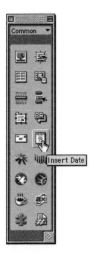

6. From the **Common Objects** palette, click on the **Insert Date** icon. This will open the **Insert Date** dialog box.

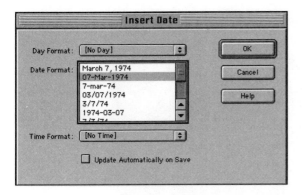

7. From the **Date Format:** list, select the date format you want to add to your page.

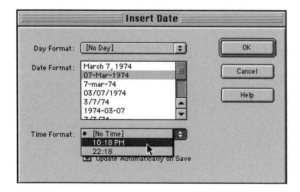

8. From the **Time Format:** menu, select a time format, if any, you want to add to your page.

9. Check the **Update Automatically on Save** checkbox. This will ensure that the date (and time, if selected) is updated each time you save your page. Click **OK**.

This will insert the current date (and time, if selected) into your page. In addition, each time the page is saved, it will update this information.

Tip | Modifying the Date Format

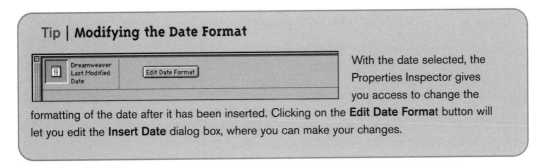

With the date selected, the Properties Inspector gives you access to change the formatting of the date after it has been inserted. Clicking on the **Edit Date Format** button will let you edit the **Insert Date** dialog box, where you can make your changes.

10. Select **File > Save**. It is really important that you save your files before you attempt to synchronize them with the remote server.

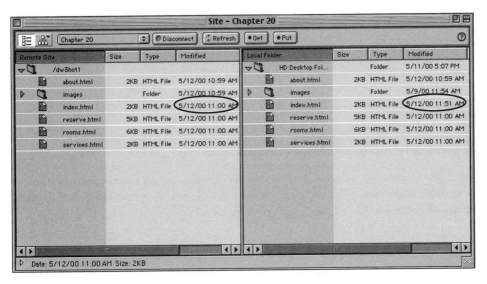

11. Press **F5** to open the Site window. Note that the **index.html** page in the local site has a newer modification time than the **index.html** currently on the remote site.

The Site window can display the modification information of the files in the local and remote sites. This is very useful when you want to know where the most current version of a file is located.

12. Select **Site > Synchronize**. This will open the **Synchronize Files** dialog box. This window controls the synchronize settings. Click **OK**.

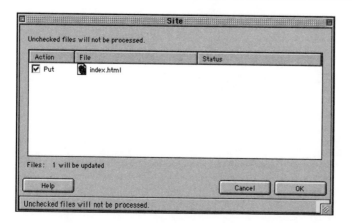

13. A separate Site window will open that outlines what files need to be uploaded in order to properly synchronize the site. In this case, only the **index.html** file should appear in this list, because that's the only file that has changed after our initial upload. Make sure you are connected to the Internet, then click **OK** to upload the **index.html** file.

Tip | **Identifying Newer Files**

It's easy to compare modification dates between two files, but what about hundreds of files? Not so easy. Dreamweaver has a great feature that will let you select the newest files in your site before you synchronize. You can access this feature by selecting **Site > Site Files View > Select Newer Local**. This is great when you only want to see a listing of the most recent files before you upload them.

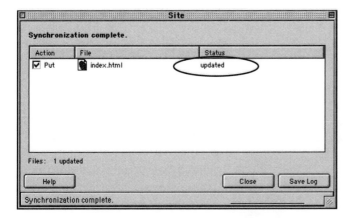

14. The file will be uploaded to the Web server. When this process is complete, the Status of the file will say **updated**. This is an indication that the synchronization worked. Click **Close**.

---

15. You can save and close all open files; you are finished with this exercise. In this exercise we showed you how to add the **Insert Date** feature to your page. This was noted as a change to the document, which Dreamweaver recognized during the file synchronization process.

*Please note that any change you make to any document will be recognized in the file synchroniza-tion process. We just chose to show you the **Insert Date** feature in this exercise too. When working on a real Web site, you can imagine how much time the synchronize feature can save you.*

---

16. Return to your browser and navigate to your GeoCities home page. You should see the updated page that was just uploaded by Dreamweaver.

It's our hope that this book helped you get up to speed with Dreamweaver quickly, and that you now feel ready to use your skills to create just about any Web site project. We wish you the best of luck with all of your future projects. Well, you've made it! Congratulations, you certainly deserve it! Rock on!

Troubleshooting FAQ

| Appendix A |

H•O•T

Dreamweaver 3

If you run into any problems while following the exercises in this book, this F.A.Q. is intended to help. This document will be maintained and expanded upon at this book's companion Web site:

http://www.lynda.com/books/dw3hot.

If you don't find what you're looking for here or there, please send an email to:

dw3faq@lynda.com.

If you have a question related to Dreamweaver, but unrelated to a specific step in an exercise in this book, visit the Dreamweaver site at: http://www.macromedia.com/ support/dreamweaver/ or call their tech-support hotline at 415.252.9080.

Q: Why do strangely named files appear inside my exercise folders?

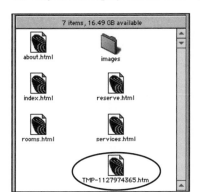

A: Whenever you preview a page in a browser, Dreamweaver creates a temporary HTML file. You can delete these files when they appear, or leave them alone, since they don't hurt anything. When and if you upload your finished work to a Web server, you will want to delete them or not upload them. If you do accidentally upload them to your server, however, they won't hurt anything since they aren't truly linked to any of your site. These files will be deleted automatically when you quit Dreamweaver.

Q: How do I call up the Properties Inspector?

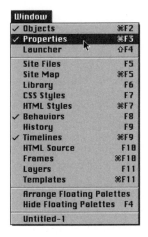

A: If you can't see the Properties Inspector or, for that matter, any of Dreamweaver's palettes, pull down the **Window** menu and click on the one you want to open. A list of short-cut keys that will help you quickly access all of Dreamweaver's palettes can be found at the end of Chapter 2, *"Interface."*

Q: I defined my site for a chapter, but files that are listed in the exercises aren't there. What happened?

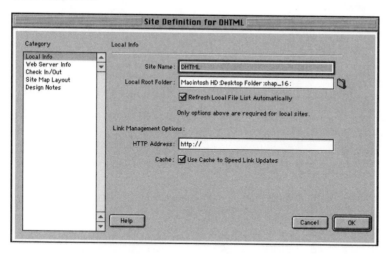

A: This could be because when you were defining the site you specified a folder that was inside the chapter folder, instead of the chapter folder itself. Go ahead and redefine the site. (If you need to revisit these steps, visit Exercise 1 in Chapter 3, *"Site Control."*) **Note:** Selecting the correct folder is done differently on Mac and Windows, as shown below.

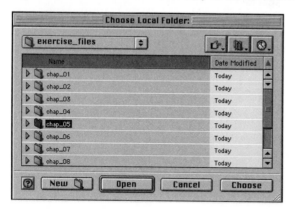

(Mac) When you're browsing to define the chapter folder and the **Choose Local Folder:** dialog box pops up, notice how there's both an **Open** and a **Choose** option. Highlight the **chapter** folder, and click **Choose**. Don't click **Open**, because you would then define as your site an interior folder, instead of the main folder. This is opposite to the way Windows users define their sites.

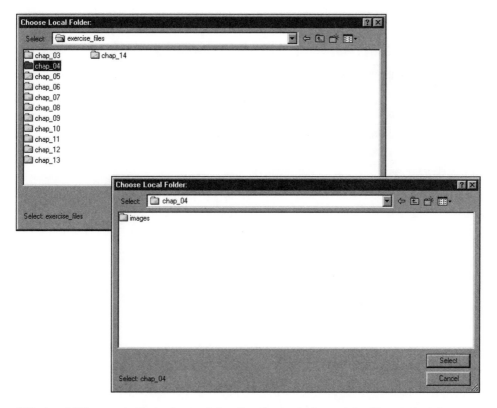

(Windows) When you're browsing to define the chapter folder and the **Choose Local Folder:** dialog box pops up, select the **chapter** folder. First click **Open**. After the folder is opened, click **Select**. This is opposite to the way Macintosh users define their site.

Q: Where's the Color palette?

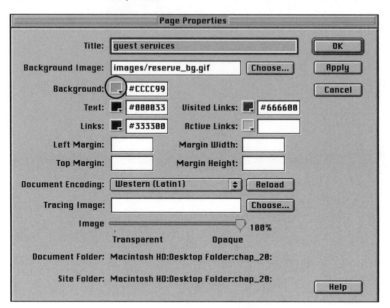

A: Because it's context sensitive, the Color palette only appears when you click in one of Dreamweaver's color wells. Color wells appear inside the Properties Inspector and the Page Properties dialog box.

Q: I thought the browser-safe palette contained 216 colors, but the Color palette in Dreamweaver looks like it contains a lot more colors than that. What's up?

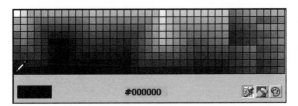

#000000

A: Dreamweaver's Color palette repeats certain colors in order to create an array that is helpful for color picking. The colors are organized by hue from left to right, and by value from top to bottom. This palette is helpful for seeing all the hues together (such as all the blues, reds, yellows, or greens), or for evaluating which colors to choose from light to dark.

Q: I just specified a Tracing Image in my Page Properties window, but I can't see it when I preview the page in my browser. Panic is starting to set in!

A: The Tracing Image is a template to be used for layout in Dreamweaver. It is invisible in the browser window, so if you don't see it, that's the whole point! It's there for your reference only, and your end users will never see it.

Q: On the Mac, Dreamweaver can't seem to find any of my files when I preview in the browser, and/or my Dreamweaver document window has the Objects palette embedded in it and I can't get rid of it.

A: You've probably run into a memory leak. Dreamweaver requires at least 32 MB of RAM, but we recommend at least 64 MB. RAM is a lot cheaper than it used to be, so if you plan to use Dreamweaver you can save yourself a lot of heartache by buying more RAM!

Q: I put one Layer on top of another! How do I delete it?

A: To delete a Layer, select it by the handle at its top and hit **Delete**. Of course, there's always the universal undo command, **Cmd+Z** (Mac) or **Ctrl+Z** (Windows).

Q: When I convert Layers to Tables, I get an error message stating that one of the Layers is offscreen. How did this happen, and how do I fix it?

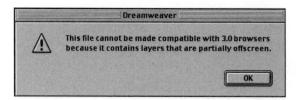

A: It is possible to create a Layer and move it, using the arrow keys, so that it is partially or fully offscreen. This is actually handy for images that you want to have bleed off the edge, or animations that begin offscreen. For converting to Tables, however, it won't work! If you can locate the offending Layer, click on its edge and use the arrow keys to move it back into the screen area. If you can't find the Layer, try opening the **Layers** window (**Window > Layers**) and selecting each Layer name that appears inside the window. Eventually, you'll be able to figure out which is on or off the screen by process of elimination.

Q: Why do I get the message, "To make a document-relative path, your document should be saved first"? I can't figure out what this gibberish means!?

A: Hey, we're with you. It would be nice if the dialog box simply stated, "Save your file now, or Dreamweaver can't keep track of your files," because that's all it's asking you to do. Sigh. If only developers knew how to speak in non-technical terms at times, eh? All you need to do is click **OK** and save your file (inside the defined site), and Dreamweaver won't bark any more.

Q: Why do I get the message that my file is located outside of the Root Folder?

A: Dreamweaver is asking you to move the file into the Root Folder that you've defined as your site. If you work with files outside your defined Root Folder, Dream- weaver cannot keep track of your links or manage your site, which is counterproductive to the way the program is structured and to your workflow. Though this message is annoying, it is actually helping you maintain a healthy site without broken links and upload problems when you publish it. **Note:** There are different ways to handle this message, depending on the sys-tem you are running.

• (Mac) You should click **Yes**, and then browse to the correct folder. At that point you will be prompted to **Save**, which you should do.

• (Windows) You should click **Yes**, and Dreamweaver will automatically pop you into the cor-rect folder. Click **Save**, and the file will be moved.

Q: Why aren't my Templates working?

A: If you leave a Template file open and work on another site (such as another chapter in this book that you've defined as a different site), Dreamweaver can't keep track of your Templates. It's best to work on a single site at a time, and not flip between sites while leaving files open from another defined site. This is true with all Dreamweaver documents, although Templates and Libraries are particularly sensitive to site-definition confusion.

Q: When I try to locate class files, why can't I see the file extensions at the end of file names, such as .gif, .jpg, and .html?

A: On Windows, you will need to change your Preferences to view file name extensions. Instructions to do this are inside the *"Introduction."*

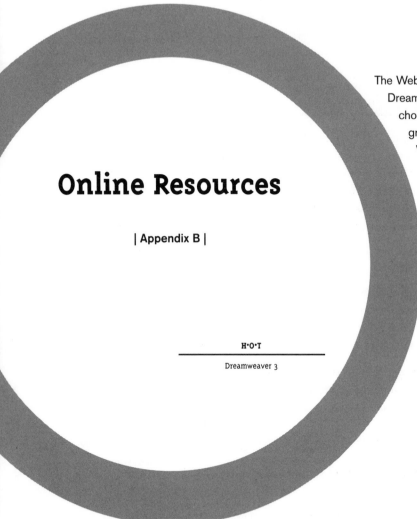

The Web is full of great resources for Dreamweaver users. You have ample choices between a variety of newsgroups, listservs, and third-party Web sites that can really help you get the most out of Dreamweaver. This appendix lists some of the best resources for learning and extending Dreamweaver.

Online Resources

| Appendix B |

H•O•T

Dreamweaver 3

Macromedia Discussion Groups

Macromedia has set up several discussion boards (newsgroups) for Dreamweaver. This is a great place to ask questions and get help from thousands of Dreamweaver users. The newsgroup is composed of beginning to advanced users, so you should have no problem finding the type of help you need, regardless of your experience with the program. Garo Green is an active participant, as well as many other Dreamweaver authors. In order to access these newsgroups, you will need a newsgroup reader, such as Microsoft Outlook or Free Agent.

Dreamweaver

news://forums.macromedia.com/macromedia.dreamweaver

Course Builder for Dreamweaver

news://forums.macromedia.com/macromedia.dreamweaver.coursebuilder

Dynamic HTML

news://forums.macromedia.com/macromedia.dynamic.html

Listservs

A listserv is different than a newsgroup, and offers another way people can ask questions and get help with Dreamweaver. Questions and answers are exchanged through the email application of your choice. Blueworld, the developers of Lasso for Dreamweaver, maintain an active and very useful listserv for Dreamweaver.

Blueworld Listserv:

http://www.blueworld.com/blueworld/lists/dreamweaver.html

Third-Party Dreamweaver Web Sites

Massimo's Corner

http://www.massimocorner.com/

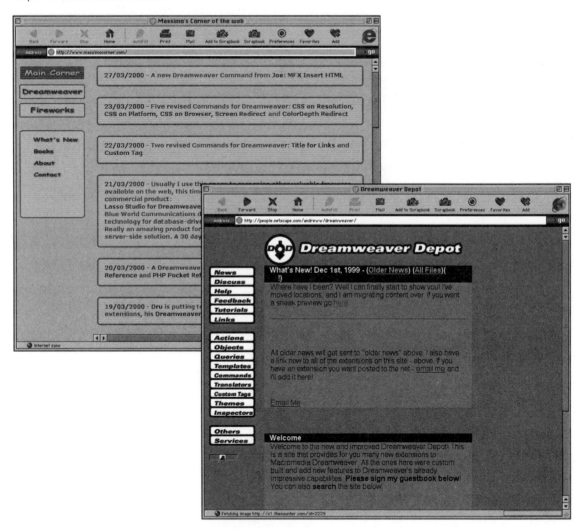

Dreamweaver Depot

http://people.netscape.com/andreww/dreamweaver/

Yaromat

http://www.yaromat.com/dw/index.html

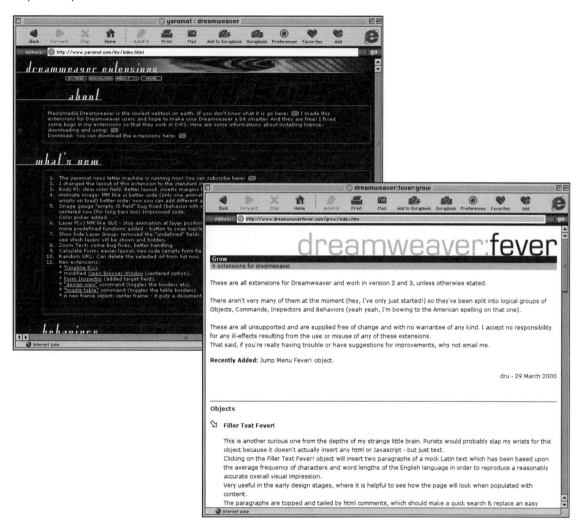

Dreamweaverfever.com

http://www.dreamweaverfever.com/grow/index.htm

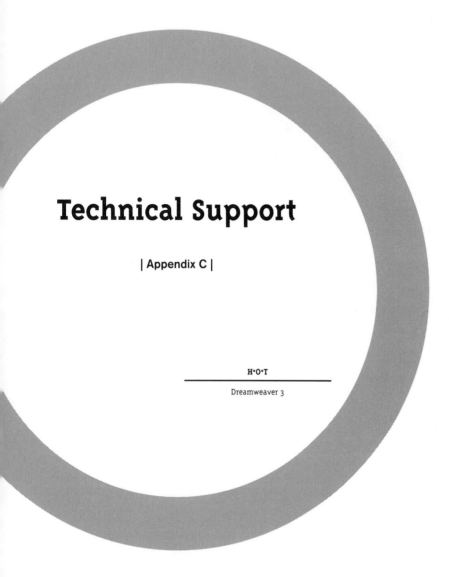

Technical Support

| Appendix C |

H•O•T

Dreamweaver 3

Macromedia Technical Support

http://www.macromedia.com/support/
415.252.9080

If you are having problems with Dreamweaver, please contact Macrome-dia Technical Support at the number listed above. Macromedia staff will be able to help you with such typical problems as: the trial version has expired on your computer, your computer crashes when you try to launch the application, etc. Please note that **lynda.com** cannot help troubleshoot technical problems with Dreamweaver.

Peachpit Press

customer_service@peachpit.com

If your book has a defective CD-ROM, please contact the customer serv-ice department at the above email address. We do not have extra CDs at **lynda.com**, so they must be requested directly from the publisher.

lynda.com

http://www.lynda.com/books/dw3hot/
dw3faq@lynda.com

We have created a companion Web site for this book, which can be found at http://www.lynda.com/books/dw3hot/. Any errors in the book will be posted to the Web site, and it's always a good idea to check there for up-to-date information. We encourage and welcome your comments and error reports to dw3faq@lynda.com. Both Lynda and Garo receive each of these emails.

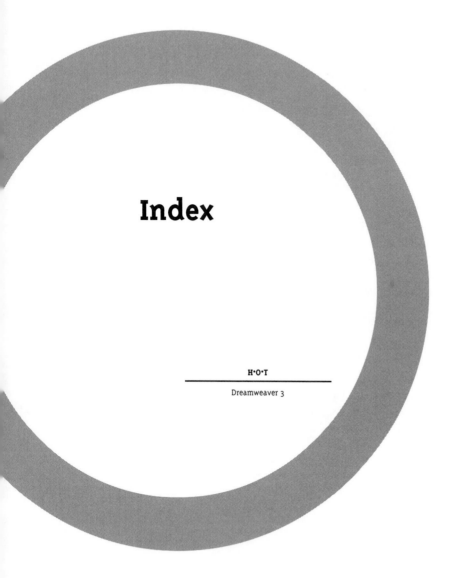

Index

H•O•T

Dreamweaver 3

Symbols

(hash mark), 106, 117, 356, 453, 468, 478
.. (dots), 45
/ (forward slash), 45
© (Copyright symbol), 183, 184
® (Registered symbol), 183, 184
™ (Trademark symbol), 183, 184

A

absolute links, 36-39
  creating, 73
  defined, 36
  displaying, 47
  illustrated, 38
  in path structures, 42
  URLs, 39
  See also links
Actions
  defined, 456
  repeating, 180-182
  See also Behaviors
active links, 67, 68, 69
  colors, setting, 67, 68, 69
  defined, 280
  See also links
Adjust Tracing Image Position dialog box, 195
.aif files, 525, 526, 529
alignment
  background image, 217
  baseline, 167
  bottom, 167
  browser default, 167
  center, 165
  default behavior, 237
  foreground image, 217
  image, 204, 220, 237-245
  Layer edge, 210
  left, 165, 167
  middle, 167
  object, 23
  options, 165, 166, 167
  percentage-based Table, 246-250
  right, 165, 166, 167
  text, 165-167, 237-245
  top, 166, 167
Alt+key shortcuts, 17
Anchor Marker, 102
  for changing name, 103
  clicking and dragging to, 106-112, 115
  defined, 102
  illustrated, 103, 105
  linking, 106-112, 115
  See also Named Anchors
anchor.mov, 102

animated GIFs
  creating, 360
  Dreamweaver treatment of, 360
  preloading, 360
animated rollovers, 357-360
  Dreamweaver treatment of, 358, 360
  images, 357
  working with, 357
  See also rollovers
animation
  keyframes, 448
  Layer, 447
  playing, 449
  previewing, 449, 452
  Timelines for, 446-451
attributes, 138-139
  ALT, 119
  bgcolor, 139
  defined, 138
  deleting, 139
  selecting, 139
  VALIGN, 141
.au format, 527
audio. *See* sound
Audio Interchange Format. *See* .aif files

B

background images, 424
  adding, 334-341
  alignment, 217
  clipped, by Frame sides, 335
  dimension, 336
  floating illusion, 207
  in Frames, 334-341
  size, establishing, 336
  specifying, 69
  types of, 69
  viewing Tracing Image and, 192
  See also images
backgrounds
  color, 69
  HTML Inspector, 127
  viewing Tracing Image and, 192
backups, creating, 149
baselines, aligning, 167
BBEdit, 26, 129-136, 406
  Find feature, 409
  for menus.xml, 408
  See also external HTML editors
Behaviors, 456-499
  accessing, 492
  Check Browser, 458-466
  components, 456
  defined, 456
  Drag Layer, 440, 444
  multiple, triggering, 371
  power of, 462

previewing, 470, 471, 476
repository, 503
Set Text of Status Bar, 467-470
Set Text of Text Field, 471-476
sharing, 11
Swap Image, 363, 366
in Timelines window, 451
See also Actions; Events
Behaviors palette
Check Browser command, 459
Events For setting, 444, 453
Go To Timeline Frame command, 454
illustrated, 366, 444
Open Browser Window command, 478
opening, 22, 366, 444, 459, 468, 473, 489
Play Timeline command, 453
plus sign, 366, 444, 453, 454, 455, 459, 468, 473, 478
for programming rollovers, 366-367
Set Text of Status Bar command, 468
Set Text of Text Field command, 473, 474
shortcut key, 23, 444, 459, 468, 473, 478, 489
Stop Timeline command, 454, 455
Swap Image command, 366, 371
_blank target specification, 332
<BLINK> tag, 143, 145, 146, 147
<BLOCKQUOTE> tag, 186
<BODY> tag, 459
Check Browser Behavior attached to, 459
defined, 8
bold, 128
bookmarks, Frames/Framesets and, 317
borders
changes, saving, 225
color, 341
creating, 222-225
default settings, 222
effect on appearance, 224
Frame, 327, 341
Frameset, 333, 341
invisible, 207
in Layers to Tables conversion, 207
line weight, 222
turning off, 249
See also Tables
Browse for File
accessing, 86
link creation, 86-87, 88
Link History and, 85
browser-safe colors, 64
<B> tag, 128

 tag, 62, 187

CD-ROM
BBEdit, 406
demo files, xxv
exercise files, xxv
Extension Manager, 457, 481
HomeSite, 406
Netscape 4.6, 28
See also folders
CellPad setting, 244, 245, 425
changing, 244
controlling, 260
using, 245
cells
centering images in, 305
centering text in, 304, 305
creating, in Layers to Tables conversion, 210
defined, 210
dotted lines, 222
empty, 222
gaps between, removing, 254
illustrated, 221
merging, 233-234
moving, 231
red dashes in, 425
selecting, 233
space between, 245
space in, 245
splitting, 234-235
transparent GIF insertion in, 210
See also columns; rows; Tables
CellSpace setting, 243, 244, 245, 425
changing, 244
controlling, 260
using, 245
centering images/text, 63
CGI (**C**ommon **G**ateway **I**nterface), 415, 423
Character Entities, 183-185
defined, 183
Macintosh, 185
shortcuts, 185
types of, 183
Windows, 185
characters, spaces between, 188
Characters Objects palette, 183
Copyright icon, 184
defined, 19
illustrated, 18, 183
Max Chars setting, 418
opening, 183
Registered icon, 184
symbol, 183-185
Trademark icon, 184
See also Objects palette
checkboxes, 421-422
inserting, 414, 421
naming, 422, 429
values, 422, 429
See also Form Objects palette; Forms

C

Calendar Object extension, 497
Cascading **S**tyle **S**heets (CSS). *See* Style Sheets

Check Browser Behavior, 458-466
    Alt URL setting, 460
    attached to `<body>` tag, 459
    in Behaviors palette, 461
    creating, 458-462
    defined, 458
    Event, 461
    URL setting, 460
    See also Behaviors
Check Browser dialog box, 459-460
    illustrated, 460
    opening, 459
Choose a Folder dialog box, 508, 509
Classes, 271
    application, 271
    creating, 273, 274
    defined, 263, 271
    editing, 272
    names, 273
Clean Up HTML command, 142-147
Clean Up HTML window, 145-147
    Combine Nested `<font>` Tags When Possible checkbox, 147
    Dreamweaver HTML Comments checkbox, 147
    Empty Tags checkbox, 147
    illustrated, 145, 146
    Non-Dreamweaver HTML Comments checkbox, 145, 147
    opening, 145
    Redundant Nested Tags checkbox, 147
    Show Log on Completion checkbox, 147
    Specific Tag(s) checkbox, 146, 147
    text field, 146
Clean Up Word HTML command, 148-151
Clean Up Word HTML window, 150-151
    CSS values, 150
    Detailed tab, 150
    illustrated, 150
    opening, 150
    XML values, 150
Color palette, 65
    buttons, 65
    Color button, 65
    Default Color button, 65
    Eye Dropper button, 65
    illustrated, 65
    opening, 64
    selecting from, 65
Color Picker palette, 51
colors
    active links, 67, 68, 69
    background, 69
    border, 341
    browser-safe, 64
    choosing, 51
    Frame, 325-327
    highlighting, 301
    link, 69
    repeating, 181

    Style, 266, 269, 272, 275
    Table, 228-231
    text, 69, 152, 157, 179
Color Schemes, 176-177
    applying, 176
    creation of, 177
    defined, 176
    illustrated effects of, 177
    setting, 504-505
    Templates, 177, 292
    uses, 176
    See also colors
columns
    adding, 235
    deleting, 235
    Frameset, 337-338
    illustrated, 221
    merging, 233-234
    selecting, 234
    size specification, 340
    sorting, 227
    See also cells; Tables
Commands, 500-521
    accessing, 492
    approaches to, 500
    Create Web Photo Album, 500, 506-511
    custom, 500
    defined, 500
    History palette for, 521
    Mailto, 500, 517-521
    Optimize in Fireworks, 500, 512-516
    pre-existing, 500
    resources, 501-503
    Set Color Scheme, 500, 504-505
    sharing, 11
Commands menu, 500
    Clean Up HTML command, 145
    Clean Up Word HTML command, 150
    Create Web Photo Album command, 506
    Email Link command, 520
    Format Table command, 228
    Get More Commands command, 501
    Manage Extensions command, 483, 484, 494
    Optimize Image in Fireworks command, 512
    Set Color Scheme command, 176, 292, 504, 505
    Sort Table command, 226
comments
    removing, 145, 147
    tags, 144
Common Objects palette, 203-204
    contents, 19
    defined, 19
    illustrated, 18, 203, 204
    Insert Date object, 553
    Insert Draw Layer object, 203, 441, 443
    Insert E-Mail Link object, 97, 98, 517
    Insert Fireworks HTML object, 385

Insert Flash object, 531
Insert Image object, 58-59, 204, 217, 302
Insert ImageReady HTML object, 487
Insert NavBar object, 375
Insert Plug-In object, 523, 528, 536
Insert Rollover Image object, 355, 357
Insert Shockwave object, 533
Insert Table object, 123, 232, 425
Insert Tabular Data object, 258
opening, 203
See also Objects palette
Configuration folder, 406-407
containers, HTML, 7
Convert Layers to Table dialog box, 207-210
Center on Page option, 210
Collapse Empty Cells option, 210
illustrated, 207
Most Accurate option, 207, 210
opening, 207
Prevent Layer Overlaps option, 207, 210
shortcut, 207
Show Grid option, 210
Show Layer Palette option, 210
Snap To Grid option, 210
Use Transparent GIFs option, 207, 210
Convert Tables to Layers dialog box, 211-212
illustrated, 212
opening, 211
shortcut, 211
Snap To Grid option, 212
Convert to 3.0 Browser Compatible dialog box, 286-287
CSS Styles to HTML Markup option, 287
illustrated, 287
opening, 286
copying
document contents, 394-397
email links, 98
History palette information, 394-397
rollovers, 385
Tables, 255-256
Copyright symbol (©), 183, 184
Create Site Cache dialog box, 53
Create Web Photo Album command, 500, 506-511
defined, 506
image processing, 508
requirements, 506
source files, 508
See also Commands
Create Web Photo Album dialog box, 506-510
Browse button, 507, 509
Destination Folder field, 509
illustrated, 506
OK button, 510
opening, 506
Other Info field, 507
Photo Album Title field, 506
Source Images Folder field, 507

Subheading Info field, 507
See also Web Photo Album
.css extension, 284
CSS Styles palette
illustrated, 265
New Style icon, 267, 271, 275, 277
opening, 22, 265, 277
Open Style Sheet icon, 270, 281, 285
pop-up menu, 265
shortcut key, 23
Ctrl+Shift+Spacebar, 189

D

date
current, inserting, 553-554
format, modifying, 555
default.html, 57
Define HTML Style dialog box, 401-405
Add to Existing Style option, 405
Alignment option, 405
Apply To: Paragraph option, 405
Apply To: Selection option, 405
Clear Existing Style option, 405
Color option, 405
default values, 401
Font Attributes options, 405
Font option, 405
Format option, 405
illustrated, 401, 404
Name field, 401, 405
opening, 400
options, 404-405
Paragraph Attributes options, 405
Size option, 405
Style option, 405
When Applying options, 405
See also HTML Styles; HTML Styles palette
Define Sites dialog box, 33-34
Done button, 53
New button, 48, 52
Definition Lists
generating, 175
illustrated, 174, 175
See also lists
demo files, xxv
descriptions, 77
deselecting images, 59, 224
detaching Templates, 302
DHTML, 12, 438-455
background, 438
browser support, 438
defined, 12, 438
dragging layers with, 440-445
exercise compatibility, 439
programming, in Dreamweaver, 12
terms, 12

uses, 438
docking windows, 450
Document **O**bject **M**odel (DOM), 12
documents
   contents, replicating, 394-397
   creating, xxiv, 54, 506
   creating, from Templates, 300
   current, making, 395, 396
   empty, saving, 170
   Fireworks, opening, 513
   Framesets and, 321
   Frameset title, assigning, 321-322
   open, 240
   saving, 55
   SimpleText view, 134
   switching between, 240-241
   title, setting, 54
Document window, 24-25
   defined, 24
   download time display, 24, 25
   file name in, 55
   highlighting within, 128
   illustrated, 15, 24
   rulers, 24, 25
   size display, 24, 25, 516
   Tag Selector, 24, 25, 138, 223
   title bar, 24, 25, 55
   viewing changes within, 127
   See also Mini-Launcher
dotted lines, 222
downloading, 549
   from Macromedia Exchange, 491-499
   Plug-Ins, 523
Down state, 374, 376
   defined, 376
   specifying, 379, 381
   viewing, 384
   See also rollover states
Drag Layer Behavior, 440, 444
   previewing, 445
   selecting, 444
   See also Behaviors
Drag Layer dialog box
   Drop Target area, 444
   illustrated, 444
   opening, 444
   Snap if Within setting, 444
Dreamweaver 3
   background, 2-13
   defined, 2
   extensions, 11, 491-499
   interface, 14-29
   RAM requirements, xxiv
   shortcut keys, 29
   system requirements, xxiv
Dreamweaver 3 **H•O•T**
   audience, x

   formatting, xvi
   how to use, xvi
   orientation, xi
   overview, x-xi
   screen captures, xvii
   Web site support, xi
Dreamweaver API, 501
Dreamweaver Depot, 11, 503
Dreamweaver Exchange, 501
Dreamweaver Extensions Database, 11
Dreamweaver's Fan Page, 11
.dwt extension, 289, 291, 297
Dynamic **HTML**. *See* DHTML

E

editable regions
   designating, 298
   illustrated, 299
   naming, 299
   See also Templates
Edit Font List dialog box, 162
editing
   Classes, 272
   date format, 555
   Font Lists, 161-162
   with HTML Inspector, 126-128
   Library Items, 308-309, 312-313
   Tables, 178, 233-235
   Templates, 291, 303-306
Edit menu
   Copy command, 255
   Cut command, 235
   Paste command, 256, 397
   Preferences command, 16, 25, 130, 301
   Repeat Apply Italic command, 182
   Repeat Font Color command, 181
Edit Style Sheet dialog box, 272, 273, 285
   illustrated, 281
   New button, 281, 283
   opening, 281
elements, HTML, 7
email addresses, 98, 517-518
   automatic insertion of, 99
   email link displaying, 99
   in empty cells, 100
   in Link field, 100
email links, 96-100, 518
   copying/pasting, 98
   creating, 96-100
   defined, 80, 96
   displaying email address, 99
   "General Information" column, 97
   inserting, 520
   mail creation of, 100
   previewing, 100, 518
   See also links

embedding sounds, 528-530
  defined, 528
  placement, 528
  previewing, 529
  process, 528-529
  See also sound
empty cells, 231
  collapsing, 241
  email addresses in, 100
  Table formatting and, 222
  transparent GIFs in, 225
  See also cells; Tables
empty folders
  defining sites for, 33
  Site window view, 49
Events
  defined, 456
  onLoad, 461
  onMouseOver, 469
  See also Behaviors
exercise files, xvii, xxv
  folder, xxv
  on Windows systems, xix-xx
exercises
  Adding a Background Image, 334-338
  Adding Layers, 199-206
  Affecting Links with Selectors, 277-279
  Aligning Images and Text with Table, 237-244
  Aligning Text, 165-167
  Animated Rollovers, 357-359
  Applying a Tracing Image, 192-197
  Applying HTML Styles, 398-403
  Blockquotes and Non-Breaking Spaces, 186-189
  Browse for File and the Link History, 85-90
  Centering Images and Text, 63
  Changing the Border of a Table, 222-225
  Changing the Color Scheme, 228-230
  Character Entities, 183-185
  Clean Up HTML, 142-147
  Clean Up Word HTML, 148-151
  Coloring Frames, 325-327
  Color Schemes, 176-177, 504-505
  Combining Pixels and Percentages, 255-257
  Converting Layers to Tables, 207-209
  Converting Tables to Layers, 211-215
  Copying and Pasting History, 394-397
  Create Web Photo Album Command, 506-511
  Creating a Check Browser Behavior, 458-466
  Creating a Form, 424-429
  Creating a Jump Menu, 430-437
  Creating a Library Item, 310-311
  Creating and Formatting HTML Text, 155-158
  Creating and Modifying a Table, 232-235
  Creating and Saving a Document, 54-55
  Creating a New Template, 296-302
  Creating a Set Text of Status Bar Behavior, 467-470

  Creating a Set Text of Text Field Behavior, 471-476
  Creating a Simple Rollover, 354-356
  Creating a Site from Nothing, 48-49
  Creating a Site Map, 46-47
  Creating Custom Keyboard Shortcuts, 406-411
  Creating Email Links, 96-101
  Creating Links with Images and Text, 70-73
  Creating Multiple-Event Rollovers, 368-373
  Creating Pointer Rollovers, 361-367
  Defining a Custom Class, 271-274
  Defining the Site, 33-35, 52-53
  Downloading from Macromedia Exchange, 491-499
  Dragging Layers, 440-445
  Editing with HTML Inspector, 126-128
  Embedding Sounds, 528-529
  External HTML Editors, 129-136
  File and Folder Management, 40-41
  File Synchronization, 552-557
  Font Lists, 159-163
  Formatting Text in Tables, 178-179
  Frames Objects Palette, 346-351
  From CSS to HTML, 286-287
  HTML Inspector, 121-125
  Image Maps, 116-119
  Inserting a Navigation Bar Rollover, 374-384
  Inserting a QuickTime Movie, 536-537
  Inserting a Simple Rollover from Fireworks, 385-387
  Inserting Director Content, 533-535
  Inserting Flash Content, 531-532
  Inserting ImageReady HTML, 484-490
  Inserting Images, 58-59
  Inserting Tab-Delimited Data, 258-261
  Inserting Text, 60-61
  Installing the Extension Manager, 481-483
  Library Items in Action, 307-309
  Linking to a Style Sheet, 281-285
  Linking to New Source Files, 91-95
  Linking to Sounds, 524-526
  Linking with Point to File, 81-84
  Links and Targets, 328-331
  Looking at the HTML, 78-79
  Mailto Command, Using the History Palette, 517-521
  META tags, 74-76
  Modifying a Library Item, 312-313
  Modifying a Page Properties, 64-68
  Modifying a Template, 303-306
  Named Anchors, 101-115
  Opening a New Browser Window, 477-480
  Optimize Image in Fireworks Command, 512-516
  Ordered, Unordered, and Definition Lists, 174-175
  Percentage-Based Table Alignment, 246-250
  Play, Stop, and Reset the Timeline, 452-455
  Putting Files to the Web Server, 547-551
  Quick Tag Editor, 137-141
  Redefining HTML Styles with Style Sheets, 264-270
  Relative and Absolute Links, 36-38

Repeat Last Action, 180-182

Saving Your First Frameset, 318-322

Seamless Background Across Two Frames, 342-345

Seamless Image Assembly, 251-254

Setting the FTP Preferences, 544-545

Signing Up with GeoCities, 540-543

Sorting the Table, 226

Templates in Action, 290-295

Understanding the Path Structure, 42-45

Using Margin Tags, 216-219

Using Selectors to Group Tags, 275-276

Using the History Palette for Undo/Redo, 389-393

Using the "PRE" tag, 168-173

Using the Timeline for Animation, 446-449

Working with Form Objects, 416-423

Extensible **M**arkup **L**anguage. *See* XML

Extension Manager, 457

    defined, 457, 481

    exiting, 486, 496

    folder for, 482

    installation confirmation, 483

    installer, 481

    installing, 481-483

    launching, 483, 484

    relaunching Dreamweaver and, 487, 496

    Windows interface, 481

extensions

    Calendar Object, 497

    downloading, 492-493

    in Extension Manager, 496

    file extensions, 494

    information on, 492

    installing, 494-496

    organization of, 492

    saving, 493

    See also Macromedia Exchange

externalcss.mov, 283

External Editors preferences, 26, 130-131

    Category option, 130

    Choose (Browse) button, 131

    Enable BBEdit Integration checkbox, 130, 131

    illustrated, 130

    opening, 130

    See also Preferences dialog box

external HTML editors, 129-136

    BBEdit, 26, 129-136

    HomeSite, 26, 129-136

    Mac vs. Windows, 129

    specifying, 26, 131

External Style Sheets, 281

    creating, 281-284

    defined, 272, 281

    linking, 284-285

    power of, 281

    See also Style Sheets

Eye Dropper, 65, 66

F

file extensions, 10, 56

    .aif, 525, 526, 527, 529

    .au, 527

    .css, 284

    .dwt, 289, 291, 297

    .lbi, 289, 308

    .midi, 527

    .MP3, 527

    .mxp, 494

    .ra, 527

    .rmf, 527

    .swa, 527

    .wav, 524, 525, 526, 527

    Windows systems, xxi-xxiii

File menu

    Convert command, 286

    Export CSS Styles command, 284

    New command, xxiv, 54, 232, 237, 311, 318, 354, 441, 487, 506

    New File command, xxiv, 49

    New Folder command, 40

    New from Template command, 300

    New Window command, xxiv, 354, 441

    Open command, 36

    Save All command, 319, 322, 323, 327, 338, 348

    Save As command, 55, 300, 354

    Save As Template command, 296

    Save command, 43, 73, 84, 95, 197, 225, 311, 323, 393, 462, 466, 555

    Save Frameset As command, 323

    Save Frameset command, 323

    Save Site Map command, 47

    Turn Off Read Only command, xx

file names

    case sensitivity, 9

    conventions, 9, 56

    document title vs., 55, 56

    in Document window, 55

files

    backing up, 149

    creating, 40, 49

    current version of, 555

    deleting, 41

    demo, xxv

    dragging, 41

    exercise, xvii, xix-xx, xxv

    importing, 148

    managing, 40-41

    modification dates, 556

    moving, 41

    nested, 43

    newer, identifying, 556

    opening, 36

    saving, 354

    selecting, 40

    sound, 524

status, 557
updating, 136
.wav, 524, 525, 526, 527
file synchronization, 552-557
defined, 552
document changes and, 557
newer file identification, 556
settings, 556
success indication, 557
File Transfer Protocol. *See* FTP
Find Source for Optimizing dialog box, 513
Fireworks
CD-ROM trial version, 506
documents, opening, 513
image processing, 510
inserting rollover from, 385-387
launching, 512
Optimize Images dialog box, 514-515
optimizing images in, 512-516
PNG file format, 513
fixed-percentage Tables, 188, 239
fixed-pixel Tables, 239
Flash Plug-In, 523
content, inserting, 531-532
defined, 532
files played by, 525
parameters, 530
scaling, 532
support, 531
Web site, 532
Folder Options dialog box, xxii-xxiii
opening, xxii, xxiii
View tab, xxii-xxiii
folders
chap_03, 33
chap_04, 52, 55
chap_05, 81, 88
chap_06, 121, 132, 142, 148
chap_07, 155, 170
chap_08, 192, 216
chap_09, 222, 224, 232, 237, 255, 259
chap_10, 264, 285, 287
chap_11, 289, 290, 300, 302, 311
chap_12, 318, 319, 328
chap_13, 356, 385
chap_14, 389
chap_15, 416, 430, 432, 434, 435
chap_16, 440, 441
chap_17, 460, 463, 464, 467, 472, 477, 485
chap_18, 507, 509, 517, 520
chap_19, 524, 528, 533, 536
chap_20, 544
Configuration, 406-407
creating, 40, 49
deleting, 41
Dreamweaver, 406

empty, 33
Extension Manager, 481
frameset2, 342
frameset3, 349, 350, 351
fw3 simple rollover, 386
html, 354, 357, 361, 368, 369, 385
images, 43, 92, 193, 201, 204, 217, 364, 369, 370, 378, 380, 513, 516
Library, 289, 398
Links, 328
managing, 40-41
Menus, 407
movies, xi, 20, 37, 65, 283, 355, 372
moving, 41
nested, 44
New Chapters, 52
paths, 43
Root, 31, 35, 80, 121, 386, 398, 548
Software/Behaviors, 458
source images, 507
Templates, 289
web gallery, 509
See also CD-ROM
<FONT> tag, 145
font colors, 152
FONT FACE element, 153
Font Lists, 159-164
adding to, 162, 163
defined, 161
display on screen, 163
editing, 161-162
functioning of, 161
goal, 161
removing from, 162
fonts, 152
Arial, 159, 163, 178
Courier, 160
default, 152, 153
Georgia, 160
HTML Style, 405
Macintosh System 8.6, 153
specifying, with Font Lists, 159
Style, 266, 269
Times New Roman, 390
Times Roman, 152
Verdana, 156, 160, 391, 400
Windows 98, 153
font sets, 153
font sizes, 152, 154
changing, 156
default, 154
HEADING tag vs., 158
Mac vs. Windows, 164
specifying, 154
font styles, 152

foreground images, alignment, 217
Format pop-up menu
    Heading 2 command, 157
    None command, 170
    Preformatted command, 172
    See also Properties Inspector
Format Table dialog box, 228
formatting
    automating, 388, 398-405
    guides, 222
    with HTML Styles, 398-405
    HTML text, 155-158
    paragraph application, 405
    quick, 398, 402
    redoing, 392
    repeating, 180-182
    selection application, 405
    Table, 222, 228
    text, with Tables, 178-179
    top row, 260
    undoing, 391, 392
Form Objects, 412, 413-414
    Button, 414, 422, 423
    Checkbox, 414, 421
    defined, 413
    File Field, 414
    Hidden Field, 414
    Image Field, 414
    Jump Menu, 414
    List, 414, 420
    names, 474
    Radio Button, 414
    Text Field, 414, 418
    types of, 412, 413, 414
    working with, 416-423
Form Objects palette
    contents, 19
    defined, 19
    illustrated, 18, 413
    Insert Button button, 414, 422, 423, 429
    Insert Checkbox button, 414, 421, 429
    Insert File Field button, 414
    Insert Form button, 414, 417, 425
    Insert Hidden Field button, 414
    Insert Image Field button, 414
    Insert Jump Menu button, 414
    Insert List/Menu button, 414, 420
    Insert Radio Button button, 414
    Insert Text Field button, 414, 418, 428
    opening, 413, 416
    See also Objects palette
Forms, 412-437
    cells, naming, 426
    CGI and, 415, 423
    creating, 424-429
    creation aspects, 412

    defined, 412
    entry fields, adding, 428
    functioning of, 412
    previewing, 423
    red dashes, 425, 426
<FORM> tag, 414, 417
    inserting, 431
    insertion indication, 425
Frames, 314-351
    advantages, 316
    background images, 334-341
    bookmark hassles, 317
    border, 327, 341
    border color, 341
    box effect, 317, 327
    breaking, 332
    coloring, 325-327
    confusion and, 317
    controversy, 316
    defined, 314, 315
    disadvantages, 317
    dividers, 318, 327
    example, 315
    fixed navigation and, 316
    highlighted, 320
    illustrated, 315, 318
    introduction, 324
    learning curve, 314
    left, 318, 328, 329, 351
    naming, 320, 329, 341
    page loading determination, 433
    printing hassles, 317
    properties, 340-341
    resizable, preventing, 341
    right, 318, 329, 343, 350
    save methods, 323
    saving, on Macintosh, 320
    scrollbars, 333, 341
    security issues, 317
    size, matching to images, 336
    size specification, 339
    source document for, 341
    special effects and, 316
    stationary, 329
    use decision, 316
    workflow and, 316
Framesets
    bookmarking, 317
    border, turning off, 333
    border color, 341
    column size, 337-338
    defined, 314, 315
    dimensions, displaying, 344
    highlighting, 319
    illustrated, 315
    inserting pages into, 324

links, 328-333
margin height, 341
margin width, 341
naming, 319
nested, 332
printing and, 317
saving, 318-324, 348
selecting, 322
targets, 328-333
titles, 321-322
without scrollbars/borders, 317
<FRAMESET> tag, 322, 324
Frames Objects palette
defined, 19
icon colors, 347
illustrated, 18, 346, 347
Insert Left Frame icon, 347
opening, 346
using, 346-351
See also Objects palette
Frames window
border, toggling, 337
clicking on outer region of, 339, 344
illustrated, 330, 337
left side, 330
opening, 330, 337, 339, 344
outermost gray border, 322
right side, 330
FTP
defined, 546
error log, 550
GeoCities access, 539
Host, 544, 545, 546
Host Directory, 544, 545, 546
Login, 544, 545, 546
Password, 544, 545, 546
setting preferences, 544-546
Site Definitions, 544

G

General preferences, 25
GeoCities, 538, 539
Build your page now! link, 543
Build Your Web Site link, 540
confirmation email, 543
defined, 539
FTP access, 539
Privacy Policy, 542
signing up with, 540-543
successful registration with, 543
Web page preview in, 551
Web site, 539, 540
Yahoo! ID, 541
your URL, 541

Get command, 549
grids
showing, 210, 212
snapping to, 210
turning off, 212

H

<H1>-<H6> tags, 158, 264, 268, 270, 271
hash mark (#), 106, 117, 356, 453, 468, 478
<HEAD> tag
defined, 8
Templates and, 306
HEADING tag, 158
Head Objects palette
defined, 19
illustrated, 18
Insert Description option, 75
Insert Keywords option, 74-75
See also Objects palette
help tags, 118, 119
adding, 119
defined, 119
highlighting
colors, 301
text, 301-302, 304, 305, 308, 390
History palette, 389-397
Clear History command, 393
clearing, 393
for Commands, 521
copying/pasting from, 394-397
Copy selected steps to the clipboard icon, 396
defined, 388
History Slider, 391, 392
illustrated, 391, 518
Mailto command with, 517-521
opening, 22, 390, 518
Paste icon, 397
Paste Steps, 397
recording illustration, 391, 392
redo with, 392
Save selected steps as a command icon, 519
saving files and, 393
selecting entries in, 395, 519
shortcut key, 23, 390, 518
undo with, 391, 392
upper-right arrow, 393
HomeSite, 26, 129-136, 406
Find feature, 409
for menus.xml, 408
See also external HTML editors
<HREF> tag, 119
HTML
containers, 7
deconstructed, 8
defined, 6, 12

elements, 7
hyperlinks, 6
ImageReady, inserting, 484-490
learning, 4
resources, 5, 139
roundtrip, 3
understanding, 4
See also DHTML
HTML code
  cleaning up, 142-151
  illustrated, 7
  learning through viewing, 4
  quick access to, 141
  for Tables, 221
  viewing, 78-79, 276
  viewing, in browser, 4
  viewing, in HTML Inspector, 125
HTML editors. *See* external HTML editors
HTML Inspector, 121-128
  background, 127
  clicking/dragging within, 127
  closing, 122, 136, 145, 149
  defined, 121
  editing with, 126-128
  External Editor option, 122, 134
  illustrated, 122
  Line Numbers checkbox, 122, 144
  moving, 124
  opening, 122, 133, 144, 146, 149
  options, 122
  updating with, 127
  viewing code in, 125
  Wrap checkbox, 122
HTML Source window, 78-79
  closing, 78, 276
  illustrated, 79
  Line Numbers checkbox, 144
  opening, 22, 78, 79, 133, 276, 462
  shortcut key, 23, 462
  Wrap checkbox, 78
HTML Styles, 398-405
  applying, 398-405
  browsers and, 398
  changing, 402
  defined, 22, 388, 398
  fonts, 405
  Library folder and, 398
  managing, 402
  naming, 401, 405
  options, 404-405
  See also Define HTML Style dialog box
HTML Styles palette, 399-401
  Delete Style icon, 402
  illustrated, 399, 400, 401
  New Style icon, 400, 402
  opening, 399
  pop-up menu, 402

  shortcut, 399
  style listings, 401
HTML tag, 8
HTML tags
  attributes, 138-139
  `<B>`, 128
  `<BLINK>`, 143, 145, 146, 147
  `<BLOCKQUOTE>`, 186
  `<BODY>`, 8, 459
  `<BR>`, 62, 187
  close, 8
  comment, 144
  defined, 139
  empty, removing, 142, 147
  `<FONT>`, 145
  `<FORM>`, 316-317, 425
  `<FRAMESET>`, 322, 324
  grouping, 275-276
  `<H1>`-`<H6>`, 158, 264, 268, 270, 271
  `<HEAD>`, 8, 306
  heading, 158
  `HEADING`, 158
  `<HREF>`, 119
  `HTML`, 8
  `<I>`, 128
  `<IMG>`, 444
  `MARGIN`, 216-219
  `<NBSP>`, 231
  nested, 142, 147
  `<NOFRAMES>`, 324
  open, 8
  `<P>`, 62, 187
  `<PRE>`, 168-173
  redundant, 142
  removing specific, 147
  Styles conversion to, 263
  `<TABLE>`, 208, 221, 256
  `<TD>`, 138, 140, 221, 234, 248
  `<TITLE>`, 8
  `<TR>`, 221, 227
hyperlinks. *See* links
HyperText Markup Language. *See* HTML

I

image links, creating, 70-71
image maps, 116-119
  defined, 80, 116
  defining, 117, 119
  help tag, 118, 119
  naming, 117
  previewing, 119
  Properties Inspector settings, 116
  See also links
ImageReady HTML dialog box, 487-488
  illustrated, 488
  Insert button, 488
  opening, 487

See also Insert ImageReady HTML extension

images
  aligning, 204, 220
  aligning, with Table, 237-245
  assembling, 251-254
  background, 69, 217, 334-341
  centering, 63
  centering, in cells, 305
  compression, 515
  deleting, 43
  deselecting, 59, 224
  dimensions, viewing, 252, 336
  folder, expanding, 92, 94
  foreground, 217
  gaps between, 251
  grouping, 252
  inserting, 42, 43, 44, 58-59, 205, 414
  naming, 363, 364
  opaque, 194
  optimizing, 514
  outside folder, inserting, 44
  replacing Placeholders with, 93, 94
  rollover, 353, 357, 359, 362, 363, 380
  selecting, 63
  of text, 164
  tracing, 69
  <IMG> tag, 444
indents, 188
index.html, 57
  advantages, 57
  defined, 55, 57
  naming, 55
  no, 57
  significance of, 57
Inline Style Sheets, 272
Insert Button object, 414, 422, 423
Insert Calendar dialog box, 497-498
  illustrated, 498
  opening, 497
Insert Checkbox object, 414, 421
Insert Date dialog box, 553-554
  Date Format setting, 553
  illustrated, 553, 554
  opening, 553
  Time Format setting, 554
  Update Automatically on Save checkbox, 554
Insert Description object, 75
Insert Draw Layer object, 203, 441, 443
Insert E-Mail Link dialog box, 97-98
  E-Mail field, 98, 99, 517, 518
  illustrated, 98, 99, 517
  opening, 97, 98, 517
  Text field, 98, 99, 518
Insert File Field object, 414
Insert Fireworks HTML dialog box, 385-386
  Browse button, 386

  Delete file after insertion checkbox, 386
  illustrated, 385
  opening, 385
Insert Flash object, 531
Insert Form object, 414, 417
Insert Hidden Field object, 414
Insert Image Field object, 414
Insert Image object, 58-59, 204, 217, 302
Insert ImageReady HTML extension, 484-490
  defined, 484
  disclaimer, 485
  display in Extension Manager, 486
  installing, 484-486
  object, 487
  See also ImageReady HTML dialog box
inserting
  Checkbox Object, 414
  current date, 553-554
  Director content, 533-535
  email links, 520
  Flash content, 531-532
  ImageReady HTML, 484-490
  images, 42, 43, 44, 58-59, 205, 414
  Jump Menu, 414
  Layers, 199, 203
  line breaks, 187, 552
  List Object, 414
  Menu Object, 414, 420
  non-breaking space, 189
  pages into Framesets, 324
  paragraph breaks, 59, 126, 186, 187
  Plug-In content, 523
  QuickTime movie, 536-537
  Radio Button Object, 414
  Submit Button Object, 414
  tab-delimited data, 258-261
  Tables, 123, 232, 238, 253, 255
  text, 60-61, 205
  text box, 414
  text field, 414, 419
Insert Jump Menu object, 414
Insert Jump Menu window, 431-435
  Browse button, 432, 435
  illustrated, 432, 433, 434, 435
  opening, 431
  Open URLs In setting, 433
  plus button, 433, 435
  Text field, 432, 434, 435
  When Selected, Go To URL option, 434
  See also Jump Menu
Insert Keywords object, 74-75
Insert List/Menu object, 414
Insert menu
  Form command, 431
  Form Object command, 431
Image command, 23, 42, 43, 44, 200, 204, 224, 229, 242, 248,
    253, 362, 364, 365, 369, 370, 441, 443

Layer command, 199
Named Anchor command, 102, 104, 105, 114
Navigation Bar command, 375
Rollover Image command, 355
Table command, 232, 238, 253, 255, 425
Insert Named Anchor dialog box, 102, 104, 105
Insert Navigation Bar dialog box, 375-383
Browse buttons, 378, 379, 380, 381
Down Image setting, 379
Element Name setting, 377, 380
illustrated, 377, 379, 382, 383
opening, 375
Over Image setting, 378
Over While Down Image setting, 379
plus sign, 380
Up Image setting, 378
Insert Plug-In object, 523, 528, 536
Insert Radio Button object, 414
Insert Rollover Image dialog box
Browse buttons, 355, 358, 359
illustrated, 355, 358
opening, 355, 357
Original Image setting, 355, 358, 359
Preload Images setting, 360
Rollover Image setting, 355, 358, 359
Insert Rows or Columns dialog box, 235
Insert Shockwave object, 533
Insert Table dialog box
Border setting, 238, 246, 253, 255, 425
Cell Padding setting, 425
Cell Spacing setting, 425
Columns setting, 238, 246, 253, 255, 425
default settings, 233
illustrated, 123, 232, 238
opening, 123, 232
Percent setting, 246, 255
Rows setting, 238, 246, 253, 255, 425
Width setting, 238, 246, 253, 255, 425
Insert Table object, 232
Insert Tabular Data dialog box, 258-261
Browse button, 259
Cell Padding setting, 260
Cell Spacing setting, 260
Data File setting, 260
Delimiter setting, 260
Format Top Row setting, 260
illustrated, 259, 260, 261
opening, 258
Table Width settings, 260
Insert Text Field object, 414
inspector_context.mov, 37
interface, 14-29
elements, 15
illustrated, 15
Mac vs. Windows, 32
overview, 14

redundancy, 23
Internal Style Sheets, 272, 281
Invisible Elements
defined, 202
deselecting, 200
illustrated, 200
Named Anchors and, 102
preferences, 202
showing/hiding, 202, 301
turning off permanently, 202
types of, 19
Invisibles palette
defined, 19
illustrated, 18
invisible Tables, 191
<I> tag, 128
italics, 128
formatting, 128
repeating, 182

J

Java, 356
JavaScript
code placement, 356
defined, 12, 13
image name requirement, 363, 364
Java and, 356
popularity, 356
rollovers, 352
uses, 13
Web browser detection and, 464
Jump Menu, 430-437
adding other items to, 433, 435
creating, 430-437
defined, 430
effects, illustrated, 436
inserting, 414
previewing, 437

K

keyboard shortcuts. See shortcuts
keyframes
defined, 448
moving, 448, 449
keywords, 77

L

language, specifying, 69
Launcher, 21-23
Behaviors button, 22
buttons, 21, 22
closing, 21
CSS Styles button, 22
defined, 21
History button, 22

HTML Source button, 22, 78
HTML Styles button, 22
illustrated, 15, 21
Library button, 22
opening, 21
shortcuts, 23
Site button, 22
See also Mini-Launcher
Layers
adding, 199-206
benefits of, 191
blinking I-beam cursor, 200
changing layout with, 212
converting, to tables, 191, 207-210, 439
defined, 191, 198
display, 207
dragging, 440-445
drawing, 203
edges, aligning, 210
flexibility, 191
handles, clicking on, 442
highlighted, 213
inserting, 199, 203
moving, 200, 444, 449
naming, 442, 443
overlapping, 207, 210
as rectangle document corner, 199
resizing, 200, 442
resizing handles, 199
selecting, 214, 442, 443, 444
Selection Handle, 199, 200, 213
snapping, 210, 212
Tables conversion to, 191, 211-215
timing, adjusting, 449
Web browsers and, 207
Layers palette
highlighted Layers in, 213
illustrated, 213
opening, 210, 439
Prevent Overlaps checkbox, 439
shortcut, 439
layout, 190-219
changing, with Layers, 212
controlling, 211
forms, 424-429
Table creation for, 211
.lbi extension, 289, 308
Library folder, 289, 398
Library Items, 307-313
applying, 311
creating, 310-311
defined, 22, 288
editing, 308-309, 312-313
format, 289
indication, 307

naming, 310
opening, 312
Templates vs., 307
time savings, 309
updating, 308-309
uses, 288
working with, 307-309
Library palette
Add To Page command, 311
illustrated, 308
New Library Item icon, 310
opening, 22, 307, 310
Open Library Item icon, 308, 312
shortcut key, 23
line breaks
creating, 61
HTML tag, 62, 186
inserting, 187, 552
paragraph breaks vs., 62
Line Height, 262
Link External Style Sheet dialog box, 285
Link History, 80, 85-90
defined, 85
pop-up menu, 89, 90
practicing, 90
previewing, 90
recording links in, 88, 89
time savings, 90
using, 88-90
links, 80-119
sign beginning, 106, 453
absolute, 36-39, 42
active, 67, 68, 69, 280
affecting, with Selectors, 277-280
Browse for File creation method, 86-87
defined, 6
email, 80, 96-100, 518
Frameset, 328-333
image, 70-71
image maps, 80, 116-119
mailto, 517
multiple, assigning to single image, 116
Named Anchors, 80, 101, 106-112
"nowhere," 468
Point to File, 80
previewing, 73, 328
relative, 36-39, 42
rollover, 356
sound, 524-527
source file, 91-95
stand-in, 356
text, 72-73
types of, 80
underlines, turning off, 277, 285
updating, 41
viewing, in Properties Inspector, 37, 38

visited, 67, 69, 280
.wav, 524, 525, 526, 527
List Object, inserting, 414
lists
    Definition, 175
    generating, 174
    Ordered, 174-175
    Unordered, 175
List Values dialog box, 420
LiveAudio Plug-In, 530
Local Info window
    folder icon, 48
    illustrated, 48
    Refresh Local File List Automatically checkbox, 53
    Site Name setting, 48
Local Root Folder, 35, 121
    defined, 31
    exporting from outside of, 386
    file selection from, 80
    importing HTML files not in, 386
    Library folder addition, 398
    selecting, 548
lynda.com
    about, xi
    Web site, xi
lynda.com/books, xi

M

Macintosh
    Character Entities, 185
    fonts, 153
    saving Frames on, 320
    screen captures, this book, xvii
    System 8, xviii
    System 9, xviii
Macromedia Exchange, 457
    account creation, 491
    defined, 457
    DOWNLOAD EXTENSION section, 493
    downloading from, 491-499
    extension organization, 492
    Web site, 457, 491
Mailto command, 500, 517-521
    defined, 517
    links, 517
    See also Commands
margins
    height, 69, 219
    indenting, 186
    left, 69, 219
    top, 69, 219
    width, 69, 219

MARGIN tags, 216-219
    browser-specific, 218
    defined, 216
Massimo's Corner, 502
Menu Object, inserting, 414, 420
Menus folder, 407
menus.xml file, 407-409
    backup, 407
    for keyboard shortcut customization, 410-411
    menu command for Rollover Image option, 410
    opening, 408
merging cells, 233-234
META Builder 2, 77
META tags, 74-76
    defined, 8
    entering, 74-77
    information, viewing, 76
    resources, 77
Microsoft Explorer, 465, 466
Microsoft Word
    file backups, 149
    HTML code, cleaning up, 148-151
.midi format, 527
Mini-Launcher, 21-22
    Behaviors button, 22
    buttons, 21, 22
    CSS Styles button, 22
    defined, 21, 25
    History button, 22
    HTML Source button, 22
    HTML Styles button, 22
    illustrated, 15, 24
    Library button, 22
    Site button, 22
    See also Launcher
Modify menu
    Frameset submenu
        Edit NoFrames Content command, 324
        Split Frame Left command, 318
    Layout Mode submenu
        Convert Layers to Tables command, 207, 214
        Convert Tables to Layers command, 211
    Page Properties command, 54, 64, 157, 171, 192, 196, 219, 232, 238, 246, 325, 334, 441
    Quick Tag Editor command, 138, 141
    Selection Properties command, 327
    Table submenu
        illustrated, 236
        Insert Rows or Columns command, 235
        Merge Cells command, 125, 233
    Templates submenu
        Detach from Template command, 302, 306
        New Editable Region command, 298, 299
movies, xi
    anchor.mov, 102
    externalcss.mov, 283

inspector_context.mov, 37
page_properties_eyedropper.mov, 65
properties_inspector.mov, 20
rollover_list.mov, 355
smooshed_table.mov, 358
swap_image.mov, 372
tracing.mov, 206
xman_win.mov, 481
moving
cells, 231
files, 41
folders, 41
HTML Inspector, 124
keyframes, 448, 449
Layers, 200, 444, 449
Site window, to front, 84
.MP3 format, 527
multiple-event rollovers, 368-373
inserting images in, 369-370
page illustration, 368
previewing, 368
See also rollovers
Musical Instrument Digital Interface. *See* .midi format
.mxp file extension, 494

N

Named Anchors, 101-115
anchor, 101
Anchor Marker, 102, 103, 105
components, 101
defined, 80, 101
error message and, 102
inserting, 102-105
link, 101
link creation, 106-112, 115
names, 103, 104
previewing, 113, 115
uses, 113
See also links
naming
checkboxes, 422, 429
editable regions, 299
Form cells, 426
Frames, 320, 329, 341
Framesets, 319
HTML Styles, 401, 405
image maps, 117
images, 363, 364
Layers, 442, 443
Library Items, 310
rollover images, 363, 364, 380
sites, 34
Templates, 297
text fields, 418, 428
navigation, fixed, 316

Navigation Bar rollover, 374-384
automatic creation of, 383
Browse button, 378
defined, 374
element names, 377, 380
elements, adding, 382
images, 374
previewing, 374, 384
states, 374
See also rollovers
<NBSP> tag, 231
nested Framesets, 332
nested Tables, 255-257
illustrated, 257
process, 255-256
See also Tables
nested tags, 142, 147
Netscape
Audio player, 525
version 3.0, 463
version 4.0, 464, 465, 466
version 4.6, 28
version 4.7, 525
New Editable Region dialog box, 298
New Style dialog box
illustrated, 265, 267
Make Custom Style (class) option, 271, 280
New Style text box, 271, 282
opening, 265, 267, 275, 281
Redefine HTML Tag option, 265, 268, 280, 282
Use CSS Selector option, 275, 277, 280, 283
<NOFRAMES> tag, 324
non-breaking space
HTML tag, 186, 231
illustrated, 189
inserting, 189
NotePad, 134

O

objects
accessing, 492
aligning, 23
Button, 414, 422, 423
Checkbox, 414, 421
Copyright, 184
Draw Layer, 203
File Field, 414
Hidden Field, 414
Image Field, 414
Insert Date, 553
Insert Draw Layer, 441, 443
Insert E-Mail Link, 97, 98, 517
Insert Fireworks HTML, 385
Insert Flash, 531
Insert Image, 58-59, 204, 217, 302
Insert ImageReady HTML, 487

Insert NavBar, 375
Insert Plug-In, 523, 528, 536
Insert Rollover Image, 355, 357
Insert Shockwave, 533
Insert Table, 123, 232, 425
Insert Tabular Data, 258
invisible, 19
Jump Menu, 414
List, 414, 420
Radio Button, 414
Registered, 184
repository, 503
sharing, 11
Text Field, 414, 418
Trademark, 184
types of, 18
Objects palette, 16-17
    Characters, 18, 19, 183-185
    Common, 18, 19, 203-204
    context sensitivity, 18
    defined, 16
    Forms, 18, 19, 413, 416
    Frames, 18, 19, 346-351
    functions, 17
    Head, 18, 19, 74
    Icons and Text option, 16, 17
    Icons Only option, 16, 17
    illustrated, 15, 16
    Invisibles, 18, 19
    opening, 355, 413
    preferences, 16
    shortcut, 517
    Text Only option, 16, 17
    types, 18, 19
    using, 17
    versions, 16-17
offset, 195
"off" state graphics, 353, 362
"on" state graphics, 353, 362
Open Browser Window dialog box
    illustrated, 479
    opening, 478
    Window Height setting, 479
    Window Name field, 479
    Window Width setting, 479
Open dialog box, 259
Optimize Images dialog box (Fireworks), 514-515
    Quality slider, 515
    Update button, 515
Optimize in Fireworks command, 500, 512-516
    defined, 512
    page size information and, 516
    See also Commands
Option+Spacebar, 189
Ordered Lists, 174-175
    generating, 174

    illustrated, 174, 175
    See also lists
outdents, 188
Over state, 374, 376
    defined, 376
    specifying, 378, 381
    viewing, 384
    See also rollover states
Over While Down state, 374, 376
    defined, 376
    specifying, 379, 381
    viewing, 384
    See also rollover states

P

page_properties_eyedropper.mov, 65
Page Properties window, 64-69
    Active Links setting, 67, 68, 69
    Apply button, 66, 67
    Background Image setting, 69, 238, 334, 441
    Background setting, 64, 69, 249, 325, 326
    Browse button, 192, 334, 441
    browser-safe color and, 64
    Choose button, 171, 192, 193, 238, 334, 441
    Color Palette, 64, 65
    Document Encoding setting, 69
    illustrated, 51, 54, 64, 192
    Left Margin setting, 69, 219
    Links setting, 67, 69, 325, 326
    Margin Height setting, 69, 219
    Margin Width setting, 69, 219
    opening, 54, 171, 192, 219, 232, 238, 325
    shortcut, 64, 171, 192, 232, 325
    Templates and, 294
    Text setting, 67, 69, 325, 326
    Title setting, 54, 69, 171, 238
    Top Margin setting, 69, 219
    Tracing Image setting, 69, 192
    Transparency setting, 69, 171, 193, 196
    Visited Links setting, 67, 69
pages
    adding Library Items to, 311
    centering on, 210
    Forms-based, 412
    inserting, into Frameset, 324
    nested, 314
    previewing, in GeoCities, 551
    reusing, 314
    size information, 516
    updating, 309, 312, 316
    uploading, 538-557
paragraph breaks
    creating, 60
    HTML tag, 62, 186

inserting, 59, 126, 186, 187
line breaks vs., 62
parameters, 530
Parameters dialog box, 528-529
    illustrated, 529
    opening, 528
_parent target specification, 332
Paste Steps, 397
path structure, 42-45
    defined, 42
    notations, 45
percentage-based Tables, 239
    alignment, 246-250
    defined, 239
    pixel-based Tables combined with, 255-257
    previewing, 247
    for width, 255
    See also Tables
pipe (|) character, 60
pixel-based Tables, 239
    combined with percentage-based Tables, 255-257
    for height, 255
    See also Tables
Placeholders
    # mark, 117
    adding, 92
    defined, 92
    highlighting, 91
    not replacing, 117
    replacing, 93, 94
    resizing, 92
Play Timeline window, 454
Plug-Ins, 522-537
    content, inserting, 523
    defined, 523
    download URLs, 523
    drawbacks, 522
    Flash, 523, 530
    LiveAudio, 530
    parameters, 530
    QuickTime, 523, 530
    Real Audio, 523
    Shockwave, 530
    working with, 522
PNG file format, 513
pointer rollovers, 361-367
    with Behaviors palette, 366-367
    defined, 361
    previewing, 361
    table, 361, 362
    See also rollovers
Point to File, 81-84
    defined, 80, 81
    for image replacement, 91

as Insert Image object replacement, 91
link creation, 84
linking with, 81-84
link preview, 84
uses, 80
See also links
<PRE> tag, 168-173
    defined, 168
    spaces, 169, 170
    using, 168-173
Preferences dialog box
    External Editors, 26, 130-131
    General, 25
    Invisible Elements, 202
    opening, 25
    Preview in Browser, 28
    shortcut, 130
    Status Bar, 27
Preview in Browser preferences, 28
    +/- buttons, 28
    Edit button, 28
    illustrated, 28
previewing, 28, 194, 205
    animation, 449, 452
    assembled image Table, 254
    Behaviors, 470, 471, 476
    Drag Layers Behavior, 445
    email links, 100, 518
    embedded sounds, 529
    Flash content, 532
    Forms, 423
    Frameset links, 331
    image maps, 119
    ImageReady HTML, 490
    imported Fireworks rollovers, 387
    Jump Menu, 437
    Layers to Tables conversion, 208
    Link History, 90
    links, 328
    Named Anchors, 113, 115
    Navigation Bar rollover, 374, 384
    nested Tables, 257
    new Web browser window, 480
    percentage-based Tables, 247, 249
    pointer rollovers, 361
    Point to File links, 84
    QuickTime movies, 537
    rollovers, 354, 356, 358
    Set Text of Text Field Behavior, 476
    Shockwave content, 534
    sound files, 526
    Table cells, 222
    Table colors, 229
    Timelines, 455
    Tracing Images and, 198
    Web page in GeoCities, 551

Web Photo Album, 511
printing, Frames/Framesets and, 317
Privacy Policies, 542
Properties Inspector, 20
    Action: Reset form option, 423, 429
    Align Center button, 63, 165, 248, 257, 311
    Align pop-up menu, 166
    Align Right button, 166, 427
    Alt field, 118, 119
    Bg color, 230
    Bold button, 128, 157
    Border Color setting, 341
    Border setting, 207, 223, 249, 327, 341, 344
    Border Width setting, 327, 344
    Browse for File icon, 70, 86, 87, 88, 465, 466
    CellPad setting, 244, 245, 254
    CellSpace setting, 243, 244, 245, 254
    Char Width setting, 418, 419
    CheckBox Name field, 422, 429
    Checked Value setting, 422, 429
    Color Box, 179
    Column icons, 338, 339, 344
    Column Value setting, 327, 344
    context, changing, 20
    context sensitivity, 20, 37
    defaults, 20
    defined, 20
    Edit Date Format button, 555
    expanding, 37, 70
    folder icon, 356
    Font List pop-up menu, 156, 159, 160, 178, 390
    Format pop-up menu, 157, 170, 172
    Frame Name field, 330, 341
    Frame properties, 340-341
    Frame Scroll options, 333
    Frameset Column setting, 337, 338
    Horz pop-up menu, 304, 305
    H setting, 247, 255, 534, 536
    illustrated, 15, 20
    Italic button, 128, 157, 182
    Layer ID setting, 442
    Link History pop-up menu, 89, 90
    Link setting, 37, 38, 73, 82, 83, 98, 100, 119, 356, 465,
            468, 478
    Links folder, 328
    Map field, 117
    Margin Height setting, 341
    Margin Width setting, 341
    Merge Cells button, 234
    No Resize setting, 341
    opening, 465, 468, 478
    Parameters button, 528
    play button, 532
    Point to File icon, 82, 83, 92, 94, 106
    Rectangular Hotspot Tool, 117, 119
    Scroll setting, 341

    shortcut, 465, 468, 478
    Size pop-up menu, 156
    Split Cell button, 234
    SRC setting, 42, 43, 44, 92, 94, 341
    Target setting, 331
    Text Color Box option, 157, 181, 230
    TextField setting, 418, 419, 428
    Type: Multi line option, 419
    Units: Percent setting, 340
    Units: Pixels setting, 340, 344
    Units: Relative setting, 338, 340, 344
    Vert setting, 241
    W setting, 242, 247, 534, 536
properties_inspector.mov, 20
<P> tag, 62, 187
Put command, 549

Q

Quick Tag Editor, 137-141
    clicking/dragging in, 141
    defined, 137
    editing tags in, 140
    illustrated, 137
    opening, 138, 141
    shortcut, 138
    uses, 137
    See also HTML tags
QuickTime
    defined, 537
    movie, previewing, 537
    movie dimensions, 536
    parameters, 530
    Plug-In, 523
    Properties Inspector settings, 534
    support, 537
    .wav files and, 525
    Web site, 523

R

Radio Button Object, inserting, 414
.ra format, 527
Real Audio
    file format, 527
    Plug-In, 523
reassembling images, 251-254
Rectangular Hotspot Tool, 117, 119
    dragging, 117, 119
    illustrated, 117
    See also image maps
Registered symbol (®), 183, 184
relative links, 36-39
    creating, 70
    defined, 36
    displaying, 47
    illustrated, 37

in path structures, 42
URLs, 39
See also links
repeating actions, 180-182
font color, 181
italics, 182
menu changes, 182
Reset button, 423, 429
Reset Timeline window, 454
resources
Commands, 501-503
HTML, 5, 139
META tag, 77
Plug-In, 523
Plug-In parameter, 530
scripts and CGI, 415
XML, 13
Rich Music Format, 527
.rmf format, 527
robots (spiders), 74
rollover images
animated, 357
creating, 353
deselecting, 359
dimensions, 353
naming, 363, 364, 380
Navigation Bar, 374
"off/on" states, 353, 362
rollover_list.mov, 355
rollovers, 352-387
animated, 357-360
with Behaviors palette, 366-367
copying/pasting, 385
creating, 354-356
creation language, 352
defined, 352
graphic components for, 353
inserting, from Fireworks, 385-387
links, 356
minimum requirements, 353
multiple-event, 368-373
naming, 363
Navigation Bar, 374-384
pointer, 361-367
previewing, 354, 356, 358
rules, 353
triggering multiple behaviors, 371
use of, 352
width/height information, 353
rollover states
Down state, 374, 376, 379, 381
Over state, 374, 376, 381
Over While Down state, 374, 376, 379, 381
Up state, 374, 376, 378, 380
viewing, 384
Root Folder. *See* Local Root Folder
roundtrip HTML, 3

rows
adding, 235
deleting, 235
illustrated, 221
merging, 233-234
selecting, 230, 234, 241
size specification, 340
sorting, 227
top, formatting, 260
See also cells; Tables
rulers
accessing, 244
illustrated, 24
showing/hiding, 25, 242
using, 244

S

Save As Command dialog box, 519
Save As Template dialog box, 296-297
illustrated, 297
opening, 296
Save As field, 297
saving, 51
borders, 225
documents, 55, 170
extensions, 493
files, 354
Frames, left, 351
Frames, methods, 323
Frames, on Macintosh, 320
Frames, right, 350
Framesets, 318-324, 348
History palette and, 393
as Template, 296
Templates, 293, 294
screen captures, this book, xvii
scrollbars
Frame, 333, 341
setting, 333
search engines
descriptions and, 77
keywords and, 77
page titles and, 56
robots (spiders), 74
security, Frames and, 317
Select File dialog box, 86, 87, 118
Select Image Source dialog box, 217
Cancel button, 336
Choose (Browse) button, 343
illustrated, 336, 343
image dimensions, 336
Image Preview, 343
selecting, 322
attributes, 139
cells, 233